Comparative Tax Law

Comparative
Tax Law

Victor Thuronyi

KLUWER LAW INTERNATIONAL
THE HAGUE / LONDON / NEW YORK

A C.I.P. Catalogue record for this book is available from the Library of Congress.

ISBN 90-411-9923-3

Published by Kluwer Law International,
P.O. Box 85889, 2508 CN The Hague, The Netherlands.
sales@kluwerlaw.com
http://www.kluwerlaw.com

Sold and distributed in North, Central and South America
by Aspen Publishers, Inc.
7201 McKinney Circle, Frederick, MD 21704, USA

Sold and distributed in all other countries
by Turpin Distribution Services Limited,
Blackhorse Road, Letchworth, Herts,
SG6 1HN, United Kingdom

Printed on acid-free paper

TABLE OF CONTENTS

CHAPTER 5
INTERPRETATION OF TAX LAW
AND ANTI-AVOIDANCE RULES 133

Biographical Note

Victor Thuronyi received his undergraduate degree in economics from Cambridge University (M.A. Cantab.) and his law degree from Harvard Law School (J.D. cum laude, 1980), where he served on the Board of Editors of the Harvard Law Review. He has practiced tax law at Miller & Chevalier (Washington, D.C.), served in the Office of Tax Policy of the U.S. Treasury Department in 1983-86, where he participated in preparation of the tax reform proposals that led to the Tax Reform Act of 1986, and was thereafter associate professor of law at SUNY-Buffalo Law School until joining the Legal Department of the International Monetary Fund in 1991.

He is the author of several articles on taxation, a coauthor of *The Taxation of Income from Business and Capital in Colombia* (Duke University Press, 1990), and editor and co-author of *Tax Law Design and Drafting* (volume 1, IMF: 1996; volume 2, IMF: 1998, and combined edition, Kluwer Law International: 2000).

Since 1988, he has travelled to the following countries to study or advise on their tax systems (not including brief visits for seminars and the like): Albania, Argentina, Azerbaijan, Brazil, Chile, People's Republic of China, Colombia, Czech Republic, Dominican Republic, Estonia, Georgia, Guatemala, Kazakhstan, Latvia, Lesotho, Mongolia, Mozambique, Palau, Peru, Romania, Saudi Arabia, Sierra Leone, Slovak Republic, Tajikistan, Ukraine, and Yugoslavia, and has supervised tax law reform projects in some 20 other countries.

He is currently Senior Counsel, Legal Department, IMF, and Adjunct Professor of Law at Georgetown University. This book was prepared independently from his employment by the IMF, and the views expressed therein are the author's personal views and do not necessarily correspond to those of the IMF or its members.

Preface

This book provides a framework for understanding tax law in other countries. It may also help you understand better your own system. Because tax law has become so complex, many tax professionals have specialized – even sub-specialized – but this book follows the opposite approach, taking a broad view of taxes as they work in many countries. It focuses on what tax systems have in common and on key structural differences. This orientation should help you deal with the details of other countries' laws in the future, as well as providing a starting point in researching any comparative tax problem. It is assumed that you already have an understanding of tax law and policy based on your own system. Therefore how taxes work and what they are about are not covered here, nor are modes of tax policy analysis, since a substantial literature already exists.[1] This book deals with core common

---

[1] Those interested in learning how the various taxes work, with a particular emphasis on design issues for developing and transition countries, are referred to TLDD (for explanations of abbreviations and references, see Abbreviations, *infra* at xviii, Appendix 3, and note 3 *infra*.) That book also contains a fair amount of discussion on comparative tax law, which is cited here where relevant. An excellent introduction (or a handy reference) to basic tax policy analysis is Neil Brooks, *The Logic, Policy and Politics of Tax Law: An Overview, in* Materials on Canadian Income Tax (Tim Edgar et al. eds. 12th ed. 2000). *See also* Joel Slemrod & Jon Bakija, Taxing Ourselves (2d ed. 2000). There is a fair amount of literature on comparative tax policy, including: Cedric Sandford, Why Tax Systems Differ (2000); The Tax System in Industrialized Countries (Ken Messere ed. 1998); and Ruud Sommerhalder, Comparing Individual Income Tax Reforms (1996). Those interested in such tax policy questions as: income versus consumption taxation, progressivity, tax mix, effective tax rates on capital income, taxation of capital gains, tax expenditures, and so on, should consult the literature, which I do not attempt to summarize here, since my focus is on legal institutions and culture. From a conceptual point of view, the tools of tax policy analysis are pretty much the same no matter what country one is analyzing. Since I assume that the reader has a good grounding in tax law and policy from the point of view of their own country, I focus on matters where modes of thinking differ from country to country. There is little to include here on tax policy analysis, since in principle the methodology should be the same for each country, even if the factual background and the values shared by policymakers and the population will differ from country to country.

knowledge that any well-informed tax lawyer should have about comparative tax law in our times, and it has a fairly practical orientation.

While tax systems have much in common, there are also different ways of looking at things in different legal systems. This book identifies and explains some of the key differences. A better understanding of modes of thought and prevailing opinions in other countries can lead to a better appreciation of one's own system and can facilitate international dialogue.

Such an understanding can also be the basis for research on the development of tax law and its role in society. This book does not seek to undertake such a study, but it may provide some ideas that others will take forward.

Tax is an interdisciplinary field. In particular, the economic view is important to tax policy. This book focuses on legal issues, without prejudice to the substantial international and comparative literature on tax policy written from an economic point of view.

The text is highly selective and abbreviated,[2] so that it can be read and not only used as a reference, although there are footnotes for the latter purpose.[3] (Those wishing information on a specific country should look up that country in the index.) The focus is on the underlying currents of the law, not all the details. The details you can look up for yourself, or ask about, but to understand them it helps to know where the main currents are. Many of the sections conclude with questions (set in italics) that you might keep in mind in researching a particular country. These questions are consistent with the tentative nature of this book – I am well aware of the limitations of my knowledge of different tax systems. Likewise, the footnotes do not purport to be comprehensive, but just refer to sources used and those that might be a starting point for further research.

This book does not purport to set forth new theories or ideas that have not been stated before. What it does is pull together material which at present

---

[2] The emphasis is on issues that are of particular interest from a *comparative* perspective; on matters whose treatment in different countries does not differ fundamentally I tend to be silent, avoiding an encyclopedic treatment, which would have made the book too heavy. This book is an introduction, not a treatise.

[3] For brevity, works included in the bibliography (Appendix 3) are cited by author and date only; in other cases the Bluebook style of legal citation is followed (abbreviations are shown in a Table of Abbreviations). Except as otherwise indicated, quotations from works not in English are given as translated by me (*caveat lector*). While tempted to follow my gut on spelling, I decided that that might be too distracting for the reader and therefore for the sake of consistency I have tried to follow American spelling.

is scattered over a somewhat disparate literature, much of which is not available in English. It is hoped that the book will serve:

- for advanced students in tax, as a primary text for a course or as supplementary reading;
- for practitioners (whether in the private sector or in government), as a book which is short enough and hopefully interesting enough that busy people will have the time and inclination to read it;
- for tax academics, as an introduction to opportunities for teaching and research in comparative tax; and
- for those academics and practitioners who already know a considerable amount about comparative tax, as a collection of key points and references.

On issues that are already dealt with in detail in *Tax Law Design and Drafting*[4] (or other literature readily available), I tend to summarize here and to footnote to that literature.

Tax law changes rapidly, and so specific references in this book can be expected to get out of date, although the fundamental structure should remain valid for some time, since that changes more slowly. My intention is to make updates available on the Kluwer Law International website (currently reachable at www.kluwerlaw.com). This will allow readers to keep up with current developments at no additional expense. It will also allow me to correct errors and omissions, which are almost inevitable in a book of this breadth, since I do not pretend to be an expert on all of the tax systems discussed here. For these, I beg the reader's indulgence in advance, and also make a request that readers spotting errors that have not already been corrected by update let me know about them (the above website will facilitate this).

Statements in this book should not be relied on for tax planning or other purposes, as they do not necessarily reflect the latest developments or all the nuances of the law in specific countries.

---

[4] For further information, see Appendix I. Key literature is listed in the Bibliography (Appendix III).

Acknowledgments

As the citations in this book attest, I am indebted to the many scholars who have written about taxation, either in their own countries or on a comparative basis. Of specific help in preparing this book have been several individuals who generously offered comments on portions of the text: Rick Krever, Ron Schultz, Geerten Michielse, Delphine Nougayrède, and Roland Ismer.

I thank Marci Hoffman of the Georgetown University Law Library for advice about international tax research, and for her assistance and her work in developing and maintaining the international law collection at Georgetown.

I am also grateful to Eric Zolt, Rita Gilligan, Yoram Margalioth, and Jeanette Yackle of Harvard Law School for support in doing my research (and to those who have financially supported Harvard Law School so that it could maintain its excellent library of international legal materials).

ABBREVIATIONS

A.C.	Appeal Cases (U.K.)
All ER	All England Reports
A.I.R.	All India Reports
Am.	American
AO	Abgabenordnung (German tax code)
BFH	Bundesfinanzhof (German Federal Tax Court)
BGE	Entscheidungen des Schweizerischen Bundesgerichts
BIFD	Bulletin for International Fiscal Documentation
B.T.R.	British Tax Review
BAO	Bundesabgabenordnung (Federal Tax Code) (Austria)
BStBl	Bundessteuerblatt
B.T.A.	Board of Tax Appeals (U.S.)
BVerfGE	Bundesverfassungsgerichtsentscheidungen (Decisions of the Federal Constitutional Court – Germany)
Cahiers	Cahiers de droit fiscal international (published by International Fiscal Association)
Can.	Canadian
C.B.	Cumulative Bulletin
CC	Constitutional Council (*Conseil constitutionnel)*
C.E.	Conseil d'Etat (Council of State – France)
CFC	controlled foreign corporation
C.G.I.	Code Générale des Impôts (General Tax Code) (France)
CGT	Capital Gains Tax
Ch.	Chancery
CIR	Commissioners of Internal Revenue
C.M.L.R.	Common Market Law Reports
Cons. const.	Conseil constitutionnel (Constitutional Court -- France)
Const.	Constitution
C.R.R.	Canadian Rights Reporter
C.T.C.	Canada Tax Cases
D.C.	Décision constitutionnel
D.O.	Diário oficial (Brazil)
D.T.C.	Dominion Tax Cases
ECHR	European Convention on Human Rights (European Convention on the Protection of Human Rights and Fundamental Freedoms)
EC	European Community

ECJ	Court of Justice of the European Communities
E.C.R.	Report of Cases Before the Court of Justice of the European Communities
EEC	European Economic Community
e.g.	*exempli gratia* (for example)
E.H.R.R.	European Human Rights Reports (Sweet & Maxwell)
EStG	Einkommensteuergesetz (Income Tax Law)(Germany)
EU	European Union
Eur.	European
Fallos	Fallos de la Corte Suprema de Justicia de la Nación (Argentina)
FinStrG	Finanzstrafgesetz (Germany) (financial crimes law)
GAAR	General anti-avoidance rule
GST	Goods and Services Tax
GYIL	German Yearbook of Int'l L.
H.L.	House of Lords
H.R.	Human Rights
IAS	International Accounting Standard
ICTA	Income and Corporation Taxes Act 1988 (U.K.)
i.e.	*id est* (that is)
I.L.R.M.	Irish Law Reports Monthly
IMF	International Monetary Fund
Int'l	International
I.R.	Irish Reports
I.R.B.	Internal Revenue Bulletin (United States)
I.R.C.	Internal Revenue Code (United States), Internal Revenue Commissioners (U.K.)
IRS	Internal Revenue Service (United States)
ITAA	Income Tax Assessment Act (Australia)
ITLR	International Tax Law Reports
J.	Journal
J.S.C.	Judgments of the Supreme Court of Cyprus
L.	Law; or used in referring to articles of the L.P.F.
Law.	Lawyer
LGT	Ley General Tributária (Spain)
L.P.F.	Livre de procedures fiscales (France)

NZLR	New Zealand Law Reports
OECD	Organisation for Economic Cooperation and Development
OID	Original Issue Discount
OJ	Official Journal
Q.B.	Queen's Bench
R	Regina (or Rex)
Rec.	Recueil des Décisions du Conseil constitutionnel (Dalloz) (France)
Rev.	Review
R.T.C.	Reportorio Aranzadi del Tribunal Constitucional (Spain)
R.U.	Raccolta ufficiale delle sentenze e ordinanze della Corte costituzionale
S.C.	Supreme Court
SCJ	Supreme Court Journal (India)
S.C.R.	Supreme Court Reports (Canada or India)
S.T.C.	Simon's Tax Cases (U.K.); Sentencias del Tribunal Constitucional (Spain)
Tax'n	Taxation
T.C.	Reports of Tax Cases (U.K.), Tax Court (U.S.)
TCGA	Taxation of Capital Gains Act
TLDD	Tax Law Design and Drafting (*see* Appendices 1, 3)
Treas. Reg.	Treasury Regulation (U.S.)
UNTS	United Nations, Treaty Series
U.S.	United States (or United States Supreme Court Reports)
U.S.C.	United States Code
VAT	Value Added Tax
WLR	Weekly Law Reports

Chapter 1

THE COMPARATIVE APPROACH

1.1 IN GENERAL

You might be asking yourself: "My own country's tax system is complicated enough – why learn about comparative tax?" I would argue that a basic knowledge of comparative tax is essential to understanding taxation. A comparative approach tends to draw one's attention to basic principles and offers welcome relief from the hypertechnicity that characterizes the study of tax today.

Knowledge of comparative law is also of practical use to tax professionals no matter what their area of endeavor. More and more often, practitioners find themselves dealing with the tax laws of other countries. To do so effectively, it is important to have a basic framework, even if only to be able to understand responses that one obtains from specialists in another country. Tax policy analysis can almost invariably benefit from study of the experience of other countries. Tax law reformers (like myself) working in different countries and who are concerned with improving international cooperation on taxation must of course reach a fuller understanding of other systems. For litigators and policy analysts, reference to decisions in other jurisdictions may provide insight.[1]

Perhaps the best reason for studying comparative tax is the same for learning about dinosaurs or distant stars: it's interesting and fun, especially if you come across surprising or strange things. Finally, there is the zen of comparative law – study of other systems paradoxically helps you better think

---

[1] See, for example, the citation of American cases in *W.T. Ramsay Ltd v. IRC,* [1982] A.C. 300 (1981), and of English and American cases in *Stubart Investments Ltd. v. The Queen,* [1984] 1 S.C.R. 536. *See also* Zweigert & Kötz (1998) at 18-20. However, given the insularity of courts I cannot in good conscience advise you to go full steam ahead in terms of citing foreign judgments in briefs, although this may sometimes be appropriate.

about your own and can provoke insights that lead to breakthroughs in under-standing.[2]

Since taxes take out of private hands a substantial chunk of national income, tax laws respond as much to political concerns as to the proposals of policy analysts. Because of this, there is as much miscellany in tax as there is unified order. It is therefore perhaps surprising that so much commonality can be found across countries. Partly, this is due to the relative newness of tax as a field of law.[3] Legislatures in different countries have tended to adapt common statutory solutions that have proven workable elsewhere. Yet, even with respect to the modern taxes (income tax and VAT), tax law is old enough that substantial case law, administrative interpretation, and statutory diversity have built up to make each country's tax system unique.

Comparing the details of each country's tax rules would be mind-numbing. Anyway, summaries for most countries exist. What these summaries tend not to offer, and what this book focuses on, are the basic approaches,[4] structural features,[5] and overall legal tradition for tax law in different countries. The concept of income is an example of a structural feature. The U.S. has a global concept, while in most of Europe income is thought of as something derived from particular sources, and so there are different types of income, depending on the nature of the source. The legal concept of income is fundamental to how the income tax law is organized and conceptualized. Members of the same legal family (for which see below) tend to share structural features, either presently or historically.

[handwritten in left margin: structural feature]

---

[2] *See* Mary Ann Glendon, *Why Cross Boundaries?*, 53 Wash. & Lee L. Rev. 971 (1996). *See also id.* at 976 ("Live in England for a year and you will not learn much about the English. But when you return to France you will see, in the light of your surprise, that which had remained hidden to you because it was so familiar." (quoting Fernand Braudel, Histoire et Sciences Sociales: La Longue Durée, Annales: Economies, Sociétés, Civilisations 725, 737 (1958)); Beltrame & Mehl (1997) at 27 (emphasizing improved critical understanding as a reason for comparative study); Tipke (2000) at 14.

[3] Taxes have been around for a long time, but the more sophisticated legal questions arising from taxes like income tax and VAT, and the role of lawyers in resolving them, largely arose starting in the 20th century. By contrast, private law has developed over a longer period.

[4] Basic approaches include, for example, fundamental judicial attitudes to statutory construction and to the relation between private law and tax law, the role of the courts in constitutional review of tax legislation, the role of the executive in providing interpretations of the law, the place of treaties in the domestic legal system, and the tax policy formulation process.

[5] *See* Ault et al. (1997) at 1-3.

[handwritten at bottom: legal family]

More broadly, a legal tradition is not merely a set of rules, but: "deeply rooted, historically conditioned attitudes about the nature of law, about the role of law in the society and the polity, about the proper organization and operation of a legal system, and about the way law is or should be made, applied, studied, perfected, and taught."[6] This book tries to identify key elements of legal traditions for tax law.

What information might I need about the "tax culture" of this country in order to understand this issue? What is the same (different) about this country? Is there anything surprising about this country's tax system? What is distinctive about the conceptual apparatus on various issues? How does the tax system work?

1.2 COMPARATIVE METHOD

Comparative law involves the study of basic structures, country differences, and the influence of systems on each other.[7] It identifies underlying patterns and analyzes how different rules function in different countries to resolve similar problems. Raw material for this study is a descriptive understanding of different countries' laws.[8] Zweigert and Kötz hold that the principal aim of comparative law as a theoretical-descriptive discipline "is to say how and why certain legal systems are different or alike," and that as an applied discipline "comparative law suggests how a specific problem can most appropriately be solved under the given social and economic circumstances."[9]

---

[6] John Henry Merryman, The Civil Law Tradition 2 (2d ed. 1985).

[7] For general material on comparative law, see Zweigert & Kötz (1998); René David & John Brierley, Major Legal Systems in the World Today (3d ed. 1985); Rudolf Schlesinger et al., Comparative Law: Cases-Text-Materials (6th ed. 1998); Peter de Cruz, Comparative Law in a Changing world (2d ed. 1999); Werner Menski, Comparative law in a global context: The legal systems of Asia and Africa (2000); Mary Ann Glendon et al., Comparative Legal Traditions: Text, Materials and Cases (2d ed. 1994); Book Review, 79 Revue de Droit international et de Droit comparé 211 (2002).

[8] Zweigert & Kötz (1998) at 6, call collected descriptions of different systems involving "no real comparison of the solutions presented" descriptive comparative law. "One can speak of comparative law only if there are specific comparative reflections on the problem to which the work is devoted." *Id.*

[9] *Id.* at 11. For Alan Watson, "Comparative Law... as an academic discipline in its own right, is a study of the relationship, above all the historic relationship, between legal systems or between the rules of more than one system...." Alan Watson, Legal

For law reform, comparative study can canvass the rules that apply in different countries in the subject area being considered and can discuss whether these rules represent good policy and how policymakers might go about deciding what rules to enact for their country. The purpose of a comparative approach is to learn about new possibilities from studying actual practice, to convince by example, and to avoid reinventing the wheel.

As with comparative law generally, one can study the local tax literature and judicial decisions to learn how people in different countries think about tax law and how actors in different legal systems behave;[10] historical, law-and-economics, or sociological methods may be apposite.

The historical method traces the development of law over time and across countries, and studies how particular legal systems have been influenced by others, or by transnational legal culture.[11] In this context, the study of legal transplants is important—both identifying where they have occurred[12] and assessing their success. This includes developing an

Transplants 9 (2d ed. 1993). He distinguishes comparative law from a knowledge of foreign legal systems, which acknowledging that the latter has practical value.

[10] *See* Zweigert & Kötz (1998) at 4-5. The authors call a comparative study of the spirit and style of different legal systems macrocomparison. Attitudes and behavior can, however, be difficult to study from written sources, which often do not provide full or comparative description and analysis. It is easier to find out what the black letter law is. For a review of a study focusing on the behavior of actors in the legal system see Norman Nadorff, Book Review, *O Jeito na Cultura Juridica Brasileira by Keith S. Rosenn*, 32 Inter-American L. Rev. 605 (2001) (The title can be roughly translated: The "Fix" in the Legal Culture of Brasil.) For a discussion of problems in application of the income tax in Germany, see Rolf Eckhoff, Rechtsanwendungsgleichheit im Steuerrecht 344-407 (1999).

[11] *See* Schlesinger et al., *supra* note 7, at 11. In general terms, it has been observed that "the tax systems of modern industrialised countries have tended to approximate each other more and more, to take over from each other forms and methods of taxation, and to take a similar approach to the distribution of the tax burden." Günther Schmölders, Allgemeine Steuerlehre 251 (4th ed. 1965). Tipke (1993) at 64 notes the influence of German tax law scholarship in Spain, Brazil, and Japan. *See also* Minoru Nakazato, *Japan,* 78a Cahiers 407 (1993) (importance in Japan of comparative studies of both European and American authorities); Beltrame & Mehl (1997) at 550-51.

[12] With respect to civil codes, transplantation has been extensive. "There is almost no private-law-code in force in any civilian country today which is not substantially copied from, or in its structure or some of its provisions directly or indirectly influenced by, the Codes of France, Germany, or Switzerland." Schlesinger et al., *supra* note 7, at 606. *See also* Frédérique Dahan, *Law Reform in Central and Eastern*

understanding of legal culture and studying how rules have changed or persisted when transplanted from one system into another.[13] Convergence by legal systems—whether as a result of influence from other systems or parallel development—is always something to look out for.[14] It is striking when systems that start out differently end up dealing with problems in a similar way. We find many examples of convergence in tax.

By way of caveat, on both of these matters—the extent of transplantation and of convergence—this book offers only the barest introduction. Both would make for fascinating study,[15] but this would go well beyond the time that has been available to me.

Europe: The 'Transplantation' of Secured Transactions Laws, 2 Eur. J.L. Reform 369 (2000). For taxation, specific transplants will be discussed throughout. As a general matter, transplants have occurred extensively within legal families (see *infra* 2.5 for a listing of legal families for tax law). For example, "[o]ver the years, the form of the anti-avoidance rule in one jurisdiction has influenced the development of the rule in another, as legislative draftsmen have referenced to other countries for useful precedents. Furthermore, court decisions, particularly from Australia and New Zealand, have exposed defects in earlier forms of general anti-avoidance rules.... As a result, general anti-avoidance rules tend to have many features in common." John Prebble, *Trends in Anti-Avoidance Legislation, in* Asian-Pacific Tax and Investment Research Centre, Practical Problems of International Taxation 161, 171 (1990) (referring principally to common-law countries). As another example, "[a] successful tax innovation in one Scandinavian country will soon be copied in the other countries." Gustaf Lindencrona, Trends in Scandinavian Taxation 21 (Kluwer 1979).

[13] *See id.* at 14-15; Watson, *supra* note 9, at 21-30, 95-101, 107-18; Alan Watson, The Evolution of Western Private Law (2001).

[14] For a general discussion of convergence between common law and civil law systems see Glendon et al., *supra* note 7, at 242-51.

[15] One would want, for example, to look for cases of wholesale borrowing, or *de novo* revision of tax laws with the aid of foreign advisors (which is work that I have been engaged in), and to evaluate the practical success of these efforts over time, including the extent to which such laws have been subject to subsequent change. A good example here would be Japan, where the system was substantially changed as a result of the Shoup report, but later many of these changes were reversed. Even if some of the ideas have been rejected, Japan is probably richer in terms of tax policy thinking for having tried out various ideas from abroad. One would also want to trace more limited borrowings across legal families, as with controlled foreign corporation legislation. One would also want to look at the development of tax legal culture in developing and transition countries. On the surface, for example, francophone and anglophone African countries might have quite different tax law, but what are the differences in practice? Just mentioning some of these questions makes it apparent how much research (including field research) would be needed to come up with answers, even tentative ones.

Law and economics is certainly relevant to tax,[16] so much so that tax policy analysts were using law-and-economics methodology even before it became fashionable in legal scholarship generally. Sociology is also quite relevant to tax because in different countries there are different attitudes to the payment of tax and different methods of tax administration, including levels of audit, levels of corruption, and attitude to aggressive tax planning.[17] For example, the literacy rate is an important predictor of revenues from the VAT (presumably because literacy goes along with better recordkeeping and compliance).[18]

The general literature on comparative tax law is sparse, although there are a number of studies on particular topics, for example corporate-shareholder taxation and controlled foreign corporation rules.[19] The sparsity of general literature may be due in part to the fact that tax law in any one country is complex enough – scholars can find plenty of material within their own system. It is also notoriously difficult to get an understanding of the tax systems of different countries, given the complexity of the subject and language barriers.[20] It gets worse: tax scholars tend to be concerned with tax policy as much as with tax law, and rightly so. Tax policy analysis includes ideas from economics and political science: the focus is on both the legislative process and the appropriateness of the resulting rules. Tax scholarship therefore tends to have an interdisciplinary[21] feel, and practitioners often use economic and policy concepts, whether they are representing clients before the legislature, the courts, or the tax authorities. This interdiscliplinary tax tradition may be somewhat isolated from the general legal tradition in any particular country. This can be seen in law firms, accounting firms, and universities, where tax is often a subculture unto

---

[16] An example of an economic approach to comparative tax is Sandford (2000).

[17] For an example of a comparative sociological study see Grant Richardson & Roman Lanis, *The Influence of Culture on Tax Administration Practices*, 15 Australian Tax Forum 359 (1999/2000). *See also* Ann Mumford, Taxing Culture: Towards a Theory of Tax Collection Law (2002) (comparative study of U.S. and U.K.). *See generally* Jean Dubergé, *Psychologie et Sociologie de l'Impôt, in* Dictionnaire Encyclopédique de Finances Publiques 1251 (Loïc Philip ed. 1991).

[18] *See* Ebrill et al. (2001) at 47.

[19] See Appendix I for a guide to some of this literature. Tipke (2000) at 14 bemoans the fact that no "Max-Planck-Institute for foreign and international tax law" exists.

[20] *See* Alvin Warren, *Preface, in* Ault et al. (1997) at vii; Glendon, *supra* note 2, at 971 ("if cross-disciplinarians waited to know as much as we feel we ought before writing, we could never put pen to paper.")

[21] *See* Tipke (2000) at 8-9 for discussion of various disciplines concerned with taxation. *See also* TLDD at xxix, 4-7.

itself. However, in order to study comparative tax law, it is necessary to pay attention to the general legal tradition as well as to the tax tradition, in addition to knowing something of general comparative law. This makes it doubly difficult for tax academics to approach comparative tax law: to do so it is necessary not only to study other countries' tax systems but also their general legal systems.[22] It seems that few people with a strong background in tax have had the inclination to do this.

The discussion in this book tends to the descriptive, although the effort is to describe highlights rather than whole systems. My effort is to survey the whole, leaving more detailed studies for further research. Accordingly, I generally refrain from opining here as to why particular systems are structured as they are, and what have been the historical lines of influence, since the general nature of this survey precludes the rigorous and detailed analysis that would be required to advance such conclusions.

What method might appropriately be applied to this tax problem? In approaching it, can I learn something from comparative scholars in other areas of law? If there has been borrowing from other systems, was the borrowed material changed in enactment or operation?

1.3 LEGAL FAMILIES

Comparative law scholars have divided countries into families to indicate broad similarities in legal traditions.[23] This type of analysis is useful for tax law as well, because it can impart structure to cross-country comparisons (for a proposed classification see 2.5 below).

Classification into legal families provides advance clues about any given country's tax system. A few examples will serve to show how useful this can be:

- Without having researched the question, I would suspect that in Luxembourg corporate capital gains are taxed as part of a corporation's business income. This is because Luxembourg is in the same family as Germany and could be expected to share this basic

---

[22] An example of an article that considers both the general legal system and tax systems from a comparative point of view is David Ward et al., *The Business Purpose Test and Abuse of Rights*, 1985 B.T.R. 68.

[23] For example, Zweigert and Kötz (1998) at 73 identify the Romanistic, Germanic, Nordic, and Common Law families, as well as separately discussing the law of the People's Republic of China, Japanese law, Islamic law, and Hindu law.

structural feature.[24]   On the other hand, I would expect a country like Nigeria to tax corporate capital gains via a separate capital gains tax if at all, since I know that under the "trust" concept of income which Nigeria likely inherited from the UK, capital gains are not income, absent a special legislative enactment.

- Even though I know nothing about the VAT of Denmark, I would assume that a full input credit is allowed for equipment or intangibles to be used in a business because this is required by the 6th Directive.[25]

- I would expect some commonality in the attitude of courts to interpreting tax laws in most of the 58 countries of the "British" family (see 2.5).

- By studying the inflation adjustment rules of Chile, you will know roughly how the inflation adjustment rules work (or should work) in all other Latin American countries which have them.[26] You will even have a start on understanding the inflation adjustment rules in Israel, which modeled its rules on the Latin American ones, albeit with changes in the mechanics.

At the same time, it is important to check out the presuppositions that one derives from the "families" approach.   Courts develop their own approaches in each country and legislatures often make major changes to the structure of tax law in derogation from their legal inheritance. Even so, the families approach can help generate relevant questions.[27]   The families approach, in other words, provides a checklist of possible skeletons that may be found in the closet of any given country's tax law.   Some of these skeletons have by now been buried, but many have not been.

While the reference to families is therefore useful in some cases, it does not provide the whole picture. This book sometimes mentions countries as representative of legal families, but in general the countries discussed are those that offer a typical and noteworthy solution to particular problems of tax

---

[24] Of course, suspicions like this should be confirmed by research. The research is, however, easier if you know approximately what you are looking for.

[25] *See infra* 8.3.

[26] *See infra* 7.15 (inflation adjustment).

[27] In this context, the following admonition (made in reference to historical concepts of tax law in the UK) is apposite: "we must remember that they are old ideas if we are to treat them correctly". Morse and Williams (2000) at 25. *See also* Zweigert & Kötz (1998) at 72 ("any division of the legal world into families or groups is a rough and ready device...[and should be used] with all the circumspection called for by any attempt to force into a schematic social order social phenomena as highly complex as living legal systems.")

law.[28] Where several jurisdictions could be discussed, I generally focus on those with the more highly elaborated doctrine and more extensive literature. In practice, this means that a fair amount of the discussion can focus on three countries: Germany, the United Kingdom, and the United States, which on many issues offer archetypical approaches to tax issues.

For those who do not have the time or inclination to study the tax systems of numerous countries, but who would like to benefit from comparative law study, I would suggest that a focus on these three countries (Germany, U.K., and U.S.) will reveal most of the basic contrasts that would arise from including other countries in the study. In other words, diminishing returns apply by adding more countries to this basic group of three. The three countries are archetypes for the basic concepts of income (accretion, trust, and source), and have been leaders in influencing the tax laws of other countries in numerous respects. For those who read French but not German, France could be substituted for Germany, although at some loss, given that the German literature is more extensive than the French and in some respects the German tax system provides a richer field for study.[29] Alternatively, any civil law country can be substituted; someone from a civil law country can therefore get an understanding of comparative tax by studying the U.K. and U.S.

As suggested above for VAT, the general legal tradition is only one dimension along which countries can be classified. A second dimension would look to significant borrowing or commonality in specific areas of legislation, either for a particular tax or for a particular set of rules (like the controlled foreign corporation rules). Borrowing often occurs across families, as countries adapt rules that have worked elsewhere. The high level of borrowing from other countries is consistent with the dynamic nature of tax law, whose rate of change exceeds that of any other field of law.[30]

---

[28] So-called *Lösungstypen*. *See* Marieke Oderkerk, *The Importance of Context: Selecting Legal Systems in Comparative Legal Research*, 48 Netherlands Int'l L. Rev. 293, 307, 316-17 (2001).

[29] Examples are the extensive decisions of the German constitutional court in the tax area (4.3 *infra*), extensive judicial decisions on anti-avoidance (5.7.5 *infra*), the highly organized tax procedure code (AO), which has had an influence on many other countries, the extensively studied relationship between tax and financial accounting (7.11.2 *infra*), and the complex rules for income taxation of international transactions.

[30] I have only anecdotal evidence from my experience both in the U.S. and numerous other countries, but find it difficult to think of any other area where legislative change might be so extensive virtually every year in many countries.

What legal family does the country belong to? Has the country kept the historical approach to given specific issues or has the legislature changed the policy? What historical influences could help one understand the law in a particular country, either in general or for a particular issue?

1.4 ECONOMIC CLASSIFICATION AND THE TAX MIX

In addition to classifying countries according to legal families, one can also usefully classify countries for purposes of tax policy analysis along economic lines.[31]   Those countries with more sophisticated economies (by and large the OECD countries) have more in common as far as their tax systems actually operate, regardless of different legal traditions, than they do with lower-income countries. In economic terms, a Francophone African country will have much more in common with its Anglophone neighbor in terms of the operation and economic effects of its tax system than it will with its former colonial power with whom it shares a legal tradition. Because my general focus here is on legal tradition, I do not emphasize the economic classification, but that is not intended to downplay its importance. In understanding tax policy in a particular country, it is critical to be aware of the role of the tax system in the economy, in addition to understanding the legal tradition.

The broad outlines of economic classification can be seen by looking at the relative size of tax revenues and the tax mix. Taxes represent substantially different shares of GDP in different countries.[32]   In broad terms, taxes represent a higher share of GDP in OECD countries than in non-OECD countries, although there is considerable variation within each group. Of the OECD countries, the lowest tax shares are found in Japan, Turkey, Korea, Mexico, the U.S.,[33] and Canada.

---

[31] For an example of such classification, see J-C Martinez & P. di Malta, 2 Droit fiscal contemporain: Les Impôts, le droit français, le droit comparé 267-383 (1989). Schmölders, *supra* note 11, at 249 distinguishes industrialised from developing countries, the latter being characterized by a tax system where customs duties and indirect taxes generally play a large role.

[32] This section is based on information in Tax Policy Handbook 293-311 (P. Shome ed., IMF: 1995).

[33] It is ironic that the U.S. has one of the world's lowest tax burdens as a share of GDP, while having the largest number of tax lawyers. The low tax burden does not prevent some politicians from making tax reduction an important and permanent part of their agenda.

The shares of revenue represented by different taxes also differ substantially from country to country. In the U.S., income tax represents a comparatively large share. European countries have comparatively high domestic taxes on goods and services. African countries tend to have comparatively low shares for income tax and social security and a high share for international trade taxes.[34] International trade taxes also tend to be significant in non-OECD Asian countries, with income tax being a minor revenue source (except in Indonesia); total tax revenue as a share of GDP being relatively low overall. A similar pattern appears in the Middle East, with the exception of Israel, whose tax mix is similar to Europe's. Latin American countries have relatively low overall tax revenue, as well as low revenue from income tax. In general, in developing countries, the role of corporate income tax (often collected from a few major companies) is relatively greater than individual income tax, and the latter tends to fall disproportionately on public servants and employees of large companies.

Transition countries tend to have a markedly different revenue pattern from developing countries. Their overall revenue tends to be higher, with high social security and other contributions based on wages and high indirect taxes, and relatively low income tax.

Broad cross-country comparisons like this can be misleading, however. For example, a country like Australia may show a relatively low tax share in GDP because it has a mandatory private pension system instead of social security.[35] Even though the economic effects of the Australian system might be quite close to those of a social security system, the revenue statistics treat them differently. In addition, a country extensively using tax expenditures (e.g., the U.S.) will show a lower tax share as compared with another countries (e.g., many European countries) that accomplish the same policies with direct expenditure programs whose economic effects may be very similar to those of the tax expenditures.[36]

What does the general economic situation of the country tell us about the actual operation of the tax system? What is the importance of various taxes as a percentage of revenue? How are taxes assigned to different levels of government (national, provincial, local)? How progressive is the tax system? Are there taxes with unusually high or low rates? What is the

---

[4] International trade taxes historically played a substantial role in Europe and America even as recently as the beginning of the 20th century.

[5] *See* Richard Vann, *General Description: Australia, in* Ault et al. (1997) at 5, 7.

[5] *See* Stanley Surrey & Paul McDaniel, International Aspects of Tax Expenditures 5- (1985).

*overall ratio of revenues to GDP in comparison with economically similar
countries?*

1.5 COMPARING THE STUDY OF TAX

Tax plays a much larger role in the U.S. law school curriculum than
in other countries. An astounding number of tax courses can be taken at the
major U.S. law schools.[37]   The number of tax law professors is
correspondingly high, compared with other countries.[38] Outside the U.S., tax
is typically studied in law school relatively little, although in recent years the
importance of tax seems to have increased in a number of countries.[39]

Another U.S. peculiarity is that what is studied is usually income tax,
rather than tax law in general. A student can go through a U.S. law school
having taken half a dozen tax courses, without considering any tax other than
the income tax, and with little attention to tax procedure. In fact, there exists
no comprehensive U.S. treatise on tax law, with the vast areas of state tax law
and constitutional tax law being left to specialists in constitutional law or state
and local finance and largely ignored by teachers of federal income tax law.[40]

---

[37] Including graduate offerings, the law school of Georgetown University offers over
50 tax courses (although, admittedly this is one of the larger programs in the U.S.)

[38] Tipke (1993) at 49 n. 109 notes that at U.S. law schools the ratio of public and
administrative law professors to tax professors is about 1:1, while in Germany it is
about 30:1. He notes that there are over 20 tax professorships in the Netherlands,
which is comparatively more than in Germany. He considers the situation in the U.K.
in terms of the number of tax law academics to be even worse than in Germany. The
complaint about Germany is telling, because when one considers the literature, the
contribution of German scholars is impressive, even more so in light of their small
numbers. The amount of academic literature devoted to tax law is by far the greatest
in the U.S. and Germany. Tax scholars kill a lot of trees in the Netherlands too.

[39] For a discussion of the situation in Germany, see Tipke (1993) at 51-64; Tipke
(2000) at 24-28. *See also* Tipke (2000) at 28-29 (Austria, Switzerland, Spain).

[40] Thomas Cooley, A Treatise on the Law of Taxation (1876) was written by a justice
of the Supreme Court of Michigan and professor of law at the University of Michigan. It covers general concepts of taxation and the power to tax, limitations on the
taxing power, the construction of tax laws, tax procedure, and particular taxes (such
as taxes on business and property – there was no federal income tax at the time). The
vast preponderance of the authorities cited are State cases, many of them
constitutional (i.e. dealing with State constitutions). Cooley was not a big fan of the
income tax: "any income tax is also objectionable, because it is inquisitorial, and
because it teaches the people evasion and fraud." *Id.* at 20. Interestingly, he
identified the Achilles' heel of the income tax, namely the fact that it fails to reach

This is, of course, consistent with the importance of the income tax in the U.S. tax system and with the complexity of U.S. income tax law. However, I cannot help but think that U.S. tax academics could learn something from their European counterparts by way of taking a more comprehensive view of tax law, both in teaching and writing, and getting away from an exclusive focus on the federal income tax. This might be of interest to students and helpful for the development of the law outside the federal income tax.

In civil law countries, an introductory course on tax law, in addition to considering major taxes such as income tax and VAT, would typically consider such general topics as the relation between tax law and other branches of law, including constitutional law, the nature of tax obligations, the sources of tax law, statutory interpretation, and tax procedure. The basic building blocks of the various taxes tend to be identified and studied as an abstract matter. These include: the nature of the authority imposing the tax, the concept of tax, its pecuniary (or in-kind) nature, the tax object, tax base, tax rate, taxpayers, taxable event, and the event that causes the tax to be due and payable.[41] In many civil law countries, these elements tend to be separately identified in tax legislation, often in a more formal and explicit manner than tends to be found in the legislation of common law countries.

---

unrealized gains: "In the United States, also, such a tax is unequal because those holding lands for the rise in value escape it altogether—at least until they sell, though their actual increase in wealth may be great and sure." *Id.* Of course, any treatise or book written today would look substantially different, and given the existence of specialized treatises, a summary book with cross references to existing treatises would make much more sense than a treatise that tried to cover the whole ground of taxation in depth. However, in terms of scope of coverage anyone contemplating writing a general book on tax law today would do well to at least have a look at Cooley's work. Moreover, they could also profitably look at Tipke (1993); Tipke (2000) (in German, but with a table of contents in English). Americans willing to think about writing on tax law in general could also profitably look at the U.K., Canadian, and Australian treatises which are listed in the bibliography – not to read them all but to see what they cover. In addition to dealing with constitutional law, including state constitutional law, an overall work on taxation would also usefully consider as such those aspects of tax law that are part of administrative law, and look systematically at interpretation of tax law and at the relation between tax law and other areas of law (e.g., criminal law, private law, public international law). *See infra* ch. 4. Bittker and Lokken (1999) covers many but not all of these issues.

[41] *E.g.*, Beltrame & Mehl (1997) at 36-61; de la Garza (2001). The latter (used in Mexico) is a good example of differences in basic tax texts. A work of 1,000 pages, it has almost no overlap in its coverage with the basic income tax texts that would be used at U.S. law schools. Martín Queralt et al. (2001) (Spain) has a bit more overlap, but the vast bulk of the coverage differs from what is found in the U.S.

Common lawyers might find topics such as the above hopelessly abstract; civil lawyers might be amazed that common lawyers feel they can study tax without first properly laying the theoretical foundations.[42] Perhaps the best approach lies somewhere in the middle?

To what extent is tax taught in law schools? In other faculties (e.g., accounting or economics)? To what discipline do the leading tax academics belong? What professions get involved in tax policy?

---

[42] *See generally* Zweigert & Kotz (1998) at 69-70.

Chapter 2

OVERVIEW

2.1 CONVERGENCE

Although there are differences among tax systems, there is a remarkable number of areas where tax systems that may have started in quite different places have converged.[1] These will be discussed throughout the book, but some highlights are given here:

- virtually all countries have adopted an income tax and a vast majority have adopted the VAT;
- individual and corporate income tax rates have been lowered and have come together;
- while earned income used to be taxed at the same rate or lower rates than unearned income[2] – for fairness reasons – the opposite approach is now commonly taken, with unearned income being subject to lower rates than earned income;
- schedular income tax systems have been replaced with global ones, but even previously global systems have come to include schedular elements;
- fringe benefits have become subject to broader inclusion in the tax base;
- capital gains have been subjected to broader taxation;
- tax rules for financial instruments have become increasingly sophisticated;

---

[1] Convergence of the tax systems of industrialized countries was already identified in Günter Schmölders, Allgemeine Steuerlehre (4th ed. 1965). For commentary on recent trends, see Thomas F. Field, *Worldwide Tax Overview,* 28 Tax Notes Int'l 1253 (Dec. 30, 2002).

[2] Lower rates applied in the U.S. to earned income under the so-called "maximum tax", as well as in the U.K. *See* Morse & Williams (2000) at 177.

- the relationship between tax and financial accounting is becoming more similar;
- deductions for bribes are being denied;[3]
- social security taxation has become common, and coordination between social security and income taxation has increased;
- customs procedures have become substantially harmonized, while customs duties have been drastically lowered;
- controlled foreign corporation and ancillary rules are widespread, particularly in capital-exporting countries;
- the double tax treaty network has grown considerably and along similar lines;
- a substantial consensus has developed on many matters of treaty application and cross border taxation (such as transfer pricing), largely through discussions at the OECD;
- the purely territorial approach[4] to international taxation has been largely abandoned;
- a number of countries have repealed estate and gift taxes;
- miscellaneous excises have tended to be repealed and excises focused on alcohol, tobacco, and petroleum, although some new excises have been introduced as a matter of environmental policy;
- the scope of stamp duty has tended to be narrowed, although financial transactions taxes have become popular in Latin America;
- the role of the courts in protecting the constitutional rights of taxpayers has increased;
- courts are increasingly adopting a purposive approach to interpreting tax laws, as opposed to strict construction;
- both general and specific anti-avoidance rules are commonplace;
- tax administrations have become more sophisticated in obtaining and processing information about taxpayers, and the use of taxpayer identification numbers has become nearly universal;
- self-assessment has been broadly accepted;
- the preceding-year basis of assessment has been dropped by most countries which used it.[5]

---

[3] *See* OECD, Update on the Implementation of the OECD Recommendations on the Tax Deductibility of Bribes to Foreign Public Officials in Countries Party to the Bribery Convention (Jan. 2002) (available on OECD website); Tiley (2000) at 137; Tipke/Lang (2002) at 298-99.

[4] *See infra* 7.14.1.

[5] *See* Tiley (2000) at 135.

This is not to say that the trend has uniformly been in the direction of convergence or that the degree of approximation of tax systems is as great as one would like.[6] Nor have the above developments taken place quickly. In some cases one is talking about developments over spans of 25 or 50 years. Yet as an overall trend we are likely to see over the coming decades tax systems coming closer together rather than moving further apart.

Except in rare instances, this convergence does not involve actual harmonization of laws, in the sense of different countries adopting identical or close to identical texts or policies. Since each country's legal system has its own history and culture and since policy choices and political considerations differ from country to country, we will still see substantial differences when we consult the actual texts of laws. Borrowed rules will be adapted to fit the policy choices of the borrowing country. They must also be superimposed on what is often a fairly complex system, requiring substantial adjustments as compared with the tax rules of the country from which the borrowing occurs.

In what respects has the country followed world trends or taken a different path?

2.2 COMPLEXITY

Tax law is simple hardly anywhere, but the degree of complexity varies substantially. The U.S. has the most complex legislation (taking together both the tax code and the regulations), followed by countries like Australia, Canada, and the U.K.[7] To some degree, complexity in the U.S. is influenced by the legislative process: there are many tax expenditures and many compromises fashioned to give limited concessions as part of the process of enacting new rules. Complexity is also influenced by the judicial process. The U.S. has, perhaps by historical accident, a Byzantine system of appeals from tax assessments, with three possible sets of courts to choose

---

[6] For a reflection on differences between the U.S. and European systems, see Leif Mutén, *Inspiration or desperation – European reactions to US tax thinking, in* Alpert & van Raad, eds. (1993), at 311.

[7] *See* Tiley (2000) at 46-47. France, with (according to one account) 15,000 pages of instructions, may be in the running too. *See* Beltrame & Mehl (1997) at 507; Frédéric Douet, Contribution à l'étude de la sécurité juridique en droit fiscal interne français 34 (1997) (referring to the fact that there are 2,000 articles of the tax code, 3,000 articles annexed to the tax code, and 8,000 pages of administrative commentary). Australia may have the longest statute. *See* Richard Vann, *Australia, in* Ault et al. (1998) at 10.

from.[8] Probably another reason for the complexity of tax legislation in the U.S., and in other common law countries as well, is the autonomy of tax law from financial accounting rules. Those countries that rely more heavily on financial accounting do not have to provide all the details for accounting in tax legislation.

Complexity is also related to the volume of material that must be consulted in order to find the answer to a question. In some countries, the tradition is that by and large the tax rules should be written in the statute. There is a substantial difference among countries as to how appropriate it is for the administrative agency to make tax law and accordingly as to how much detail is written in regulations. Again, the U.S. furnishes a contrast, with the statute being only a starting point. In addition to the statute, there are judicial decisions, regulations, and published and private administrative rulings. As far as the statute itself is concerned, the above-mentioned common-law countries involve substantially more complexity than civil law countries as a group, which favor a less detailed drafting style.[9] Those common law countries following the so-called Westminster rule that each subdivision, however long, must be expressed in one sentence suffer from the difficulty of following the convoluted expressions often required.[10] This is not to say that tax law in countries like France and Germany is simple. Tax authorities in these countries issue a substantial amount of administrative guidance and there are also numerous court cases to be consulted. Moreover, in a number of countries tax expenditures have assumed an increased importance. The use of tax laws to accomplish subsidy purposes has obviously led to complexity, and conversely the differences in the extent to which countries have used tax expenditures can explain at least in part differences in tax law complexity.

Of course, it is an oversimplification to ascribe complexity just to the volume of words of the law. One might more usefully inquire as to the burden of compliance costs that the tax system imposes. This is, however, difficult to estimate, especially across jurisdictions. In any event, it seems legitimate to evaluate different systems for complexity both in terms of the absolute verbiage and degree of impenetrability of legislation and in terms of compliance burden.

---

[8] *See infra* 6.8.

[9] "In civil law countries it is customary for statutes to be drafted in terms that are much more general than the detail to which the common lawyer is accustomed." John Prebble, *Trends in Anti-Avoidance Legislation, in* Asian-Pacific Tax and Investment Research Centre, Practical Problems of International Taxation 161, 165 (1990).

[10] *See* Krishna (2000) at 1; Thuronyi, *Drafting Tax Legislation, in* TLDD at 77-78.

Many developing and transition countries have fairly simple tax laws. These may if anything be too simple for taxpayers with more sophisticated transactions. There is often a corresponding lack of administrative capacity to provide guidance to taxpayers on complying with the tax laws and to audit returns in an effective manner.

In all countries, complexity is also a function of time. Virtually never has a country succeeded in actually simplifying its tax legislation. Rather, the tendency is for the laws to grow more and more complex each year.[11] This is true for countries with different levels of complexity. The reasons are many but an important one is that as new cases come up and as legislators and administrators have occasion to consider the application of the existing legislation, more detailed and nuanced approaches almost invariably seem attractive. Simple rules are often perceived as unfair. Those who make rules tend to be swayed by the need to avoid unfairness rather than by the more elusive goal of reducing complexity.

Some countries (Australia, U.K., New Zealand[12]) have recently made efforts to simplify their legislation, although the results are mixed. It is particularly difficult to attempt, as these jurisdictions have done, to achieve simplification without tax policy reform. The two are best done together. On the other hand, one difficulty with a concerted approach is that the reduction of complexity is detailed work that takes time, while tax policy reform often can be done only by striking while the iron is hot. The truth is that only by a sustained effort which combines policy reform and simplification can substantial simplification be achieved. The management of tax law complexity is an important tax policy issue that can benefit from international comparison.

---

[11] *See* Ault et al. (1997) at 43 (France), 29 (Canada), 10 (Australia), 83-84 (Netherlands). *But see id.* at 101 (Sweden). See Beltrame & Mehl (1997) at 496-502 for a discussion of the organization of the laws, increase of complexity over time, and management of complexity in different systems.

[12] *See* Tax Law Review Committee, Final Report on Tax Legislation (1996), the discussion in which should be of general interest in other countries as well for those interested in simple and effective tax legislation. In Nov. 2002, the New Zealand government introduced in Parliament a revised income tax law, intended to make existing law more understandable without making substantial policy changes The new law is supposed to be more user-friendly, but it does not read like a novel. While the language used may be "plain English," the underlying approach remains highly technical; only highly skilled professionals can be expected to plow through this law and make any sense of it. It may look good only because the existing law is so bad.

How complex are the tax laws?   What has been the development of complexity over time?

2.3 LEGISLATIVE PROCESS

Since it is legislatures which adopt tax laws, it should not be surprising that differences in politics and in the process for passing legislation exercise a profound influence on the tax laws. It is instructive to compare the tax laws of the United States—with their mind-boggling complexity and array of special provisions—with those of virtually any European country. The European parliamentary systems—with their greater party discipline and less power in individual legislators to add their favorite items to the tax code— surely go a long way to explaining the differences in result.[13] The politics of taxation is undoubtedly a key factor in explaining why U.S. tax law is substantially more complex than that of any other country. The rules of procedure in Congress are also relevant. In the House of Representatives, tax bills are typically considered under rules which limit the amendments that can be offered; otherwise, the consideration of a tax bill would be quite chaotic given that each of the 435 Member of Congress would surely have at least one amendment to take care of vital interests of constituents. Even so, since the Ways and Means Committee is large and powerful,[14] many "member's" amendments are introduced to any significant tax bill to take care of special interests. Once a tax bill gets to the Senate, additional amendments can be introduced at the behest of special interests in the Senate Finance Committee and on the Senate floor by any Senator, there being no limitations comparable to those applicable in the House. Depending on the procedural stance, there may, however, be limitations arising from the budget rules. These may require balancing offsets to revenue-losing amendments. While well-in-tentioned, the result of these rules often is tax policy by revenue estimate,

---

[13] In the U.K., for example, tax legislation is under the tight control of the government. *See* David Williams, *Taxing Statutes are Taxing Statutes*, 41 Modern L. Rev. 404, 405-06 (1976). This is not to deny the power of special interests in Europe. It is simply that the role of individual legislators, in the context of campaign finance practices, which give an important voice to business interests and the wealthy, is peculiarly strong in the United States.

[14] The Committee used to be more powerful than it is today since it had a number of prerogatives outside taxation which were taken away in the post-Watergate reforms. It is possible that the more closed pre-Watergate system made for a more tightly controlled tax policy since the chairman of the committee had a lot of power, more so than today.

with rules being formulated so as to hit the desired revenue target. It can be imagined that the result is not likely to be simple or rational rules. (The effect of budgetary rules of procedure varies from country to country, but should be borne in mind in identifying factors that influence tax legislation.)

Each Senator and Member of Congress is elected on their own and must raise their own campaign funds, and is therefore responsive to interests in their own district, especially those backed by substantial campaign contributions. Industries or wealthy individuals with particular interests in the details of the tax code can therefore often secure helpful amendments to tax legislation. While the U.S. Treasury Department has traditionally upheld the public interest in terms of tax policy, the Treasury's position is of course part of the political agenda of whichever administration is in power, and the White House is often reluctant to defer to the policy judgments of the experts in Treasury when these conflict with the administration's political agenda. When the White House has gotten involved, the result has usually not been a simpler and more even-handed tax policy. A lot of the complexity found in the Internal Revenue Code results from compromise—with so many divergent interests tugging in different directions, there is rarely agreement on a decisive step in one direction or the other. Rather, the staffs usually come up with an extremely complex solution that gives each of the important interests a portion of what they had been trying to get.

What influence does the legislative process have on how tax policy decisions are made?

2.4 INVESTMENT INCENTIVES

Tax laws almost invariably contain provisions favoring certain industries or activities, often with the avowed purpose of encouraging investment. There is considerable controversy over whether investment incentives are effective or desirable.[15] It is clear that there is a substantial competitive element—if there is to be a meaningful prospect of reducing such incentives, some coordination among States is required. This is taking place in the EU under the umbrella of the Code of Conduct on business taxation (a nonbinding understanding), as well as in the framework of rules on state aid

---

[15] *See* Alex Easson, *Tax Incentives for Foreign Direct Investment,* BIFD 266 (July 2001).

(binding rules under the EC Treaty).[16] The OECD has also launched an effort on curbing harmful tax practices.[17] In developing countries, the effectiveness of investment incentives depends in part on tax rules in the investor's home country (tax sparing under double taxation agreements or exemption, either under tax treaties or unilateral rules). While tax sparing has come under critical reappraisal at the OECD level, the actual rollback of such provisions has been limited, in part because existing treaties are renegotiated infrequently, and tax sparing continues to be granted under newly negotiated treaties.[18]

While coordination among governments on limiting investment incentives remains controversial, there is perhaps greater consensus on the appropriate design of incentives. It is clear that some incentives (tax holidays being an obvious example) suffer from serious design flaws and are open to abuse.[19] Presumably, even if developing and transition countries continue to provide tax incentives, they will in the future be better designed so as to reduce abuse possibilities. For example, instead of tax holidays, incentives can be provided in the form of more attractive cost recovery allowances for investment in equipment.

Customs duties and VAT also play an important role in tax incentives in developing and transition countries. The imposition of customs duties on

---

[16] *See infra* 4.4.

[17] The OECD initiative has taken a narrower approach than the EU, focusing on financial services and on transparency of information. See the OECD website for details (www.oecd.org).

[18] *See* Linda L. NG, *Singapore's Tax Incentives: Optimizing Benefits, Tax Sparing, and U.S. Treaty Hopes,* 22 Tax Notes Int'l 1498 (Mar. 26, 2001). Tax sparing under the Australia-Malysia treaty is to expire on 30 June 2003. *See* Krever, *Australia,* 27 Tax Notes Int'l 651 (Aug. 5, 2002). The Denmark-Singapore treaty signed in 2000 eliminated tax sparing. *See* Tan How Teck, *Commentary on Denmark-Singapore Tax Treaty,* 22 Tax Notes Int'l 144 (Jan. 8, 2001). Under the new Japan-Malysia income tax treaty signed in 1999, tax sparing was set to expire after 2006. *See* Grant Beaumont, *Japan,* 22 Tax Notes Int'l 1109 (Mar. 5, 2001). The Belgium-Indonesia treaty signed in 1997 eliminated tax sparing. *See* Sorin Anghel, *Belgium*, 22 Tax Notes Int'l 2695 (May 28, 2001). The OECD recommended restraint in the granting of tax sparing, not its complete abolition. *See* OECD, Tax Sparing: A Reassessment (1998). About one-third of the treaties signed in 2000-2002 (not including those involving the U.S., which has a long-standing position against tax sparing, or countries using the exemption method) included tax sparing provisions. *See* Victor Thuronyi, *Recent Treaty Practice on Tax Sparing,* 29 Tax Notes Int'l 301 (Jan. 20, 2003).

[19] *See* David Holland & Richard Vann, *Incentives for Investment, in* TLDD at 986.

imports of capital equipment undermines a policy of encouraging investment, even if it may be called for by good principles of customs administration. The payment of VAT at the border upon importation of capital equipment would normally involve no tax burden if the VAT system were running properly. This is because the VAT paid on import would give rise to an immediate credit on the taxpayer's monthly VAT return which would give the right to a refund to the extent the credit resulted in a negative balance of tax. Tax refund systems unfortunately do not work smoothly in many developing and transition countries.[20] Measures to take care of cash flow problems arising from VAT on imports may therefore be appropriate and are contemplated in a number of these countries.

What kinds of incentives are in effect in the country?

2.5 COUNTRY FOCUS

2.5.1 IN GENERAL

This section summarizes key features for a number of countries and families of tax laws. While not all countries are specifically discussed, virtually all are included in the table of families.[21]

The family classification provides an insight to the historical roots of any particular country's system, thereby providing a better understanding of underlying legal culture. As can be seen from the discussion below, the tax law of most countries fits more or less clearly within one of several families. Legal concepts are inevitably shared within each family. Of course, it is important to check the extent to which a particular country has developed rules of its own, which may differ radically from those of its brothers and sisters. More likely than not, however, particular rules, even if they cause the law to differ from the rest of the family, will be rooted in the common legal heritage and may be framed as an antithesis or modulation of rules that are part of that heritage. To understand those rules, it is helpful to know about the common family heritage.

Division into families is therefore of assistance to those seeking to understand the tax law of different countries, whether for the purpose of

---

[20] *See* Ebrill et al. (2001) at 155-65.

[21] This section is a revised and expanded version of material in the introduction to volume 2 of TLDD; the classification into families is broadly similar to that for families of income tax laws which I previously prepared, but I have made some changes with the benefit of rethinking, to reflect developments, and to adjust for the fact that this table covers tax law as a whole, not just income tax.

comparative study or as part of tax practice.   Identifying common characteristics of each family gives a head start to someone trying to sort out the law of an unfamiliar country. In the case of comparative tax law research, the classification suggests that such research should include at least one country from each of the groups if it is to embody a truly global perspective.[22] As suggested above, however, in a pinch a survey of the U.S., U.K., and Germany may often suffice, depending on the issue.

The classification scheme is not a novel one and largely tracks the classification of legal families by comparative law scholars.[23]   At the same time, the focus on taxation means that some countries that might be grouped into different families for private law purposes may fall into the same family for taxation because their tax laws are similar.[24]   The families into which countries appear to fall are set forth in Table I.[25]   The grouping is based on primary historic commonality or influence; much influence from one country to another is not captured in this grouping.

In a few cases, countries are placed in more than one family, to show a strong influence of more than one legal system.   The table also divides countries into three agglomerations of families: all countries are divided into common law and civil law, to highlight basic differences in legal style. It is hard for me to put a finger on it, but there seems to be a basic difference of outlook concerning tax law in common and civil law systems. The civil law outlook is rather formal and systematic.   It tends to define and categorize taxes.   It establishes fairly abstract concepts such as the tax obligation and the tax obligor (anyone with a tax obligation, taxpayer being a subcategory), and governs the circumstances in which the tax obligation arises and is extinguished.   This outlook is epitomized in the tax codes of Germany (*Abgabenordnung*) and of Latin American countries (*códigos tributarios,* the latter having been heavily influenced by the former), and to a greater or lesser extent is shared by civil law countries generally. The underlying concepts are not much different from those in common law countries, but they are articulated in a more systematic way. More general differences in legal

---

[22] Of course, by focusing on solutions adopted within the same paradigm, research confined to a single group can also be of interest, although it will not provide a global view.

[23] *See supra* Chapter 1, note 23.

[24] *Cf.* Zweigert & Kötz (1998) at 65.

[25] By way of disclaimer, I have not studied all these countries in detail and it is certainly possible that the classification can be improved on the basis of further study and can be enriched by analysis of cross-family influences. Perhaps there is a doctoral dissertation here for someone?

background between common and civil law countries are also relevant for tax law. Courts in common law countries tend to play an important role in the development of tax law, generally more so than in civil law countries. Statutes tend to be drafted in greater detail. In a number of ways, the legal backdrop to tax law differs in these two groups.

The table also includes a third overall group of countries which straddles common and civil law countries, namely the EU members. These countries hold in common a significant portion of tax law whose source is European law (especially in the case of customs duties and VAT). Moreover, European law is exercising an influence on judicial interpretation of statutes which may grow over time. EU member countries also have experienced some approximation of tax law beyond that required by EC directives.

While there are considerable variations in the details of the tax rules from country to country, it is important not to lose sight of the considerable commonality in the tax laws of all countries, and the even greater commonality among the various groups of countries. Also, considering the systems of nine groups of countries is considerably less daunting than considering all the countries of the world individually. Therefore, obtaining a general overview of the tax laws of the countries of the world is not as difficult as it may seem at first.

One could go on to identify numerous instances of legislative imitation (which in many cases involve borrowing from, or being influenced by, countries outside the group) beyond the influence of predominant countries in these groups, some of which may not be apparent from the legislative language itself. The grouping in the table therefore does not begin to tell the full story as to the influences of various systems on each other.

The balance of this section highlights basic structural features of the tax laws of countries in each family.

2.5.2   COMMONWEALTH FAMILY

The first group consists of countries whose tax law has been influenced by that of the United Kingdom.[26]   For the most part, these countries fall under the common law legal system. The income tax laws of a number of countries in the group go back to a British Colonial model law of

---

[26] I use the term "Commonwealth" as a convenient label, rather than as a fully accurate one, given that this group does not coincide completely with current members of the Commonwealth.

1922,[27] although some precede it. Each country has modified its income tax law independently since initial enactment; the extent of independent development varies. Countries that achieved independence from Britain before 1922 (Australia, Canada, New Zealand) developed their income tax laws independently and have not been influenced by the 1922 model, although all these countries have important links to the U.K. in terms of the conceptual underpinnings of their tax laws.[28] For these countries, the common statutory language or structure is minimal, but there are similarities in, for example, the concept of income and allowable deductions that justify placing them into the same tax family as the United Kingdom. The income tax law of the United Kingdom itself of course has also undergone considerable independent development since the 1920s, which has not been closely followed by the other countries, except Ireland. Only the income tax law of Ireland therefore bears a close resemblance to that of the current U.K. law. Some of the countries in the group (Brunei Darussalam, Kuwait, Oman, Saudi Arabia) have an income tax statute of limited application that has a common law influence dating from a later period (after World War II), with a much looser link to U.K. law.

Although the United Kingdom itself has separate laws for income tax and corporation tax, the 1922 model was a unitary law covering both individuals and corporations, and this approach of having only one income tax law is generally followed by countries in the group.

The modern income tax originated in Great Britain in 1798.[29] Initially, the tax was imposed on a global basis. A schedular structure was introduced in 1803, but the tax again had a global form by 1842, although still based on a schedular definition of income.[30] The 1922 model ordinance represented a considerably simpler statute than the law then in effect in the United Kingdom, namely the Income Tax Act, 1918. The 1918 act defined different types of income in schedules to the act and specified different rules

---

[27] Report of the Inter-Departmental Committee on Income Tax in the Colonies not Possessing Responsible Government, Cmnd. 1788 (Dec. 1922).

[28] The concept of income in these countries is influenced to varying degrees by the same theories that lie behind English judicial decisions on the meaning of income. *See* Ault et al. (1997) at 8-10, 27-29.

[29] *See* Tiley, *United Kingdom, in* Ault et al. (1997) at 109. The tax was imposed by the Income Tax Act, 1799 (39 Geo. 3, c. 13). For a history of the law, see also 12 Halsbury's Statutes of England (2d ed. 1949).

[30] *See* Sylvain Plasschaert, Schedular, Global and Dualistic Patterns of Income Taxation 30 (1988). *See infra* 7.2.1 for a discussion of the distinction between a schedular system and a global system with a schedular definition.

for allowable deductions in each schedule. By contrast, the model ordinance provided unified definitions of income and deductions. The definition of income in the model was schedular in nature, in that there were six paragraphs listing separate types of income, so that any receipts not listed in one of these paragraphs were not subject to tax.

Many of the Commonwealth countries have departed from a schedular definition of income. Income is often defined globally, and there is no segregation of rules for determining allowable deductions according to particular schedules. Instead, the rules for deductions are stated in terms that apply generally to all types of income. Even where the statute has adopted such a global form, however, judicial concepts of income may hearken back to the old schedules. Concepts of what is employment income, what is a capital gain, what is a business, what is a revenue item, and what expenses are deductible, among other matters, tend to be similarly treated in the judicial decisions, although in some countries these judicial rules have been overridden by statute. An underlying theme for the judicial concept of income (again, except as overridden by statute) is the source concept, under which a receipt is considered to be income only if it is periodic in nature and derived from capital or from an income earning activity.[31] The source concept is shared with Continental systems, and is in sharp distinction to the United States, which has enjoyed a judicial concept of income that is broad in scope, reflecting any realized accessions to wealth. The source concept used to be most important for the taxation of capital gains, which are not considered income under a source concept; however, by now many countries with a source concept of income have overridden it by statute with respect to capital gains (or at least some capital gains). Some but not all the countries in this group also share the trust concept of income with the U.K.

As a general matter, courts in Commonwealth jurisdictions tend to have regard to U.K. decisions, not necessarily as binding precedent but for their persuasive value.[32] To a greater or lesser extent depending on the country, there is therefore a common judicial culture among Commonwealth countries. (Even though the U.S. is a common law country, it is not part of

---

[31] *See infra* 7.2.2.

[32] *See, e.g.,* Cahiers 78a (1993) at 189 (Australia), 467-68 (New Zealand), 537 (Singapore). The Judicial Committee of the Privy Council hears appeals from Antigua & Barbuda, Bahamas, Barbados, Belize, Brunei, Grenada, Dominica, Jamaica, Kiribati, Mauritius, New Zealand, St. Christopher & Nevis, St. Lucia, St. Vincent and the Grenadines, Trinidad & Tobago, and Tuvalu. *See* www.privy-council.org.uk.

this same judicial culture, although in a broader sense one can also speak of a common law tradition.)

2.5.3   AMERICAN FAMILY

The United States, together with the few countries whose tax laws are closely modeled on that of the United States, is listed as the second group. It shares with most of the countries in the first group the common law legal system. Therefore some aspects of drafting, administrative law, and the role of judicial decisions are similar to those in the first group. In contrast with civil law countries, where concepts defined in non-tax codes tend to be applied relatively uniformly in tax law,[33] the tax law in the United States and other common law countries tends to be autonomous from other branches of law. The United States is categorized in a separate family from the U.K. because its income tax has developed along different lines. There was never an influence of the old U.K. schedules, because the U.S. definition of income was always a global one. U.K. court decisions on the concept of income and allowable deductions have had little influence in the United States. Although the influence of the U.S. tax rules on other countries in specific areas has been extensive in the past few decades, and although a number of countries— including, for example, many Latin American countries, Canada, Indonesia, and Japan—have taken some inspiration from U.S. tax law, only those few countries whose tax laws were modeled closely on that of the United States are included in the same group.

The United States is characterized by a global definition of income, a comprehensive system for taxing capital gains (although capital gains have been subject to tax at preferential rates, and although the realization rules are not as broad in the United States as they are in Canada, for example), a classical corporate tax system, a single law for corporate and individual income tax, and a worldwide jurisdictional approach based on both citizenship and residence, with the use of a foreign tax credit system for granting relief from international double taxation. The United States has among the most highly developed rules in virtually all areas of income taxation, which have as a whole become impossibly complex to deal with. A good deal of the law— both basic concepts and detailed interpretations of the statute—is judge-made, probably more so than in any other country.

---

[33] *See infra* 4.7.

The U.S. boasts a high percentage of returns filed compared with the total population. Taxpayers are required to self-assess tax on their return. Joint filing for spouses is virtually required (separate filing is an option but different rates apply and it is almost never advantageous for a married couple for file separately). The U.S. has been a leader in the use of advance rulings, although the expense of obtaining a ruling means that rulings are most heavily used by larger corporate taxpayers. U.S. tax policy is a bitterly contested battleground, often involving trench warfare.[34] One of the outcomes is the alternative minimum tax, which involves an expanded tax base but lower rates than the regular tax. Almost no one is happy about this tax.[35] Although the U.S. is also a leader in terms of a global concept of income, it can paradoxically be said to have one of the most schedular systems, in the sense that the tax law draws a large number of distinctions among different categories of income. These include, for example, employment income, investment income, trade or business income, income from passive activities, and capital gains, but the full list of different kinds of income subject to different treatment would be quite indigestible.

The income tax is far and away the most important tax in the U.S., more so than in most other countries. The U.S. is the only OECD country without a VAT, and is not likely to adopt one.[36] States are sovereign taxing powers, subject to constitutional limitations. Most States have an income tax, sales taxes, and, at the local level, real property taxes, as well as miscellaneous taxes such as inheritance taxes, excises, and real property transfer taxes.

2.5.4 FRENCH FAMILY

The third group consists of France and countries that have modeled their tax laws on those of France, largely deriving from a colonial period. There is a substantial degree of commonality among the tax laws of countries

---

[34] *See generally* Michael J. Graetz, *100 Million Unnecessary Returns: A Fresh Start for the U.S. Tax System,* 112 Yale L. J. 261 (2002); Daniel Altman, *A Tax Code Not Intended for Amateurs*, N.Y. Times, Feb. 4, 2003, at C1.

[35] The unhappiness is likely to increase as a result of the tax cut enacted in 2001, which did not deal with the problem of increasing numbers of individuals that will be hit by this tax. Presumably, this problem will be dealt with, but the necessary revenue to do so will have to be taken from somewhere. Canada copied the idea of an alternative minimum tax in 1986, except that in Canada the tax applies rarely. *See* Hogg et al. (2002) at 460-62.

[36] *See infra* ch. 8, note 5.

in this group. The resemblance generally is to the tax law of France at an earlier time rather than to the tax law of France today. In France and in many other countries in the group, the tax laws are all gathered into a single tax code (some countries have separate codes for direct and indirect taxes). However, the individual and corporate income taxes are set forth in separate chapters of this code and are considered to be separate taxes. The French definition of income is structured according to eight categories.[37] The rules for determining income and allowable deductions differ from one category to another. Before 1960, income in each schedule was separately taxed, and a global tax was superimposed on the schedular taxes (this is known as a composite system).[38] This composite approach has been replaced in France with a global approach. The scheme of division into schedules is similar to that of Germany (see below), except that Germany has an additional category of miscellaneous income that includes pensions. Capital gains in Germany are taxed under either business income or miscellaneous income. Apart from these and a few other details, however, the German and French schedules follow the same basic approach. The French system does, however, have a number of distinctive features, including a special "family quotient" method for granting relief for dependants,[39] the relatively extensive use of presumptive assessment methods,[40] the preferential treatment of business capital gains,[41] and its approach to taxing income earned abroad (exemption for business income of corporations; no foreign tax credit except under treaties).[42] The French income tax is also noteworthy for the absence of withholding on wages and for the high threshold, which exempts roughly half of households from income tax.[43]

2.5.5 LATIN AMERICAN FAMILY

The Latin American countries share a similar legal system and the same or similar language. They do not belong in the same family as Spain and

---

[37] *See infra* 7.2.1.

[38] *See* Guy Gest, *France, in* Ault et al. (1997) at 39. For a discussion of schedular and composite taxation, *see infra* 7.2.

[39] *See infra* 7.4

[40] *See infra* 7.17.

[41] *See infra* 7.9.

[42] *See infra* 7.14.

[43] *See* Ken Messere, *Tax Policy in Europe: A Comparative Survey,* BIFD 526, 534 (2000).

Portugal, however, despite the language similarity and colonial background, although they would be placed together if the topic were private law rather than tax law. The reason is that colonial independence was achieved well before the development of the income tax. Therefore, the development of the income tax in Latin America, Portugal, and Spain occurred with substantial independence and along different lines.[44]   Brazil's income tax resembles Argentina's much more than it does Portugal's.   The tax law of Latin American countries has developed independently, while being influenced by a number of sources, including the U.S., Germany, Italy, and other countries in the region.

These countries generally use a single income tax law, covering both individuals and corporations.   There are, however, substantial differences within the Latin American group, even in terms of the basic architecture of the income tax law.   Some countries have a global definition of income; for example, in Colombia the global definition of income goes back to the origins of the income tax in that country.[45] By contrast, Chile still follows a composite[46] system of income taxation, under which schedular taxes on different categories of income are creditable against a global complementary tax.[47] The Chilean law divides income into only two categories: capital and business income (first category) and earned income (second category). In the middle fall countries like Argentina. The Argentine law follows continental Europe in defining income differently depending on whether individuals or companies are involved.[48] In the case of companies, any increment to wealth constitutes income (this brings about an equivalent result to the balance sheet approach of France and Germany).[49] In the case of individuals, the source theory is followed, under which an item is income only if it is periodic and comes from a permanent source.[50]

---

[44] For a synopsis, *see* Plasschaert, *supra* note 30, at 32.

[45] *See id.* at 30-31.   The income tax was first adopted in Chile in 1924. Its features resembled the income tax of France, and there were six categories of income.   A global complementary tax was added in 1925, imposing a progressive tax on global income.   The number of categories was reduced to two in 1984.   Under article 2 of the law, the concept of income is the net worth increment. *See* Massone (1996) at 23-24, 44, 57-58, 66.

[46] *See* Plasschaert, *supra* note 30, at 17.

[47] *See* Income Tax Law §§ 52, 56(3), 63.

[48] This discussion of Argentina draws on Reig (2001) 23-30, 43-46.

[49] *See infra* 7.11.2.

[50] *See* Income Tax Law § 2 (Argentina).

Many of the countries have fairly simple corporate-shareholder taxation systems which avoid double taxation by simply exempting dividends; Mexico, however, has a fairly sophisticated imputation system.

Many of the Latin American countries have experienced substantial inflation and have enacted comprehensive inflation-adjustment rules (as contrasted with the ad hoc rules adopted in some European countries) that have by and large been retained even as inflation has declined in recent years.[51] These rules are quite similar in all the Latin American countries that have them. The Latin American countries have historically followed a territorial approach to international taxation, although this is now being abandoned. Many of the countries in the group have over the past decade enacted a tax on assets as a minimum business income tax.[52] Virtually all the countries in the group have implemented a VAT, often not without difficulty. The VATs do not necessarily follow standard European practice; for example, a full input credit for capital goods may not be allowed, and there may be some cascading (for example, in Brazil, where there is a VAT at the regional level). Several have used "tax handles" such as a tax on financial transactions to cover emergency revenue needs. In line with this, there is a fairly prevalent use of stamp taxes and a tendency to impose withholding taxes on an extensive basis.

The general procedural framework is governed by tax codes which are to a greater or lesser extent inspired by the tax code of Germany and which exhibit substantial cross-influence and uniformity among the countries in this group. These tax codes typically include general provisions on application of tax legislation, influenced by German law and *fraus legis* concepts, but there is not a uniform approach.[53] Some countries apply a fairly literal interpretation of the tax laws, and confine the concept of abusive transactions to simulation, while others (such as Argentina) employ broader anti-avoidance rules. In a few countries (Brazil, Venezuela) these rules have been expanded. In a number of countries, including Mexico and Argentina, the courts have been quite active in the tax area on constitutional grounds.[54]

---

[51] *See* Victor Thuronyi, *Adjusting Taxes for Inflation, in* TLDD at 434.

[52] *See* Peter Byrne, *The Business Assets Tax in Latin America: The End of the Beginning or the Beginning of the End?,* 15 Tax Notes Int'l 941 (Sept. 22, 1997); TLDD at 412-21. Colombia has had a presumptive assets-based tax for some time. *See* McLure et al., The Taxation of Income from Business and Capital in Colombia 46-49, 140-44 (1990). The concept may have been borrowed from Italy. *See infra* note 77. As of 1999, Argentina restored its minimum tax based on business assets.

[53] *See infra* 5.6.

[54] *See infra* 4.3.9.

2.5.6 TRANSITION AND POST-CONFLICT COUNTRIES

This group consists of countries which, within the past decade or so, have been undergoing a transition to a market-oriented economy, either from a socialist economy or after a war. Although each country has a history in terms of taxation, to a substantial extent they started from scratch in terms of their tax law at the beginning of their transition. For the most part, the tax legislation of these countries has been revised relatively recently and in some cases is still undergoing substantial revision, usually with the benefit of outside advice. In most cases, the result is fairly eclectic.

The group is divided into three subgroups, the first of which consists of the 15 countries that formerly made up the Soviet Union. The tax laws of these countries have been subject to rapid development over the past decade. The pace of change in different countries can be tracked fairly exactly because all these countries started with virtually identical tax laws as of the time of the breakup of the Soviet Union in early 1992. This common origin justifies their inclusion in one group, even though there are already substantial differences among them. In the case of the Baltics, the commonalities with the other countries have rapidly been eroding and can be expected to erode further with EU accession. Therefore, it seemed appropriate also to include these countries in the Northern European group as well as the European Union group, thinking of them for the moment as straddling these groups. Since 1992, virtually all members of the former Soviet Union group have made radical changes to their tax legislation, often heavily influenced by international models.

The legislation in place in 1992 was appropriate to the tax system existing under the Soviet Union. The former tax system was hardly comparable to the tax system of a market economy, both in its function and in how it was administered. Tax administration was a largely clerical function, part of the system of price determination and economic management, consisting of effecting the appropriate transfers to the budget from the accounts of each enterprise.[55]

In 1992, separate laws governed income taxation of physical persons and legal persons. The income tax for individuals had a limited role given the restrictions on individual property ownership and entrepreneurial activity.

---

[55] *See* Delphine Nougayrède, Construire L'Impôt en Russie 149 (2001).

Under the 1992 legislation,[56] the definition of income for individuals was global in concept. Residents were taxed on their worldwide income, nonresidents only on their domestic-source income. However, a wide variety of exemptions applied, covering many types of payments and benefits, including both items received from the state and also many benefits offered by employers (social benefits, pensions, compensation for injuries, severance pay, unemployment benefits, scholarships, interest on state bonds, lottery winnings, and interest on bank deposits, to mention only a few of the long list of exemptions). Under the Russian legislation, capital gains were in principle subject to tax, with exclusions. Enforcement of a capital gains tax is, however, difficult in the region, and some countries eliminated the tax.[57] Special exemptions applied for veterans, other individuals who provided heroic service of specified kinds, and the disabled. Deductions were provided for charitable contributions, dependency allowances, and home construction expenses. Despite the global nature of the definition of income, special rules (primarily having to do with withholding, but also in some cases specifying allowable deductions) were provided for wages received at the primary source of employment, wages received at other sources of employment, business income, income of foreign resident persons (i.e. noncitizens), and nonresidents. A number of the rules were holdovers from the former economy (e.g., special rules for noncitizens). The general orientation of the law was focused on collecting tax from withholding in all possible cases, even for business income.[58] This obviously made sense only in the context of the former economy, where little independent business activity existed. As the economy developed, it is therefore not surprising that substantial changes in the income tax would be made. While the income tax law in each of the countries of the group has taken its own direction, many of the features outlined above have been preserved in most of the countries of the group.

The tax on enterprises was designed with state-owned enterprises in mind. Its accounting rules and concept of income were the same as those under the accounting rules used for general purposes by state enterprises. Indeed, there was no conception that there *could* be a difference between financial accounting and tax accounting. The concepts involved developed out of a planned economy and had little to do with the concept of profit under

---

[56] Russian Federation Act no. 1998-1, Act on Income Tax on Natural Persons, Dec. 7, 1991.

[57] For example, neither Kazakhstan nor Georgia taxed capital gains of individuals before adopting tax codes in 1995 and 1997, respectively, and in practice many such gains still go untaxed today.

[58] *See* Act on Income Tax, *supra* note 56, §13(1)(a).

a market economy. Under these accounting rules, many expenses that are normally deductible under international practice were not deductible. Deductibility was subsumed under the question of what expenses entered into production costs, and hence into the cost.[59] Advertising costs are one example of a nondeductible expense; excessive wages are another,[60] the latter having to do primarily with concerns for regulating state owned enterprises.

At the time of dissolution of the Soviet Union and transition of these countries toward market-based systems, a fundamental overhaul of these laws was required in short order. Even a decade later, the process is only in its incipient stages in many of the countries in this group, although a few (particularly the Baltics) have advanced much further in the direction of European standards than the rest.[61] Even where progress has been made in reforming the law, administrative practice may take longer to change. The result is that the old Soviet accounting principles may still exercise an important influence in a number of countries. Those countries that have adopted substantially reformed laws may have freed themselves from these principles in theory, but now face the task of elaborating and applying the somewhat skeletal provisions found in the new legislation.

Tax compliance has been notoriously poor in the region. This has historical roots in the Soviet system, where bending the rules was necessary

---

[59] The relevant concept is that of *sebestoimost'*, which is the cost or value of production. Under the Soviet economy, the theory of which costs enter into the *sebestoimost'* was developed under criteria quite different from those applicable to the analysis of deductible expenses under the income tax laws of market economies, and the holdover of the old ideas became part of the obstacle to adoption of a market-oriented tax system. *See* Nougayrède, *supra* note 55, at 52-54, 260-65 (2001).

[60] The concept of denying a deduction for excessive wages seems to have to do with a concern that managers of state-owned enterprises would pay excessive wages as an alternative to making profit distributions to the state.

[61] Kazakhstan adopted a comprehensive tax code in 1995 (and a revised code in 2001), the Kyrgyz Republic in 1996, Uzbekistan and Georgia in 1997, Tajikistan in 1998, and Azerbaijan in 1999. Russia adopted its tax code in stages, starting in August 1998. Ukraine has revised its laws but not yet adopted a new code. These codes contain the rules for all the taxes, as well as the procedural rules. I have worked on the codes for Kazakhstan (both 1995 and 2001 versions), Tajikistan, Georgia, and Azerbaijan (the others were modelled on the Kazakh code). Even these relatively more modern codes respond to the stage of development of the tax systems of the countries concerned and will need to be upgraded in the future (as Kazakhstan's already has been).

for survival of enterprises and individuals and therefore acquired a certain legitimacy.[62]

The new tax codes contain more or less complete rules for tax procedure. In the case of Russia, these have been heavily influenced by the tax code of Germany, which has served as a source of inspiration for many countries, while reflecting many concerns peculiar to Russia. The other codes contain somewhat a mixture of the Russian rules and more generic ones drafted independently. (Because the Russian tax code had such a long gestation period, its influence was felt in some of the other former Soviet Union countries even before it was enacted in Russia.)

Value added tax has had a troubled history in this group of countries.[63] Initially, the tax was applied on an origin basis, but this now applies only to petroleum products and the like from Russia. Over time, most of the peculiarities of VAT have been eliminated, so that the tax takes a more standard form analogous to European VATs, but there are substantial administrative problems with the tax in most of the countries in the group.

The other transition countries face similar issues, although they are distinguished from the former Soviet Union group in that they did not inherit the Soviet tax laws as of 1991. These countries similarly started with an accounting system designed for central planning. They have generally by now undertaken at least one round of fundamental revision of their tax laws, with further rounds lying ahead. In many cases, the definition of income under the individual income tax is global in form, although substantial schedular elements are often present to simplify administration. To varying degrees, individual countries have looked to particular European countries as models. For example, the income tax law adopted by the Czech and Slovak Republics bears resemblances to the laws of Germany.

The income tax legislation has developed at a different pace for different countries in this subgroup. Hungary and Poland are probably the most advanced, followed by the Czech and Slovak Republics and Slovenia. The income tax laws of these countries are starting to rival those of the OECD countries in complexity and sophistication, and no doubt this will continue as compromises are made to foster various political interests and as tax administration in these countries improves. Other Eastern European countries are also keeping up a steady pace of development. For example, Albania

---

[62] *See* Nougayrède, *supra* note 55, at 50, 177-79.

[63] *See* Victoria Summers & Emil Sunley, An Analysis of Value-Added Taxes in Russia and Other Countries of the Former Soviet Union (1995)(IMF Working Paper WP/95/1).

adopted a new income tax law for individuals and companies at the end of
1998.   At the same time, Bulgaria amended its individual and corporate
income taxes.   These laws now are fairly detailed.   The income tax law
contains a system of presumptive taxation for small businesses.   The
corporate income tax base is determined by starting with commercial
accounting profits, with specified adjustments.   Countries such as Cambodia,
Laos, Mongolia, and Vietnam are generally further behind, consistent with the
development of their economies, although even in these countries important
steps forward are being taken in the development of tax legislation, and the
extent of change over the past 5-10 years is impressive.

China's position is, of course, sui generis.[64]   The development of the
tax system has responded to the government's general economic policies.
The current era dates from 1978, when the Four Modernizations program was
launched under Deng Xiao Ping (two years after the death of Mao Zedong and
the end of the Cultural Revolution).   The economic program called for
reducing the scope of central planning and opening to the rest of the world.
Tax law reform followed soon after, taking the form of new laws on the
income taxation of individuals, enterprises, and foreign joint ventures in
1980-81.   The laws on taxation of foreign enterprises have been more
sophisticated and oriented to international tax practices.   The pace of tax law
reform accelerated in the early 1990s (together with the reform of other
economic laws).   A new version of the income tax law for enterprises with
foreign investment was adopted in 1991.   A new individual income tax law
was adopted in late 1993, and in early 1994 a new income tax law for
domestic enterprises was adopted by the State Council.   These can still be
considered relatively rudimentary.   Compliance with the individual income
tax has been poor, and the government has now realized the problem that this
poses in the case of wealthy individuals, and has begun cracking down.[65]
Despite the often short text of the laws, there is an increasingly detailed web
of implementing regulations and policy statements, promulgated both at the
national and the regional levels.   A great deal of the evolution of
administrative policy is taking place at the regional level, particularly in the
special economic zones and financial centers.   Thus, the income tax system of
China in practice runs the range from a quite rudimentary, schedular system
of taxation of individuals in rural regions to a fairly sophisticated system for
taxing the income of multinational companies that operate in cities such as
Shanghai, Shenzhen, or Beijing.   It is to be expected that legislation at the

---

[64] *See generally* Jinyan Li, Taxation in the People's Republic of China (1991).
[65] *See* Peter S. Goodman, *China's Wealthy Facing Income Tax Crackdown,* Washngton Post, Oct. 22, 2002, at E1.

national level will continue to grow in sophistication, taking advantage of these regional developments.

I have included also a group of post-conflict countries because—like the transition countries—these have experienced a revision of tax legislation virtually from scratch with the assistance of foreign advisors. In many cases, their tax administrations have had to be constructed or reconstructed virtually from scratch as well. The influence of foreign advisors has led to a fair amount of eclecticism in their laws.

2.5.7   NORTHERN EUROPEAN FAMILY

The northern European group consists of countries whose law has been influenced to varying degrees by Germany and is further broken down into subgroups to reflect the degree of resemblance within each of these. Generally these countries have separate taxes on individuals and on legal persons. Germany's definition of income is schedular in form and is based on seven categories of income;[66] the same approach is followed in other countries in the same subgroup. The other countries in the group also use a basically schedular definition, but with fewer categories (typically three or four). In these countries, there is generally no separate concept of capital gains in a business context; gains on the disposition of business assets are taxable as part of business income.[67] Germany has a very important concept (largely shared by other countries in the group and by France) that distinguishes between business assets and private assets. The withdrawal of business assets from business use is a realization event (this is also true in France). By contrast, gains on the sale of private assets are generally not taxable. Exceptions are made for the disposal of shares that represent a significant holding in a company and for short-term gains.[68] Accounting for business income generally follows financial accounting.

Germany draws a distinction between types of income taxed on a net profit basis[69] and those taxed on a cash basis as the difference between

---

[66] *See infra* 7.2.1.

[67] Belgium is an exception. *See* TLDD at 902.

[68] *See* Ault et al. (1997) at 199.

[69] These are known as *Gewinneinkünfte* and include agriculture and forestry, commercial activity, and activity from independent work. *Einkünfte* is a concept unique to German tax law and does not exactly correspond to "income" (*Einkommen*) *Gewinneinkünften* can be taxed on the following basis:

receipts and expenses.[70] Capital gains on sales of assets used to produce income in the latter group (so-called private assets) are generally not taxed. In the case of real estate, a business activity is found where there are more than 3 sales in a 5-year period.[71] Depreciation is allowed for buildings rented out, but there is apparently no recapture.[72] Gain is taxed only if it is speculative; in 1999 the holding period for this purpose was extended to 10 years.[73]

The income tax in Germany is not self-assessed, but is assessed by the tax administration based on information submitted by the taxpayer.

2.5.8   SOUTHERN EUROPEAN FAMILY

As in northern Europe, the southern European group has separate taxes on individuals and on legal persons. In contrast to the global approach of Germany, the southern European countries have a history of schedular taxation.[74]

The Italian system has historically been schedular (i.e. separate taxes with independent rate structures) and territorial, with a strong element of presumptive taxation.[75] Italy's approach to taxation of capital gains has been similar to that of Germany: private gains are taxed only if attributable to speculative activity; gains of companies are taxed as part of business income. Italy has had a corporate income tax only since 1954.[76] This also had an important presumptive element in that it consisted of two components, the first being the assets of the company and the second being income that

---

Balance-sheet comparison (*Betriebsvermögenvergleich*, §§ 4 I, 5 EStG).

Excess of receipts over expenses (*Einnahme- Überschussrechnung*, § 4 III EStG).

On a concessional   presumptive basis (for agriculture) (*Berechnung nach Durchschnittssätzen mit Subventionscharakter für Land- und Forstwirtschaft*, § 13a EStG).

[70] Known as *Überschusseinkünfte*, they include income from employment, capital, rent, and "other incomes." *See* §22 EStG; BVerfGE 26, 302 (1969); BVerfGE 27, 111 (1969).

[71] *See* Tipke/Lang (2002) at 419-20.

[72] *See* §§ 9 I, 3 Nr. 7, 7 EStG.

[73] *See* §22 Nr. 2, §23 I Nr. 1a EStG.

[74] *See* Plasschaert, *supra* note 30, at 28-29. Greece also had a schedular system until 1955. The line between north and south is not a clean one, in the sense that France and Belgium had composite systems, going global in 1960 and 1962, respectively.

[75] *See* Harvard Law School, Taxation in Italy (1964).

[76] *See id.* at 196-97.

exceeds 6 percent of the taxable assets.[77]   The income of corporations was determined in the same manner as for individuals, that is, on a schedular basis. While the income and corporate taxes have now taken a more global form, the historical roots described above have influenced the form of these taxes.

Spain also started with a schedular income tax system, including presumptive elements, to which was eventually added a complementary global tax. Finally, the law of September 8, 1978, established the tax on a global basis, but still on a schedular definition of income.[78] Accordingly, the tax is imposed on the following types of income: income from labor, income from nonbusiness capital, income from business and professional activity, capital gains, and income taxed on a flow-through basis.[79] The corporate income tax in Spain goes back to the beginning of the 20th century. By 1957, it was calculated on a global basis.[80] The tax law provides its own accounting rules (i.e. the tax law is autonomous from commercial accounting); however, in practice the differences between tax and commercial accounting are minimized because the regulations call for the commercial accounting rules to be followed for tax purposes unless the tax law stipulates otherwise.[81]

2.5.9   JAPANESE/KOREAN FAMILY

Japan and the Republic of Korea form a separate group. There is a close resemblance between the tax laws of these two countries, which have been influenced by Germany and the United States, but have unique features of their own. The Japanese income tax dates back to 1887.[82] In the aftermath of World War II, the Shoup Mission played an influential role, although many of the reforms it recommended were subsequently reversed; much income from capital is effectively exempt from tax, so that the Japanese tax is a

---

[77] *See id.* at 199-200. The assets tax has now been dropped in Italy. *See* Income Tax Law, art. 89.

[78] *See* Albiñana (1992) at 260-63.

[79] *See* Spain, Individual Income Tax Law, art. 5.

[80] *See* Albiñana (1992) at 203.

[81] *See* Reglamento del Impuesto Sobre Sociedades, §37, *reprinted in* Código Tributário (Ollero et al. eds.; Aranzadi, 1995); Albiñana (1992) at 208.

[82] The discussion of Japan is based on Nakazato and Ramseyer, *Japan, in* Ault et al. (1997) at 71; Ishi (1993); Tax Bureau, Ministry of Finance, An Outline of Japanese Taxes 1997; and Yoshihiro Masui, *International Taxation in Japan: A Historica. Overview,* 21 Tax Notes Int'l 2813 (Dec. 18, 2000).

hybrid between an income tax and an expenditure tax.[83] Tax accounting for business income is determined by financial accounting, with such adjustments as are specified by the tax law. The taxation of business income is characterized by an extensive availability of reserves. Double taxation of corporate income is relieved by a dividend credit at the individual shareholder level and an exclusion at the corporate level for intercorporate dividends (80% or 100% depending on percentage of share ownership).

The individual income tax is characterized by a high level of schedularity, although there are also global features. Individual income is divided into ten categories: interest, dividends, real estate income, business income, employment income, retirement income, timber income, capital gains, occasional income, and miscellaneous income. The statute's approach to defining income is a hybrid between schedular and global. The statute does not define total income. Instead, the taxpayer is told to divide his income into categories (article 21 of the income tax law); any amount not falling into a particular category is considered to be miscellaneous income (article 35 of the law). Virtually all of the categories are subject to special computations, deductions, or rates. For example, there is a generous deduction from wages in lieu of itemizing employment expenses. Significant fringe benefits are exempt from tax (e.g. commuting subsidies, meals, clothing, low-interest loans for acquisition of employee housing, expense allowances, recreation facilities). Much interest income is either exempt or is taxed at source at a flat rate of 15%. Certain dividends are taxed at a flat rate of 35% at the taxpayer's option. The progressive rate schedule is applied separately to retirement income, timber income, and other income. The tax unit is the individual, although there is an allowance for dependent spouses. Personal deductions are allowed for an extensive list of items. Some special credits are allowed (research and development, acquisition of a dwelling house). Extensive withholding applies (wages, interest, dividends, professional fees, and other specified payments). A special system of "blue returns," relevant mostly to business income, involves special privileges, including special deductions, for taxpayers submitting such returns (which require maintenance of records in a specified format). The general approach to relief of international double taxation is a foreign tax credit system, with an overall limitation. Taxation of individuals distinguishes among residents, nonresidents, and those who are not permanently resident (resident less than five years) (the last group is taxed on their non-Japanese source income only if remitted to Japan). The government wins in an overwhelming percentage tax cases that are litigated;

---

[83] *See* Ishi (1993) at 97.

most audits are resolved by taxpayers agreeing to file corrected returns, thereby leading to no formal dispute.[84]

2.5.10 MISCELLANEOUS

The miscellaneous category represents countries whose income tax laws do not closely resemble those of any other group. Many of these belong to the Islamic legal family.[85] This is not to say that there has not been a substantial cross-country influence for this group. For example, Turkey has been influenced by Germany and perhaps France. Indonesia has been influenced in recent years by the United States, particularly in the 1983 reform of its income tax law.

2.5.11 EUROPEAN UNION

I include the European Union member countries (as well as the next wave of applicant countries) as a separate family, in no small part because these countries have a great deal of their tax law in common, even if they still retain substantial autonomy in taxation. Although the process is a slow one, it seems likely that overall the tax laws of these countries will move even closer together over time.

---

[84] *See* The State of Taxpayers' Rights in Japan 52-53, 57, 100 (Koji Ishimura ed., 1995).

[85] An argument could be made for putting Islamic countries into a separate family, but it is not clear that there is sufficient commonality with respect to the tax laws to warrant doing so. A feature that is unique to Islamic countries (since it is based in the Koran) is the zakat (whose form varies from country to country, but could be characterized as a hybrid income and wealth tax). In some Islamic countries particularly Saudi Arabia, the zakat plays an important role in the income tax system but the relationship between the zakat and the income tax differs substantially from one country to another, and in only a few countries is zakat collected by the State. *See infra* 4.9.

Table 1: Tax Law Families

I. Common Law

1. Commonwealth: Antigua and Barbuda, Australia, Bahrain, Bangladesh, Barbados, Belize, Botswana, Brunei Darussalam, Canada, Cyprus, Dominica, Fiji, The Gambia, Ghana, Grenada, Guyana, India, Iraq, Ireland, Israel, Jamaica, Jordan, Kenya, Kiribati, Kuwait, Lesotho, Malawi, Malaysia, Malta, Mauritius, Myanmar, Namibia, Nepal, New Zealand, Nigeria, Oman, Pakistan, Papua New Guinea, St. Kitts and Nevis, St. Lucia, St. Vincent and the Grenadines, Samoa, Saudi Arabia, Seychelles, Sierra Leone, Singapore, Solomon Islands, South Africa, Sri Lanka, Sudan, Swaziland, Tanzania, Tonga, Trinidad and Tobago, Uganda, United Kingdom, Zambia, Zimbabwe

2. American: Liberia, Marshall Islands, Micronesia, Palau, Philippines, United States

II. Civil Law

3. French: Algeria, Benin, Burkina Faso, Burundi, Cameroon, Central African Republic, Chad, Comoros, Republic of Congo, Democratic Republic of the Congo, Cote d'Ivoire, Djibouti, France, Gabon, Guinea, Haiti, Lebanon, Libya, Madagascar, Mali, Mauritania, Morocco, Niger, Rwanda, Senegal, Togo, Tunisia

4. Latin American: Argentina, Bolivia, Brazil, Chile, Colombia, Costa Rica, Dominican Republic, Ecuador, El Salvador, Guatemala, Honduras, Mexico, Nicaragua, Panama, Paraguay, Peru, Uruguay, Venezuela

5. Transition and post-conflict countries

  a. Former Soviet Union: Armenia, Azerbaijan, Belarus, Estonia, Georgia, Kazakhstan, Kyrgyz Republic, Latvia, Lithuania, Moldova, Russia, Tajikistan, Turkmenistan, Ukraine, Uzbekistan

  b. Other: Albania, Bosnia and Herzegovina, Bulgaria, Cambodia, People's Republic of China, Croatia, Czech Republic, Hungary, Lao People's Democratic Republic, Former Yugoslav Republic of Macedonia, Mongolia, Poland, Romania, Slovak Republic, Slovenia, Vietnam

  c. Post-conflict: Rwanda, Afghanistan, East Timor

6. Northern European

    a. Germanic: Austria, Germany, Luxembourg, Switzerland

    b. Dutch: Netherlands, Suriname

    c. Nordic: Denmark, Finland, Iceland, Norway, Sweden

    d. Belgian: Belgium

    e. Baltic: Estonia, Latvia, Lithuania

7. Southern European

    a. ˙Portuguese: Angola, Cape Verde, Guinea-Bissau, Mozambique, Portugal, São Tomé and Principe

    b. Italian: Eritrea, Ethiopia, Italy, San Marino, Somalia

    c. Spanish: Equatorial Guinea, Spain

    d. Greek: Greece

8. Japanese/Korean. Japan, Korea

9. Miscellaneous: Islamic State of Afghanistan, Bhutan, Egypt, Indonesia, Islamic Republic of Iran, Syrian Arab Republic, Thailand, Turkey, Yemen.

III. European Union

    a. Current Members: Austria, Belgium, Denmark, Finland, France, Germany, Greece, Ireland, Italy, Luxembourg, The Netherlands, Portugal, Spain, Sweden, United Kingdom

    b. Applicants:[86] Cyprus, Czech Republic, Estonia, Hungary, Latvia, Lithuania, Malta, Poland, Slovak Republic, Slovenia

---

[86] As approved at the Dec. 13, 2002, Copenhagen summit.

Chapter 3

TAX AND TAXES

3.1 WHAT IS A TAX?

Since this is a book on tax, it seems appropriate to ask what "tax" means. It turns out that the concept is a slippery one. In economic terms, any imposition of costs on individuals or firms by the government can be considered a tax. For example, economists frequently talk about the inflation tax, since inflation appropriates resources to the government. Legally, though, it is clear that inflation is not a tax, since it does not involve a payment by the taxpayer to the government. Similarly, regulatory requirements can have the same economic consequence as taxes. For example, a legal requirement for employers to provide health insurance to their employees may have almost the same economic effect as a tax imposed on the employer the revenues from which are used to provide health benefits to employees. Such a requirement is not a tax, even though it is economically equivalent to a tax.[1]

Tax might be defined as a required payment to government. While this definition distinguishes taxes from other government action with an equivalent economic effect, it is at the same time both under- and over-inclusive. Some legally required payments may be made not to the government itself, but to a government-controlled entity. Such payments differ only in form from earmarked taxes that are paid to the government and then passed on to the spending agency in question. On the other hand, not all required payments to the government are taxes. Tax should not include a civil or criminal fine. The distinction between a fine and a tax can be a matter of

---

[1] *See, e.g.,* Armour Packing Co. v. United States, 209 U.S. 56, 79-80 (1908) (Art. I, sec. 9 of the Constitution, which prohibits the imposition of a tax on exports, did not prohibit regulation of rates for transportation by rail, because such regulation was not a tax, even though it might place a burden upon export trade. "There is no attempt to levy duties on goods to be exported, and the mere incidental effect in the legal regulation of interstate commerce upon such exportations does not come within this constitutional prohibition." 209 U.S. at 80) (This analysis of course leaves open the possibility that a regulatory measure that was not bona fide might be considered a tax under the export clause, since then the effect would not be "incidental".)

form. For example, are the foundation excise taxes found in the Internal Revenue Code[2] really taxes or are they fines?[3] The answer may differ depending on the context in which the question arises.

Further, taxes should not include payments to the government for which the taxpayer receives something in return. There is a continuum, ranging from pure taxes where the taxpayer receives nothing, to a fee for services whose value corresponds to what was paid.[4]

As an abstract matter, the concept of "tax" is accordingly somewhat malleable. This may not be a big deal but for the fact that in a number of different legal contexts,[5] it may be critical whether a particular payment is

---

[2] For example, I.R.C. § 4941 imposes a tax on self-dealing between private foundations and certain persons. There are several other excise taxes which look like fines in the guise of taxes, including I.R.C. § 4980C, which imposes a "tax" of $100 per day per insured on providers of long-term care insurance who fail to meet certain regulatory requirements.

[3] According to Tipke (1993) at 1058, fines should not be considered taxes. *See also* S.T.C. (Nov. 16, 2000) R.T.C. 2000, 276 (Spain) (a penalty may be distinguished from a tax on the basis that the former is designed to punish illegal conduct, while the latter is designed to contribute to public revenues on the basis of the taxpayer's economic capacity).

[4] One of the intermediate positions along this continuum involves the case where the tax corresponds to the right to engage in certain activity or to a legal benefit obtained by the taxpayer. For example, a property transfer tax may be payable as a condition for registering ownership of property. In this case, the taxpayer obtains a registered title in exchange for paying the tax. Another case involves a fee the amount of which exceeds the value of the services provided. A passport issuance fee may, for example, be set at a level substantially higher than the costs of issuing the passport. Evaluation of the relationship between the level of the fee and the cost of the services may be complex, however. In the case of the passport fee, should just the costs of issuance be taken into account, or also the cost of operating the immigration system and embassies abroad? Some "fees" seem indistinguishable from taxes. For example, in my home town, the city set a "stormwater" fee, which funds stormwater management. All property owners are charged this fee. The fee allowed a reduction in the property tax, which previously funded these expenses. Why the change? Tax-exempt institutions pay the stormwater fee, but not property tax.

[5] For example, in a constitutional context. In federal countries, the constitution may assign competence for levying tax among levels of government. *See* Tipke (1993) at 1074-1135. Tipke (1993) at 1060-61 notes that the mere fact that a levy qualifies as a tax does not necessarily mean it is constitutionally authorized, if it is a backdoor way of expanding the regulatory authority of a particular level of government, thereby encroaching on the authority of another level. The same problem of regulatory measures disguised as taxes has been considered by the U.S. Supreme Court, *see infra* 4.3.3. The constitution may also contain procedures for adoption of taxes or impose

considered a tax. The answer may differ according to the context and the country where the question is asked.

Several continental European and Latin American countries have fairly well-elaborated statutory definitions of taxes and other compulsory contributions.[6] Under such schemes, taxes are viewed as a subset of a more

---

restrictions on what kinds of taxes may be imposed. Taxes generally may be imposed only by law, while fees may be imposed by administrative agencies. To determine whether a particular restriction applies, it is necessary to decide whether the item in question is a tax.

Besides constitutional matters, some other contexts in which one might care whether something is a tax are as follows:

- procedure. There may be an issue as to whether tax procedures apply to the item in question. Usually this will be a straightforward matter of statutory construction of the law applicable to tax procedure. For example Tipke (1993) at 1054 notes that the German Abgabenordnung applies to taxes only (and not to other compulsory contributions) but that there has not been dispute as to the scope of its application. Another example of a broad procedure-oriented definition is the definition of "tax" for purposes of sec. 811 of the Taxes Consolidation Act, 1997 (Ireland): "any tax, duty, levy or charge which... is placed under the care and management of the Revenue Commissioners and any interest, penalty or other amount payable pursuant to the [tax] Acts." Sec. 811 is the GAAR.

- classification for purposes of budget law.

- contractual. A contract may provide that one party shall bear the burden of taxes, and it will then be a matter of interpreting the contract. One possibility would be to refer to general legal concepts of tax in the jurisdiction where the tax is imposed, but the contractual terms may call for a different approach.

- application of double taxation treaty or a treaty on exchange of information. Treaties generally specify which taxes they apply to but they may contain some clauses that are applicable to taxes generally; hence the need to ascertain whether a particular item is a tax.

- extradition. Extradition may not be available for tax crimes. In the case of a prosecution for failure to pay an amount, the issue may therefore arise whether the amount is a tax.

- human rights protection. The ECHR has been held not to apply to taxes in certain respects.

[6] The definition is typically contained in the tax code or in a general law on tax procedure. For example, AO § 3 (Germany); LGT art. 26 (Spain); Tax Code, art. 8 (Russia).

general category — compulsory contribution[7] — which has been defined as "a monetary contribution unilaterally imposed under public law which serves (at least in part) to raise revenues and is payable to a public authority."[8]   A fundamental criterion is that the contribution is *compelled* by law. In turn, compulsory contributions are typically subdivided into fees, special contributions, and taxes.[9] Fees are compulsory contributions paid by the beneficiary of public services. While a fee need not correspond precisely to the value of the benefit, some systems consider that it should not be entirely disproportionate to this value.[10]   Special contributions are compulsory

---

[7] In German: *Abgabe*. German law contains a definition of tax (*Steuer*) in §3 AO. *Abgabe* is a compulsory contribution; therefore, taxes are a subset of *Abgaben*. *See* Tipke (1993) at 1052. The corresponding term to *Abgabe* in Spanish and Portuguese is *tributo*, the term for tax being *impuesto* (in Portuguese *imposto*). Soler Roch (2002) at 13 uses the term "tribute" in English for *tributo,* but I just don't think that works. "Tribute" means something in English, but it means something else. I admit that compulsory contribution is not idiomatic, but I çan't think of anything better.

[8] Ferdinand Kirchhof, Grundriss des Abgabenrechts 1 (1991). The following definition from Spain is about the same: "a public receipt under public law, obtained by a public entity, on the basis of a relationship as a creditor in respect of the person obligated to contribute, as a result of the application of the law to a fact which is indicative of economic capacity, and which does not constitute a penalty for illegal activity." Martín Queralt et al. (2001) at 79.

[9] This is under Spanish law, but the approach of other civil law countries is broadly similar. For example, Brazil uses the general concept of *tributo* to cover *impostos, taxas, contribuição de melhoria,* and *contribuições especiais.   Taxa* refers to a payment made in exchange for a service provided by the government. *See* Ives Gandra da Silva, Curso de direito Tributário 1 (1982). *Imposto* is a tax proper. For the somewhat different Mexican terminology, see de la Garza (2001) at 319-20.

[10] *See* Tipke (1993) at 1067, 1070-74. In France, obligatory contributions are divided into fees (*taxes fiscales* and *redevances*), parafiscal fees (*taxes parafiscales*), social contributions (*cotisations sociales*), and taxes (*impôts*). The difference between *taxe* and *redevance* is that the latter should be equivalent in value to the service rendered, while the former need not be. According to Trotabas & Cotteret (1997) at 18-19, *taxe* has a fiscal nature while *redevance* is a non-fiscal fee for services. Parafiscal fees are the same as *taxes*, except that they are extrabudgetary and not paid to the State itself. *See* Michel Bouvier, Introduction au droit fiscal et à la théorie de l'impôt 18-20 (1996); Beltrame & Mehl (1997) at 35, 40; Guy Gest, *Imposition, in* Dictionnaire Encyclopédique de Finances Publics 923 (Loïc Philip ed. 1991). The Constitutional Court has held that the television fee imposed by Radio-television francaise (RTF) was in the nature of a *taxe parafiscal* within the meaning of the organic budget law of 1959. *See* Cons. const., Aug. 11, 1960, Dec. 60-8 DC, Rec. 25. The decision is reproduced with commentary in Louis Favoreu & Loïc Philip, Les grandes decisions du Conseil constitutionnel 85-102 (16th ed. 1999). *See also* Loïc Philip, Droit Fiscal

contributions tied to the contributor's receipt of a benefit as a result of the carrying out of public works or the establishment or expansion of public services (sidewalk improvements being a classic example). Tax is the residual category of compulsory contributions where the taxpayer does not receive anything in return for the payment.[11]

Common law countries tend not to be as systematic about the concept of tax. Some make no attempt to define in law what is a tax.[12] With its largely unwritten and non-federal constitution, the U.K. has seen little need to

---

Constitutionnel 101-08 (1990). Since the organic law required any *taxe parafiscal* to be approved annually by parliament, the Constitutional Court found that this procedure had to be followed by RTF, i.e. that it was illegal for this fee to be imposed administratively without parliamentary approval. The Constitutional Court thus adopted a narrow concept of user fee, requiring a close relation between the services rendered and the fee, and hence a broad concept of *taxe parafiscal*. As a policy matter, this decision can be justified on the basis that it is appropriate as a matter of democratic governance to take a broad view of the kind of levy requiring Parliamentary approval.

[11] In Germany, there is no legally binding subdivision of *Abgaben* on a constitutional level. *See* Kirchhof, *supra* note 8, at 1. Taxes are defined in the Abgabenordnung. However, the generally accepted concept of tax for constitutional purposes in Germany is that of a monetary contribution, imposed by law, by a public authority, for public purposes, and not in exchange for a benefit. *See* Tipke (1993) at 1055. Revenue raising may be only incidental. The German constitutional court has found that a measure passed under the authority to levy tax would lack constitutional authority only if it is practically impossible that it would raise any revenue. *See id.* at 1059; BVerfGE 16, 147, 161 (1963). The law does not fix what other kinds of *Abgaben* there may be. The constitution does refer to *Gebühren*, which are levied only where the State renders some service to the taxpayer. *See* Kirchhof, *supra* note 8, at 7. One of these would be social security contributions, which are not considered taxes in Germany (although they are *Abgaben*). *See id.* at 9-10. Customs duties are taxes. *See id.* at 39. Beltrame & Mehl (1997) at 45-46 offers the following definition out of the French tradition: "Tax is a monetary contribution, levied for the purpose of covering public expenditure or for regulatory reasons, required from individuals or legal persons ... according to their ability to pay, on the basis of authority, in a determined amount and without receiving something in return." *See also* de la Garza (2001) 319-85 (applying a similar methodology for Mexico).

[12] "There is no formal legal definition of a tax in any of the taxing statutes or, indeed, in the Constitution." Corrigan (2000) at 4 (Ireland). In Australia, the concept of tax is relevant under the Constitution and has been developed through judicial decisions. *See* P.H. Lane, Lane's Commentary on the Australian Constitution 165-70 (2d ed. 1997).

do so, for example.[13] In common law countries, the concept of tax may differ according to the context. Moreover, in common law countries, the more general category (which I have called compulsory contribution) which includes taxes, fees, and special contributions, does not seem to be much used as a legal category. Indeed, it is not typical to use just one word for this concept in English; more commonly, one would say "taxes and fees."

In the U.S., for example, the concept of tax has been developed judicially in different contexts. For example, in the *U.S. Shoe* case,[14] the U.S. Supreme Court adopted a broad concept of tax. The Export Clause of the constitution (art. I, § 9) provides that no tax may be imposed on articles exported from any State. The question was whether a harbor maintenance tax (HMT) is a tax within the meaning of the Export Clause. The Court found that the HMT would be constitutional if it were a "user fee," i.e. a "charge designed as compensation for Government-supplied services, facilities, or benefits."[15] The HMT was levied at a rate of 0.125 percent of the value of cargo passing through U.S. ports; its proceeds were deposited in the Harbor Maintenance Trust Fund and used for harbor maintenance and development projects. The Court found that the HMT could not be considered a user fee because it bore no relation to the extent of port use, being based on the value of the cargo.

The Canadian courts have upheld levies such as license fees, registration fees and the like as "regulatory charges," being charges for a government service which bear a reasonable relation to the cost of providing the service. The Canadian courts have given the legislature "reasonable leeway" in setting rates. For example, a fee for gravel extraction based on the volume extracted was upheld as a regulatory charge, even though there was no direct connection to road repair and no requirement that the funds be used for road repair.[16]

---

[13] *See generally* Tiley (2000) at 3-7 (also discussing Canadian and Australian cases, where the concept of tax is constitutionally relevant). Aston Cantlow and Wilmcote with Billesley Parochial Church Council v. Wallbank, 4 ITLR 353 (Court of Appeal, May 17, 2001) held, somewhat surprisingly, that the liability at common law of the owner of land historically associated with the rectory of a church to repair the church chancel was a tax. The decision illustrates the flexibility of the concept of tax.

[14] United States v. U.S. Shoe Corp., 523 U.S. 360 (1998).

[15] 523 U.S. at 363.

[16] *See* Allard Contractors v. Coquitlam, [1993] 4 S.C.R. 371, discussed in 2 Peter Hogg, Constitutional Law of Canada at at 30-20 (looseleaf, updated to 2001). Similarly, an "educational development charge" levied on land undergoing development, the revenues to be used for school construction, was upheld in Ontario Home Builders' Association v. York Region Board of Education, [1996] 2 S.C.R.

European law prohibits the imposition of customs duties on intra-community trade, or charges having an equivalent effect.[17]   On this basis, similar to *U.S. Shoe,* the ECJ has struck down *ad valorem* charges since they could not be considered proportionate to the services rendered.[18]

The distinction between tax and fee also arises in the context of the foreign tax credit. Obviously, a foreign tax credit should be allowed only for a foreign levy which is a tax. While the legislation of most countries does not discuss the meaning of "tax" in this context, there is an extensive discussion in the U.S. income tax regulations. Taking an economic approach for policy reasons, these regulations provide that, to the extent that a levy is paid in exchange for receipt of a specific economic benefit, it will not be considered a tax.[19]   A levy that is a tax under the laws of the country imposing it may not be considered a tax for U.S. foreign tax credit purposes. This narrow concept of a tax is influenced by policy considerations under the foreign tax credit, which is designed to relieve double taxation, not reimburse U.S. taxpayers for fees paid to foreign countries for services received.

A levy on exports imposed to compensate for exchange rate differences as part of the Common Agricultural Policy of the EU has been held not to be a tax.[20]   EU law seems generally to look at substance in

---

929. However, Re Eurig Estate, [1998] 2 S.C.R. 565 held that an *ad valorem* probate fee could not be justified as a regulatory charge because it bore an insufficient relation to the cost of issuing letters probate. This made the fee a tax.

[17] Article 25 of EC Treaty. *See* Lyons (2001) at 21, 103 n.87.

[18] Case 63/74 W Cadsky S.p.A. v. Istituto nazionale per il commercio estero [1975] E.C.R. 281 (Feb. 26, 1975) involved a customs inspection charge. The court left open the possibility that a charge could be imposed where "a specific service actually rendered may form the consideration for a possible proportional payment for the service in question." *See* Case 170/88 Ford España SA v. Estado español [1989] E.C.R. 2305 (July 11, 1989) (amount of customs charge for customs clearance in special premises "cannot, as it is calculated on an *ad valorem* basis, be regarded as proportionate to that service or correspond to those costs" [i.e. customs clearance costs]); *see also* citations in Lyons (2001) at 103 n.87. Separately, the ECJ has held that notarial charges are a tax within the meaning of Council Decision 69/335, concerning indirect taxes on the raising of capital, when they are collected by notaries employed by the state and finance the state's general expenditures. *See* Eileen O'Grady, *Notarial Charges Constitute Taxes,* 21 Tax Notes Int'l 1992 (Oct. 30, 2000).

[19] Treas. Reg. §1.901-2(a)(2).

[20] Byrne v. Conroy, [1997] 1 C.M.L.R. 595 (Irish High Court), [1997] 2 I.L.R.M. 99, *aff'd,* [1998] 2 I.L.R.M. 113. The issue was whether a conspiracy to evade payment of monetary compensation amounts (MCAs) was "an offence in connection with taxes, duties or exchange control" within the meaning of the Extradition Act. If it

determining what is a tax, as opposed to relying on the formal characterization of a levy under national law.[21]

The precise contours of what is a tax may even differ depending on the constitutional provision in question, as the Court in the *U.S. Shoe* case suggested.[22] Therefore it should not be surprising for the concept of tax to differ somewhat from country to country, and even to have slightly different meanings within a single constitution (although civil law jurisdictions might have more difficulty assigning differing meanings to a given term than would common law jurisdictions).

A clash between common law and civil law terminology and concepts is presented by Brazil's enactment of a "contribution for intervention in the economy" which was imposed at a 10% rate on royalties paid by Brazilian residents to nonresidents.[23] To bolster the status of this levy as a "contribution" rather than a tax, proceeds from this contribution were earmarked to the National Fund for Scientific and Technological Development. The enactment of this levy raises the question as to whether it is subject to provisions of double tax treaties that impose a limit on the withholding tax on royalties. Under article 2 of Brazil's tax treaties, following the OECD Model, the treaties apply not only to existing taxes but also to similar taxes enacted in the future. But is this levy a "tax" within the meaning of article 2? In the Portuguese version of Brazil's treaties, the term "*imposto*" is used in correspondence to "tax" in the English version. *Imposto*

---

was, the defendant could not be extradited. Agricultural levies imposed on exports were levied as if they were customs duties. The court held that despite its labelling as a tax the MCA "is not in fact a tax in any real meaning of that term. The principal object of a tax is to raise revenue. But that was not the object of the levy here." [1997] 1 C.M.L.R. at 609.

[21] *See* IRC v. Océ Van Der Grinten NV, Chancery Division, England (Nov. 2, 2000), 2 ITLR 948 (2000), which involved the issue whether a charge involving a rebate of a tax credit allowed to a nonresident shareholder was a "withholding tax" within the meaning of the parent-subsidiary directive (*see infra* 4.4.1). The court found that for this purpose, European law would consider the substance of "how the national law operates," and not whether under the national law the charge is considered to be a "tax" (a question which is not even "relevant under United Kingdom tax law").

[22] The Court found that the distinction between a tax and a user fee would appropriately be drawn differently for purposes of the Export Clause, as opposed to other constitutional situations, in light of textual and policy differences between the provisions involved. The other situations involved the "nontextual negative command of the dormant Commerce Clause," the Takings Clause, and the issue of intergovernmental immunity from taxation. *See* 523 U.S. at 367-69.

[23] Law No. 10,168, Dec. 29, 2000 (D.O., Dec. 30, 2000).

(as opposed to *tributo*) is a tax in the narrow sense, and does not include "contributions."[24] Therefore, it appears that if this levy is properly considered a contribution rather than a tax, Brazil's treaties do not apply. Possibly, those of Brazil's treaties that provide that the English text prevails could be relied on to apply to contributions as well, on the basis that the English word "tax" is generally read broadly so as to include levies such as "contributions."[25] Moreover, even using the Brazilian nomenclature, one would presumably have to determine whether the name used is appropriate; the label used should not determine the legal nature of a levy.[26] To avoid such issues in the future, if treaty negotiators wish to make sure that Article 2 of a double tax treaty applies to a broader range of levies than taxes in the narrow sense, it may be advisable for them to familiarize themselves with the country's concept of tax and other levies and draft the treaty appropriately.

Are social security payments taxes? If legally required, they would seem to be, although if viewed as in the nature of an insurance premium they might not be, and in fact they are not treated as taxes in many countries.[27] Their status is determined by the legislation of each country. In other words, form may be decisive. If the law says that a contribution is a tax and if it is collected by the tax authorities according to the procedures applicable to taxes generally, then it is a tax. The foundation excise taxes are taxes because they are included in the Internal Revenue Code and are called taxes. If instead they were structured as fines, they would not be taxes.

Largely for historical reasons, taxes are not always called tax, but the use of different nomenclature does not usually imply a legal difference. The use of different terms for different taxes is in most cases a matter of custom.[28]

---

[24] *See supra* notes 7 and 9.

[25] *See* Marcio Neves, A Comparative Analysis of the Relationship Between Tax Treaties and Domestic Law in the United States and in Brazil (unpublished student paper: Georgetown University Law Center 2002).

[26] *See* S.T.C., Nov. 10, 1994, R.T.C. 1994, 296 (Spain); de la Garza (2001) at 320 (Mexico) (whether a levy is a tax or a fee must be determined according to substance and not labels).

[27] *See* David Williams, *Social Security Taxation, in* TLDD 340, 346-48. They are not considered taxes in Germany, France, or the U.K. S*ee* Tipke (1993) at 1053; Beltrame & Mehl (1997) at 35; Tiley (2000) at 6.

[28] In English, the terms excise, impost, duty, levy, cess, and rate are used to refer to different taxes. Tiberghien (1995) at 4-5 notes that in Belgium the terms *taxe, contribution, impôt* and *droit* are used but that all of these terms mean "tax." In Russian, the term for tax is *nalog*, duty is *poshlina* (used in the case of customs duty and state duty, which is a sort of stamp tax or in some cases such as court fees and passport fees is a fee for services), and these are subsets of obligatory payments

Is the concept of tax relevant under the country's constitution? For what other purposes is it relevant whether something is a "tax"? How has it been interpreted? Is there a definition of tax in the tax legislation? Does the country distinguish between taxes and other types of contributions and, if so, how?

3.2 DIRECT VS. INDIRECT TAXES

Taxes are often classified as direct or indirect.[29] There seems to be a fair amount of consensus that the income tax is a quintessential direct tax and that taxes on consumption (sales, VAT, or excises) are indirect taxes. However, when one probes deeper to ask on what basis taxes should be classified as direct or indirect the distinction between the two becomes quite murky, and one is left with the impression that the distinction does not make a great deal of sense. In the 18th and 19th centuries, the distinction seems to have been made on the basis that indirect taxes are those whose incidence is shifted.[30] However, modern economic theory holds that even income taxes

---

(*obiazatel'niy platej*). Therefore the full name of the tax code of Kazakhstan is the Code on Taxes and Other Obligatory Payments.

[29] For example, the general tax code of France is divided into direct and indirect taxes. In France, direct taxes include income tax and property tax, while indirect taxes include VAT and inheritance tax, among others.

[30] Beltrame & Mehl (1997) cite at 62-63 the explanation given by the French constituent assembly in 1790, to the effect that direct taxes are levied on persons or property, while indirect taxes are levied on manufacture, sale, consumption, and the like, and are indirectly paid by the consumer. *See also* Bruce Ackerman, *Taxation and the Constitution,* 99 Colum. L. Rev. 1, 16-18 (1999), discussing the origins of the concept of direct taxation in the writings of John Locke and the French Physiocrats, and noting that the Physiocrats believed that only agriculture generated wealth, and that a tax on land was accordingly a direct tax on wealth generation. In later doctrine, the distinction was based on the more general concept of shifting. "The grouping of taxes into two classes, direct and indirect, and the principles upon which the classification is made goes back a long way in the literature. The main guide as to the appropriate category has tended to be whether the person who actually pays the money over to the tax collecting authority suffers a corresponding reduction in his income. If he does then – in the traditional language – impact and incidence are upon the same person and the tax is direct; if not and the burden is shifted and the real income of someone else is affected (i.e. impact and incidence are upon different people) then the tax is indirect." David Walker, *The Direct-Indirect Tax Problem.*

might be shifted to different degrees and in different circumstances (and in some cases, such as those of the corporate income tax, the incidence is unknown) so basing classification of taxes on their incidence does not seem to make a lot of sense.[31]

Despite the lack of sound economic basis for the distinction between direct and indirect taxes, such a distinction is made in various contexts and often has legal significance.[32] The distinction is not always drawn on the same basis, which should not be surprising in light of the lack of theoretical justification for a distinction.

The U.S. Constitution places limits on the way the Federal government may impose direct taxes, requiring direct taxes to be apportioned according to population, which is quite awkward and virtually rules out direct taxes at the Federal level. The clause in question can be viewed as a constitutional anomaly, having been negotiated to facilitate a compromise between slave and free states in order to reach agreement on adoption of the constitution.[33] Constitutional jurisprudence is unclear and perhaps contradictory on what is a direct tax. For most of the 19th century, the Supreme Court construed "direct tax" very narrowly, essentially confining it to taxes on property (historically, direct taxes in the U.S. colonies were primarily property taxes). However, in *Pollock v. Farmers' Loan & Trust Co.*,[34] the court ruled that the income tax — at least to the extent it fell on property — was a direct tax and hence unconstitutional. The Sixteenth

---

Fifteen Years of Controversy, 10 Public Finance 153, 154 (1955). *See also* Tiley (2000) at 17-18; Randolph Paul, Taxation in the United States 45-62 (1954).

[31] "As the literature of public finance reveals, the distinction between "direct" and "indirect" has been drawn in a number of ways but has remained without much analytical usefulness." Richard Musgrave & Peggy Richman, *Allocation Aspects, Domestic and International, in* The Role of Direct and Indirect Taxes in the Federal Revenue System (Brookings Institution: 1964). Richard Musgrave & Peggy Musgrave, Public Finance in Theory and Practice 215-16 (5th ed. 1989) refers to the distinction as "ambiguous" but intended to distinguish between those taxes that are intended to be shifted and those that are not.

[32] In France, the administrative courts have jurisdiction over appeals concerning direct taxes and VAT, while the ordinary courts have jurisdiction over indirect taxes (other than VAT). *See* art. L.199 L.P.F. In determining whether for this purpose taxes are direct or indirect, the courts have relied on the "legal nature of the tax." Gilles Bachelier & Eve Obadia, Le Contentieux Fiscal 126 (2d ed. 1996).

[33] *See* Ackerman, *supra* note 30, at 7-13. The relevant clause is Art. I, § 9 (together with Art. I, § 2).

[34] 158 U.S. 601 (1895).

Amendment to the Constitution was ratified in 1913 to allow the implementation of an income tax without apportionment.

A totally different approach to defining direct taxes has been taken in Canada, where provincial governments are allowed under section 92 of the Constitution to impose direct taxes, while indirect taxes may be imposed by the Federal government alone. An unduly narrow reading of "direct" tax would have stifled provincial public finances, and the courts have accordingly tended to read the concept fairly broadly, albeit with its own technicalities. The starting point has been John Stuart Mill's definition: "A direct tax is one which is demanded from the very persons who it is intended or desired should pay it. Indirect taxes are those which are demanded from one person in the expectation and intention that he shall indemnify himself at the expense of another; such are the excise or customs."[35]

In determining whether a tax is direct or indirect, the courts have refrained from applying economic analysis to determine whether the particular tax could be shifted. Rather, they have established typologies based on "the general tendencies of the tax and the common understandings of men as to those tendencies."[36] In so doing, they have distinguished taxes that are likely to be recouped as part of the cost of doing business, from those that are likely to be "passed on" as an element of the price of the transaction subject to tax.[37] For example, a tax based on the volume of gravel extracted could be expected to be passed on to purchasers, while a flat amount per month would not be passed on as such.[38] The courts have taken rather formal approaches. While a sales tax based on the seller (it would be passed on) is indirect, if the tax is structured so that legal incidence falls on the consumer, it has been held to be a direct tax (directly on the consumer), even if the seller is required to collect as agent for the government and is legally liable for failure to collect.[39] An estate tax is indirect, since it is imposed on the executor, who will pass on the tax to the estate, but an inheritance tax (imposed on the beneficiary) is direct, even if the executor is liable to collect the tax.[40] However, a probate fee was considered to be a direct tax, since it was payable by the executor "in

---

[35] Principles of Political Economy (1848), Book V, ch. 3, *as quoted in* Bank of Toronto v. Lambe, 12 App. Cas. 575, 582 (Privy Council 1887). *See also* Hogg, *supra* note 16, at 30-6.

[36] *Bank of Toronto*, 12 App. Cas. at 582.

[37] *See* Hogg, *supra* note 16, at 30-7.

[38] *See id.*

[39] *See id.* at 30-11 to 30-14.

[40] *See id.* at 30-14 to 30-15.

his or her representative capacity."[41]   While taxes on land had been considered direct as a matter of typology, in *Ontario Home Builders' Association v. York Region Board of Education,*[42] the court considered a charge for building permits to be indirect. Without going into further detail,[43] it should be apparent that it is virtually impossible to draw a principled distinction between direct and indirect taxes. The Canadian courts have come up with an approach that removes most controversies, although it is notable that disputes still arise after more than 100 years of case law.

In Switzerland, art. 129 of the Constitution allows the Federation to harmonize only direct taxes.   These are understood as including taxes on income and capital, but not on inheritances and gifts.[44]

The WTO agreements permit countries to impose indirect taxes on the destination method, i.e. to grant a rebate of such taxes to exporters.   For this purpose, the agreements define direct and indirect taxes according to a specific list,[45] thereby removing most arguments about the classification of taxes.

Does the country's constitution or legislation distinguish between direct and indirect taxes? If so, is there precedent for how the distinction is drawn?

3.3 THE PANOPLY OF TAXES

The most important[46] tax worldwide is *income tax*.   In some countries, this term covers both the tax on the income of individuals and that

---

[41] *See id.* at 30-15 (discussing Re Eurig Estate [1998] 2 S.C.R. 565).

[42] [1996] 2 S.C.R. 929.

[43] The interested reader can refer to Hogg, *supra* note 16, sec. 30.

[44] *See* Höhn & Waldburger (2000) at 65.

[45] "For the purposes of this Agreement: The term 'direct taxes' shall mean taxes on wages, profits, interests, rents, royalties, and all other forms of income, and taxes on the ownership of real property:... The term 'indirect taxes' shall mean sales, excise, turnover, value added, franchise, stamp, transfer, inventory and equipment taxes, border taxes and all taxes other than direct taxes and import charges." Marrakesh Agreement Establishing the World Trade Organization, Annex 1A, Multilateral Agreements on Trade in Goods. Agreement on Subsidies and Countervailing Measures, Annex I, note 58. *reprinted in* Edmond McGovern, International Trade Regulation ¶25:39 (looseleaf. as updated to 2002).

[46] The income tax (including corporate income tax under this concept) is the most important tax in revenue terms in most – but not all – countries, and would far outweigh other taxes if total revenues from various taxes in different countries were

on corporations. In other countries, the tax on legal persons is separate (being referred to, for example, as *corporate tax* or as *profit tax)*, the term income tax being reserved for the tax on individuals.

Because the individual income tax is a progressive tax,[47] many individuals pay more in *social security tax* than in income tax. Social security tax is not called or considered a tax in many countries, but is instead referred to as a contribution, being likened to a premium for old age and disability insurance (*national insurance contributions)*. Nevertheless, regardless of the name and the benefit features of the social insurance scheme funded, the contributions are typically collected in a similar manner to taxes, even if they are not legally designated as taxes.

Value added tax has become the most important tax in a number of countries, and a substantial revenue source in all countries which impose it. Economically, VAT is broadly equivalent to a *retail sales tax.* Most countries without VAT impose some form of sales tax, and a few countries have both sales tax and VAT (retail sales tax often being imposed by a lower level of government). The trend, however, has been to abandon retail or other forms of sales taxes in favor of VAT.

Excise can be viewed as a sales tax imposed on a limited category of goods. Typically, it is imposed at the manufacturing stage only (or on import into the country), but it is sometimes imposed at the retail level (e.g., gasoline tax in the U.S.).

Property tax is a tax on land and buildings, often with different rates for different types of land or buildings. It is often imposed at the local level, which is suitable in light of the lack of mobility of the tax object.

Some jurisdictions also levy a *personal property tax* on selected possessions, for example, automobiles, yachts, airplanes, or intangible assets. A few jurisdictions, primarily in Europe, levy a *net wealth tax* on the value of the taxpayer's total assets net of liabilities. A number of jurisdictions have wealth transfer taxes (*estate and gift* taxes or *inheritance* taxes).

Customs duty was once the principal revenue source in many countries, but no longer, although it remains important in small countries without a VAT. Customs duty is now more important as a matter of trade law rather than revenue. It retains procedural significance for taxation, however, because the customs authorities collect VAT and excise at the border on imports. Customs duty is typically collected by a different agency than that

---

aggregated. The tax is widespread, having been adopted by virtually all countries. *See infra* 7.1. It is more complex than any other tax, raises the most significant policy issues, involves the most litigation, and exercises profound influences on economies.

[47] Even a flat-rate income tax is progressive if there is a personal exemption.

responsible for internal revenue, and a separate customs code governs procedure, which focuses on the physical entry of goods into the country. Valuation and classification are important issues, and norms have been established by international conventions. Customs can involve both *import duties* and *export taxes*, the latter being levied on the export of specific commodities.

Stamp duties are imposed on transactions such as the transfer of immovable property or securities, the issuance of securities, the recording of a mortgage, or the execution of a contract. The tax is typically a small percentage of the value of the transaction. Somewhat analogous is the *financial transactions tax*, which taxes a small percentage of the value of bank transactions.

There are other miscellaneous taxes,[48] often levied at a local level (*dog tax, hotel tax* and others*).* The term "nuisance tax" is applied to taxes which raise little revenue compared with the compliance burden involved, and many miscellaneous taxes fall into this category.

What taxes are imposed in this country (at both national and regional or local levels)? Are there fees or contributions with similar effect to a tax? What economic and political factors might explain the country's tax composition?

---

[48] For a summary description of taxes in force in the EU, see European Commission, Inventory of Taxes Levied in the Member States of the European Union (17th ed. 2000).

Chapter 4

THE LEGAL CONTEXT

4.1 TAX LAW AS PART OF THE LEGAL SYSTEM

Tax lawyers tend naturally to focus on tax legislation, but it is important to remember that, in any country, tax law is part of the overall legal, socioeconomic, and political system. Knowledge of certain aspects of the legal system outside taxation is therefore needed in order to understand tax law. This chapter reviews some of the main areas where non-tax law has an impact on tax. Chapter 5 (which considers interpretation of tax laws) also looks outside the context of taxation, namely at general approaches that courts take in interpreting laws.

Civil law countries tend to take a more systematic approach to law than common law countries.[1] Fields of law in civil law systems are classified into branches—the main division being between public and private law.[2] Tax is indisputably part of public law (this is also true in common law countries, but the distinction tends not to be emphasized).[3] As to which branch of public law tax falls under, there is some difference in approach—French, Italian, and Spanish academics tend to consider tax law as part of public finance, thereby studying it together with budget law, while German academics tend to favor

---

[1] I would not wish to imply that being more systematic is necessarily better (or worse) – there is simply a difference of approach in different systems.

[2] Although this division exists clearly in all civil law countries, in France the division is particularly stark because it corresponds to a division in jurisdiction of the courts. The system of administrative courts (headed by the *Conseil d'Etat*) is responsible for public law, while a separate system of courts (headed by the *Cour de cassation*) deals with private law disputes.

[3] In countries such as France, the classification of tax into public law has relevance for the court system that hears tax cases: for most tax cases, it will be the system of administrative courts. *See infra* 6.8. The assignment of tax to public law is also relevant for the European Convention on Human Rights, since that convention applies its fair trial requirements to "civil" disputes, and this has been held not to include disputes under public law. *See infra* note 203 and accompanying text. On the distinction between public and private law in the U.K., see Ian Saunders, Taxation: Judicial Review and Other Remedies 103-05 (1996).

treating it as a branch of administrative law, acknowledging that it may also be classified under public finance.[4]   There is no uniform approach even within particular countries, although in France there is a close connection between tax law and public finance, a number of French academics having written treatises in both tax and budget law. Common law lawyers tend not to be too preoccupied with such questions, taking each statute on its own.

Putting tax law in its place among branches of law makes a difference in the organization and contents of treatises on tax law and on how tax law is taught. Treating tax as part of administrative law may encourage tax lawyers in civil law countries to focus more on procedural issues than on tax policy. This is consistent with generally more formal tax procedures in civil law countries. The common law approach tends to isolate tax law and foster the development of a separate tax legal culture, which includes a strong emphasis on tax policy and economic analysis of tax law issues.[5]

The unity of the legal system is an underlying principle in civil law countries.[6] According to Tipke, this concept means for tax law that it should not undermine policies established in other areas of the law, for example that it should not bestow favored tax treatment on an activity that is forbidden in

---

[4] *See* Tipke (2000) at 35; Liccardo, *Introduzione allo studio del diritto tributario, in* Amatucci (1994) at 4-5, 11; de la Garza (2001) (Mexico: textbook covers both tax and budgetary law). Tipke also finds that tax law may be considered part of the public law of obligations—together with social law and subsidy law. "In tax law the State is the creditor. In social and subsidy law it is the debtor." Tipke (2000) at 37. While tax is often considered as part of business law, Tipke finds that as a systematic field of law business law would be too vague. *See id.* at 37. He also advocates joint study of tax and social welfare law, the integration of which is important since they both use concepts of income for determining benefits or obligations. *See id.* at 38-41. Ferdinand Kirchhof finds that *Abgabenrecht* (the law of contributions—since tax is part of contributions generally, see supra 2.1) together with police law is part of *Eingriffsrecht* (literally, intervention law), and that it is also part of the public law of obligations (*öffentliches Schuldrecht*), and administrative procedure law. In Japan, tax law is considered part of administrative law. For a review of the development of the study of the law of public finance in various European countries, together with a proposed subject matter division of the field and a bibliography of treatises available in Spanish, see 1 Luis Sánchez Serrano, Tratado de Derecho Financiero y Tributario Constitutioncional 55-154.

[5] See for example Neil Brooks, *The Logic, Policy and Politics of Tax Law: An Overview, in* Materials on Canadian Income Tax Tax (Tim Edgar et al. eds., 12th ed. 2000), which emphasises policy analysis. A good deal of the writing of legal tax academics in the U.S. is along economic lines.

[6] *See* Ault et al. (1997) at 69. In German, the expression is *Einheit der Rechtsordnung.*

another area of the law.[7] While this may be accepted as a general principle, its application in particular cases is not obvious. For example, Germany, as do most other countries, taxes income from illegal activities and allows a deduction for expenses of such activities. The allowance of a deduction is not considered to violate the unity of the legal system because it is not "favored tax treatment."[8] The concept of unity of the legal system also covers the relationship between tax law and civil law.[9]

The connection between tax and other areas of law is emphasized by some civil law academics in dividing tax law into various fields: constitutional tax law, interstate tax law (i.e. having to do with compacts among states in a federal system); material or substantive tax law (i.e. the general rules concerning the tax liability); formal or administrative tax law; criminal tax law; procedural tax law; international tax law; and (last but not least) the special part of tax law (i.e. the rules for specific taxes).[10]

As a matter of comparative study, there are of course differences between countries and systems for the relevant areas of law outside the tax system; further, in each area there may be specific differences for tax law. For example, for statutory interpretation, there are differences in general approach and there may be differences between the general approach to statutory interpretation in a particular country and the approach to interpreting tax laws.

Is tax law considered to form part of a specific branch of law in the country? With what implications?

4.2 SOURCES OF TAX LAW

The sources of tax law are similar in all countries, but their relative roles differ depending on the legal system in general and the tax culture in particular. In civil law countries, the classical sources of law are laws, treaties, regulations, jurisprudence, and doctrine.[11] Jurisprudence refers to judicial decisions and doctrine refers to writings, including those of academics and materials issued by the tax administration that do not have normative

---

[7] *See* Tipke (2000) at 57-60. The idea is not unknown in common law countries: the analogue would be the concept of an overriding "public policy."

[8] *See id.* at 102.

[9] *See infra* 4.7; Ault et al. (1997) at 69.

[10] *See, e.g.,* 1 Catalina García Vizcaíno, Derecho Tributário 164-66 (1999)(Argentina).

[11] *See* Beltrame & Mehl (1997) at 487.

character. The same sources exist in common law countries, but with a different emphasis. The importance of case law is obviously greater in common law countries, but there is some convergence in this respect in the sense that case law has become important in civil law countries, even where precedents are not formally binding as in common law jurisdictions. In common law countries, doctrine is not acknowledged as an independent source of law but in practical terms treatises and writings are relied on by courts and practitioners to the extent they are persuasive. As for norms and other interpretative materials issued by the government, Ministry of Finance, or tax administration, their legal significance varies from system to system.[12] Legislative history (committee reports, preparatory works and the like) is also important in statutory interpretation in many systems.[13]

Apart from legal significance of various sources as a theoretical matter, there are big differences in tax culture simply in terms of what kind of material is available. For example, in the U.S., legislative history on tax legislation tends to be extremely voluminous and detailed and can provide important clues as to what various actors involved with a tax bill had in mind. It has also been collected so that it is not too much trouble to research. In other countries, the legislative history may be much skimpier. Another example: both in Germany and in the U.S., the tax laws are commented on by extensive treatises. As a practical matter, if one wants to learn what the tax law is in a particular area, these treatises are the place to start. In many countries, however, extensive treatises of this sort are not available. In the U.S., practitioners have also been blessed (cursed?) by the public availability of private letter rulings. Although their precedential value is supposedly limited, they can provide clues to how the IRS sees the tax law, and a practitioner would fail to consult them at his peril. In sum, the sheer volume of published material in a number of countries colors the practice of tax law. Instead of just reading the statute and reflecting on it, it may be virtually obligatory to sift through all of the published material in case something is relevant.

What is the respective role of each source of tax law in the country?

---

[2] *See infra* 4.6.

[3] *See infra* 5.3.

4.3 CONSTITUTIONAL LAW

4.3.1 IN GENERAL

4.3.1.1 Overview

In countries where courts can overturn statutes as unconstitutional,[14] tax lawyers often must be constitutional lawyers as well. Constitutions can impose several types of limits on tax lawmaking power. There may be restrictions on the types of taxes that may be levied or principles with which taxes must comply (such as the principle of equality). The constitution may also delimit the competence of the legislature vis-a-vis the executive branch. Typically, the constitution will guarantee to citizens substantive and procedural rights, which provide protection from legislation in all areas, including tax, that violates these rights (e.g., freedom of speech and religion), and may include other provisions that come into play for tax legislation (for example, where tax laws are used to provide support to political parties).[15] For EU member countries, the requirements of EU law are also of a constitutional nature.[16] In federal states, the constitution invariably makes arrangements for the division of tax lawmaking power between the national government and the constituent states or provinces. Under such arrangements, the states may, for example, be prohibited from imposing taxes that discriminate against interstate commerce, and the power to impose specific types of taxes may be divided among the states and the federation.[17]

---

[14] In such countries, one can identify two submodels: the decentralized (or American) approach under which the entire court system exercises constitutional review and the centralized (Austrian, "Kelsenian", or European) model under which constitutional review is exercised by a specialized court. *See* Louis Favoreu, *Constitutional Review in Europe, in* Constitutionalism and Rights 38, 40-41 (Louis Henkin and Albert Rosenthal eds. 1990). The centralized approach includes Austria, France, Germany, Italy, and Spain. The decentralized approach is followed in Argentina, Brazil, Canada, India, Sweden, and the U.S.

[15] For a discussion of rulings concerning support to political parties provided through the tax system, see Donald Kommers, The Constitutional Jurisprudence of the Federal Republic of Germany 201-15 (1997). The German court overturned an income tax deduction for contributions to political parties on the basis that it favored wealthy contributors and, hence, parties that appealed to such contributors.

[16] *See infra* 4.4.

[17] *See infra* 4.3.5. For Canada and GST, see Schenk and Oldman (2001) at 17.

The constitutional courts of different countries have exhibited considerable diversity of approach in testing tax legislation against their respective constitutional norms. This diversity arises both from differences in the constitutional texts and from the courts' philosophy and style, both generally and in the tax area in particular, as well as from differences in political systems.

In some countries, the courts do not have the power to overturn acts of the legislature on the basis of unconstitutionality. This is the case in the United Kingdom and New Zealand, for example, which do not have a written constitution. Now, however, in the U.K. as well as in the rest of the EU, courts can invalidate statutes on the basis that they violate European law.[18] In addition, the European Human Rights Convention[19] contains a number of principles of the type found in constitutions, such as prohibitions on discrimination.

It almost goes without saying that anyone actually contemplating a constitutional challenge to legislation must become familiar with the applicable procedure. The procedure can substantially affect the availability of constitutional remedies.[20] In some countries, the procedural rules for access to the constitutional courts are rather generous (for example, Germany, where the *Bundesverfassungsgericht* (Constitutional Court) may hear concrete cases upon referral from a court, may hear cases complaining of the validity of

---

[18] Besides the UK, this is the case in the Netherlands. *See* Kees van Raad, *The Netherlands*, in Ault et al. (1997) at 88. *See infra* 4.3, 4.4.

[19] European Convention on the Protection of Human Rights and Fundamental Freedoms. *See infra* 4.4.2.

[20] For procedure in Spain, see Sánchez, *supra* note 4, at 506-69. For example, under article 53 of the Spanish Constitution, the writ of *amparo* is available to challenge legislation that violates certain constitutional rights, such as the right to equal protection under art. 14. The Spanish Constitutional Court has held, however, that a number of challenges based on unequal treatment in tax legislation were properly founded not on article 14, but rather on article 31 (establishing principles of equality in taxation) and hence could not be brought under the writ of *amparo. See, e.g.,* STC, Feb. 15, 1993, R.T.C. 1993, 54. In the U.S., constitutional challenges may be blocked by doctrines of standing. For example, in Apache Bend Apartments, Ltd. v. United States, 987 F.2d 1174 (5th Cir. 1993) (*en banc*), the U.S. Court of Appeals for the Fifth Circuit held that prudential principles of standing barred a challenge to the elective granting of transition relief in the Tax Reform Act of 1986 in a case where plaintiffs where not litigating their own tax liability. The court noted: "The injury of unequal treatment alleged by the plaintiffs is shared in substantially equal measure by a 'disfavored class' that includes all taxpayers who did not receive transition relief." It also observed that other branches of government (the Executive and Congress) had the function of vindicating the public interest.

legislation in the abstract on petition by legislators or a government, or may respond to constitutional complaints brought by individuals or other persons[21]). Other countries provide narrower access to the courts on constitutional matters (for example, France, where the *Conseil Constitutionnel* (Constitutional Council) can strike down statutes in response to complaints of legislators or the government, but where courts cannot strike down laws for unconstitutionality after their enactment). Even where a tax is found to be unconstitutional, in some situations some or all affected taxpayers may not be able to recover the tax, for example where the decision finding the tax unconstitutional is applied prospectively.[22]

It may also be possible to bring a constitutional challenge indirectly in a normal tax appeal, by asking the court to interpret a taxing statute so as to be consistent with the constitution.[23] When the constitutional principle involved is the principle of equality, then interpretation consistent with the Constitution can become an occasion for broadly reading terms in the statute, so as not to draw arbitrary distinctions. The constitutional environment can therefore

---

[21] *See* Kommers, *supra* note 15, at 13-15.

[22] *See, e.g.,* 2 Peter H. Hogg, Constitutional Law of Canada §55.7 (looseleaf, as updated 2001). For example, the taxing authority may replace the unconstitutional tax with a retroactively imposed constitutional tax. *See* Air Canada v. British Columbia, [1989] 1 S.C.R. 1161. In Re Eurig Estate, [1998] 2 S.C.R. 565, the court granted to the plaintiff a refund of the tax paid under protest which was held unconstitutional, but otherwise suspended the finding of unconstitutionality for six months in order to give the legislature time to replace the revenues that would have been lost. In Murphy v. Attorney General, [1982] I.R. 241, which struck down the Irish "marriage penalty," the taxpayers were allowed to recover the tax only for tax years after the proceedings had been instituted, and other taxpayers were prohibited from claiming refunds, since they had not commenced judicial proceedings. *See also* Harper v. Virginia Dept. of Taxation, 509 U.S. 86 (1993); Gary Knapp, Annotation, *Supreme Court's views as to retroactive effect of its own decisions announcing new rules as to taxation,* 125 L. Ed 2d 845 (1998).

[23] *See* Guy Gest, *France, in* Ault et al. (1997) at 44; Gianluigi Bizioli, *Tax Treaty Interpretation in Italy, in* Tax Treaty Interpretation 195, 204-05 (Michael Lang ed. 2001); Kommers, *supra* note 15, at 51; Sánchez, *supra* note 4, at 544-46. For an example of interpretation of a law so as to make it consistent with the principle of equality, see Karl Korinek and Michael Holoubek, *Austria, in* The Principle of Equality in European Taxation 35, 41-42 (Gerard Meussen, ed.,1999) [hereinafter The Principle of Equality]. Favoreu, *supra* note 14, at 57, notes that this technique is "used increasingly by German, Austrian, Italian and French courts." It seems to be fairly generally accepted. *See, e.g.,* K.P. Varghese v. Income-Tax Officer, A.I.R. 1981 S.C. 1922 (India); BGE 124 I 145 (March 20, 1998) (Switzerland); Elisabeth Willemart, Les Limites Constitutionnelles du Pouvoir Fiscal 225-28 (1999)(Belgium).

exercise an important influence on statutory construction, and can lead to significant country differences in how courts read tax laws.

While mentioning other countries, the discussion below focuses on constitutional tax cases in three countries which furnish stark contrasts to each other—France, Germany, and the United States.

4.3.1.2 France

In France, the Constitutional Council determines the constitutionality of laws prior to their enactment.[24] Because France is a unitary state, limitations concerning federalism are not applicable.[25] The Constitutional Council has most often struck down tax laws where there was an irregularity of competence (e.g., parliament could not delegate to the executive branch the decision to set the effective date of a law[26]) or where the law violated procedural protections of citizens (for example, the right of citizens to be secure in their homes against unreasonable searches,[27] or to defend themselves against penalties[28]). More rarely, the Constitutional Council has found that substantive rights, such as the right to equal treatment, were violated by a tax law.[29] The administrative courts (headed by the *Conseil*

---

[24] *See* Beltrame & Mehl (1997) at 493. The petition for review may be filed by the President, the Prime Minister, the President of the National Assembly, or sixty deputies or sixty senators. Constitution, Art. 61. Private litigants thus may not bring a case challenging the constitutionality of a law or proposed law.

[25] A unitary state is a centralized one; it is of course an oversimplification to refer to states as either federal or centralized for tax purposes since there are many variations. *See generally* Frans Vanistendael, *Legal Framework for Taxation, in* TLDD 15, 62-70.

[26] *See* Cons. const., Dec. 29, 1986, 223 D.C., Rec. 1986, 184, *excerpted in* Loïc Philip, Droit Fiscal Constitutionnel 211 (1990). Similarly, in Cons. const., Dec. 30, 1987, 239 D.C., Rec. 1987, 69 the court held that the power to set the tax rate could not be delegated. *See* Philip, *supra*, at 212.

[27] *See* Cons. const., Dec. 29, 1983, 164 D.C., Rec. 1983, 67. The decision is reproduced with commentary in Louis Favoreu & Loïc Philip, Les grandes décisions du Conseil constitutionnel 563-79 (10th ed. 1999).

[28] *See* Cons. const., Dec. 29, 1989, 268 D.C., Rec. 1989, 110, *excerpted in* Philip, *supra* note 26, at 212.

[29] *See generally* Philippe Marchessou, *France, in* The Principle of Equality, *supra* note 23, at 75.

d'État[30]) can strike down regulations (but not statutes) as unconstitutional.[31] The courts can also construe statutes so that they are in conformity with the constitution.

4.3.1.3 Germany

The German Constitutional Court has developed a jurisprudence remarkable for its judicial activism in the tax area.[32] It has tested tax laws against general principles of due process, equality, and protection of marriage and property. Given the substantial arbitrary element in tax laws, due to political compromise and administrative considerations, it is not surprising that the tax laws have often been found wanting when measured against the ideal principles of the constitution. The willingness of the German Constitutional Court to overturn tax laws on the basis of the principle of equality in particular has brought substantial litigation. The complexity of the resulting jurisprudence and commentary is such that I cannot hope to summarize it in the discussion below, but just to give a flavor of some of the contemporary cases. The German jurisprudence furnishes a contrast to most other countries, where the constitutional courts have generally shied away from applying such elastic principles to tax law.

4.3.1.4 United States[33]

Although the U.S. Supreme Court did take an activist stance in striking down the income tax when it was first imposed, and has also actively policed state taxing powers on the basis of considerations of federalism, it has—in contrast to some European courts—been unwilling to strike down tax

---

[30] Council of State. It has over time become equivalent to an independent court. It has the last word in tax cases, except for constitutional issues within the competence of the Constitutional Court, and those matters that are appealable to the ordinary courts. *See infra* 6.8.

[31] *E.g.,* Conseil d'Etat, Rec. 279 (June 30, 1995)(the unjustified exclusion of agricultural income from tax by the territorial assembly of French Polynesia violates "the general principle of equality which every administrative authority must respect.") The same function can be exercised by the ordinary courts in the case of appeals from tax assessments within their competence. *See infra* 6.8.

[32] See the summary of key decisions in Albert Rädler, *Germany, in* Ault et al. (1997) at 61-62. For a comprehensive summary of holdings, see Karin Grasshof, Nachschlagewerk der Rechtsprechung des Bundesverfassungsgerichts (looseleaf).

[33] *See generally* 1 Bittker & Lokken (1999) at ¶ 1.2.

laws for equal protection violations, finding that "in taxation, even more than in other fields, legislatures possess the greatest freedom in classification."[34] The Court's reluctance to make the federal income tax a constitutional battleground[35] may be due in part to the inauspicious start that constitutional litigation concerning the tax took after its enactment following ratification of the Sixteenth Amendment. In *Brushaber v. Union Pacific Railroad Co.*,[36] an abstract challenge was brought, alleging twenty-one constitutional objections. Having just experienced the enactment and ratification of a constitutional amendment to permit the imposition of the income tax (a rare event in the United States and requiring substantial political activity throughout the country) the Court was doubtless reluctant to evoke popular ire by again striking down the statute as unconstitutional. The numerosity of the plaintiff's arguments undermined their credibility and allowed the Court, in a unanimous opinion, to give them short shrift. Belittling the constitutional objections as "numerous and minute, not to say in many respects hypercritical"[37] the Court was able to treat them as so obviously ill founded as hardly worth answering.[38] While this may be true of some of the arguments raised, the Court probably dismissed too summarily the arguments based on equal protection, stating that they failed because of "the adequate bases for classification which are apparent on the face of the assailed provisions."[39] In fact, substantial instances of unequal treatment were adduced, including discrimination between married and single people, and between persons with different kinds of income. After *Brushaber*, any constitutional challenge to

---

[34] Madden v. Kentucky, 309 U.S. 83, 88 (1940), *quoted in* Regan v. Taxation with Representation, 461 U.S. 540, 547 (1997).

[35] For a discussion of the constitutional litigation on the Federal income tax, see Bittker and Lokken (1999), chapter 1.

[36] 240 U.S. 1 (1916).

[37] 240 U.S. at 24.

[38] "In fact, comprehensively surveying all the contentions relied upon... we cannot escape the conclusion that they all rest upon the mistaken theory that although there be differences between the subjects taxed, to differently tax them transcends the limit of taxation and amounts to a want of due process, and that where a tax levied is believed by one who resists its enforcement to be wanting in wisdom and to operate injustice, from that fact in the nature of things there arises a want of due process of law and a resulting authority in the judiciary to exceed its powers and correct what is assumed to be mistaken or unwise exertions by the legislative authority of its lawful powers, even although there be no semblance of warrant in the Constitution for so doing." 240 U.S. at 25-26.

[39] 240 U.S. at 25.

income tax provisions based on equal protection arguments must have seemed like an uphill fight.[40]

The U.S. Courts seem to regard taxation as intensely political and based on many considerations in addition to equality, and are therefore reluctant to impose a common denominator of equality on tax law.

Is there a constitutional court that can overturn tax legislation? If so, what role has it taken?

4.3.2   TAX MUST BE IMPOSED BY LAW (PRINCIPLE OF LEGALITY)

Constitutions usually require taxes to be imposed by law, often saying so explicitly.[41] This implies that they cannot be imposed by an administrative regulation.[42] The French Conseil Constitutionnel found that a television fee was in the nature of an extrabudgetary fee (*taxe parafiscal*), which was required by law to be approved by parliament, and hence could not be imposed by an administrative agency.[43] The Turkish Supreme Court held that an administrative regulation imposing a withholding tax violates the

---

[40] The Supreme Court did, however, respond positively to a more targeted challenge in 1920, striking down a provision of the income tax subjecting stock dividends to tax as unconstitutional. Eisner v. Macomber, 252 U.S. 189 (1920). This challenge was not, however, brought on equal protection grounds, but on the basis that stock dividends were not income and therefore that the Sixteenth Amendment did not authorize their taxation. In subsequent cases, the Court seems to have abandoned scrutinizing income tax statutes on the basis of whether they tax "income" within the meaning of the 16th Amendment.

[41] *E.g.*, Belgium Const. art. 170; Mexico Const. art. 31; Italy Const. art. 23; France Const. art. 34, *see* Michel Bouvier, Introduction au droit fiscal et à la théorie de l'impôt 36-41 (1996); Beltrame & Mehl (1997) at 488-90.

[42] Unconstitutional delegation to the executive has been struck down in Mexico. *See* de la Garza (2001) at 266-68. In France, Cons. const., Dec. 29, 1986, 223 DC, Rec. 1986, 184 held that the specification of an effective date for legislation could not be delegated to the executive. The Spanish court has held that while article 31 of the Constitution required essential elements of a tax to be determined by law, the constitution should be interpreted flexibly and allowed the legislature to delegate to the executive such a matter as adjustment for inflation. *See* S.T.C., Dec. 11, 1992 R.T.C. 1992, 221. The Belgian constitution requires taxes to be established by law but delegations of law-making authority to the executive have been upheld in some circumstances. *See* Elisabeth Willemart, *supra* note 23, at 100-23.

[43] *See supra* 3.1, note 10.

constitutional provision requiring taxes to be imposed by laws.[44] Some constitutions (e.g., Romania, Argentina, Brazil) allow the use of emergency decrees, including in the tax area. The use of such decrees was recently limited by constitutional amendment in Brazil.[45]

In some countries, the principle of legality has been construed to mean:

- that the tax authorities do not have the power to enter into an agreement with an individual taxpayer, because such an agreement would imply that tax is being imposed otherwise than under the general rule of law;[46]

- that administrative discretion to determine whether to grant a tax privilege cannot be unlimited (e.g., France);[47] or

- that tax laws should be construed strictly, since otherwise the judge—not the legislator—would be making the law (e.g., Mexico, Belgium, Japan).[48]

---

[44] *See* Mustafa Çamlica, *Turkish Supreme Court: Withholding Tax Imposed on Investment Allowances is Unconstitutional,* 20 Tax Notes Int'l 2423 (May 29, 2000).

[45] *See* David Roberto R. Soares da Silva, *Constitutional Amendment Limits Use of Provisional Measures,* 24 Tax Notes Int'l 554 (Nov. 5, 2001).

[46] *See* Vanistendael, *Legal Framework for Taxation, in* TLDD 15, 18-19; Faes (1995) at 7-8; Tipke (2000) at 131-36 (Germany, Austria, Italy, Switzerland, France, Belgium, Luxembourg, Spain). *See also* Ferdinand Kirchhof, Grundriss des Abgabenrechts 47-49 (1991)(previous thinking disallowed agreements but they are becoming allowed in some cases). Such agreements are, however, permitted in many countries, e.g., the U.S. (closing agreements), such countries also tending to allow plea bargaining in criminal law. France allows an exception from the general rule (*transaction* pursuant to art. L. 247-3 L.P.F.). *See* Frédéric Douet, Contribution à l'étude de la sécurité juridique en droit fiscal interne français 23-25 (1997). The availability of binding rulings also tends to contradict the principle against binding agreements, although in principle these should be consistent with the law. The principle of legality may also be seen as limiting discretion to prosecute. *See* A.A. Aronowitz et al., Value-Added Tax Fraud in the European Union 29 (1996).

[47] *See* 237 DC of Dec. 30, 1987; Philip, *supra* note 26, at 84-97. *See also* Dec. 87-39 DC (Dec. 30, 1987)(while the legislature may delegate the authority to set rates, the delegation must be within limits); Dec. DC 191, July 10, 1985 (provision that was so vague that it allowed the administration to in effect legislate was unconstitutional); Dec. 223 DC of Dec. 29, 1986 (administration may not be delegated power to fix effective date of legislation).

[48] *See infra* 5.1.

A related principle is that of annuality, according to which tax laws have to be renewed annually. More a principle of budget law than of tax law, it applies in a few countries.[49]

4.3.3   GENERAL LIMITS ON TAXING POWER

Constitutional limitations on legislative power apply equally to taxation. For example, the legislature could not tax in such a way as to violate constitutional limitations on abridging freedom of speech.

Constitutions may impose procedural rules specific to taxation. For example, in the U.S., tax legislation must originate in the House of Representatives. In France, the organic budget law (which is a type of law with higher rank than ordinary laws)[50] imposes procedures that must be followed in enacting tax legislation.

In federal countries, the general legislative power of the national government may be limited, even though it may enjoy a broad taxing power. This raises the issue as to whether the taxing power can be used to legislate in areas where the national government might otherwise not have the power to do so. The U.S. Supreme Court has held that Congress could not disguise a regulatory measure as a tax and thereby extend its regulatory reach beyond that accorded to it under the Constitution.[51]

What limitations in the Constitution might apply to taxation? Have any tax provisions been overturned as violative of these limits?

---

[49] *See* Beltrame & Mehl (1997) at 523-24. The principle is embodied in art. 171 of the Belgian Constitution. *See* Willemart, *supra* note 23, at 135-40; Introduction to Belgian Law 349 (Hubert Bocken & Walter de Bondt eds., 2001) [hereinafter Belgian Law]. In France, it is part of the organic budget law (loi organique du 1 août 2001) *See* Bouvier, *supra* note 41, at 46-47. *See also* Morse & Williams (2000) at 25-2((principle of annuality has influenced construction of income tax laws and application of the source doctrine).

[50] France is one of the few countries with the concept of laws of different rank (Brazil and Romania being two others). In France, organic laws, specificall provided for in article 46 of the constitution, provide a framework in various area and typically must be passed with a supermajority or under special procedures.

[51] *See* Laurence Tribe, American Constitutional Law 843-46 (2000). Similar argu ments have been raised in Australia, although rarely accepted by the courts. *See* P.F Lane, Lane's Commentary on the Australian Constitution 170-73 (2d ed. 1997).

4.3.4 EXPLICIT LIMITS ON TYPES OF TAXES

Constitutions often impose specific limitations on the types of taxes that may be enacted. This is often the case in federal states, where the constitution may restrict the taxes that may be imposed either at the federal or the state level.[52] Such limitations have proved troublesome. Taxes are like viruses—they can mutate rapidly and are difficult to confine by labels. The economic content of a tax can differ from its label and be hard to pin down. Nevertheless, the courts have had to give some content to the labels found in constitutions, in the face of legislatures which often tried to push the limits as far as possible.

For example, the U.S. Supreme Court has had to determine whether various levies on exports constituted taxes, since the constitution specifically prohibits such taxes.[53] The Court has also had to decide whether certain taxes were direct taxes, since there is a constitutional limitation on how direct taxes may be imposed.[54]

Does the Constitution impose specific limitations on taxes?

4.3.5 FEDERALISM

Constitutions of federal states almost invariably allocate taxing power among the national and regional governments in some fashion,[55] and these rules may be policed by the supreme constitutional court. There are actually three general elements of sovereignty in respect of a tax: legislative authority, administrative authority, and the right to receive revenues.[56] Legislative authority can be subdivided further; for example, a local government may have the authority to set tax rates alone, with the rest of the law being enacted

---

[2] For example, in the U.S., the constitution prohibits the imposition of taxes on exports and prohibits the imposition of direct taxes at the federal level, unless apportioned on the basis of population (the Sixteenth Amendment removed the apportionment requirement in the case of income taxes). *See also* TLDD at 17 n.8 (India and Pakistan); Linus Osita Okeke, *The VAT Decree and the Nigerian Constitution,* 27 Tax Planning Int'l Rev. 7 (March 2000). Articles 96-100 of the Constitution of Ethiopia provide for a detailed division of taxing authority between the Federal Government and the States, undoubtedly leading to a host of problems in practice.

See supra 3.1.

See supra 3.2.

See Frans Vanistendael, *Legal Framework for Taxation, in* TLDD 15, 62-70.

See Tipke (1993) at 1085.

at the national level. In Germany, these different elements are often split with respect to particular taxes. For example, for income tax the law is made at the federal level, the tax is administered at the provincial (*Land*) level, while revenues are allocated partly to the federation and partly to the provinces. While the German system of tax allocation is complex in some senses, particularly at the level of budget and constitutional law, it is relatively simple for taxpayers, in the sense that for the important taxes taxpayers face only one set of rules and one rate no matter where in the country they set up business. This is the case both for corporate income tax and VAT.

Only in relatively few OECD countries do different rates of VAT (or sales tax) and corporate income tax apply in different subnational jurisdictions. These include the U.S., Canada, and Switzerland. Likewise, such a degree of tax raising provincial autonomy is seen in only a handful of developing and transition countries. In these countries, it becomes important for the taxpayer where its income or sales will be taxed, since the total tax will differ, often substantially. In each of these countries the provincial (in the U.S., state, in Switzerland, cantonal) tax authority is more or less autonomous. It is not just a matter of what rate applies—the substantive rules may differ as well. As a result, the taxpayer's income may end up being taxed in more than one state, or in no state, much the same as with taxation internationally. For purposes of comparative law, therefore, the countries where provinces have substantial tax autonomy can be considered as a group with common problems.

In the U.S., most of the constitutional litigation involving taxes has had to do with state taxing powers and their consistency with principles of federalism. The Court has construed the Commerce Clause of the Constitution as permitting State taxation only where it "(1) applies to an activity having a substantial nexus with the taxing state, (2) is fairly apportioned, (3) does not discriminate against interstate commerce, and (4) is fairly related to services provided by the state."[57] The Court has been even tougher on the States when they seek to tax foreign commerce, finding that, in addition to satisfying the above principles, the tax must not enhance the risk of multiple taxation and must not impair federal uniformity.[58] The other area where State taxation has been curtailed on grounds of federalism has been where states have sought to tax the Federal government in some way. While a tax imposed directly on a federal agency seems like a clear violation of federalism, this

---

[57] Tribe, *supra* note 51, at 1106 (discussing Complete Auto Transit, Inc. v. Brady, 43 U.S. 274 (1977)).

[58] *See id.* at 1156 (discussing Japan Line, Ltd. v. County of Los Angeles, 441 U. 434 (1979)).

area has thrown up difficult questions of where to draw the line, for example, where state taxes reached contractors working for the federal government.[59]

In Canada tax rates vary from province to province, both for income tax and for sales tax, although substantial conformity is achieved for income tax law via agreements whereby the provinces adopt the federal tax base.[60] The portion of a corporation's taxable income that is considered earned in a particular province is determined under a two-factor formula under a Federal regulation. One-half the taxable income is allocated to the province on the basis of the portion of the gross revenue that is attributable to a permanent establishment of the corporation in the province. The other half is allocated to the province on the basis of the portion of wages paid to employees of the permanent establishment. Special rules apply to insurance companies and other special taxpayers.[61]

Switzerland has an intricate regime for federalism in taxation, with substantial independence of taxing powers vested in the cantons. Intercantonal double taxation is avoided by federal court rulings within the framework of article 127 of the constitution, a federal law on tax harmonisation, as well as intercantonal concordats. The tax base of enterprises doing business in more than one canton is divided among them, in a manner which does not appear to be very simple.[62]

Sweden's municipalities have some tax raising autonomy, with variations in tax rates for individuals, but corporations pay the national income tax only.[63]

To what extent is the country a Federal (as opposed to a unitary) state? Are there federalism-type limits on taxes? What authority do regional or local governments have to enact tax laws?

---

[59] *See generally id.* at 1220-37.

[60] *See* Brian Arnold, *Canada, in* Ault et al. (1997) at 25-26. Under agreements with the provinces the Federal government collects provincial personal income tax (except in Quebec) and corporate income tax (except in Quebec, Ontario, and Alberta). *See* Hogg, *supra* note 22, at § 6.4; Hogg et al. (2002) at 20.

[61] *See* Income Tax Regulations, Part IV, *reprinted in* 9 Canada Tax Service at 124-04 (looseleaf 2002).

[62] *See generally* Höhn & Waldburger (2001) at 799-874.

[63] *See* Peter Melz, *Sweden, in* Ault et al. (1997) at 97-99.

4.3.6 NONRETROACTIVITY

Taxpayers are of course interested in knowing the applicable tax rules when they plan their transactions, and retroactive tax legislation can disrupt these plans. However, there is often a public interest for tax legislation to be enacted retroactively. One case is that of technical corrections. A tax law might be passed, but with a technical mistake. Such mistakes should generally be fixed retroactively to the effective date of the original legislation. Another case is one of cracking down on tax avoidance transactions. In the constant struggle between the tax authorities and taxpayers, abusive transactions may be devised. When they are discovered by the tax authorities, legislation to eliminate them may be proposed. Often, the legislation is enacted retroactive to the date that the proposal was announced.[64] The public announcement of the proposed legislation may be considered fair warning to taxpayers. If the new law were not applied retroactively to the date of announcement, taxpayers would be given a window of opportunity to enter into tax avoidance transactions before the new law is enacted. Another situation where retroactive legislation might be justified is to reverse a judicial decision with which the legislature disagrees.[65] Laws may also be passed to interpret existing law with retroactive effect.[66] In such cases where the law is

---

[64] For example, tax amendments are routinely made retroactive to date of announcement in Australia. *See* Richard Vann, *Australia, in* Ault et al. (1997) at 11.

[65] For examples of instances where legislation was enacted retroactively in France to overturn judicial decisions, see Cyrille David, *Taxpayer Protection and Tax Fines in France, in* Dirk Albregtse and Henk van Arendonk, Taxpayer Protection in the European Union 99, 101 (1998).

[66] This has occurred, for example, in France. *See* Ault et al. (1997) at 45; Douet. *supra* note 46, at 113-18 (1997). Laws which interpret retroactively the provisions of an earlier law are known as *lois interprétatives* (interpretative laws); those which retroactively modify earlier laws in order to validate an administrative interpretation which had been overturned by a court decision are called laws of validation and are typically applied retroactively except for those cases that had already been decided by the courts. There are also occasional examples of "implicit validation" (*see id.* at 120-25). This occurs when material in inserted into the general tax code by decree but the legality of this action is questionable. A subsequent law may implicitly uphold the codification by making some modification to the text. In Brazil, the retroactive effect of interpretative laws is provided for in art. 106 of the National Tax Code. In the U.K., similar legislation is referred to as declaratory legislation. *See* David Stopforth, *Retrospection by Stealth*, [1998] B.T.R. 103. In Italy an interpretative law is known as *Legge di interpretazione autentica. See* Fantozz (1991) at 125-26. The U.S. does not have an analogous concept, lumping it with technical corrections.

retroactively fixed or clarified, taxpayers often cannot be said to have a reliance interest that would prohibit retroactive application of the law, particularly in cases where a judicial decision departing from previously announced administrative interpretation is being reversed, or where the law was unclear.

Constitutional law concerning retroactive tax legislation varies substantially. In most countries, decisions about the effective date of tax legislation are considered a policy issue for the legislature. There is no constitutional protection against retroactive legislation, as long as the legislature does not act capriciously.[67] In France, the Constitutional Council has ruled that laws (other than penal laws) may be retroactive, as long as they do not disturb specific cases where a court decision has already been entered or where the statute of limitations has run out.[68] Retroactive legislation has been found compatible with the European Convention on Human Rights, as long as it serves a legitimate purpose and is not disproportionate.[69]

---

[67] *See* TLDD at 25; The European Commission on Human Rights has held that anti-tax-shelter legislation could be applied retroactively. *See* TLDD at 25. For the Netherlands, *see* Kees van Raad, *The Netherlands, in* Ault et al. (1997) at 84 (government takes the position that retroactive legislation is justified in cases of anti-abuse, technical corrections, and where announcement of the new rule in advance would lead to tax avoidance). Retroactive tax legislation has also been upheld in Canada, *see* Kathleen Lahey, *The Impact of the Charter of Rights and Freedoms on Canadian Income Tax Policy, in* Charting the Consequences: the Impact of Charter Rights on Canadian Law and Politics 109, 121-22 (David Schneiderman and Kate Sutherland eds., 1998); Krishna (2000) at 21; Belgium; *see* Tiberghien (1995) at 36-37; Faes (1995) at 10, and India; *see* Krishnamurthi & Co. v. State of Madras, [1973] 2 S.C.R. 54 (Sept. 5, 1972); Hira Lal Rattan Lal v. State of Uttar Pradesh, [1973] 2 S.C.R. 502, 509 (Oct. 3, 1972).

[68] *See* Dec. 91-298 (July 24, 1991); Dec. 86-223, Rec. 184 (Dec. 29, 1986). The prohibition of nonretroactivity of penal laws also applies to tax penalties. *See* D.C. 155, 237. *See also* Beltrame & Mehl (1997) at 525-26. In Ireland, Article 15.5 of the constitution provides that the legislature may not "declare acts to be infringements of the law which were not so at the date of their commission." This provision may prohibit retroactivity in tax legislation in certain cases but it has received limited judicial attention thus far. *See* Corrigan (2000) at 106-15. In Argentina, the Supreme Court has accepted retroactive tax legislation, except in limited cases such as where the tax liability has been settled, in which event retroactivity is considered to violate the constitutional right to property. *See* García Vizcaíno, *supra* note 10, at 194-202.

[69] *See* Philip Baker, *Taxation and the European Convention on Human Rights*, [2000] B.T.R. 211, 225; The National and Provincial Building Society v. United Kingdom, 25 E.H.R.R. 127 (1998).

Regulations can also apply retroactively; the effective date of interpretative regulations is often coextensive with that of the law they interpret. However, explicit statutory authority is often required for retroactive application,[70] particularly for legislative regulations, and in practice regulations arc often promulgated with prospective effective dates.

The U.S. Supreme Court has given wide latitude to the Congress in deciding whether to enact retroactive tax legislation, finding that retroactivity does not constitute a violation of substantive due process if "retroactive application ... is rationally related to a legitimate legislative purpose."[71] Not too long ago, the Court considered a case arising out of a retroactive technical correction enacted in 1987 to fix a mistake in the Tax Reform Act of 1986 that would have allowed estates to wipe out their estate tax liability by entering into transactions after the decedent's death but before the estate tax return was filed. The provision in question was intended to encourage decedents to provide for the transfer of the shares in their business to employees via an ESOP. The provision allowed a deduction for stock sold to an ESOP. By oversight, the statute omitted to require that the stock for which a deduction would be allowed had to be owned by the decedent at the time of death. Obviously, the assumption was that the stock would have been held by the decedent, but the statute did not mention this condition. While a court could have read this requirement into the statute in order for it to make sense, Congress decided to fix the matter by amending the statute, with retroactive effect. This rendered ineffective artificial maneuvers such as those practised by the estate in litigation, which had purchased stock after the decedent's death and then sold the stock to an ESOP, claiming a deduction and thereby wiping out much of its estate tax. The Court held that "[t]he due process standard to be applied to tax statutes with retroactive effect, therefore, is the same as that generally applicable to retroactive economic legislation: ... that the retroactive application of a statute is supported by a legitimate legislative purpose furthered by rational means...."[72] It found that "Congress' purpose in enacting the amendment was neither illegitimate nor arbitrary" and that it was "not unreasonable" for Congress to prevent revenue loss by imposing tax on

---

[70] *See* Beltrame & Mehl (1997) at 525 (decree may not be retroactive unless the law on which it is based specifically allows it to be); I.R.C. § 7805(b); John S. Nolan & Victor Thuronyi, *Retroactive Application of Changes in IRS or Treasury Department Position*, 61 Taxes 777 (1983).

[71] United States v. Carlton, 512 U.S. 26, 35 (1994).

[72] 512 U.S. at 30-31.

"those who had made purely tax-motivated" transactions to take advantage of the uncorrected version of the statute.[73]

A sharp contrast is provided by decisions of the German Constitutional Court, which has developed an extensive jurisprudence protecting the taxpayer's ability to rely on the existing tax legislation. The court has found this reliance interest to be a basic element of the rule of law, and has allowed retroactive tax legislation only under limited circumstances where there was a compelling public interest.[74]

The Court's jurisprudence is summarized in its decision of May 14, 1986, concerning the retroactive application of amendments dealing with the taxation of German citizens who had taken up residence abroad (mostly in Switzerland) in order to escape from German taxation, while still receiving income from activity in Germany. The amendments removed the previously favorable position of such taxpayers. They were adopted by the legislature in September 1972, with retroactive effect to the beginning of 1972 (the type of tax liability imposed was known as "extended limited tax liability"— previously, tax liability had been either limited (for nonresidents) or unlimited (for residents)).[75] The government had announced on Dec. 17, 1970, a proposal to change the tax treatment of Germans who had taken up residence abroad; a new treaty with Switzerland, which withdrew protection for Germans who had taken up residence in Switzerland, was signed on Aug. 11, 1971. According to its terms, it was to apply starting with the tax year 1972. Proposed legislation was submitted on Dec. 2, 1971. The Court found that the amendments could not constitutionally apply to incomes arising before the date that the parliament adopted the law (i.e. September 1972).

The German Court has based its prohibition of retroactivity on the *Rechtsstaatsprinzip* (principle of a state based on the rule of law).[76] It has distinguished two kinds of retroactivity: actual retroactivity, where the law

---

[73] 512 U.S. at 32.

[74] *See* Tipke (2000) at 145-63. The Austrian court has reached similar results under the principle of equality. *See id.* at 147. The position of the Federal Court of Switzerland is close to that of the German court. It has held that retroactive tax legislation is allowed only where it (1) is clearly called for by the enacting law, (2) does not reach back too far under the circumstances, (3) does not lead to unwarranted unequal treatment, (4) has sufficient justification, and (5) does not overturn settled rights. *See* BGE 101 I a 82 (June 4, 1975).

[75] For an explanation of these terms see 7.14.4 *infra*.

[76] BVerfGE 72, 200 (May 14, 1986) (translation at www.ucl.ac.uk/laws/global_law). The Court grounded this principle in Const., art. 20, clause 3: "The legislature shall be bound by the Constitutional order, the executive and the judiciary by law and justice." Constitutions of the Countries of the World, Germany (Gisbert H. Flanz ed. 1994).

changes previously determined taxes, and *de facto* retroactive application. There is more flexibility for the legislator in the latter case. The case in point was of the latter variety, since the income tax obligation arises only as of the end of the year.   The Court nevertheless found inapplicable the possible exceptions enunciated in previous decisions which might justify retroactivity:

- the retroactive consequences could be considered *de minimis*;
- the law was unclear or contradictory before enactment of the legislation;
- retroactive application was required in order to correct a constitutionally defective legal rule (for example, a rule that violated the principle of equality);
- retroactive application was required because of "urgent requirements of the public interest."

The Court found "that the publication of legislative proposals and the public notification of the preparation of new legal rules through the lawmaking bodies do not undermine the worthiness of protecting reliance on the existing legal situation."[77]

In a more recent case, the Court relied on the exception for "urgent requirements in the public interest" in upholding retroactive repeal of a subsidy for shipbuilding.[78] It found that, once the government has determined that a subsidy makes no economic sense, the legislature may repeal the subsidy retroactively to the announcement date, since a later effective date could give rise to abuse as taxpayers structured transactions to take advantage of the subsidy before its repeal. The twist in the case, though, was that when the government announced on April 25, 1996, its intention to propose repeal of the subsidy, it stated that the repeal would apply to contracts entered into after April 30. The contract in question was entered into on April 30. The legislature set the effective date as of the date of announcement (April 25), thereby catching this contract. The Court said that once the government announced its intention to repeal, the taxpayer had no more reliance interest, but it seems strange that the taxpayer should be placed on notice with respect to the government's intention to repeal but not with respect to the government's announced effective date. It is also strange that the Court could find a compelling interest in catching contracts entered into between April 25 and the end of the month when the government's announcement evidently saw no substantial harm from such contracts. These considerations evoked a rare dissent (by one judge). The downplaying of the details of the government's

---

[77] BVerfGE 72, 200, 261.

[78] *See* BVerfGE 97, 67 (Dec. 3, 1997).

announcement is consistent with the Court's above-described decision on Swiss residents, although this time it cuts against the taxpayer. The case provides an ironic example of the fact that taxpayers may receive better protection from the political process in countries—such as the U.S.—where there is virtually no judicial control over retroactive tax legislation, but where generous transition rules are typically provided.

The Italian and Spanish courts have taken an intermediate position, finding that in principle there is constitutional protection against unduly retroactive tax legislation, while in practice according a considerable degree of discretion to the legislator.[79]

A number of countries have enshrined the right to be free from retroactive tax (or other) legislation in explicit constitutional language.[80] While sometimes admitting of exceptions, this approach runs the risk of imposing an unduly rigid constraint on the legislator.

Are there constitutional limitations on the retroactivity of tax legislation (either textual or under judicial doctrine)?

---

[79] The Italian court has judged retroactivity of tax legislation under the principle of ability to pay (taxable capacity), finding that laws reaching back too far might violate this principle, since the ability to pay might no longer exist; in practice, the court has very rarely found tax laws to violate this principle. *See* Tipke (2000) at 148; Constitutional court, decision of July 7, 1994, R.U. 112, No. 315 (a law taxing gains realized three years ago was forseeable and in view of this fact and its relatively short retroactive effect, the principle of taxable capacity was not violated).

Like the German court, the Spanish Constitutional Court draws a distinction between two degrees of retroactivity. But it has taken a flexible approach, finding that the constitutionality of a retroactive law must be determined on a case-by-case basis, taking into account the degree of retroactivity and the justification for the law. On this basis, it has upheld the change of individual income tax rates retroactive to the beginning of the calendar year (the court noting that this was not authentic retroactivity since the taxable event is the close of the tax year on Dec. 31), but has struck down a substantial addition to the tax on gambling machines which was imposed after the tax for that year had already been paid. *See* S.T.C., Oct. 31, 1996, R.T.C. 1996, 173; S.T.C., Oct. 28, 1997, R.T.C. 1997, 182. *See generally* Martín Queralt et al. (2001) at 183-86.

[80] *See* Brazil Const. art. 150 III; Greece Const. art. 78; Mexico Const., art. 14 (*see* de la Garza (2001) at 301-06); Código Fiscal de la Federación, art. 7 (Mexico); Mozambique Const. art. 201; Paraguay Const. art. 14; Peru Const. art. 74; Romania Const. art. 15; Russia Const. art. 57; Delphine Nougayrède, Construire L'Impôt en Russie 214-16, 288-89 (2001); Slovenia Const. art. 155; Sweden Const. ch. 2, art. 10 allowing limited exceptions); Venezuela Const. art. 24.

4.3.7 EQUALITY

4.3.7.1 In general

Taxation is all about drawing distinctions. Often, situations that are very similar from an economic point of view are taxed unequally. Sometimes this discrimination is justified by policy reasons, for example concerns of administrability. Sometimes political considerations motivate special rules favoring certain taxpayers. The appropriate way to tax various transactions can of course be controversial, which is attested by a huge volume of literature on tax policy. At which point do tax policy disputes become disputes about constitutional law? On this issue, we see substantially different approaches by the constitutional courts of different countries. On one side of the spectrum is the United States. The Supreme Court has applied a low level of equal protection scrutiny to tax laws, finding that unequal treatment does not raise constitutional concerns where it is justified by a possible legitimate state interest (this is known as "rational basis" scrutiny[81]). On the opposite extreme have been countries like Austria and Germany. There the constitutional courts have been active in striking down tax legislation that violates the principle of equality. Countries like France fall somewhere in the middle. The French Constitutional Council has occasionally struck down tax laws for violating the principle of equality, but has shown greater deference to the judgment of the legislator than has the German Constitutional Court.

4.3.7.2 Germany

The German Constitutional Court has been active in striking down tax legislation for violating the principle of equality. In implementing this principle, the Court has established a doctrine that taxation must be imposed in line with ability to pay, thereby raising much of tax policy to the level of

---

[81] *See, e.g.,* Apache Bend Apartments v. United States, 964 F.2d 1556, 1563 (5th Cir. 1992).

constitutional law.[82] The discussion below focuses on decisions in the most recent phase of the Court's jurisprudence.[83]

In its decision of June 27, 1991, the Constitutional Court found that the scheme for taxing *interest income* was unconstitutional, being in violation of the equality clause.[84] This was because there was so much tax evasion by way of nondeclaration of interest income that those taxpayers who did declare their income were taxed unfairly. Nevertheless, the Court found that this complaint did not render the current scheme invalid, and that it could continue to apply for a transitional period.[85] The Court found that the legislature could remedy the defect in a number of ways: it could provide for effective provision of information by banks to the tax authorities, so that declarations could be subject to effective checking, or it could impose a flat-rate withholding tax, among other possibilities. The decision is noteworthy for the fact that the Court was willing to go beyond what the law stated on the books to find a constitutional violation from uneven administration.[86]

The Court's later decision on the *net wealth tax* also considered the actual application of the tax. The Court found this tax unconstitutional because the valuation rules as applied resulted in substantially different valuations for different kinds of property as compared with market value, thus violating the principle of equality before the law.[87] In particular, no revaluation of real estate had been carried out for a substantial period, leading

---

[82] *See* Klaus Vogel & Christian Waldhoff, *Germany, in* The Principle of Equality, *supra* note 23, at 99-114; Grasshof, *supra* note 32, at art. 3 I GG No. 178 ("The command of equality in taxation requires at least for direct taxes a taxation according to the financial ability to pay [*Leistungsfähigkeitsprinzip*].")

[83] For a discussion of these phases and more general analysis of the court's constitutional jurisprudence in the tax area, see Vogel & Waldhoff, *supra* note 82, at 89. One of the earlier decisions held that the principle of equality prohibited the exemption of compensation for legislators. *See* Kommers, *supra* note 15, at 135-36; BVerfGE 40, 296 (1975).

[84] BVerfGE 84, 239 (1991).

[85] The German Constitutional Court has the flexibility to declare a law to be either void or incompatible with the constitution. In the latter case, the statute may remain in effect for a transitional period. *See* Kommers, *supra* note 15, at 52-53.

[86] For an exploration of the concept of equality in the actual application of the law, see Rolf Eckhoff, Rechtsanwendungsgleichheit im Steuerrecht (1999).

[87] Decision of June 22, 1995, 93 BVerfGE 121. On the same day, the Court decided a case concerning the inheritance tax, finding that the same type of valuation problems that plagued the net wealth tax (resulting in unconstitutional discrimination among different types of assets) also invalidated the inheritance tax as applied, and required corrective legislative action. BVerfGE 93, 165 (June 22, 1995).

to a substantial undervaluation of this class of asset. The relatively favorable treatment of real estate could not be justified by a legislative decision to encourage real estate holding, since no such decision had been explicitly taken by the legislator. The Court also stated that the constitutional protection of liberty prohibited confiscatory taxation, and therefore that the tax could take no more than about 50% of the income from property, when combined with other taxes. Finally, the Court found that the protection of the family was also relevant to the wealth tax, requiring the legislator to respect the continuity of the property of the marriage and family. However, the primary basis of the decision was the violation of the principle of equality.

In a number of other cases, litigants have invoked the principle of equality to protest distinctions made in the tax laws.[88] These cases find the

---

[88] *Lump-sum limitations.* The Court found that legislative or administrative establishment of lump-sum limitations on deductions (as opposed to case-by-case determinations) did not violate the principle of equality because it was justified on the basis of administrative considerations. This decision also upheld the right of the tax administration to establish mechanical rules in administrative guidelines even where such rules were not contained in the statute itself. BVerfGE 78, 214 (May 31, 1988).

Government employee allowances. The exemption of allowances paid to government employees which could be unrelated to actual costs incurred and could serve simply as an incentive to serve in particular regions was found to violate the equality clause. BVerfGE 99, 286 (Nov. 11, 1998).

Medical assistance. On the other hand, the Court found that a valid distinction could be drawn between private and public employees concerning the treatment of medical assistance payments. Because for public sector employees—unlike for the private sector—such payments were subject to audit and control, the legislator could constitutionally draw a distinction between them and exempt from tax the receipt of such payments by public employees. BVerfGE 83, 395 (Feb. 19, 1991).

Legal form. The Court held that it was unconstitutional discrimination to condition a VAT exemption on the legal form in which the taxpayer's business was carried out. BVerfGE 101, 151 (Nov. 10, 1999). Legal form was also held not to justify a distinction for inheritance tax purposes between the widow of an employee and the widow of a deceased partner in a partnership. BVerfGE 79, 106 (Nov. 9, 1988).

Home office. In a 1999 case, the court considered the rules for deduction of home office expenses. In general terms, these were allowed up to a specified amount if certain conditions were met (use of home office must represent at least 50% of business activity or no office is otherwise available), allowed in full where the home office was the principal place of business, and not allowed at all where neither condition was met. The Court found that these arbitrary limits were justified because a case-by-case determination would have required intrusive home inspections, and because they fell within the legislature's consitutional freedom of action to establish administrable general rules for taxation. BVerfGE 101, 297 (Dec. 7, 1999).

Court wrestling with the issue of what reasons might justify the distinctions drawn. Because the arguments are specific to the context of each case, it is difficult to generalize. It is clear, however, that this type of case finds the Court second-guessing the legislator on the basis of tax policy considerations: the distinction will be upheld only where justified by sufficiently clear and persuasive grounds.[89] The Court found an absence of justification for a rule preventing losses to be offset from the category of "other income."[90] In a similar vein, the Court held that a provision prohibiting an owner of a two-family dwelling to deduct (for purposes of withholding) allowances that would finally be deductible at the end of the year constituted unconstitutional discrimination vis-à-vis those taxpayers making estimated payments of tax (who were allowed to deduct such allowances).[91] On the other hand, the Court found that the legislature could eliminate special allowances intended to

---

[89] Contrast the rational basis inquiry applied by the U.S. courts. *See supra* 4.3.7.1; *infra* 4.3.7.4.

[90] *Loss offset.* Under the income tax law, losses from activity generating "other income" could not be offset against any other type of income, or even carried over to be offset against the same type of income from one year to the next. The Court found that this treatment disadvantaged taxpayers receiving "other income" as compared with other taxpayers, who generally were allowed to carry over their losses. The case involved the rental of movable property, which was classified for income tax purposes as "other income." Since no basis justifying this distinction could be adduced, the Court held that the principle of equality was violated and overturned the provision. BVerfGE 99, 88 (Sept. 30, 1998). Incidentally, in this case the court made the comment that incomes from private capital gains could not be taxed as "other income" if they were not the result of an income-generating activity (the "source" principle of income). BVerfGE 99 at 96. It appears that this observation was made as a matter of statutory construction rather than being on a constitutional level.

[91] *Withholding deductions.* BVerfGE 84, 348 (Oct. 8, 1991). The Court could easily have found that the discriminatory treatment was justified because it involved not a permanent difference in taxation but just a timing difference which was justified on the basis of administrative simplicity and, moreover, was compensated for at least partially by special deductions that were allowed to employees. In a subsequent case, the Court would state: "Equality of taxation over time is affected only minimally by the monthly collection of tax through withholding." BVerfGE 96, 1, 9 (April 10, 1997). In the event, the court held the other way: it found that timing differences were significant enough to constitute unconstitutional discrimination, that the special deductions were not relevant because they were not correlated with those employees disadvantaged by the particular rule in question, and that administrative considerations were not compelling.

compensate for the disadvantages arising from the monthly collection of tax through withholding.[92]

In some cases, such as those involving constitutionally protected rights, the Constitutional Court has applied *stricter scrutiny*. For example, the court stated that discrimination relating to the tax treatment (or other regulation) of political parties is subject to a higher standard of review under the equality principle: it must be justified by a "special, urgent reason."[93] Stricter scrutiny (though presumably not as strict as for political parties) has not been reserved for cases involving fundamental rights. In a case involving a rule whereby overtime was fully tax-free if the rates were determined by law or collective bargaining but tax-free only to a limited extent in other instances, the Court explained that the principle of equality called for varying levels of scrunity, with more intensive scrutiny where the exercise of constitutionally protected rights was concerned or where one group of persons was treated unequally as compared with another group.[94] In this case, there were *two groups* of workers – those whose overtime pay was determined by law or collective bargaining, and other workers. The statute discriminated against a group by restricting the tax-free amounts for the latter group only. The legislature did have the discretion to prescribe some sort of limitation, but the particular limit it had determined was invalid since it did not reasonably correspond to the average amount of tax-free income that the first group of workers was able to receive.

A series of decisions has involved review of the adequacy of deductions for *subsistence minimums*, often in connection with child rearing

---

[92] *Christmas allowance.* A decision subsequent to that on withholding deductions considered the elimination of special Christmas allowances and a general allowance for employees. The complaint was that the elimination of these allowances was unconstitutional, because they were intended to compensate for the disadvantages that employees suffered from having to pay tax through monthly withholding. The Court held that, while there was a responsibility to ensure a rough equality of taxation, to determine whether there was constitutionally impermissible inequality the entire set of rules governing the taxation of a particular type of income had to be considered. In addition, the legislator enjoyed a certain freedom of maneuver in establishing general rules in the interest of administrability, and was not obligated to tailor tax rules to the individualities of all particular cases. Under this analysis, taking the rules concerning taxation of wage income as a whole, a disadvantageous treatment rising to constitutionally significant level could not be discerned. In this context, the disadvantage from collection of tax through monthly withholding was a minor one. BVerfGE 96, 1 (April 10, 1997).

[93] BVerfGE 78, 350, 358 (June 21, 1988).

[94] BVerfGE 89, 15, 22.

expenses. In these cases, the Court sometimes has relied on other constitutional provisions beyond the equality clause. In a 1990 decision, the Court held that for income tax purposes a subsistence minimum must be tax free (unless the State determines to cover minimum child rearing expenses directly). In this respect, the equality principle must be applied in conjunction with the clause in the Constitution protecting the family. The combination of these clauses produced a principle of horizontal equity in family taxation which required a reasonable differentiation among families of different sizes for income tax purposes. In the same case, the Court found constitutional a provision which, for purposes of means testing of child allowances, used income tax rules but denied a compensation of losses between different categories of income. The Court found that there were grounds to be suspicious of artificial tax losses. While a more precise approach would have been to distinguish more finely among different types of losses, administrability justified the blunter approach taken by the legislature.[95] A 1992 case found that art. 2(1) of the Constitution (providing a right to the free development of one's personality), read together with art. 14 (right to property), required the income tax to leave the taxpayer at least a subsistence minimum free of tax, and that this amount could be determined on the basis of amounts payable under the welfare laws.[96]

The Court held that Art. 6, para. 2, of the Constitution required child maintenance expenses to be taken into account for tax purposes in the case of all parents, and therefore invalidated tax rules limiting the cases where a child dependency allowance was deductible.[97]

A difficult problem was posed for the Court when the deduction for expenses of maintaining a child who was a student living away from home was cut in half. Particularly in light of Art. 6(1) of the Constitution, which protected the family, how could this be reconciled with the principle that each taxpayer must be taxed according to his ability to pay?[98] "The unavoidable additional expense arising from maintenance obligations, above all for

---

[95] BVerfGE 82, 60 (May 29, 1990) (dealing with the child allowance) and BVerfGE 82, 198 (June 12, 1990) (dealing with the dependency deduction for income tax purposes). Subsequent decisions determined precisely how large a child dependency deduction for income tax purposes was constitutionally required, finding that this could be derived from amounts allowed by the State under the welfare laws. BVerfGE 99, 246 (Nov. 10, 1998) and BVerfGE 99, 273 (Nov. 10, 1998).

[96] BVerfGE 87, 153 (Sept. 25, 1992). *See* Vogel and Waldhoff, *supra* note 82, at 97.

[97] BVerfGE 99, 216 (Nov. 10, 1998).

[98] BVerfGE 89, 346, 352 (Jan. 26, 1994) ("From the general principle of equality there follows for the sphere of tax law that taxation must be oriented according to the economic ability to pay of the taxpayer.")

children, reduces the taxpayer's ability to pay. The lawgiver violates art. 3, para. 1 of the Constitution, if he disregards such obligations."[99] However, the Court found that educational expenses for college were different from other maintenance expenses for children, and indeed could be seen as a form of investment.[100] Nevertheless, parents still had an obligation to pay for such education, and the state had a corresponding obligation either to bear a certain portion of such expenses itself or to recognize such portion as a reduction of the ability to pay of the parents for tax purposes. In this area, the lawgiver has a certain freedom of action as to how much of the expenses to recognize for tax purposes. Taking into account amounts paid by the State outside the tax system, the Court found that the particular amount chosen by the legislature as deductible for tax purposes was within the area of permissible discretion.

The principle of equality is often closely related to statutory interpretation where it is possible to read a statutory enumeration either narrowly or more broadly. The Court has found that a narrow interpretation of the law by the lower courts violated the equality principle, when this principle   called for a broader interpretation.[101] It is interesting that this problem was dealt with as a constitutional matter, when another approach would simply have been for a higher court to find the lower court's interpretation to be wrong (the Constitutional Court had jurisdiction over an appeal on constitutional grounds, but not otherwise). This highlights an important aspect of the principle of equality: the principle influences statutory interpretation under the theory that a statute should wherever possible be interpreted so as to be constitutional. In effect, this opens the door to the possibility for interpreting statutory language in a broad manner.

4.3.7.3 France

The Constitutional Council has invalidated tax legislation for violating the principle of equality in several cases, particularly in instances

---

[99] *Id.* at 352-53.

[100] *Id.* at 354.

[101] BVerfGE 71, 354 (Jan. 14, 1986). Similarly, the court held that an interpretation of the VAT statute, which provided exemptions for various listed medical professions, including "similar" ones, according to which professions would be recognized as similar only if subject to professional licensing, violated the equality clause since the criterion of professional licensing had no relevance in terms of the policy of the VAT statute and the statute as so construed would therefore discriminate against similarly situated persons. BVerfGE 101, 132 (Oct. 29, 1999).

where the tax law was seen as violating the principle of procedural equality before the law (procedural due process).

The Court found the right to procedural due process to be violated by provisions of the 1974 finance bill. One of these involved the rules concerning deemed taxation, based on specified indicia of the taxpayer's lifestyle. The 1974 finance bill would have added a provision to the tax code allowing taxpayers to avoid an assessment on this basis by proving that the taxpayer did not have hidden sources of income. However, this procedure of proof would have been unavailable to taxpayers with income above a specified level. The Constitutional Council found that the denial of this possibility of proof to a limited group was a violation of the constitutional principle of equality before the law.[102] The right to procedural equality before the law was also found to be violated by a rule allowing the tax authorities to correct mistakes in assessments despite expiration of the limitations period.[103] The Court also overturned as violative of the principle of equality before the law a rule shortening the period of limitations for taxpayers who received solely wage or pension income. The Court noted that there was some basis for this distinction, since this type of income was subject to third-party reporting, but found that the distinction was nevertheless irrational, since a taxpayer with a small amount of other income was in a "virtually identical" position to a taxpayer whose sole source of income was wages.[104]

In a few cases, the Constitutional Council (CC) has struck down legislation on the substantive right to equality. For example, the CC found that it was arbitrary to distinguish among gifts on the basis of whether or not they were made before a notary, and hence that this distinction violated the principle of equality.[105]

In general, however, the CC has been reluctant to find that tax distinctions violate the principle of equality. For example, a ceiling on the stamp duty on stock exchange transactions was challenged as discriminatory against smaller transactions. However, the CC found that Parliament was free to establish rates so as to provide an incentive for the development of economic activity and that the reduced rate "tends to encourage the development of the national stock market, in particular through the carrying

---

[102] Cons. const., Dec. 27, 1973, Dec. No. 51 DC, Rec. 25, *reprinted with commentary in* Favoreu & Philip, *supra* note 27, at 288-308.

[103] Cons. const., Dec. 29, 1989, Dec. No. 89-268 DC, Rec. 110 (Consideration 61).

[104] Cons. const., July 3, 1986, Dec. No. 86-209 DC, Rec. 86 (Considerations 25, 26), excerpted in Philip, *supra* note 26, at 211.

[105] Cons. const., Dec. 30, 1991, Dec. No. 91-302 DC, Rec. 137 (Considerations 2-9). Other cases are summarized in Favoreu & Philip, *supra* note 27, at 301-02.

out of substantial transactions which have heretofore taken place abroad because of a more favorable tax regime." The legislature was free to provide "concessions which are in the public interest."[106]

The CC has also been reluctant to get into the question of tax-free subsistence minimums. It has held that, while the Constitution calls for a principle of national support for the family, the legislator can provide this support in different ways, not necessarily through the tax system, and therefore that a change in the family quotient system that reduced the tax benefit for dependent children was not unconstitutional.[107]

Since about 1995, the CC seems to be somewhat more willing to question the rationality of legislative classifications.[108] The CC struck down a scheme allowing a 50 percent valuation reduction for closely held businesses for inheritance tax purposes, finding that the scheme did not correspond closely enough to the legislative goals of allowing business continuation.[109] It has found that the principle of taxation according to taxable capacity was violated by including property subject to a usufruct in the wealth tax base of its legal owner, given that this person was not in a position to obtain income from the property.[110] In a decision involving what seemed to be a poorly designed local tax on commercial activity, the CC struck down the tax because it did not take into account the period of time for which the activity was carried out in the locality.[111] Taking a fairly activist line, the Court struck down a tax on energy, on the basis that there was not a close enough correlation between the tax imposed and the purpose of the tax (reduced carbon emissions). In particular, the CC objected to the fact that one enterprise could pay more tax than another, even though its carbon emissions were lower, and to the fact that electricity was taxed, even though its contribution to carbon emissions was minimal (presumably given the high use of nuclear power in France).[112]

---

[106] Cons. const., June 21, 1993, Dec. No. 93-320 DC, Rec. 146 (Considerations 17-19).

[107] *See* Cons. const., Dec. 98-405, Rec. 326 (Dec. 29, 1998).

[108] *See also* Dec. 96-385, Rec. 145 (Dec. 30, 1996)(distinction between widowed persons and other single persons was not relevant to the family quotient); Dec. 97-395, Rec. 333 (Dec. 30, 1997)(limits on amount of *avoir fiscal* (imputed corporation tax) that could be refunded to individual taxpayers could not be justified).

[109] *See* Cons. const., Dec. 95-369, Rec. 257 (Dec. 28, 1995).

[110] *See* Cons. const., Dec. 98-405, Rec. 326, 328 (Dec. 29, 1998).

[111] *See* Cons. const., Dec. 99-424, Rec. 156 (Dec. 29, 1999).

[112] *See* Cons. const., Dec. 2000-441, Rec. 201 (Dec. 28, 2000).

Thus, while the CC has tended to favor challenges on the basis of procedural equality before the law, it has only rarely found that substantive discrimination is invalid,[113] although a more activist phase may have commenced around 1995. Part of the reason for the relatively small number of cases where tax legislation has been found to violate the principle of equality is procedural, since in France statutes can be challenged on constitutional grounds only before enactment. While the annual laws on finance are routinely subject to challenge (most of the CC's decisions are issued at the end of December), the German system, which allows private litigants to bring challenges to the particular provision that is relevant to their facts, seems to make for a more robust challenge than that placed before the French Constitutional Council.

4.3.7.4 United States

Taking an opposite position to the German Court, the U.S. Supreme Court has been reluctant to find that discrimination in tax law violates the equal protection of the laws: "in taxation, even more than in other fields, legislatures possess the greatest freedom in classification."[114] This is consistent with the Court's general approach to constitutional review of economic legislation.[115]

Nordlinger v. Hahn[116] involved an equal protection clause challenge to the manner in which real property is assessed under the California Constitution. A change in ownership or new construction triggers reassessment. Thus, longer-term property owners pay lower taxes, reflecting historic values. The Court found that in this context equal protection "requires only that the classification rationally further a legitimate state

---

[113] *See* Beltrame & Mehl (1997) at 527; Favoreu & Philip, supra note 27, at 298-99; David et al. (2000) at 106-13.

[114] Madden v. Kentucky, 309 U.S. 83 (1940), *quoted in* Regan v. Taxation with Representation, 461 U.S. 540, 547 (1983). The general standard that the Supreme Court has used in reviewing economic legislation is that "Normally, a legislative classification will not be set aside if any state of facts rationally justifying it is demonstrated to or perceived by the courts." United States v. Maryland Savings-Share Ins. Corp., 400 U.S. 4, 6 (1970). *See* Bittker and Lokken (1999) ¶ 1.2.5. The federal courts have rejected a host of equal protection challenges to the income tax. See cases collected in *id.* n. 52.

[115] *See* Apache Bend Apartments v. United States, 964 F.2d 1556, 1562-67 (5th Cir. 1992).

[116] 505 U.S. 1 (1992).

interest."[117] It found that a possible[118] purpose of discouraging turnover or protecting existing owners from unanticipated tax increases served to justify the statutory scheme.

In *Apache Bend Apartments v. United States*,[119] the Fifth Circuit considered the consistency of rifle-shot[120] transition rules in the Tax Reform Act of 1986 with the equal protection clause. These rules were adopted largely in response to the political influence of certain well-connected taxpayers.[121] The Court found that "[n]ot every application for transitional relief was granted, however, political clout notwithstanding," and that staff had been given "rules by which transitions are to be selected."[122] "[A]s far as we can tell from the legislative history, Congress made their decisions based on the merits of the applications for transitional relief made to the Finance Committee."[123] "We hold that the classifications made by Congress were not arbitrary. It accorded transitional relief to those deserving taxpayers who applied for such relief and established most convincingly that they relied substantially on the old tax laws in making major investment decisions."[124]

Have tax laws been struck down as violative of the principle of equality?

4.3.8 TREATMENT OF MARRIED COUPLES

In addition to general protection from unequal treatment, constitutions typically protect specific rights. In some countries, marriage and family are

---

[117] 505 U.S. at 10.

[118] "The Equal Protection Clause does not demand for purposes of rational-basis review that a legislature or governing decisionmaker actually articulate at any time the purpose or rationale supporting its classification." 505 U.S. at 15.

[119] 964 F.2d 1556 (5th Cir. 1992).

[120] This commonly used nickname refers to the fact that the rules are targeted to hit very specific taxpayers. Each rule is typically drafted in such a way as to apply to one company only.

[121] *See* 964 F.2d at 1562; Jeffrey Birnbaum & Alan Murray, Showdown at Gucci Gulch 146-47, 240-47 (1987).

[122] 964 F.2d at 1568.

[123] *Id.* Reading between the lines of the opinion, it appears that the factual record before the court was not very well developed. The conclusion that the transitional rules of the 1986 Act were primarily responsive to non-political considerations would have been difficult to justify on a fuller factual record. However, given the state of the law, even a well-litigated case would have been an uphill fight.

[124] 964 F.2d at 1569.

specifically protected by the constitution. Courts in these countries have generally found that this special protection is violated by joint taxation of married couples that results in a higher tax than the combined tax for single persons. Some courts have also seen such joint taxation as a violation of the principle of equality.

In a landmark decision of Jan. 17, 1957,[125] the German Constitutional Court held that the joint taxation of married couples violated art. 6, clause 1 of the Constitution. This provision provides constitutional protection to marriage and family. The Court found that this provision prevented the State from imposing higher taxation on a married couple than what would apply if the couple had remained unmarried. The Court stated that the constitution would not prohibit "incidental" effects of taxation on marriage, but that the joint taxation of a couple was not incidental. Moreover, the Court found that the aggregation of a married couple could not be justified on the basis that the couple formed a household unit, because unmarried couples could also form such a unit, and the law did not reach such units (the Court noted as an historical aside that originally the tax law did speak of household units, but this had not been the case for a long time). Finally, the Court found that a social policy to encourage women to stay at home could not justify the taxing provision, since such a policy would be discriminatory against women and hence would violate art. 3, clauses 2 and 3 of the Constitution which prohibit such discrimination.

Courts in Cyprus, Ireland, Italy, Korea, and Spain have also found joint taxation of married couples to be unconstitutional.[126]

---

[125] 6 BVerfGE 55, *excerpted in* Kommers, *supra* note 15, at 495-98.

[126] *See* Vanistendael, *Legal Framework for Taxation, in* TLDD 23; Chang Hee Lee, *Korea,* 28 Tax Notes Int'l 1300 (Dec. 30, 2002); The Constitutional Court of Italy, Case No. 179/1976 (July 14, 1976); *see also* Decision of Feb. 22, 1999, 132 R.U. No. 41 (irrebuttable presumption that transfer of property between spouses is a gift violates the principle of taxation according to taxable capacity, since it imposes a tax based on personal status, not on the capacity to pay tax); Republic of Cyprus v. Demetriades (1977) 12 J.S.C. 2102. The Court in *Demetriades* found unconstitutional a regime under which income of a wife was taxed to the husband. The Court relied on the American case of Hoeper v. Tax Commission, 284 U.S. 206 (1931), as well as on the German Constitutional Court's decision of 1957. Its finding of unconstitutionality was based on several alternative grounds, including contravention of art. 24(1) of the Constitution, providing that every person is bound to contribute towards the public burden according to his means (but not someone else's means), and art. 28 of the Constitution, which provides for equality before the law and against discrimination (married men were treated unequally depending on the income of their wives, and married and unmarried women were treated unequally).

4.3.9   OTHER COUNTRIES[127]

The most active constitutional courts in the tax area in EU member countries have been those in Austria, France, Germany, Italy, and Spain.

The Austrian constitutional court, like its German counterpart, has applied a fairly searching scrutiny of laws for violation of the principle of equality, finding that good reasons must be adduced to justify a legislative classification.[128] The Austrian court tests retroactive laws against this same principle, finding that the retroactivity is permitted only where there are special circumstances that justify it.[129]

For Spain, see Carlos Palao Taboada, *Leistungsfähigkeitsprinzip und Gleichheitssatz im Steuerrecht in der Rechtsprechung des spanischen Verfassungsgerichts, in* Die Steuerrechtsordnung in der Diskussion 583, 589-90 (Joachim Lang ed., 1995); S.T.C., Feb. 20, 1989, R.T.C. 1989, 45. The Spanish Court's conclusion followed from the premise that taxation is to be evaluated on the basis of an individual tax unit. The Court found that imposing a higher tax on a married couple violated the principle of equality in taxation as well as constitutional protection of the family.

In Canada, although married taxpayers are taxed as individuals, there are a number of provisions that look to the position of the spouse, and that disadvantage married couples in some instances. Challenges to these provisions have been rejected by the Canadian courts. *See* Lahey, *supra* note 67; Kathleen Lahey, *Tax Law and "Equality": The Canadian Charter of Rights, Sex and Sexuality*, [2000] B.T.R. 378.

For Ireland, see Corrigan (2000) at 11; Murphy v. Attorney General, [1982] I.R. 241. The scheme considered in Ireland taxed a married man on the earnings of his wife. It had the effect of imposing a higher tax in most cases on married couples than if each spouse had been taxed as a single person. The Court struck down this scheme on the basis of art. 41 of the Constitution, which provided protection to the family. It refused, however, to hold that the scheme violated art. 40 of the Constitution (equal protection): "In so far as unequal treatment is alleged as between, on the one hand, married couples living together and, on the other, unmarried couples living together the social function of married couples living together is such as to justify the legislature in treating them differently from single persons for income tax purposes Numerous examples could be given from the income-tax code of types of income-tax payers who are treated differently, either favourably or unfavourably, because of their social function." [1982] I.R. at 284.

[127] *See generally* Tipke (2000) at 307-09.

[128] *See* Karl Korinek and Michael Holoubek, *Austria, in* The Principle of Equality *supra* note 23, at 35.

[129] *See id.* at 40-41; *supra* note 74.

While the Constitution of Italy explicitly guarantees equality in tax matters, the Italian constitutional court has struck down relatively few tax provisions as violative of this principle.[130]

The Spanish Constitution, like the Italian, contains a clause specifically guaranteeing equality in matters of taxation. The Spanish Constitutional Court has applied the principles of generality, equality, progressivity, non-confiscation, and economic capacity to taxation under the constitution.[131] As of 1995, the Court had struck down a tax law on the basis of the equality principle only once, in its decision on taxation of married couples.[132]

---

[130] *See* Livio Paladin, *Der steuerrechtliche Gleichheitssatz in der Rechtsprechung des italienischen Verfassungsgerichts, in* Besteuerung von Einkommen (Klaus Tipke & Nadya Bozza eds. 2000); Adriano di Pietro, *Italy, in* The Principle of Equality, *supra* note 23, at 115, 122-23. It seems that the attitudes of the courts in both Italy and Belgium are closer to that of France: relatively deferential to the legislator. However, the Italian Court—similar to the French CC—seems to be less tolerant of departures from equality in tax procedure (principle of equality before the law). *See id* at 123.

[131] *See* Tulio Rosembuj, *Spain, in* The Principle of Equality, *supra* note 23, at 157; Martín Queralt et al. (2001) at 108-32; Tomas Gui Mori, Jurisprudencia Constitucional 1981-1995 (1997). Its jurisprudence concerning the principle of equality began in 1981. *See* Palao, *supra* note 126, at 585.

[132] *See id.* at 597-98; *supra* note 126. In 2000, the court struck down a rule (already repealed at the time the court heard the case) taxing capital gains at an 8% rate if the tax on the taxpayer's ordinary income was zero, and otherwise taxing capital gains at the average tax rate on ordinary income. Under this scheme, it was possible for taxpayers whose ordinary income was higher (but taxed at an effective rate of between zero and 8%) to enjoy a lower rate on capital gains than those whose ordinary income was zero or negative. The court found this result contrary to art. 31 of the Constitution (taxation according to economic capacity). *See* S.T.C., Feb. 17, 2000, R.T.C. 2000, 46. In general, however, the Spanish court has been fairly deferential to the legislator, finding that the legislator had considerable scope for discretion. For example, in S.T.C., Oct. 4, 1990, R.T.C. 1990, 150, the court refused to find a taxing scheme to be confiscatory, while acknowledging that there was a general principle prohibiting confiscatory taxation. In S.T.C., July 14, 1994, R.T.C. 1994, 214 the court found that the constitutional principle of taxation according to economic capacity was not violated by denying partners a deduction for partnership losses. The court likewise upheld limits on the deduction for interest. In the same decision, the court upheld a distinction between public and private scholarships. The court has been most active in distinctions involving the family. *See supra* note 126. The court struck down a limitation on the deduction for salary paid to family members as arbitrary and disproportionate, finding that the legislator could have addressed problems of abuse by less restrictive means, such as requiring special proof. *See* S.T.C., May 12, 1994, R.T.C. 1994, 146.

The Belgian constitutional court[133] has struck down several tax provisions as violative of the principle of equality, but has been more deferential to the judgment of the legislator than the courts of Austria or Germany.[134]

In a decision reminiscent of the German jurisprudence, the Constitutional Court of Slovenia held that provisions of the income tax law that denied a deduction to independent contractors for expenses violated the constitutional principle of equality.[135] The court gave the legislature a few months to bring the law into conformity with the ruling. While recognizing that the legislature had discretion to enact different tax rules for employees and independent contractors in order to encourage work under employment contracts, the court found that the complete denial of deductions (beyond a lump-sum amount of 10 percent) went too far.

The Constitutional Tribunal of Poland has overturned tax laws on a number of occasions, recently striking down provisions on tax amnesty and property declaration, finding them poorly defined, and contravening principles of equity and privacy.[136]

The Supreme Court of Mexico has developed over the course of more than 50 years a jurisprudence applying the constitutional requirements of equity, equality, and proportionality, striking down many tax laws in the process.[137] Art. 31, para. IV of the Constitution provides that Mexicans are obliged "To contribute toward the public expenditures both of the Federation and of the State and municipality where they reside, in the proportional and equitable manner provided by the laws."

Likewise, the Supreme Court of Argentina has over a substantial period developed the concept of equality in taxation as a control on arbitrary legislation.[138] The Supreme Court has also struck down as confiscatory taxes

---

[133] Arbitragehof/Cour d'Arbitrage.

[134] *See* Stefaan van Crombrugge, *Belgium, in* The Principle of Equality, *supra* note 23, at 51; Belgian Law, *supra* note 49, at 349; Willemart, *supra* note 23, at 167-250; Faes (1995) at 6-7.

[135] Decision of Dec. 1, 1994, Official Gazette of the Republic of Slovenia, Jan. 13, 1995.

[136] *See* IBFD Tax News Service, TNS-581 (Dec. 18, 2002).

[137] *See* de la Garza (2001) at 265-98. For a discussion of a recent case, see Jaime González-Bendiksen & Alejandro Enriquez-Mariscal, *Mexican Supreme Court Reverses Decision on Employee Subsidy,* 24 Tax Notes Int'l 549 (Nov. 5, 2001).

[138] *See* Jarach (1996) at 319-25; Dino Jarach, Curso de Derecho Tributario 87-105 (3d ed. 1980); García Vizcaíno, *supra* note 10, at 290-95. An early decision on the principle of equality (albeit not in a tax case) was rendered in 1875. *See* 16 Fallos de

which took away an excessive portion of the taxpayer's income or capital (compare the ruling of the German Constitutional Court discussed above).[139]

In Denmark, Norway, and Sweden, although there is constitutional review, in few or no cases have laws (whether tax or nontax) been held unconstitutional in recent times.[140]

In the Netherlands, art. 120 of the Constitution prohibits courts from striking down laws as unconstitutional. However, the courts have reviewed laws against the principle of equality found in both the International Covenant on Civic and Political Rights (ICCPR) and the ECHR. The number of cases where laws have been struck down is quite small (five altogether, with two of these involving the right of access to the courts). Thus, the Supreme Court of the Netherlands allows the legislator a considerable margin of discretion.[141]

In Switzerland, constitutional review does not extend to Federal laws.[142] However, the Swiss Federal Court has been quite active in the constitutional area concerning cantonal tax laws. In general terms, its jurisprudence is comparable to that of Germany, although it has not followed the German court in finding a right to a tax-free existence minimum,[143] and

---

la Suprema Corte 118 (Feb. 6, 1875). *See generally* Rodolfo Spisso, Derecho Constitucional Tributario (1993).

[139] *See id.* at 284-89; Héctor Villegas, *El Principio Constitucional de no Confiscatoriedad en Materia Tributária, in* Estudios de Derecho Constitucional Tributário 217 (Horacio A. García Belsunce ed. 1994); Alberto Tarsitano, *El Principio Constitucional de Capacidad Contributiva, in id.* at 301; Juan Carlos Luqui, Derecho Constitucional Tributario 47-71 (1993). In Marta Navarro Viola de Herrera Vegas v. Nación Argentina, Fallos 312: 2467 (Dec. 19, 1989), the Supreme Court struck down as confiscatory a tax promulgated on June 9, 1982, which was based on financial assets held by taxpayers on Dec. 31, 1981, given that the tax made no exception for assets that the taxpayer no longer owned at the time of promulgation of the law.

[140] *See* Favoreu, *supra* note 14, at 47-49. In Sweden, ch. 8, art. 18 of the Constitution requires legislation to be submitted for pre-enactment review to a Council on Legislation consisting of justices. Under ch. 11, art. 14 of the Constitution, courts may refuse to apply a statute that is unconstitutional, but only "if the error is manifest." Given the pre-enactment review, this standard is difficult to meet.

[141] *See* Richard Happé, *The Netherlands, in* The Principle of Equality, *supra* note 23, at 125.

[142] *See* Favoreu, *supra* note 14, at 50.

[143] The court recognized the constitutional right to a subsistence minimum, but found that the State could assure this by other means than an outright tax exemption, for example by not collecting tax in individual cases of need. *See* BGE 122 I 101 (May 24, 1996).

has been cautious in its doctrine on confiscatory taxation.   There are
numerous decisions, however, requiring equality in taxation.[144]

In 1982, Canada adopted the Charter of Rights and Freedoms.
Although numerous challenges to tax legislation based on the   anti-
discrimination rules have been brought since the Charter of Rights was
adopted in 1982, they have virtually all been rejected by the courts.[145]   This
is in line with the Supreme Court's general focus on discrimination based on
criteria enunciated in section 15 of the Charter of Rights, or analogous
criteria, rather than on purely economic discrimination.   However, the
litigation did result in legislation extending spousal treatment to same-sex
couples.[146]

The Irish Supreme Court has taken an approach similar to that of
Canada to claims of discrimination in interpreting its Constitution.[147]   An Irish

---

[144] *See generally* Höhn & Waldburger (2001) at 102-29.   *See, e.g.,* BGE 124 I 145
(March 20, 1998) (provision allowing valuation of rental value of owner-occupied
housing to deviate by more than 60% from market value violates the constitutional
principle of equality in taxation); BGE 124 I 159 (March 20, 1998) (differential
valuation of property for net wealth tax lacks sufficient justification to be
constitutionally admissible).

[145] *See* Lahey, *supra* notes 67 & 126; 5 The Canadian Charter of Rights Annotated
15-107 to 15-110.2 (John Laskin et al. eds. looseleaf, updated to May 1999).   For
example, in Thibaudeau v. Canada, [1995] 2 S.C.R. 627, 29 C.R.R. 2d 1 (S.C.C. May
25, 1995), the Supreme Court rejected a challenge to the system for taxing alimony
for the maintenance of minor children.   The system was alleged to discriminate
against custodial parents in relatively high tax brackets. In Symes v. Canada, [1993]
4 S.C.R. 695, the limitation on deductions for child care was challenged.   The
Supreme Court found that the provision did not discriminate on the basis of sex and
hence was not unconstitutional.   The courts have, however, struck down
discrimination based on sexual orientation. For example, in Rosenberg v. Canada, 51
C.R.R.2d 1 (Ontario Court of Appeal, April 23, 1998), the court held that the denial
of pension benefits under the Income Tax Act to same-sex partners could not be
justified and was unconstitutional.   For a discussion of the general framework for
interpretation of sec. 15 of the Charter of Rights, which provides for equal protection,
see 2 Peter Hogg, *supra* note 22, at § 52.

[146] *See* Lahey, *supra* notes 67 & 126.

[147] *See* Corrigan (2000) at 10.   Although article 40 of the Constitution states in general
terms that "[a]ll citizens shall, as human persons, be held equal before the law," the
Supreme Court has interpreted this provision as not being "a guarantee of absolute
equality for all citizens in all circumstances but it is a guarantee of equality as human
persons...and a guarantee against any inequalities grounded upon an assumption...that
some...classes of individuals, by reason of their human attributes or their ethnic or
racial, social or religious background, are to be treated as the inferior or superior o.

court struck down a scheme for withholding tax on professionals, which was implemented as part of the transition from assessment based on the prior financial year to current year assessment. The court found that while there was a legitimate objective in preventing windfall gains to taxpayers as part of the transition (it involved one year of assessment dropping out), the means adopted must be proportionate to the objective. In this case, the scheme caused financial hardship out of proportion to what was needed to implement the transition and hence interfered with the taxpayer's property rights guaranteed by Article 40, s. 3, subsection 2 of the Constitution.[148] The Supreme Court relied on the same provision in striking down property tax based on outdated and arbitrary valuations. "In the assessment of a tax such as a county rate reasonable uniformity of valuation appears essential to justice. If such reasonable uniformity is lacking the inevitable result will be that some ratepayer is required to pay more than his fair share ought to be. This necessarily involves an attack upon his property rights which by definition becomes unjust."[149]

A Venezuelan tax court has ruled that a statutory denial of a deduction for a payment on the basis that the taxpayer has not withheld tax on the payment as required violated the constitutional rule that taxpayers should be taxed on the basis of their economic capacity.[150]

The Japanese courts apply a rational basis standard of review and hence have not found tax laws to violate principles of equal protection.

---

other individuals in the community.....this guarantee refers to human persons for what they are in themselves rather than to any lawful activities, trades or pursuits which they may engage in or follow." Quinn's Supermarket v. Attorney General, [1972] I.R. 1, 13-14.

[148] *See* Daly v. Revenue Commissioners, [1995] 3 I.R. 1 (High Court July 27, 1995).

[149] Brennan v. Attorney General, [1984] I.L.R.M. 355, 365. (A rate is a tax on real property.) In Madigan v. Attorney General, [1986] I.L.R.M. 136, the Supreme Court rejected a challenge to a property tax imposed only on higher-income occupiers of higher-value properties. It found that the valuation techniques used and income aggregation applied in determining eligibility for exemption from the tax were not unjust. In this case, the lower court judge cited with approval U.S. Supreme Court cases referring to the wide latitude to be given to legislatures in determining tax classifications. [1986] I.L.R.M. at 152 (citing State Board of Tax Commissioners v. Jackson, 283 U.S. 527, 537 (1931)). Despite some success on grounds of property rights, constitutional challenges to tax legislation remain an uphill battle in Ireland. See Corrigan (2000) at 84-100.

[150] *See* Ronald E. Evans, *Venezuelan Tax Court: Denying Tax Deductions for Taxpayer's Failure to Withhold is Unconstitutional,* 20 Tax Notes Int'l 1237 (March 13, 2000).

The Constitutional Court of Russia in its tax decisions has thus far focused mostly on issues of competence of tax law making power, including that of regional authorities.[151]

In India, Article 14 of the Constitution guarantees equal protection of the laws. "[C]ourts seldom invalidate laws under this ground though challenges are numerous."[152] In taxation, "[t]he Courts...admit, subject to adherence to the fundamental principles of the doctrine of equality, a larger play to legislation discretion in the matter of classification."[153] The Supreme Court did, however, strike down as discriminatory and unconstitutional as denying equality before the law a land tax imposed at a uniform rate without reference to potential productivity (the land in question was forest land).[154] Similarly, property taxes imposed on the sole criterion of floor area have been struck down as arbitrary and therefore violative of the guarantee of equality under article 14 of the Constitution.[155] Differential procedures applicable to similarly situated taxpayers have also been struck down.[156]

Have tax laws been struck down on any other constitutional grounds?

4.4 EUROPEAN TAX LAW

4.4.1 TAX LAW OF THE EUROPEAN UNION

EC tax law has become important for virtually every tax practitioner in Europe, and a basic familiarity with it is critical to understanding the

---

[151] *See* Nougayrède, *supra* note 80, at 275-89. The Court also struck down the sales tax as unconstitutionally vague, while deferring the effect of the ruling. *See* Joel McDonald, *Sales Tax in Russia Ruled Unconstitutional,* 22 Tax Notes Int'l 1115 (March 5, 2001).

[152] K. Parameswaran, Power of Taxation Under the Constitution 194 (1987).

[153] V.V. Ravi Varma Rajah v. Union of India, (1969) 1 SCC 681, (1969) II SCJ 721, 725.

[154] K.T. Moopil Nair v. State of Kerala, AIR 1961 SC 552, (1961) II SCJ 269.

[155] *See* State of Kerala v. Haji K. Kutty Naha, AIR 1969 SC 378, (1969) 1 SCR 645, (1969) I SCJ 691; New Manek Chowk Spinning & Weaving Mills v. Municipal Corporation, Ahmadabad, AIR 1967 SC 1801, (1968) I SCJ 332.

[156] Anandji Haridas & Co. v. S.P. Kushare, AIR 1968 SC 565, (1968) I SCJ 820, 828 ("the classification must be based on some real and substantial distinction bearing a just and reasonable relation to the object sought to be attained and cannot be made arbitrarily and without any substantial basis").

European tax systems of today.[157] Tax lawyers might be tempted to jump right in and look at the directives and case law dealing with taxation. This would be a mistake. Just as constitutional tax law can be understood only in the context of constitutional law as a whole, so a basic understanding of European institutions and procedures is needed before dealing with the specifics of European tax law.[158] For example, an important concept is the relationship between the constitutional law of EU member countries and European law. The ECJ has ruled that "the validity of a Community instrument ... cannot be affected by allegations that it runs counter to ... fundamental rights as formulated by the constitution of [a member] State...."[159]—except insofar as these fundamental rights are recognized at a European level, based on common constitutional traditions of the member countries.[160]

The importance of European tax law can only grow in the future, although there are disagreements as to just how fast it should grow and in what directions. In particular, there is substantial debate on the extent to which taxes in the EU should be harmonized. There is no doubt, however, that European law creates policy pressures that will likely lead to changes in

---

[157] An excellent introduction to EC tax law from a policy point of view is David W. Williams, EC Tax Law (1998) (from which this section draws). The terminology (EC vs. EU) is confusing and changing; in this section I use "European" where possible as a synonym. See for a more detailed treatment Terra & Wattel (2002); Farmer & Lyal (1994); Peter Takacs, Das Steuerrecht der Europäischen Union (1998) (helpful because it discusses European tax law in the general context of European law, analyzing the latter in reasonable detail insofar as relevant for tax).

[158] A good place to start would be Philip Raworth, Introduction to the Legal System of the European Union (2001). The European Community is established by the EC Treaty (Treaty Establishing the European Community) (this is the Treaty of Rome of 25 March 1957, as amended most recently by the Treaty of Amsterdam of October 2, 1997, and Treaty of Nice, OJ, Oct. 3, 2001. The consolidated text of the treaty is reprinted in European Union Law Guide (Philip Raworth ed., looseleaf, as updated July 1999). The institutions of the EC are: a European Parliament, a Council, a Commission, a Court of Justice, and a Court of Auditors. EC Treaty, art. 7. For tax purposes, the most relevant institutions are the Court of Justice (ECJ), the Council Council of the European Union), and the Commission (Commission of the European Communities). On the relationship between the ECJ and the national courts of EU member countries, see Raworth, *supra,* at 197-99. A new constitutional arrangement for the EU is under development.

[159] Internationale Handellsgesellschaft m.b.H. v. Einfuhr- und Vorratsstelle für Getreide und Futtermittel, 11/70, [1970] E.C.R. 1125, 1134, discussed in Raworth, *supra* note 158, at 116-17.

[160] See Raworth, *supra* note 158, at 215-17.

tax laws and provides opportunities to challenge in court existing statutes and treaties. The proper interpretation of some domestic legislation (such as VAT or cross-border merger provisions) may depend on European directives. In order to understand tax law in any EU member country it is therefore necessary to keep European law in mind.

One can debate the extent to which the EU resembles a federal state.[161] An important feature of a state which is missing is the power to tax. Moreover, when the Council adopts provisions harmonising taxes, it must act unanimously, thereby requiring the support of the governments of all the member countries.[162] This unanimity rule has slowed down tax harmonisation in Europe. European governments have tried to reach agreement to change the unanimity rule—but unanimous consent could not be obtained.[163] An important paradox of the unanimity rule is presented by the situation where the ECJ makes a ruling, and member governments wish to overturn it. When a national court interprets the law in a way that the legislature does not like, the legislature can simply change the rule—by majority vote. However, in the EU, if member governments want to overturn a ruling of the ECJ they need to muster unanimous support. This places the ECJ in a virtually impregnable position when it comes to interpreting European law. In this context, the unanimity rule represents a delegation of power by member governments to the judiciary, probably not what member governments which insist on the rule have in mind.

Despite the limitation of the unanimity rule, taxation represents an important part of European law. For one thing, even though the EU has no power to tax on its own, it does have its own sources of tax revenue. The EU's own revenue sources are: customs duties (i.e. all trade taxes on imports and exports); industry-based levies on coal, steel, sugar, and isoglucose; income tax on its own staff; and revenue sharing which is linked to VAT according to a formula.[164] Much more important than EC-level taxation is the minimisation of distortions in the internal market through both positive and negative integration—positive integration being harmonisation actions taken by the Council in the form of directives or regulations, and negative integration being the policing of distortive taxation measures by the member

---

[161] *See* Raworth, *supra* note 158, at 183, 221-39.

[162] *See* Williams, *supra* note 157, at 6; EC Treaty arts. 93, 94, 95(2).

[163] *See* Joann M. Weiner, *EU Leaders Debate Qualified Majority Voting at Nice Summit*, 21 Tax Notes Int'l 2647 (Dec. 11, 2000).

[164] *See* Williams, *supra* note 157, at 46-52.

States, which is carried out by the Commission and the European Court of Justice.[165]

The EU has achieved *unification* of law in respect of customs duties — the European Customs Code is an EC regulation[166] which applies in every EU country and there are no internal customs duties.[167] The law of VAT has been *harmonized*—while separate VAT laws exist in each country, they must be consistent with the 6th VAT directive and other VAT directives (adopted on the EC level). These directives allow only limited freedom for countries to vary their VAT rules. There is also some harmonisation of excise taxes, although not as close as for VAT.

By contrast, there is very little harmonisation in the individual and corporate income tax areas.[168] The key harmonisation measures here are the Parent-Subsidiary Directive, the Merger Directive, and the Arbitration Convention. The Parent-Subsidiary Directive[169] relieves from taxation dividends paid by subsidiaries of European companies to their parent companies. The Merger Directive[170] provides harmonized tax rules for cross-border reorganizations. The Arbitration Convention[171] provides for binding arbitration in the event that competent authorities cannot agree on secondary adjustments to be made in transfer pricing cases. This convention is not technically part of EC law, although all EU members are parties to it. It is considered to have been effective in encouraging resolution of transfer pricing disputes even though (or perhaps because) it has rarely been made use of.

---

[165] *See* Terra and Wattel (1997) at 1-2.

[166] Regulation (EEC) 2913/92 of 12 October 1992, establishing the Community Customs Code (OJ L302/92, October 1992). Regulations are directly applicable. *See* Raworth, supra note 158, at 122. Customs duties are collected by national customs services as agents for the EU, and the applicable procedures governing, for example, criminal liability are found in national law.

[167] *See* Art. 3(1)(a) EC Treaty ("the prohibition, as between Member States, of customs duties and quantitative restrictions on the import and export of goods, and of all other measures having equivalent effect").

[168] *See generally* Sandra Eden, *Corporate Tax Harmonisation in the European Community*, [2000] B.T.R. 624.

[169] Council Directive 90/435/EEC on the Common System of Taxation applicable in the case of Parent Companies and Subsidiaries of Different Member States (23 July 1990)(1990 OJ L225/6).

[170] Council Directive 90/434 EEC on the Common System of Taxation applicable to Mergers, Divisions, Transfers of Assets and Exchanges of Shares concerning Companies of different Member States (23 July 1990)(1990 OJ L 225/1).

[171] Convention on the elimination of double taxation in connexion with the adjustment of profits of associated enterprises (23 July 1990) (published at 1990 OJ C 225/10).

The above-mentioned directives are considered to have *direct effect*,[172] which means that taxpayers can rely on them even if domestic law is inconsistent. Sometimes, however, particularly where a country is determined to keep its rules despite inconsistency with applicable directives, the taxpayer's route to relief can be a rocky one.[173]

The European Commission has been pushing for a long time ideas to further harmonize income taxation and recently issued a comprehensive study.[174] In 1997, European Finance Ministers signed a Code of Conduct, pledging to address harmful tax competition.[175] Although not legally binding, it may prove instrumental to limit competitive erosion of the tax base.

Social security taxation and benefits have been coordinated in the EU on the basic principle that employees pay social security contributions in one state only—where they are employed.[176] Although in practical terms social security contributions can be regarded as taxes (and are closely coordinated with income tax in some European countries), the relationship between social security and income tax differs throughout Europe, leading to coordination

---

[172] For the meaning of this term (and for the distinction between direct effect and direct applicability), *see* Raworth, *supra* note 158, at 114-15, 123. "Essentially, this principle states that where the provisions of a binding Community measure (including Directives) are sufficiently clear and precise to allow it to be applied in the resolution of disputes, then it may be invoked in the domestic courts of the Member States. In the case of Directives this may only be done after the time for transposition has elapsed and then only as against the State or agencies or emanations thereof." Corrigan (2000) at 12.

[173] *See* Nicolas Not, *The Deduction of French VAT on Business Expenses: Will EC Law Finally Prevail?*, 3 Tax Planning Int'l E.U. Focus 5 (2001). France restricts the right to an input credit for entertainment expenses, while the Sixth VAT Directive allows no such limitation. In 1989, the Council of Ministers allowed France to maintain its restriction on a temporary basis. However, in 2000 the ECJ found this Council decision to be invalid. The focus has now shifted to the circumstances under which taxpayers will be able to take advantage of the ECJ decision with respect to prior years, a question involving the statute of limitation rules in the French tax code as well as questions of EC law. *See also* Case C-62-00, Marks & Spencer plc v Commissioners of Customs & Excise (ECJ July 11, 2002) (a sufficiently precise Directive may be relied on before national courts to obtain a refund of tax, and the right to refund may not be removed by a retroactive shortening of the limitation period).

[174] Commission of the European Communities, Company Taxation in the Internal Market, COM (2001) 582 (May 23, 2001).

[175] *See* Eden, *supra* note 168, at 631-32.

[176] *See* Henk Bedee et al., The International Guide to Social Security 20-25 (1995 Williams, *supra* note 157, at 112-114.

problems (consistently with their separation from taxation in most European countries).[177] The problem is probably not helped by the fact that for purposes of European law social security is generally not treated as part of the tax system.[178]

An important feature of European tax law is the limitations it imposes on taxation by member countries. These include the absence of internal customs duties, and more generally the prohibition on member states to tax in such a way as to impede the free movement of goods,[179] workers,[180] services,[181] or capital,[182] or the freedom of establishment[183] within the common market.[184] Discrimination on the basis of nationality is also prohibited.[185] The law which prohibits discriminatory taxation and taxation that violates these so-called "fundamental freedoms" is more flexible than European tax law that is embodied in directives or regulations: it is judge-made law and can therefore develop without the constraint of the unanimity

---

[177] *See id.* at 114-118.

[178] *See id.*

[179] Art. 28 EC Treaty ("Quantitative restrictions on imports and all measures having equivalent effect shall be prohibited between Member States.")

[180] Arts. 39-42 EC Treaty. Art. 39(1) provides: "Freedom of movement for workers shall be secured within the Community."

[181] Arts. 49-55 EC Treaty. Art. 49 provides in part: "...restrictions on freedom to provide services within the Community shall be prohibited in respect of nationals of Member States who are established in a State of the Community other than that of the person for whom the services are intended."

[182] Arts. 56-60 EC Treaty. Art. 56 provides in part: "...all restrictions on the movement of capital between Member States and between Member States and third countries shall be prohibited."

[183] Arts. 43-48 EC Treaty. Art. 43 provides in part: "...restrictions on the freedom of establishment of nationals of a Member State in the territory of another Member State shall be prohibited. Such prohibition shall also apply to restrictions on the setting-up of agencies, branches or subsidiaries by nationals of any Member State established in the territory of any Member State. Freedom of establishment shall include the right to take up and pursue activities as self-employed persons and to set up and manage undertakings..."

[184] Art. 3(1)(c) EC Treaty ("an internal market characterized by the abolition, as between Member States, of obstacles to the free movement of goods, persons, services and capital"); Art. 14(2) EC Treaty.

[185] Art. 12 EC Treaty ("...any discrimination on grounds of nationality shall be prohibited.") This has been construed by the ECJ to include discrimination on the basis of residence, since that would be an indirect discrimination on the grounds on nationality.

requirement. Because tax cases come to the ECJ only as matters are litigated,[186] the case law develops in a somewhat haphazard manner, as judge-made constitutional law tends to do. This area is inherently problematic, since the principle of nondiscrimination does not sit well with national tax systems that are in fundamental ways constructed on the basis of different treatment of residents and nonresidents. An example of an area where further development can be expected is the interaction of European law with tax treaties—because of nondiscrimination principles it is possible that existing treaties have greater scope than they appear to do on their face.[187] A common external double tax treaty, which could be concluded by the EU itself,[188] may ultimately be required. Further, any number of rules applicable to cross-border transactions may be vulnerable to attack on nondiscrimination grounds; for example, arguments have been made that controlled foreign corporation legislation violates nondiscrimination rules of European law, particularly insofar as applicable to subsidiaries operating within the EU.[189]

Another important limitation on state taxing power is the prohibition against state aid, found in article 87 of the EC Treaty. This prohibits "any aid granted by a Member State...in any form whatsoever which distorts or threatens to distort competition by favouring certain undertakings or the production of certain goods...." Article 87 is interpreted as applying only to state aid that is targeted to particular industries or otherwise to a narrow

---

[186] Tax cases typically "come before the ECJ by virtue of a reference from a national court which asks for advice on the construction of E.C. law." Eden, *supra* note 168, at 627. *See generally* Das EuGH-Verfahren in Steuersachen (Michael Holoubek & Michael Lang eds. 2000). Art. 234, EC Treaty provides: "The Court of Justice shall have jurisdiction to give preliminary rulings concerning:

(a) the interpretation of this Treaty;

(b) the validity and interpretation of acts of the institutions of the Community...

Where such a question is raised before any court or tribunal of a Member State, that court or tribunal may, if it considers that a decision on the question is necessary to enable it to give judgment, request the Court of Justice to give a ruling thereon.

Where any such question is raised in a case pending before a court or tribunal of Member State against whose decisions there is no judicial remedy under national law that court or tribunal shall bring the matter before the Court of Justice."

[187] *See* Compagnie de Saint-Gobain, Zweigniederlassung Deutschland v. Finanzamt Aachen-Innenstadt, Case C-307/97, 1999 ECR I-6161 (Sept. 21, 1999).

[188] For the EU's authority to enter into treaties, see Raworth, *supra* note 158, at 131-32.

[189] *See* Sarah Kirkell, *EU Commission Urged to Remove CFC Barriers Between Member States*, 26 Tax Notes Int'l 1256 (June 17, 2002).

class,[190] so that a provision such as generally applicable accelerated depreciation would presumably be safe from attack. However, if a very short depreciation life were given to a particular type of asset, this might run afoul of article 87. Although the prohibition against state aid was not used too often in the past, the European Commission has in recent years started investigations that may result in calling into question any number of tax expenditure provisions.[191] Because such measures are directly prohibited by the EC Treaty, unanimity to attack them is not needed. Tax measures may also be attacked in the courts as unlawful state aid.[192]

The effects of European law can be seen not only in the obvious places such as the areas of tax law that are governed by directives. Just as with constitutional law, European law tends to exercise a pervasive influence on the legal systems of the member countries,[193] which can only be expected

---

[190] *See* Notice, O.J. C 384/5, para. 13 (Oct. 12, 1998); *see also* Germany v. Commission of the European Communities, Case C-156/98, Court of Justice of the European Communities, Sept. 19, 2000, 2000 ECR I-6857, 3 ITLR 159 (2001), which involved aid to small businesses located in eastern Germany. An important factor in this decision is that the state aid was discriminatory, in that it only applied to companies with registered offices in the targeted region of Germany. This was found to be discriminatory as against companies established elsewhere in Europe. *See also* Tiley (2000) at 30 (selective increase of insurance premium tax held to be state aid).

[191] For example, the European Commission has required Italian banks to repay tax privileges which were found to be in violation of the state aid rules. *See* Emma Barraclough, *EU orders banks to repay tax breaks*, Legal Media Group (16 Dec. 2001).

[192] *E.g.,* R (on the application of Professional Contractors Group Ltd and others) v. Inland Revenue Commissioners, [2001] EWHC Admin 236, Queen's Bench Division, Administrative Court (Apr. 2, 2001), 3 ITLR 556. In this case, the argument was made that the limited application of a particular set of anti-avoidance rules constituted unlawful state aid to those taxpayers who were unaffected by the rules. The court found that in the circumstances this was not state aid, because it was a general measure applied according to objective criteria, and did not have the effect of providing a benefit to identifiable recipients. *See generally* Lyons (2001) at 37-38.

[193] For example, in Byrne v. Conroy, [1997] CMLR 595 (Irish High Court), the court was faced with an argument that the Irish Extradition Act prevented the extradition of defendant to Northern Ireland, because the offence he was charged with was a "revenue offence". The court found that were there any ambiguity in the statute it should be read against the defendant to the effect that the levy the defendant was charged with violating was not a tax, since the levy had been enacted to comply with European law and European courts had to construe national legislation so far as possible so as to be "consistent with the obligations of the State to the European Union". The court cited the cases of Faccini Dore v. Recreb, [1994] 1 ECR 3325, [1994] 1 CMLR 665; Marchleasing SA v. La Commercial International de

to grow over time. In the constitutional area, as we have seen, European countries have had substantially different regimes, both with respect to the availability of judicial review and with respect to the substantive law, in particular the application of the principle of equality. Now in all the EU member countries, courts can review domestic laws against constitutional-type principles, including the principle of equality. A common jurisprudence may develop.

European law also exhibits common development with respect to statutory construction. First, with respect to construction of European legislation, a literal interpretation tends to fall by the wayside, since there are many possible literal interpretations of a text that is authentic in several languages, and the court can therefore pick one that seems appropriate to further the policy of the legislator.[194] For this and other reasons, the ECJ has favored a teleological interpretation of European legislation and considers legislative history in determining the meaning of legislation.[195] Second, European law affects the interpretation of domestic legislation in areas that are harmonized by directive. One possibility is to use the directive as evidence of legislative intent. Since the domestic legislator presumably intended to implement the directive, the domestic legislation should be interpreted to fulfill that intent, i.e. in conformity with the directive wherever possible.[196] This approach fails, however, in cases where the domestic legislation apparently was not enacted to conform to the directive (it may

---

Alimentacionsia, [1991] ECR 4135, [1992] 1 CMLR 305; and Von Colson v. Landnordrhein-Westfalen, [1984] ECR 1891, [1986] 2 CMLR 430.

[194] *See* Wolfgang Schön, Die Auslegung europäischen Steuerrechts 50-51 (1993). *E.g.,* WN v. Staatsscretaris van Financiën, 2 ITLR 685, 704-05 (2000) (ECJ) (in the face of different wording of a Directive in different languages, the court adopted a construction in line with the purpose of the Directive). *See also* IRC v. Océ Van Der Grinten NV, Chancery Division, England (Nov. 2, 2000), 2 ITLR 948, 953 ("in tax as it does in general, Community law looks to substance.")

[195] *E.g.,* Lyons (2001) at 96.

[196] *See* Schön, *supra* note 194, at 36. This can also result in involving the ECJ in a case that is purely domestic. In Case C-28/95, Leur-Bloem v. Inspecteur de Belastingdienst/Ondernemingen Amsterdam 2 [1997] ECJ I-4190 (July 17, 1997), Netherlands court referred to the ECJ a question of interpretation of a European directive (the merger directive). The directive was not applicable to the case, since involved a purely domestic situation. The Netherlands court, however, decided that the intention of the legislature in passing the provision of domestic law in question had been to implement the directive, and accordingly it had to be construed consistently with the directive. The ECJ held that where a domestic court had determined to refer such a case to the ECJ, the ECJ had jurisdiction.

have been unchanged or the legislator may have departed from full implementation of European law). In this case, interpretation of domestic law to conform to European law goes beyond implementing the purpose of the domestic legislator, but can be justified on the basis of implementing the will of the European legislator.[197] This raises a number of questions for domestic courts beyond those traditionally arising in statutory interpretation. Third, interpretation of European law raises issues of the relationship between the tax law and civil law, where European tax law uses concepts that are borrowed from civil law.[198] The ECJ has generally tended to adopt a "European" meaning of terms in the tax directives, thereby seeking to ensure uniformity of application, instead of looking to the civil laws of member countries for the meaning of terms.[199] Of course, this is not necessary where, as in the case of the merger directive and the parent-subsidiary directive, a specific enumeration of references to domestic law is made (the directives list specific forms of company for the various member States).[200] The specific enumeration approach, however, has its own problems, such as rigidity. Fourth, the purposive approach of European statutory interpretation may have influenced jurisdictions within Europe which previously had not been so enthusiastic about a purposive approach.[201]

4.4.2   THE EUROPEAN HUMAN RIGHTS CONVENTION

The European Court of Human Rights has jurisdiction to decide cases under the European Convention on Human Rights, which contains rules protecting property, prohibiting discrimination, and requiring due process;

---

[197] *See* Schön, *supra* note 194, at 38-39.

[198] *See infra* 4.6.

[199] *See* Schön, *supra* note 194, at 2-11, discussing Case C-320/88, Staatssecretaris van Financiën v. Shipping and Forwarding Enterprise Safe BV (ECJ Feb. 8, 1990), [1993] 3 CMLR 547; Case 102/86, Apple and Pear Development Council v. Commissioners of Customs and Excise, [1988] ECR 1443, [1988] 2 CMLR 394 (March 8, 1998); Case 270 81 Felicitas Rickmers-Linie & Co. v. Finanzamt für Verkehrsteuern, Hamburg, [1982] ECR 2771 (July 15, 1982).

[200] *See* Schön, *supra* note 194, at 12.

[201] *See, e.g.,* McKay, *Tax Law Review Committee Report on Tax Avoidance,* [1998] B.T.R. 86, 88 ("Other factors contributing towards purposivism include the greater influence of European law and its teleological method of interpretation."); Tiley 2000) at 40; John Avery Jones, *Tax Law – Rules or Principles?*, 17 Fiscal Studies 63 1996) (1996 Institute for Fiscal Studies Annual Lecture).

national courts also apply the Convention.[202] The Convention's provisions requiring a fair trial in civil matters generally do not apply in tax matters; the Convention's procedural protections for criminal trials apply to cases of serious tax penalties.[203] The ECHR is a European court, but not an EC court. The jurisdiction of the ECHR is also broader than the members of the EU, since some non-EU members are signatories to the Convention. The ECJ can, however, also apply the provisions of the Convention.[204] The existence of the Convention is of particular significance for those countries that lack a court that can review legislation on constitutional grounds, for example, the U.K. and the Netherlands.[205] The Human Rights Act 1998 incorporates provisions of the Convention into U.K. law, so that U.K. courts must give effect to them. This means that U.K. legislation must be construed, so far as possible, so as to be consistent with the Convention. Moreoever, U.K. courts may declare provisions of U.K. legislation incompatible with the Convention.

There have not been many successful challenges of tax provisions under the ECHR; most involved the right to a fair trial. One such challenge involved a procedure under which the French tax administration could acquire at a 10-percent premium real estate which it considered to have been underdeclared upon its registration.[206] The European Court of Human Rights

---

[202] *See generally* Philip Baker, *Taxation and the European Convention on Human Rights in the Domestic Law of the Council of Europe Countries,* 41 Eur. Tax'n 459 (2001) and other articles in the Dec. 2001 issue of Eur. Tax'n.

[203] *See* Ferrazzini v. Italy, [2002] 34 E.H.R.R. 45, European Court of Human Rights (12 July 2001), 3 ITLR 918; Philip Baker, Editorial, 29 Intertax No. 11 (2001); Sylvie Lopardi, *The applicability of Article 6 of the European Convention to tax-related proceedings,* 26 Eur. L. Rev. 58 (2001) ; Philip Baker, *Should Article 6 (Civil) ECHR Apply to Tax Proceedings?,* (2001) Intertax 205; Frederik Zimmer, *Norwegian Supreme Court Decides on So-Called Penalty Tax Under European Convention on Human Rights,* 21 Tax Notes Int'l 1517 (Oct. 2, 2000). *See also* Taxation and Human Rights (IFA seminar proceedings, 1988); Clare Ovey & Robin White, The European Convention on Human Rights 139-75 (3d ed. 2002).

[204] *See* Raworth, *supra* note 158, at 214-17.

[205] *See* Stephen Oliver, *The Human Rights Act in Prospect: Some Reflections,* [2000] B.T.R. 199; Jonathan Peacock & Francis Fitzpatrick, *The Impact of the Human Rights Act 1998 in the Tax Field,* [2000] B.T.R. 202; Philip Baker, *Taxation and the European Convention on Human Rights,* [2000] B.T.R. 211. The ECHR is also relevant for the jurisdiction of France's *Conseil d'Etat,* since this court can set aside provisions of laws that are inconsistent with treaties, constitutional review being reserved to the *Conseil constitutionnel. See* Maurice-Christian Bergeres, *Vers un Contrôle Élargi de la Loi Fiscale par le Conseil D'État?,* (2002) Droit Fiscal 1433.

[206] Hentrich v. France, 296A Eur.Ct. H.R. (1995), 18 Eur. H.R.Rep. 440 (Sept. 22 1994).

found that the French rule violated article 6(1) of the Convention, which guarantees the right to "a fair and public hearing" in the determination of anyone's civil rights and obligations. Further, article 1 of Protocol No. 1 to the Convention (protection of property rights) was violated. While this provision allowed measures to enforce taxes, the Court found that "there must also be a reasonable relationship of proportionality between the means employed and the aim sought to be realised.... A fair balance must be struck between the demands of the general interest of the community and the requirements of the protection of the individual's fundamental rights, this balance being destroyed if the person concerned has had to bear an individual and excessive burden."[207] The U.K. Court of Appeal has also struck down a liability which it characterized as a tax on the basis that it "operates entirely arbitrarily."[208]

Is the country an EU member or potential entrant? If so, to what extent has it implemented EU directives? Might any of its tax provisions constitute impermissible state aid, or impermissible discrimination under ECJ doctrine? If not an EU member, is the country a party to the ECHR?

4.5 TREATIES[209]

4.5.1 SCOPE OF TREATIES

Tax lawyers tend to focus on so-called "double tax" treaties along the lines of the OECD Model. While these are the most prominent for tax practice, it is important to remember that there exist quite a number of bilateral or multilateral treaties which may be relevant for taxation, including:

- other double taxation and ancillary conventions (e.g., conventions concerning inheritance, estates and gifts, limited agreements concerning certain types of income only, such as shipping or air transport, and ancillary agreements on administrative assistance);[210]
- treaties on mutual legal assistance and on information exchange;

---

[207] 296A Eur. Ct. H.R. at 42, 18 E.H.R.R. at 461.

[208] Aston Cantlow and Wilmcote with Billesley Parochial Church Council v. Wallbank, 4 ITLR 353 (Court of Appeal, May 17, 2001).

[209] For an introduction to tax treaties, see Arnold & McIntyre (1995) at 89-125. *See also* Rohatgi (2002) at 11-130; Asif Qureshi, The Public International Law of Taxation: Text, Cases and Materials (1994).

[210] *See* Philip Baker, Double Taxation Conventions at B-10 to B-11 (looseleaf 2001).

- WTO agreement, other trade agreements, other multilateral treaties;
- EC Treaty;[211]
- European Convention on Human Rights;
- Vienna Convention on Diplomatic Relations;
- treaties of friendship, commerce and navigation;
- social security treaties.[212]

Treaties may be called by different names (e.g., convention, agreement, treaty) but the name does not necessarily indicate a difference in legal status.[213]

To what tax-relevant treaties is the country a party?

4.5.2 DOMESTIC LEGAL EFFECT OF TREATIES

The legal effect of treaties in domestic law will depend on the circumstances and in general will depend on a country's constitution. Treaties may become operative in domestic law in one of three basic ways, depending on the country's constitutional rules.[214] Under the automatic integration model, treaties become operative in national law automatically (e.g., France, Netherlands, Spain, Switzerland).[215] Under the formal incorporation model, treaties are incorporated into domestic law by a formal or procedural executive or legislative act (e.g., Austria, Belgium, Germany, U.S.).[216] Finally, under some constitutions (e.g., Australia, Canada, Denmark, Israel, New Zealand, Norway, Sweden, U.K.) a treaty does not have effect as domestic law of its own force. Treaties are incorporated into domestic law by

---

[211] For a discussion of the EC Treaty as international law, see Raworth, *supra* note 158, at 138-40.

[212] *See generally* Henk Bedee et al., *supra* note 176. Strictly speaking, these are not *tax* treaties, if social security contributions are not treated as a tax in the countries party to the treaty, but they are in any event treaties concerning the broader category of compulsory contributions. *See supra* 2.1.

[213] *See* Baker, *supra* note 210, at B-10 n.1.

[214] *See* Treaty Making – Expression of Consent by States to Be Bound By a Treaty 87 (Council of Europe and British Institute of International and Comparative Law eds. 2001) [hereinafter Treaty Making]; Baker, *supra* note 210, at F-1; Vogel and Prokisch, *General Report,* 78a Cahiers 59 (1993).

[215] *See* Treaty Making, *supra* note 214, at 89-90.

[216] *See id.* at 90-92.

special enactment (substantive incorporation).[217]   Therefore each such enactment must be studied to ascertain the domestic legal effect of a treaty.

Generally, treaties do not increase a taxpayer's tax, but the contrary may be the case if specified by law and if consistent with the country's constitution (examples are France and the Netherlands).[218]

In some countries (e.g., France), the constitution explicitly or through interpretation provides that treaties prevail over domestic law.[219]   In these countries, the prevalence of treaties is clear and the question of a "treaty override" cannot arise.   In other countries (those following the substantive incorporation approach, and some of those following formal or automatic incorporation) treaties have the same rank as ordinary laws and the legislature has the power to override the provisions of treaties by passing subsequent legislation.[220]   In these countries, it may be necessary to construe the

---

[217] *See id.* at 92-93.

[218] *See generally* Baker, *supra* note 210, at B-1 to B-4 (looseleaf 2001). For example, CGI arts. 4 bis, 165 bis, 209(1) provide for taxation where France has the right to tax under a treaty. The effect of these provisions is not settled. *See generally* Daniel Gutmann, Tax Treaty Interpretation in France, in Tax Treaty Interpretation 95, 100-02 (Michael Lang ed. 2001). It is possible that in the U.S. a treaty itself could not impose a tax, given the requirement that revenue bills must originate in the House of Representatives.

[219] *See* Treaty Making, *supra* note 214, at 97-98   (Albania, Austria, Azerbaijan, Croatia, Cyprus, France, Georgia, Greece, Japan,   Mexico, Netherlands, Poland, Portugal, Romania, Slovenia, Spain); Baker, *supra* note 210, at F-4; Hiroshi Oda, Japanese Law 51-53 (1992); M. Maresceau, *Belgium, in* The Effect of Treaties in Domestic Law 1 (Francis Jacobs & Shelley Roberts eds. 1987); Theodor Schweisfurth & Ralf Alleweldt, *The Position of International Law in the Domestic Legal Orders of Central and Eastern European Countries,* 40 GYIL 164 (1997); Igor Lukashuk, Treaties in the Legal System of Russia, 40 GYIL 141, 146-53 (1997). For France, this has led to a holding that the CFC regime could not be applied in light of the treaty with Switzerland. *See infra* ch. 7, note 235. In Argentina, art. 75 of the Constitution provides supremacy of treaties.   *See* Garcia Vizcaino, *supra* note 10, at 160.   Supremacy of treaties also applies in Greece, *see* Katerina Perrou, *Tax Treaty Intrepretation in Greece, in* Tax Treaty Interpretation 153, 155 (Michael Lang. ed. 2001) [hereinafter Interpretation], and Spain, *see* Maria Teresa Soler Roch and Aurora Ribes Ribes, *Tax Treaty Interpretation in Spain, in id.* at 303, 305.

[220] *See generally* Treaty Making, *supra* note 214, at 98-99; John H. Jackson, *Status of Treaties in Domestic Legal Systems: A Policy Analysis,* 86 Am. J. Int'l L. 310 (1992); OECD, Tax Treaty Override Report (1989); Rohatgi (2002) at 38-43; Richard L. Doernberg, *Overriding Tax Treaties: The U.S. Perspective,* 9 Emory Int'l L. Rev. 71 1995); Detlev F. Vagts. *The United States and its Treaties: Observance and Breach,* 5 Am. J. Int'l L. 313 (2001); Jonathan A. Greenberg, *Section 884 and Congressional*

subsequent legislation to ascertain whether the legislature intended to override treaties.[221] The possibility of treaty override is not clear for all countries; since override should in principle be avoided under the *pacta sunt servanda*[222] principle of international law, the point may come up infrequently. The constitution may not be explicit and a "monist" view, under which there is a unitary legal order and domestic legislation therefore cannot override treaties, may be based on judicial pronouncements which in principle might be reversible.[223] In countries where override is possible, sometimes the legislature clearly expresses its intent to do so; where it does not, it is up to the courts to decide whether an override was intended. Because a treaty override often would constitute a failure by the country to comply with its obligations under international law, courts usually try to construe legislation as not overriding treaties.

In some countries, courts have by judicial decision established the general principle that subsequent laws are considered not to override treaties under the maxim *lex posterior generalis non derogat legi priori speciali*.[224] Another judicial approach is to require evidence of a clear legislative intention to override before construing a law as overriding a treaty.[225] In Belgium, the

---

"Override" of Tax Treaties: A Reply to Professor Doernberg, 10 Va. Tax Rev. 425 (1990); Timothy Guenther, *Tax Treaties and Overrides: The Multiple-Party Financing Dilemma*, 16 Va. Tax Rev. 645 (1997); I.R.C. §7852(d). Treaty override is in principle possible in Denmark, *see* Aage Michelsen, *Tax Treaty Interpretation in Denmark, in* Interpretation, *supra* note 219, at 63, 65-67, and in Norway, *see* Frederik Zimmer, *Tax Treaty Interpretation in Norway, in id.* at 261, 263; John Ward & Brendan Mccormack, *Tax Treaty Interpretation in Ireland, in id.* at 171, 173-77. The situation in Ireland is complicated by, among other things, a judicial dictum that the Constitution might prohibit an override. *See* Murphy v. Asahi Synthetic Fibres, [1985] I.R. 509, 515 (High Court Feb. 22, 1985).

[221] *See generally* Benedetto Conforti, International Law and the Role of Domestic Legal Systems 41-47 (René Provost trans. 1993); Baker, *supra* note 210, at F-4 to F-11.

[222] Agreements must be kept.

[223] For example, in Belgium the courts adopted a different approach (in favor of the supremacy of treaties) in 1971. *See* Baker, *supra* note 210, at F-4 n. 6; Faes (1995) at 9; Maresceau, *supra* note 219.

[224] "A subsequent general law does not repeal a previous special law." The idea is that where a law governs a specific area in detail it is unreasonable to ascribe to the legislature the intention to repeal this detailed regulation merely because it contradict a more general principle contained in a later law. *See* Vogel and Prokisch, *supra* note 214; Gianluigi Bizioli, *Tax Treaty Interpretation in Italy, in* Interpretation, *supra* note 219, at 195, 197-202; Conforti, supra note 221, at 43.

[225] *See* Conforti, supra note 221, at 43-47.

priority of self-executing treaties over prior or later laws has been found as a matter of judicial decision on the basis of a monistic view of the legal order, under which treaties and domestic law are considered to be part of the same legal order.[226] In Brazil, the tax code, which has a rank superior to that of ordinary laws, provides for the primacy of treaties over domestic laws.[227]

What is the constitutional framework for treaties? Can there be treaty overrides?

4.5.3 INTERPRETATION OF TREATIES

4.5.3.1 *In general*

There is some literature on interpretation of double taxation conventions in various countries,[228] but generalisations are difficult because in many jurisdictions there are relatively few cases interpreting treaties and because the specificity of each case may make it difficult to draw a generalisation as to how courts in that country may behave in future cases involving different issues. Nevertheless one can observe some overall

---

[226] *See* Bernard Peeters, Belgium, 78a Cahiers 221, 222-23 (1993); Belgian Law, *supra* note 49, at 37; Olivier Bertin, *Tax Treaty Interpretation in Belgium, in* Interpretation, *supra* note 219, at 41, 43-45. Bertin notes the possibility that the Belgian Supreme Court could refuse to enforce treaty provisions if it found them inconsistent with the constitution. The monist approach prevails also, for example, in Luxembourg, see Alain Steichen, *Tax Treaty Interpretation in Luxembourg, in id.* at 229, 231, and Portugal, *see* Ricardo Henriques da Palma Borges and Raquel Maria Maymone Resende, *Tax Treaty Interpretation in Portugal, in id.* at 273, 277.

[227] National Tax Code art. 98. *See* Roberto Paraiso Rocha, *Brazil,* 78a Cahiers 249, 250 (1993); Alberto Xavier, Direito Tributário Internacional do Brasil 113 (5th rev. ed. 2000). Under article 146 of the constitution of Brazil, complementary laws (of which the tax code is one) have a higher rank than ordinary laws.

[228] *See generally* Baker, *supra* note 210, Topic E, which gathers citations to books, articles, and cases. *See also* Ault et al. (1997) at 469-71; Interpretation, *supra* note 219; Rohatgi (2002) at 21-36; Michael Edwardes-Ker, Tax Treaty Interpretation (looseleaf 1997); David A. Ward, *Introduction to the Law Relating to Tax Treaties, in* Ward's Tax Treaties 1996-97 (supplement to Ward's Tax Law and Planning 1996); Jinyan Li & Daniel Sandler, *The Relationship Between Domestic Anti-Avoidance Legislation and Tax Treaties,* 45 Can. Tax J. 891, 898 n.9 (1997) (citations to literature); Caroline Docclo, *Nature and Interpretation of Double Tax Treaties in Belgium,* 16 Tax Notes Int'l 669 (March 2, 1998).

differences and point to things to look for in assessing how the courts of any specific country might approach a particular issue.

Treaty interpretation is a complex area, involving the need to examine intersecting legal traditions both outside the tax area and those peculiar to taxation.[229] First, there is the general tradition of courts in interpreting laws. Second, the extent to which courts follow that tradition in interpreting treaties or take a more specific approach to treaties, either because treaties are drafted differently than domestic legislation,[230] or because principles of customary international law apply to treaty interpretation. Third, there is the role of the Vienna Convention on the Law of Treaties and in particular whether and under what circumstances the Vienna Convention allows the consultation of extraneous material, such as the OECD Commentary or legislative history. Finally, there are factors peculiar to taxation, including the relevance of the OECD Commentary and the possible development of a general international consensus on the meaning of certain terms or method of interpretation of treaties. Each of these strands is somewhat independent; only the last is peculiar to taxation. It is out of their intersection that we observe court decisions interpreting tax treaties. But to understand what is going on, it is necessary to consider all of these elements on a comparative basis.

4.5.3.2 *Judicial approaches*

The general attitude of courts to statutory interpretation includes, for example, such matters as the extent to which legislative history will be consulted, the extent to which interpretation of a statute is based on finding the "purpose" of the legislator (rather than focusing on the literal language), the extent to which policy arguments are taken into consideration, and the tradition of interpreting statutes in line with the constitution.[231] In some countries (including the U.S), courts seem to take a similar approach to interpreting laws and treaties (which are after all domestic law and go through a ratification process similar to the process of enactment of legislation

---

[229] See the summary in Ault et al. (1997) at 469-71.

[230] Treaties are often drafted in a more general matter than domestic legislation, and in any event the actors involved in the drafting process are typically different from those drafting domestic laws. More than one language may also be involved, which in most countries is not the case for domestic laws.

[231] *See infra* 5.1-5.3.

generally).[232] In several Commonwealth countries, the courts take a broader approach to interpreting treaties than they might take to domestic legislation, both in recognition of the fact that the drafting style of treaties differs from that of domestic laws and of the fact that principles of international law apply.[233] In France, the courts used to refer questions of treaty interpretation to the executive, but in 1990 the *Conseil d'Etat* decided that courts could interpret treaty provisions on their own.[234] However, in doing so they seem to take a generally literal approach to interpretation; sometimes this ends up favoring the taxpayer and sometimes the government.[235] By contrast, the German courts do not seem excessively wedded to a literal interpretation, and often seek to implement the purpose of the treaty or principles of equality in taxation.[236]

An important issue is whether general judge-made or statutory anti-avoidance rules will be applied in the tax treaty context.[237] The *fraus legis* principle has been applied cautiously in the Netherlands in the treaty context, tempered by the principle that it would not apply if this was not the intention

---

[232] *See* Baker, *supra* note 210, at E-6. This includes for the U.S. recourse to legislative history, even though this is unilateral in nature. *But see* Xerox Corp, v. U.S., 41 F3d 647 (Fed. Cir. 1994)(rejecting unilateral material).

[233] *See* Baker, *supra* note 210, at E-4 to E-9; Sol Picciotto, International Business Taxation 311-23 (1992); James Buchanan & Co. v. Babco Forwarding and Shipping (UK) Ltd [1978] A.C. 141; Fothergill v. Monarch Airlines, [1981] A.C. 251; CIR v. Exxon Corp., 56 T.C. 237 (Ch. Div. 1982); David H. Bloom, *Australia,* 78a Cahiers 179, 180-82 (1993); Crown Forest Industries Ltd. v. The Queen, [1995] 2 S.C.R. 802; James Hausman, *Interpreting Tax Treaties—A Canadian Perspective*, 55 B.I.F.D. 93 (2001); Jean-Marc Déry & David A. Ward, *Canada,* 78a Cahiers 259, 260-89 (1993). A few treaty interpretation issues in Canada are governed specifically by statute (the Income Tax Conventions Interpretation Act). *See id.* at 264-65.

[234] *See* Baker, *supra* note 210, at E-5 to E-6; Gutmann, *supra* note 218, at 104 (noting that the *Cour de cassation* adopted the same position in 1995).

[235] *See* Guttman, *supra* note 218, at 108-11.

[236] *See* Ekkehart Reimer, *Tax Treaty Interpretation in Germany, in* Interpretation, *supra* note 219, at 119.

[237] *See* S. van Weeghel, Improper Use of Tax Treaties 163-90; David Ward, *Abuse of tax treaties, in* Alpert & van Raad eds. (1993), at 397; International Fiscal Association, Abusive Application of International Tax Agreements (2000); Klaus Vogel, *Steuerumgehung bei Doppelbesteuerungsabkommen, in* Grenzen der Gestaltung im Internationalen Steuerrecht 79 (W. Haarmann ed. 1994). Vogel concludes that courts have been willing to apply anti-avoidance principles in the treaty context but have not explicitly examined whether they were applying national anti-avoidance rules or principles of customary international law.

of the parties to the treaty.[238] The U.S. courts have been willing in appropriate cases to apply judge-made anti-avoidance doctrines in construing treaties.[239] In Germany as well, domestic anti-avoidance rules will apply unless they are considered to be inconsistent with the treaty.[240] Switzerland has developed special anti-avoidance provisions applicable to treaties.[241] Experience in other countries is more limited.[242]

4.5.3.3 The Vienna Convention

The Vienna Convention on the Law of Treaties provides, among other things, principles for the interpretation of treaties. These principles deal, for example, with the permissibility of consulting *travaux préparatoires* and other extraneous texts in order to ascertain the intent of the parties. They also deal with the purposive interpretation of treaties, i.e. interpreting terms in such a manner as to give effect to the purpose of the treaty within its context.

Obviously, it will be relevant whether the particular country is a party to the Vienna Convention or not.[243] However, even among countries that are

---

[238] *See* van Weeghel, *supra* note 237, at 167-78.

[239] *See id.* at 178-88; Johansson v. United States, 336 F.2d 809 (5th Cir. 1964); Aiken Industries v. Commissioner, 56 T.C. 925 (1971); Del Commercial Properties Inc. v. Commissioner, 251 F.3d 210 (D.C. Cir. 2001), *cert. denied*, 122 S.Ct. 903 (2002) (interest paid to a Netherlands company did not qualify for the zero withholding rate under the U.S.-Netherlands treaty because the loan was in substance extended by a Canadian affiliate, there being no business purpose for interposition of the Netherlands company).

[240] *See* Schaumburg (1998) at 822-45; Tipke/Lang (2002) at 151. Detailed anti-treaty shopping rules in a treaty may be considered to take precedence over domestic antiabuse rules. *See id.* at 828. *But see infra* 5.8.1, note 251.

[241] *See* Oberson & Hull (2001) at 153-71, 277-311.

[242] *See* van Weeghel, *supra* note 237, at 188-190. The Austrian Supreme Administrative court has applied the domestic antiabuse rule in BAO § 22 (similar to § 42 AO) in applying the Austrian-Swiss treaty on the issue of beneficial ownership *See* N AG v. Regional Tax Office for Upper Austria, Decision of the Austria: Supreme Administrative Court of 26 July 2000, 2 ITLR 884. *See also* Li & Sandler *supra* note 228 (suggesting that the drafting of the Canadian GAAR creates doubt about its applicability to treaties); Toaze, *Tax Sparing: Good Intentions, Unintende Results*, 49 Can. Tax J. 879, 903-913 (2001).

[243] Vienna Convention on the Law of Treaties, 1155 UNTS 331 (concluded May 2 1969). As of 2001, there were 94 parties. *See* United Nations, Multilateral Treati Deposited with the Secretary-General: Status as at 31 December 200 ST/LEG/SER.E/20, at 279-80. 21 of the 30 OECD countries are parties; Franc

parties there are differences in how the Vienna Convention is used by the courts. Among those that are not parties the Convention may still play a role to the extent that the Convention is viewed as a codification of customary international law. Even in countries which are parties to the Vienna Convention, courts may not pay close attention to the rules of the Convention in interpreting tax treaties.

In the U.S., courts will look to legislative history in interpreting treaties, just as they do for statutes. This is arguably inconsistent with the Vienna Convention (or with customary international law), since the documents in question relate to the period after signature and before ratification by the Senate. The other party to the treaty does not have a chance to approve of the statements made in these documents.

For income tax treaties based on the OECD Model, an important practical question is the extent to which the OECD Commentary will be used in interpreting the treaty. Since the Commentary is approved by the member countries, it can be expected to be followed by tax authorities. Under the Vienna Convention, reference to the Commentary can be justified on the basis that it reflects a "special meaning" intended by the parties or is part of the "preparatory work" or the "context" of the treaty,[244] but it seems unlikely that this would permit an ambulatory use of the Commentary.[245] Use of the Commentary in interpretation could, of course, be explicitly mandated by a protocol to a treaty.[246]

4.5.3.4 A common approach to double tax treaties

It would be desirable for double tax treaties to be interpreted commonly by the courts of both treaty partners and for common terms and rules found in different treaties to be interpreted in the same manner by all courts. To some extent the OECD Commentary is a vehicle to achieve that

---

Iceland, Ireland, Luxembourg, Norway, Portugal, Turkey, and the U.S. are not (Luxembourg and the U.S. are signatories, however).

[244] *See* Hugh Ault, *The role of the OECD commentaries in the interpretation of tax treaties, in* Essays on International Taxation 61, 64-66 (Alpert and van Raad eds., 1993); Arvid Skaar, Permanent Establishment 45-49 (1991).

[245] *See* Edwardes-Ker, *supra* note 228, at §§ 26.05, 26.11. An ambulatory reference was rejected by the Austrian Administrative Supreme Court. *See* Ines Hofbauer, *Tax Treaty Interpretation in Austria, in* Interpretation, *supra* note 219, at 13, 28.

[46] *See* John Avery Jones, *Are Tax Treaties Necessary?,* 53 Tax L. Rev. 1, 19-21 1999); Memorandum of Understanding Re Interpretation of the Convention, May 31, 996, U.S.-Austria, 1 Tax Treaties (CCH) ¶ 703A.

common interpretation and hence the acceptance of the Commentary as an aid in interpreting treaties is desirable as a matter of encouraging international cooperation. In addition, a common approach would be fostered to the extent that courts took notice of each others' decisions. In this respect, there has been a fair deal of success in terms of use of the OECD Commentary, and a growing practice of courts in citing tax treaty interpretation cases of other countries.[247] There is growing recognition that terms used in treaties have a special meaning as "part of an 'international tax language.'"[248]

Is the country a party to the Vienna Convention? What approaches do its courts take in interpreting tax treaties?

4.5.4   TREATY POLICY

The OECD Model has exercised a dominant influence on the formation of income tax treaties. However, even the OECD members do not have a uniform policy in negotiating treaties. Each country will reflect in its negotiating policy the need to deal with peculiarities of its own system and how that system interacts with the particular negotiating partner. A detailed review of each country's different approach is beyond the scope of this book.[249] Several countries have "models" that they use as a starting point for negotiations, some of which have been published.[250] As in many other areas, the U.S. approach is distinctive.[251] There is an emphasis on anti-treaty-shopping and other anti-abuse rules in the U.S. model,[252] there is a consistent U.S. policy against any tax sparing relief, and there are of course the necessary adaptations to permit peculiarities of U.S. policy such as the taxation of its citizens wherever resident and the autonomy of its constituent

---

[247] *See* Baker, *supra* note 210, at E-10-11, E-27-28; 78a Cahiers at 276-77 (1993) (Canadian courts receptive to common interpretation but UK courts cautious). *See also* Li & Sandler, *supra* note 228, at 910-11 (discussing Canadian decision in The Queen v. Crown Forest Industries Limited et al., 95 DTC 5389; [1995] 2 CTC 64 (SCC), which approved of use of a wide range of extraneous material including the OECD Commentary).

[248] Thiel v. Commissioner of Taxation (1990) 171 CLR 338, 349, *quoted in* Bloom, *supra* note 233, at 185; Ostime v. Australian Mutual Provident Society, 38 T.C. 492, 517 (H.L. 1959). *See* Edwardes-Ker, *supra* note 228, at § 7.02.

[249] *See generally* Vogel (1997); Ault et al. (1997) at 476-80, 528-31.

[250] *See* Ault et al (1997) at 476-82.

[251] United States Model Income Tax Convention of Sept. 20, 1996 (available together with a technical explanation at www.treas.gov).

[252] *See* Schaumburg (1998) at 828.

States in tax matters. The U.S. also tends to be relatively reticent in expanding its treaty network, in comparison with countries like France,[253] Germany, and the U.K.

Many developing countries will seek to follow the UN Model[254] at least in part, and OECD countries often accomodate this desire in their treaties with such countries. If the bilateral treaty network is to be expanded to include most developing and transition countries, a multilateral approach will ultimately be needed, this also being called for by a number of structural problems of the bilateral network.[255]

What do the country's treaties show about its treaty policy?

4.6 ADMINISTRATIVE LAW

In civil law countries, tax law may be considered a branch of administrative law.[256] Whatever one feels about this classification, it is clear that in both common and civil law countries general principles of administrative law apply to tax. These principles govern such matters as agency power to issue regulations, requirements of procedural due process, and judicial review of agency action. Even in civil law countries, these principles may derive from judge-made law as much as from statute.[257]

The power to issue regulations in common law countries is generally found as a matter of delegation from the particular statute.[258] In civil law

---

[253] France had 101 tax treaties as of 2001. *See* Castagnède (2002) at 14.

[254] A new UN Model was published in 2001. Department of Economic & Social Affairs, United Nations Model Double Taxation Convention between Developed and Developing Countries (2001). In large part, the UN Model tracks the OECD Model. Key differences are that the UN Model broadens the taxing rights of the source jurisdiction with respect to permanent establishments and allows the source state to tax interest, royalties, capital gains on shares in some circumstances, as well as "other income." For a detailed review of the differences and of the practical impact of the UN Model, see Willem Wijnen & Marco Magenta, *The UN Model in Practice*, 51 B.I.F.D. 12 (1997). *See generally* Edwin van der Bruggen, *A Preliminary Look at the New UN Model Tax Convention*, [2002] B.T.R. 119; Vogel (1997).

[255] *See* Victor Thuronyi, *International Tax Cooperation and A Multilateral Treaty*, 4 Brooklyn J. Int'l L. 1641 (2001).

[256] *See supra* 4.1.

[257] *See generally* Jürgen Schwarze, European Administrative Law (1992).

[258] In the U.K., delegated authority to issue regulations can be broad, including the authority to amend Acts of Parliament. Regulations are typically required to be laid before Parliament before they are adopted, thereby giving Parliament a chance to

countries, there tends to be a general constitutional power in the executive to issue regulations, although the details will differ depending on the constitution.[259] Thus, in France, the constitution gives an autonomous power to the executive to issue decrees in areas that do not fall within the domain of the law, although for practical purposes administrative regulations to implement the law are of greater importance; laws may also delegate to the executive the authority to regulate specific matters.[260] Although it may be as much a matter of practice as of law, the relationship between statute and regulations is a key element of tax law. One might have different views about the best mix of statute and regulations in terms of where the details should lie and how much they should be elaborated, but as a matter of practice countries differ substantially on this point.[261] For example, in Sweden, the constitutional requirement that tax rules be made by statute is interpreted as precluding any extensive delegation of the authority to make regulations.[262] In Russia, the first years of the transition period saw a primacy in lawmaking on the part of the bureaucracy (in continuation from the Soviet era); the newly adopted tax code has reacted sharply against this, limiting the administration's authority to issue normative acts.[263] A comparative study would be of interest to see whether an optimal approach could be identified, as well as to situate the degree of elaboration of regulations within the overall operation of different tax administrations.

---

disapprove them. Regulations are subject to judicial review, and can be struck down where they are inconsistent with the statute authorizing them or otherwise ultra vires. *See* William Wade & Christopher Forsyth, Administrative Law 839-83 (8th ed. 2000).

[259] *See* Beltrame & Mehl (1997) at 491; Garcia Vizcaino, *supra* note 10, at 157-58 (Art. 99 of Constitution of Argentina authorizes executive to issue regulations; circulars issued by the tax administration are not included in this category, however.)

[260] *See* Philip, *supra* note 26, at 47-73. The power to issue regulations does not, however, extend to the Minister of Finance, so that the instructions issued by that Ministry do not bind the taxpayer. *See* Douet, *supra* note 46, at 174-89. The approach of the Mexican constitution is broadly similar. *See* de la Garza (2001) at 42-47.

[261] There has been little use of delegated legislation in the U.K. in the income tax area, although more for VAT. *See* David Williams, Taxation Statutes are Taxing Statutes, 41 Modern L. Rev. 404, 407 (1978).

[262] *See* Ault et al. (1997) at 103.

[263] *See* Nougayrède, *supra* note 80, at 209-14, 330. *See also* Tax Code, art. 2(1) (2001) (Kazakhstan) (limiting regulations to those specifically referred to in the Code).

Regulations must be consistent with the statute. In most systems, courts will strike down regulations that are not.[264] This doctrine presents a fundamental philosophical problem. Regulations almost invariably modify the scope of the statute. Thus, a court adopting a very strict approach that regulations contrary to the statute are unlawful would strike down most regulations. On the other hand, in most systems courts recognize the role of the executive in providing detailed implementation rules to carry out the purpose of the statute. It is a matter of judgment whether these rules go too far in terms of creating limitations that cannot be found in the statute. In each country, one can observe (1) the extent to which regulations in fact specify rules that are not found in the statute, (2) the extent to which such regulations are challenged in court, and (3) the results of such challenges. It is only by carrying out such an analysis that one can arrive at a judgment as to whether a particular regulation is likely to survive in court if challenged.

In the U.S., a so-called "reenactment doctrine" insulates longstanding regulations from searching judicial review: such regulations are deemed to have been approved by the legislature by reason of the reenactment of the statute on which the regulations are based. The theory is that if the legislature did not like the regulations, it would have changed the statute accordingly at the time of reenactment.[265]

In France, taxpayers who are adversely affected because an administrative circular extends a benefit to another taxpayer, but not to them (or because the circular extends a benefit to another taxpayer who does not

---

[264] *See* Bittker and Lokken (1999) ¶ 110.4.2; Aprill, *Muffled* Chevron: *Judicial Review of Tax Regulations*, 3 Fla. Tax Rev. 52 (1996). Under the *Chevron* doctrine, U.S. courts "defer to reasonable agency 'gap-filling' interpretations of a statute as expressed in agency regulations". Bankers Trust New York Corp. v. United States, 225 F.3d 1368, 1376 (Fed. Cir., Sept. 20, 2000). However, such deference may not apply where an agency issues regulations inconsistent with previous judicial decisions. *See id. See also* United States v. Mead Corp., 533 U.S. 218 (2001); David et al. (2000) at 129-48. In the U.S., a distinction is drawn between legislative and interpretative regulations, only the former having the force of law. *See* Thomas Merrill & Lathryn Tongue Watts, *Agency Rules With the Force of Law: The Original Convention,* 116 Harv. L. Rev. 467 (2002). Tax regulations are generally considered interpretative, unless there is a specific grant of authority for legislative regulations. *See id.* at 570-75.

[265] "Treasury regulations and interpretations long continued without substantial change, applying to unamended or substantially reenacted statutes, are deemed to have received congressional approval and have the effect of law." United States v. Correll, 389 U.S. 299, 305-306 (1967), quoting Helvering v. Winmill, 305 U.S. 79, 83 (1938).

qualify for the benefit) may challenge the circular in court;[266] many systems would not grant standing to sue in such a case.

A U.K. peculiarity is extra-statutory concessions. These are published rules that provide more lenient treatment than that contemplated by the statute in specified circumstances, and can be relied on by taxpayers. Their legal status is, however, questionable.[267]

In a number of countries, the tax administration is bound by its pronouncements, even where they do not have legal force (i.e. the taxpayer not being bound by them). For example, in India, the tax administration has been held to be bound by their own circulars, even where these contradict the statute.[268] In France, the taxpayer is protected against retroactive changes in published administrative positions, and may therefore rely on such positions.[269] And the U.S. Tax Court has stated that the IRS may not litigate against its published position without first having withdrawn the ruling in question.[270] The Canadian courts have not, however, held the revenue authorities to their interpretation bulletins.[271]

What is the authority to issue regulations and other normative acts, and the practice in doing so? Have any been struck down by the court?

---

[266] *See* David et al. (2000) at 134-35.

[267] *See generally* Basil Sabine, *Extra-statutory concessions 1987-1997*, [1998] B.T.R. 83; Vestey v. I.R.C., [1980] A.C. 1148, 1194-95 (per Lord Edmund-Davies); Tiley (2000) at 53-54 (noting that these are subject to anti-avoidance rules—which provides a marked contrast to the situation in France, *see infra* 5.7.4 ("turbo funds" decision). Somewhat analogous are the *mesures de tempérament* of France. *See* Beltrame & Mehl (1997) at 506-07.

[268] *See* K.P. Varghese v. Income-Tax Officer, A.I.R. 1981 S.C. 1922, 1932-33. The same is true for Mexico. *See* de la Garza (2001) at 48-49. However, in Belgium, administrative circulars might not have binding force, under the principle of legality. *See* Willemart, *supra* note 23, at 123-34; Faes (1995) at 4; Dassesse & Minne (2001) at 48-51 (pointing out that in practice this doctrine allows the administration freedom to decide which situations fall within a concession extended by circular and which do not).

[269] *See* Bouvier, *supra* note 41, at 157-60; CGI art. L80A, L80B; Gilles Noël, *Doctrine Administrative, in* Dictionnaire Encyclopédique de Finances Publiques 636 (Loïc Philip ed. 1991); David et al. (2000) at 149-63; *infra* 5.7.4, note 218.

[270] *See* Ravenhorst v. Commissioner, 119 T.C. No. 9 (Oct. 7, 2002).

[271] *See* Hogg et al. (2002) at 17.

4.7 PRIVATE LAW

Tax law often uses private law[272] concepts to define tax liability, for example, someone's ownership of property or acquisition of the legal right to income (such as under a contract).   It is clear that private law is relevant to tax law, and that the private law consequences of transactions are often critical to application of tax.[273]   In civil law countries, the precise relationship between private (civil) law and tax law has been debated. While the view that civil law outranked tax law was prevalent historically, it has now been accepted to a greater or lesser extent that tax law must be interpreted according to its own policies.   Nevertheless, in a number of countries, including in particular, France, there is an underlying notion of *droit commun*[274] (embodied in the civil code), which provides an interstitial source of law where specific statutory solutions are not provided.

In a number of civil law countries, the question has been posed by scholars as to whether tax law is "autonomous."[275]   To call tax law

---

[272] Private law may also be called civil law in civil law countries. It includes, in addition to matter contained in the civil code, that contained in the commercial code, i.e. commercial law, insurance law, and financial law. *See* Tipke (2000) at 44 n.38. Private law is sometimes referred to as "state law" in the U.S., since there is little federal private law. In the U.S. system, private law is governed by the common and statutory law of each State.

[273] *See* Tipke (2000) at 44-46. There are many issues where private law is relevant to tax law. For example, the status of an individual as an employee is determined under private law and may be relevant for tax purposes. A corporation's ability to redeem shares or to pay a dividend is determined under private law, and these constraints are important for tax planning. A person's rights and liabilities under private law may be relevant for taxation in different contexts.   An individual's legal rights as a shareholder in a corporation will be relevant to the question of whether that individual is considered to control the corporation for tax purposes. Rights to property and income under marital law may be relevant to taxation.

[274] This can be literally (but confusingly) translated as "common law," but the meaning is more akin to "general law."

[275] *See* Trotabas & Cotteret (1997) at 10-13. For a summary of the French literature, see Douet, *supra* note 46, at 236-60. See, from the viewpoint of Argentina, García Vizcaíno, *supra* note 10, at 138-53 (citing authors from a number of countries, suggesting that this is a general preoccupation in civil law countries). *See also* Heinrich Weber-Grellet, Steuern im modernen Verfassungsstaat 194-203 (2001); de la Garza (2001) at 30-31 (Mexico); Nicola D'Amati, *Il Diritto Tributario, in* 1 Amatucci (1994) at 55, 64-68. The issue has been debated in Russia as well, in connection with the extent to which the tax code should develop rules independent of the civil code. *See* Nougayrède, *supra* note 80, at 320, 329.

autonomous is not to deny that tax law is part of the legal system. Rather, it has more to do with the independence of tax law from civil law. Some have suggested that it might be more accurate to call tax law "specific" rather than "autonomous."[276]

Tipke identifies three related subquestions in the debate about the autonomy of tax law: (1) Does tax law have to take over the basic principles of civil law? (2) Should tax law use the terminology of civil law? (3) Where tax law uses civil law concepts, must these be interpreted in the same way as under civil law?[277] There is undoubtedly a tendency in civil law countries for concepts used in tax law to be interpreted according to their civil law meaning.[278] At least in Germany, however, the courts have recognized the need to interpret terms used in a tax law in accordance with the policies of that tax law. The Constitutional Court in 1991 rejected the notion that there was any presumption that civil law terms used in tax law should be interpreted according to their civil law meaning.[279] It found that the relevance for taxation of the civil law form used by the parties had to be determined by interpreting the tax laws according to their purpose.[280]

The relationship between tax law and private law becomes even more complex in cases where the private law is foreign law, since there are often

---

[276] Beltrame & Mehl (1997) at 559 ("Il serait plus exact de parler de la *spécificité* du droit fiscal.")

[277] *See* Tipke (2000) at 46-47. *See also* Florence Deboissy, La Simulation en Droit Fiscal 17-22 (1997)(focusing on the last of these questions); Kirchhof, *supra* note 46, at 49-51.

[278] *See id.;* Faes (1995) at 8-9; Dassesse & Minne (2001) at 58-59; David et al. (2000) at 36-38; Ault et al. (1997) at 47 (France) (suggesting that civil law concepts may be followed more by civil law courts in dealing with tax cases than by administrative courts—in France, most tax cases are dealt with by administrative courts); *id.* at 79 (Japan); Minoru Nakazato, *Japan,* 78a Cahiers at 410-11 (1993). For example, in the *Richard* case, Conseil d'Etat, March 31, 1978, *Lebon* 168, *reprinted in* David et al (2000) at 25, the court was faced with the effective date of VAT provisions. The question was when certain yachts were supplied. The court looked to the civil law concept of "delivery" (even though this was not the same term used in the VAT law) and found that under this concept the taxpayer had not delivered the yachts before the VAT rate increased. Perhaps the court was just finding a way to impose a tax in a situation where the taxpayer had obviously employed a stratagem in order to accelerate the taxable event so as to qualify for the lower rate of tax. However, it is notable that the court relied on the civil code rather than either relying on the policy of the VAT law or on European law (perhaps now the court would do the latter; *see supra* note 199.

[279] Decision of Dec. 27, 1991, BStBl II 1992, 212. *See* Tipke (2000) at 55.

[280] *See* Tipke (2000) at 55-57.

substantial differences between the institutions and concepts of foreign law and local law. One approach would be to treat foreign situations under the tax rules of the foreign country. However, this is almost never done. Instead, the typical approach is to evaluate the foreign law entity or situation, find the analogue under the local law under a functional analysis, and then apply the tax rules that would apply to that local analogue.[281]

In the U.S., the attitude of the federal courts about interpreting private law terms used in the tax laws was influenced by the fact that private law differs from state to state and that a deference to private law might lead to a lack of uniformity of federal tax law. For example, where the income tax used the term "sale", this was held to have a meaning peculiar to the income tax, rather than referring to whether a transaction was considered a sale under state law.[282] And in construing the term "property acquired by gift," the Court stated that the statute "does not use the term 'gift' in the common-law sense."[283] The same issue is faced by Canada; the courts there may be more deferential to provincial law than the U.S. federal courts are to state law.[284] In the U.K., the tax laws apply to the separate legal systems of England and Wales, Scotland, and Northern Ireland. The courts have construed the tax laws so as to achieve uniform application.[285] The issue is of no small importance in Europe, at least in those areas of tax law that are harmonized by regulation or directive. Somewhat similarly to the U.S., although probably more explicitly, given the larger divergences in civil law in Europe, the ECJ has pronounced in favor of a uniform application of European law.[286]

---

[281] *See* Arndt Raupach, *Darf das Steuerrecht andere Teile der Rechtsordnung stören?, in* Die Steuerrechtsordnung in der Diskussion 105, 109 (Joachim Lang ed., 1995); Tiley (2000) at 1027-29; Jürgen Killius, *Common law trusts: New developments affecting the German tax—status of grantors and beneficiaries, in* Alpert & van Raad eds. (1993), at 239. *See also infra* note 318.

[282] *See* Burnet v. Harmel, 287 U.S. 103 (1932); Bittker and Lokken (1999) ¶ 4.1.1. In *Burnet*, the taxpayer argued that a bonus payment under a Texas oil and gas lease was a capital gain since under Texas law the lease was a present sale of the oil and gas in place. The Court rejected this analysis, finding that the policy behind the capital gain provisions did not call for capital gain treatment in such a case and that in the absence of statutory language to the contrary, the tax laws are "to be interpreted so as to give a uniform application to a nationwide scheme of taxation." 287 U.S. at 110.

[283] Commissioner v. Duberstein, 363 U.S. 278, 285 (1960). *See* Bittker and Lokken 1999) ¶4.1.4.

[284] *See* Ault et al. (1997) at 35.

[285] *See* Tiley (2000) at 50; Morse & Williams (2000) at 27.

[286] *See supra* note 199.

An important issue in applying tax law is the extent to which tax law takes at face value the apparent consequences of private law transactions. This comes down to interpreting tax statutes: do they allow taxpayers to reduce tax by making various legal arrangements which, for example, divert income to other persons, or do they "look through" these arrangements to the underlying economic reality? One view is that the only reality that tax law can regard is that which results from legal relationships under civil law. This point is discussed in the next chapter in depth.

The opposite side of the relationship between private law and tax law is the influence of tax considerations on private law. The income tax in particular has had a pervasive influence on private law, as part of its general influence on private behavior.[287]

For comparative tax, it is important to be aware of differences in the underlying private law system. Some issues will not even come up for purposes of tax law because of differences in private law. For example, some tax systems will not specify the tax treatment of a redemption, because companies are not allowed to buy back stock under company law; company law may also limit the dividends that may be paid.[288] And the tax rules for reorganizations will differ depending on what forms of reorganization are allowed under company law. Another example is that some jurisdictions allow the transfer of the "seat" of the company abroad, while others do not allow such a transfer without liquidation, which can be disadvantageous taxwise.[289]

What is the relationship between tax law and private law? Are there peculiarities of private law (e.g., company law) that are relevant for taxation?

---

[287] *See* Bittker and Lokken (1999) ¶ 1.1.1; Sneed, *Some Reflections About the Impact of Federal Taxation on American Private Law*, 12 Buff. L. Rev. 241 (1962); Tipke (2000) at 54-55; Raupach, *supra* note 281.

[288] For example, in Sweden company law limits dividend distributions to the amount of after-tax profits. This constraint has caused some companies to fail to take full advantage of tax allowances that could have been used for corporate income tax because full use of the allowances would have prevented dividend distributions. *See* Jonas Agell, Peter Englund & Jan Södersten, *Tax Reform of the Century–The Swedish Experiment, in* Tax Policy in the Real World 331, 343 (1999).

[289] *See* Pierre-Jean Douvier, Droit Fiscal dans les relations internationales xi (1996) who mentions that Netherlands holding companies cannot be continued abroad without liquidation, while Luxembourg holding companies can.

4.8 CRIMINAL LAW

Most tax lawyers don't have to worry about criminal law very much, although cases do arise where a client (or the tax advisor[290]) may face criminal liability. In such cases, protections of criminal procedure may apply, such as against warrantless searches or requirements to be informed of the right to counsel. In addition, tax crime offenses will have to be tried under criminal procedure. Even where the provisions defining tax crimes are located in the tax laws, these provisions are part of criminal law, and therefore subject to all the doctrines and procedures of criminal law. To apply them properly requires an understanding of both tax law and criminal law in the particular jurisdiction.

Procedural protections may apply even if tax penalties are not structured as criminal offenses. Thus, the procedural protections of the European Convention on Human Rights apply to serious tax penalty cases, although this is somewhat anomalous since criminal penalties are not necessarily involved.[291]

Is the country a party to the European Convention on Human Rights? Can capital punishment apply in a tax fraud case?

4.9 RELIGION AND RELIGIOUS LAW

In many countries the separation of church and state is a constitutional principle, and state aid to religion is prohibited. This is the case for the U.S., although tax exemption of church property has been held not to constitute impermissible state aid.[292] In a number of other countries, churches receive state funds.[293] Although the German constitution also prohibits establishment of religion, it has carried over the institution of the church tax, which is recognized in the Constitution.[294] The tax is levied under the authority of framework legislation adopted by each *Land*, and regulations issued by each church, which specify the details of the tax and the tax rate.[295] The authority to levy the tax belongs to each church, but the legal basis for the

---

[290] *See infra* 6.11.

[291] *See* Baker, *supra* note 203.

[292] *See* Walz v. Tax Commission, 397 U.S. 664 (1970).

[293] *See* Ute Suhrbier-Hahn, Das Kirchensteuerrecht: Eine Systematische Darstellung 23-26, 238 (1999).

[294] *See id.* at 2; GG art. 140; Tipke/Lang (2002) at 435-39.

[295] *See* Suhrbier-Hahn, *supra* note 293, at 7-8.

tax is a *sui generis* mixture of state and church law.[296] The regulations are adopted by church bodies the majority of the members of which must be elected.[297] The regulations are subject to approval by the *Land* authorities.[298] All churches established as legal persons under public law have the right to levy tax, but some churches do not do so.[299] Because of principles of religious freedom and non-establishment of religion, the tax may in principle also be levied by a group that is not a religion, if the group is established as a legal entity under public law, which is rare.[300] Under agreement with the churches, the tax is generally collected by the tax authorities, the revenues being turned over to each recognized church, although a few churches collect the tax on their own.[301] In any particular *Land*, the rates tend to be uniform, except where the church itself administers the tax.[302] The tax may be imposed on church members only.[303] The church tax most commonly takes the form of an additional rate to the income tax, and is taken into account in determining the tax to be withheld from wages.[304] The tax can, however, be levied on other bases, such as property or net wealth.[305] Church tax also applies in Switzerland on a somewhat similar basis as in Germany, with one important difference being that legal persons may also be taxable.[306] In Iceland church tax is levied mostly as a capitation.[307] Sweden imposes church tax as well, even subjecting non-church-members to tax at a reduced rate.[308] In Italy and

---

[296] *See id.* at 1.

[297] *See id.* at 8.

[298] *See id.* at 11.

[299] *See id.* at 51-52. Islamic entities have not received recognition as public law corporations in Germany. *See* Tipke/Lang (2002) at 436.

[300] The group must be a *Weltanschauungsgemeinschaft*, i.e. it must be a group that "seeks to understand the universe as a whole and to recognize and evaluate the position of human beings in the world on the basis of this overall world view, and to testify and act according to this understanding." *Id.* at 3.

[301] *See id.* at 14-18, 94-95.

[302] *See id.* at 274-82.

[303] *See id.* at 80. The tax has been held to be applicable to members only as a constitutional matter and not, for example, to spouses of members. *See generally* Kommers, *supra* note 15, at 484-89, 587n. 57. There is a right to strike one's name from the membership list under public law. *See* Tipke/Lang (2002) at 437.

[304] *See* Suhrbier-Hahn, *supra* note 293, at 98.

[305] *See id.* at 92.

[306] *See id.* at 234-35; Höhn & Waldburger (2001) at 123-24.

[307] *See* Suhrbier-Hahn, *supra* note 293, at 235.

[308] *See id.* at 236-37

Spain, individuals may earmark a portion of their income tax to the church or other social purposes.[309]   Surprisingly, there seems to be a church tax in England: the liability at common law of the owner of rectory land has been characterized by the Court of Appeal as a tax.[310] The court struck down this "tax" as violative of the European Convention on Human Rights because of its arbitrary incidence (while in medieval times ownership of the land was associated with the right to receive a tithe, the right to the tithe had disappeared).

While for many religions the obligation to contribute to the church, or to give alms, is cast in terms of a general moral obligation, rather than being given a precise form,[311] Islam provides an exception. Zakat, the obligation to give alms, is even considered one of the main pillars of the religion.   In general terms, zakat is 2.5% of zakatable wealth.[312]   The 2.5% rate poses a problem in application of the tax to an animal herd, given that animals are indivisible; Hanafi lawyers solved this problem by devising a creative rate schedule (for example, the tax on a herd of from 5 to 9 camels is one medium-size goat).[313] Zakat also has anti-avoidance rules; thus, the 12-month holding period which must be satisfied in order for property to be zakatable does not apply in the case of "transactions undertaken specifically to avoid" it.[314]   In those jurisdictions adopting Sharia (Islamic law), zakat is therefore part of the law.   In several countries, zakat is collected by state authorities.[315]   Only

---

[309] *See id.* at 238-40.

[310] Aston Cantlow and Wilmcote with Billesley Parochial Church Council v. Wallbank, 4 ITLR 353 (March 29, 2001).

[311] For example, in the Roman Catholic Church the obligation to contribute to the church is found in 1983 Codex Iuris Canonici can. 1260. *See* Suhrbier-Hahn, *supra* note 293, at 220. The fulfillment of this obligation by means of a tax is considered unusual according to canon law, and in fact specific accomodation was made in the revised code of canon law in order to accomodate the German system. *See* Norbert Feldhoff, Kirchensteuer in der Diskussion 52-53 (1996). In most countries, the obligation is voluntary rather than being legally binding in amount.

[312] Zakatable wealth includes only wealth above a certain minimum and held for at least 12 months. There are a number of exemptions for specific kinds of property. The tax on "apparent" property may be collected by agents of the state, while that on non-apparent property is the private responsibility of the owner. Zakat funds are to be used for the needy. *See* Hossein Askari et al., Taxation and Tax Policies in the Middle East 62-63 (1982).

[313] *See id.* at 63.

[314] *See id.* at 81 n.14.

[315] In 1982, these included Saudi Arabia, Sudan, and the Yemen Arab Republic. *See id.* at 220; Ali Ahmed Suliman, *The Sudan: Experience with Zakat*, 42 BIFD 34

Muslims are liable for zakat. Where the state collects zakat, it typically collects only half of what is due (i.e. 1.25%), leaving the rest to individual conscience.[316] The relationship between zakat and income tax varies. In Pakistan, zakat is deductible in determining taxable income.[317] In Saudi Arabia, those liable to zakat are not taxed under the income tax. This principle is even extended to corporations: Saudi Arabia imposes no income tax on the portion of a corporation's income that corresponds to the portion of the shares owned by individuals liable for zakat.

Separately from zakat, Islamic law raises other issues for the tax system. Because usury is prohibited, interest income is not mentioned in the income tax law in some Islamic countries. The law may instead mention profits received with respect to loans. The problem of how to deal with Islamic banking and other financial transactions is not confined to Islamic countries, since such transactions may occur anywhere. Those countries (such as the U.S.) which have a flexible "economic substance" approach to taxation may deal best with such transactions, since they can readily be recharacterized. On the other hand, countries that adopt a more form-based taxation may tax such transactions according to their form under private law, which may lead to tax treatment that does not correspond well to the economic reality of the transaction and that, in general, may differ from the treatment accorded to interest.[318]

In most systems, churches are exempt from tax along similar lines to charities generally. However, some countries have special rules to avoid entanglement between church and state. These may end up providing preferential treatment to churches. As with other charities, pretended status as a church can give rise to administrative difficulties and has led to much litigation.

(1988). There is no requirement, however, that the state itself collect zakat. *See id.* In Malaysia, zakat is collected by state (i.e. not federal) government units. *See* Ameen Ali Talib and Atique Islam, *Islamic Tax System in Secular Countries*, 2 Asia-Pacific Tax Bulletin 182 (June 1996).

[316] *See id.* at 132, 219.

[317] *See* Income Tax Ordinance, 2001, sec. 60.

[318] Germany follows what is probably an intermediate approach: the tax treatment of various forms of Islamic finance conducted abroad requires identification of the corresponding structure under German law, with appropriate application of the "economic substance" approach (*wirtschaftliche Betrachtungsweise*) and the provisions of double tax treaties. The analysis is not simple, and there is as yet little legal precedent. *See generally* Frank Roser, Die Steuerliche Qualifikation der Finanzierungsinstrumente des Islam (1994).

Chapter 5

INTERPRETATION OF TAX LAW AND ANTI-AVOIDANCE RULES

5.1 IN GENERAL

This chapter deals with country differences in how judges interpret tax laws. Because the most controversial issues in tax law interpretation arise in the context of tax avoidance transactions, I focus on judicial anti-avoidance doctrines and the closely linked question of statutory general anti-avoidance rules (GAARs).

An important role of tax lawyers is to advise their clients as to the likelihood that a contemplated return position[1] will be upheld in litigation. A lawyer advising on a proposed transaction that will give rise to tax consequences in another jurisdiction needs to understand how the courts in that jurisdiction are likely to react. Because judges are independent, it is not possible to predict with certainty how the courts might resolve a particular case, but one can form a view as to probabilities. Such a view can be informed by judicial style and precedent in the jurisdiction. Judicial style differs from country to country, both in general and for tax law in particular.[2] It can even differ within a single country: different courts and judges can have identifiably different approaches, and in some countries there are even several different types of courts that can hear tax appeals[3] (if administrative appeals and appellate review of trial court decisions are included, then virtually all countries experience the conduct of tax litigation in different fora). One can

---

[1] I.e. the manner in which it is proposed to report a planned transaction on the tax return.

[2] For an overview, see G.S.A. Wheatcroft, *The Interpretation of Taxation Laws With Special Reference to Form and Substance: General Report*, 50a Cahiers 7 (1965). The country reports in this volume are still worth consulting, although they are dated on some points.

[3] This is the case in the U.S. (where trials can be heard by the Tax Court, a U.S. District Court, or the Claims Court), the U.K. (General and Special Commissioners); and France (*Conseil d'Etat* and ordinary courts). *See infra* 6.8.

generalize about how judges in different countries decide tax cases, subject to appropriate cautions:

- Things can change. Law evolves in each country.
- In considering specific issues, it is important to be aware of precedents in the particular area of tax law, which may be a variation on the general theme. For example, the jurisdiction may have one or more statutory or judge-made general anti-avoidance rules. These rules may be applied in quite specific ways in particular areas. If there is precedent in the specific area as to how the issue is treated, this will be essential to know.
- Because tax law is statutory, it is important to be aware of both general and specific anti-avoidance rules and other rules of statutory construction that may have been enacted, which will interact with the judicial style.
- Each case has its own facts, which can influence the decision in a particular direction.
- Because the principles of statutory construction in each jurisdiction contain contradictory maxims, and because many situations require judgment, it is never possible to predict with certainty how a particular case will be decided.

Bearing these caveats in mind, some overall differences in approach in various jurisdictions can be identified by way of generalisation. Ultimately, however, an understanding of differences in judicial style must be based on a detailed analysis of actual decisions. Any such analysis will soon show the limitations of generalisation. Moreover, it will become apparent that judicial style cannot be studied in isolation from the rest of the tax system. In part, judges approach statutes differently in different countries because the statutes are written in different styles and the judges have different mandates. Countries will also differ substantially in the extent to which tax litigation is conducted in the courts, as opposed to administratively. Judicial style will interact with administrative style. If the administration takes a very passive approach and refrains from legal challenges to the taxpayer's position (or if taxpayers refrain from taking aggressive positions on their returns), then there may not be much to litigate.[4] The opposite will be the case if both the administration and taxpayers aggressively interpret the law in their favor.[5]

The average tax case will not turn on a dispute over the meaning of the law, and even those cases that do involve a pure issue of interpretation

---

[4] This is generally characteristic of Japan, for example.

[5] *E.g.*, Richard Vann, *Australia, in* Ault et al. (1997) at 14.

will present this issue in light of specific facts.[6] Judges in different systems may be more or less creative in identifying the relevant facts, applying private law, identifying the relevant aspects of tax law and analyzing precedent. This means, for example, that quite apart from explicitly applying anti-avoidance rules, there are many ways that courts can strike down transactions that they feel are going too far in terms of tax avoidance.[7] The role of the consequences of transactions under private law will also differ. In systems or situations where the economic substance of a transaction is relevant for tax purposes, the judicial approach may be a complex iterative process of analyzing the facts in the light of possibly relevant legal rules in order to determine what legal rules and facts are actually relevant to decide the case.

The above discussion assumes a high level of competence and integrity on the part of tax judges. Where these are lacking, in particular where there is extensive corruption in the judicial system, legal doctrines about how judges should go about deciding cases may be of little practical relevance. Judicial lack of competence to decide tax questions is a problem in many countries. Even in countries with the most advanced legal systems, judges often do not have a full understanding of how the tax system works or an enlightened attitude about their role in it. The remedy on the part of the government should involve both a careful and restrained litigation policy, and an allocation of sufficient resources so that briefs in tax cases are as persuasive as possible and explain the context so that the judge can understand the consequences of the judge's decision. In countries where judicial corruption is a problem, the remedy is more difficult, and may be effective only where it is part of a larger anti-corruption effort. Because these questions would take me far beyond the scope of this book, and because a meaningful analysis would require a close focus on specific countries, I will not attempt further discussion here, but the abbreviated treatment is not meant to downplay the seriousness of these issues in many countries.

What are the closest precedents in the country to the particular case? Is there a choice of fora?

See generally John Tiley, *Judicial Anti-Avoidance Doctrines* [1987] B.T.R. 180, 90-95.

See, e.g., Brian Arnold, *Reflections on the Relationship Between Statutory Inter- retation and Tax Avoidance*, 49 Can. Tax J. 1, 15-16 (2001).

5.2 CONFLICTING MAXIMS

A well known feature of statutory construction is the coexistence of different and contradictory maxims about how judges should decide cases. This means that the judge often has the freedom to decide a particular case one way or another based on which maxim he or she uses. Because a number of possible approaches may have received the approval of the higher courts, it is not possible to predict how particular judges will decide based on appellate court doctrine. The actual results of litigation therefore need to be consulted to see how judges decide in practice. Nevertheless, we can identify some differences and trends in terms of which approaches are emphasized: in some countries particular maxims and approaches are given greater weight than in others. The following are of particular significance for tax law:

- *literal meaning.* The literal meaning of the statute is always an available interpretative technique. Where systems differ is on the extent to which other techniques (for example, legislative history) can be used "where the statute is unambiguous". The more modern approach rejects the maxim *interpretatio cessat in claris.*[8]

- *in dubio contra fiscum.*[9] This used to be a popular approach. Being inconsistent with a purposive approach to interpretation, it has largely been abandoned, but pops its head up now and again. In some countries, for example, Belgium, it is still important.

- *legislative intent.* Courts increasingly tend to construe the statute so as to fulfill the intent of the legislator, even departing from the literal language of the statute. While courts in some countries have routinely considered legislative history in order to ascertain intent, in the U.K. the use of legislative history has been accepted only since 1993 and even so not in all cases.

- *teleological.* Here the court looks not just at the historically expressed intent of the legislator but attempts to determine the purpose of the legislation. This has been accepted for a long time in countries like Germany. In the U.S. it would be called a "policy" approach.

---

[8] "Interpretation ceases if things are clear."

[9] "In doubt [construe a provision] against the revenue [i.e. the government]." This maxim goes back to the Digest of the Emperor Justinian: "Non puto delinquere eum qui in dubiis quaestionibus contra fiscum facile responderit." (Modestinus) Dig. 49 14, *reprinted in* Corpus Iuris Civilis 879 (T. Mommsen & P. Krueger eds., 1911).

- *decision based on the facts.*   Available in every system.   This approach sidesteps questions about the meaning of the statute by finding that, properly regarded, the facts of the case do not come within the statutory provision.

- *true legal nature.* The court looks at the private law consequences of the transactions entered into, based on a careful analysis of the facts and the applicable private law (i.e. not the tax law). Available in any system, but is of greater importance in systems which reject taxation based on economic substance. The expression is often found in U.K. decisions.

- *economic substance.* The court analyzes the economic effects of the transactions entered into, ignoring subtle differences under private law if these do not have economic significance. There are important differences between systems as to the acceptability of this method.

- *deference to administrative agency.*   The court may defer to the agency's interpretation of the statute, particularly where regulations have been issued. With respect to regulations, the approach is typical in the U.S.

- *constitutional construction.* The statute may be construed so as to fulfill requirements of the constitution, usually the principle of equality in taxation. The availability of this approach depends on the country's constitutional jurisprudence.

- *reenactment doctrine.* The legislature is presumed to have approved prior construction of the statute by the courts or the administrator by reenacting the statute. It is sometimes used both in the U.S. and the U.K.

- *taxpayer entitled to rely on administrative interpretation.* Administrative interpretations may be held to be binding on the administration. This is codified in France.

- *procedural errors in assessment.* In some systems, assessments are often struck down for procedural errors. Examples are France and Germany.

Are there predominating maxims in the actual practice of courts in the particular country?

.3 COUNTRY PRACTICE

In the U.K.—and to a large extent in other Commonwealth countries well—the dominant approach to statutory construction traditionally has been a literal interpretation of the tax laws,[10] and an unwillingness to adopt a purposive interpretation to craft glosses onto the statute that are not based on the text (in particular, for the purpose of combatting tax avoidance—for which see 5.7.2.1 below).

The traditional attitude of the British courts was based on a view of the proper role of the courts. Courts were not legislators and it was not their responsibility to fix defects in legislation—if Parliament thought that there was a defect in the law then it was up to them to fix it.[11]

However, since about 1980 if not earlier,[12] the U.K. courts have been willing to adopt a more purposive interpretation of the statute. In *Pepper v.*

---

[10] As stated by Lord Cairns in Partington v. Attorney General, LR 4 HL 100, 122 (1869), "as I understand the principle of all fiscal legislation, it is this: If the person sought to be taxed comes within the letter of the law he must be taxed, however great the hardship may appear to the judicial mind to be. On the other hand, if the Crown, seeking to recover the tax, cannot bring the subject within the letter of the law, the subject is free, however apparently within the spirit of the law the case might otherwise appear to be. In other words, if there be admissible, in any statute, what is called an equitable construction, certainly such a construction is not admissible in a taxing statute, where you can simply adhere to the words of the statute." This judicial attitude goes back at least as far as 1807, and arose mostly in the context of stamp duty cases. *See* David W. Williams, *Taxation Statutes are Taxing Statutes*, 41 Modern L. Rev. 404, 409 (1978). In contrast to the modern approach of purposive interpretation, Lord Halsbury denied that a taxing Act could be considered to have a purpose, beyond that of imposing tax on whatever its provisions expressly reached. *See* Tennant v. Smith, [1892] A.C. 150, 154.

[11] *See, e.g.,* Lord Vestey's Executors v. IRC, 31 T.C. 1, 90 (1949) (H.L.). "Parliament in its attempts to keep pace with the ingenuity devoted to tax avoidance may fall short of its purpose. That is a misfortune for the taxpayers who do not try to avoid their share of the burden and it is disappointing to the Inland Revenue, but the Court will not stretch the terms of taxing Acts in order to improve on the efforts of Parliament and to stop gaps which are left open by the statute. Tax avoidance is an evil, but it would be the beginning of much greater evils if the Courts were to overstretch the language of the statute in order to subject to taxation people of whom they disapproved." *See also* Williams, *supra* note 10, at 406-07, noting that this attitude of the courts was consistent with the frequency of tax legislation and its common use to fix mistakes. Parliament's alacrity to step in may have encouraged the courts in the attitude that defects in how the tax laws were drafted were not their problem and that Parliament would soon fix them. In New Zealand, "[t]he courts do not see it as the role to 'fill the gaps' or to produce results which they sense might be more welcomed...by government if they cannot do so on the present words of the legislation." David Simcock, *New Zealand,* 87a Cahiers 473, 473-74 (2002).

[12] *See* W.T. Ramsay Ltd. v. Commissioners, [1982] A.C. 300, 323 ("A subject is only to be taxed on clear words...What are 'clear words' is to be ascertained upon norm

Hart the House of Lords accepted the possibility of consulting legislative history to determine the purpose of the legislature where the statute "is ambiguous or obscure or the literal meaning of which leads to an absurdity."[13] U.K. courts have also defeated tax avoidance schemes by finding that the taxpayer had not, as a factual matter, achieved the desired result, such as by refusing to recognize a purported transformation of an employment relationship into an independent contractor arrangement.[14] As a general

---

principles; these do not confine the courts to literal interpretation."); Chevron UK Ltd. v. Commissioners, [1995] S.T.C. 712, 721, 67 T.C. 414, 426-27 (tax provisions should be "read in a way which, taken as part of the Act as a whole, produces a coherent and reasonable result...There is nothing new or revolutionary in this approach to construction, although in recent years no doubt greater emphasis has been placed upon the need to discern the legislative purpose and to fit the particular provision under consideration into a reasonable and coherent scheme and less upon semantic delicacy.") Hugh McKay, *Tax Law Review Committee Report on Tax Avoidance*, [1998] B.T.R. 86, 88 cites the cases of I.R.C. v. Joiner, 50 T.C. 449 (1975), and Luke v. I.R.C., [1963] A.C. 557 (House of Lords construed statutory provision in light of its object and what must have been the intention of Parliament) as examples of purposive interpretation.

[13] [1993] A.C. 593. Lord Griffiths stated: "The days have long passed when the courts adopted a strict constructionist view of interpretation which required them to adopt the literal meaning of the language. The courts now adopt a purposive approach...." [1993] A.C. at 617. Although it may seem that tax legislation will nearly always qualify as ambiguous, obscure, or absurd, the British courts have not read *Pepper v. Hart* as allowing unlimited reference to legislative history. *See, e.g.,* Padmore v. Commissioners, 73 T.C. 470 (High Court, Chancery Division 2001); Aston Cantlow and Wilmcote with Billesley Parochial Church Council v. Wallbank, 4 TLR 353 (Court of Appeal, May 17, 2001). The rule in *Pepper v. Hart* has not (yet) been accepted in Canada. *See* Ault et al. (1997) at 31.

[14] For example, in Customs and Excise Commissioners v. Jane Montgomery (Hair Stylists) Ltd., [1994] S.T.C. 256 (Court of Exchequer – Scotland), *reprinted in* Schenk & Oldman (2001) at 120-22, a hair salon had entered into franchise agreements with its former employee hair stylists, in an effort to treat them as self employed for the purpose of removing their receipts from the company's turnover, with the result that each stylist's receipts would fall below the VAT registration threshold. The court said: "the approach we must take is to look at the substance of what has been established here rather than at mere matters of form" and that the purported arrangements had not effected "any material and substantial change in the nature of the business carried on", that "there was only one business which was being carried on in the hairdressing salon at East Craigs, Edinburgh. That was the company's business, and it follows from that it was the company who made the taxable supplies provided by the stylists."

matter, the U.K. courts have refused to blindly accept the label proposed by the taxpayer, instead making their own characterization of the facts under private law or tax law.[15]

A purposive approach to statutory construction has also been adopted in other common law countries, e.g., Australia,[16] Canada,[17] India,[18] and

---

[15] *See* Tiley (2000) at 94-95. On interpretation generally, *see id.* at 48-53.

[16] *See* Richard Vann, *Australia, in* Ault et al. (1997) at 12-19.

[17] *See id.* at 30. The purposive approach was announced by the Supreme Court of Canada in *Stubart Investments*, 84 D.T.C. 6305 (1984), where the court stated: "Today there is only one principle or approach, namely, the words of an Act are to be read in their entire context in their grammatical and ordinary sense harmoniously with the scheme of the Act, the object of the Act and the intention of Parliament." Note, however, that the Court declined in this case to apply a judicially crafted anti-avoidance approach along the lines of the *Ramsay* decision (*see infra* 5.7.2.2). The Court has qualified this approach with a "plain meaning" approach, under which statutory purpose need not be referred to where the words of the statute are "clear and plain." *See* Hogg et al. (2002) at 557-65. The *in dubio contra fiscum* rule has survived in Canada in weakened form. *See* Corporation Notre-Dame de Bon-Secours v. Quebec, [1994] 3 S.C.R. 3 ("a reasonable doubt, not resolved by the ordinary rules of interpretation, will be settled by recourse to the residual presumption in favour of the taxpayer").

[18] *See* Markandey Katju, Interpretation of Taxing Statutes 35-38 (2d ed. 1998); S.R. Wadhwa & P.K. Sahu, *India,* 87a Cahiers 337 (2002); McDowell & Co. v. Commercial Tax Officer [1985] 154 ITR 148 (SC, Apr. 17, 1985) (For sales tax purposes, the taxable turnover includes the excise on the product; taxpayer could not avoid this rule by arranging for the purchaser to pay the excise. Although somewhat *obiter,* a concurring opinion stated that "the time has come for us to depart from the *Westminster* principle...In our view, the proper way to construe a taxing statute, while considering a device to avoid tax, is not to ask whether the provisions should be construed literally or liberally, nor whether the transaction is not unreal and not prohibited by the statute, but whether the transaction is a device to avoid tax, and whether the transaction is such that the judicial process may accord its approval to it."); K.P. Varghese v. Income-Tax Officer, A.I.R. 1981 S.C. 1922; Chunni Lal Parshadi Lal v. Commissioner of Sales Tax, [1986] 1 SCR 891, 906 (March 18, 1986 ("An interpretation which will make the provisions of the Act effective and implement the purpose of the Act should be preferred when possible without doing violence to the language."); Hindustan Polymers v. Collector of Central Excise (1989) 4 SCC 323 (words of a statute cannot simply be read literally but must be considered in the context of the Act); C'r of Income Tax v. J.H. Gotla, A.I.R. 1985 S.C. 1698 ("Where the plain literal interpretation...produces a manifestly unjust result which could never have been intended by the legislature, the Court might modify the language used by the legislature so as to achieve the intention of the legislature and produce a rational construction....If the purpose of a particular provision is easi

Israel[19] although both the Australian and the New Zealand courts continue by and large to respect the civil law form of transactions for tax purposes, absent sham or the invocation of the statutory GAAR.[20] While the Irish courts are willing to consider legislative history, their general approach, contrary to U.K. precedents, is to stick to a strict approach to tax law interpretation.[21]

Despite its nominal adoption of a purposive approach, the Canadian Supreme Court has been criticized for an excessively literal interpretation of

---

discernable from the whole scheme of the Act...then bearing that purpose in mind... if other construction is possible apart from strict literal construction then that construction should be preferred to the strict literal construction."); State of Tamil Nadu v. Kodaikanal Motor Union (P) Ltd., [1986] 2 SCR 927 ("it is always the duty to find out the intention of the legislature and if it can be done without doing much violence to the language as we find it can be done in this case, though as we have noted that when the purpose was writ large in the scheme of the section 'some violence' is permissible...").

[19] *See* Arye Lapidoth & Ruth Lapidoth, *Israel,* 78a Cahiers 363, 365-73 (discussing purposive interpretation including in some cases an economic interpretation of terms used in tax law, and a general trend to depart from the *Duke of Westminster* case); Herman Doron, *"Substance Over Form" Establishing Permanent Foothold in Israeli Tax Cases,* 26 Tax Notes Int'l 384 (April 29, 2002).

[20] *See* Richard Vann, *Australia, in* Ault et al. (1997) at 20-21; 2 Wine Box Inquiry 2:2:6, 3:1:54–3:1:58 (New Zealand); Mills v. Dowdall [1983] NZLR 154; Simcock, *supra* note 11.

[21] See Corrigan (2000) at 14; Inspector of Taxes v. Kiernan, [1981] I.R. 117 (Supreme Court Dec. 4, 1981). *Kiernan* involved the question whether the taxpayer was a "dealer in cattle." The taxpayer's business was pigs. Although other statutes had defined cattle as including pigs, the term was undefined in the income tax law. The Court stated that in a statute "addressed to the public generally" a term "should be given the meaning which an ordinary member of the public would intend it to have when using it ordinarily." Moreover, in the case of ambiguous words used in a penal or taxation statute, "the word should be construed strictly so as to prevent a fresh imposition of liability from being created unfairly by the use of oblique or slack language." On this basis, the court concluded that pigs were not cattle. In McGrath v. McDermott, [1988] I.R. 258 (July 7, 1988), the Supreme Court refused to apply the *Ramsay* approach to a tax avoidance transaction, finding that this would amount to reading into the statute provisions that were not there. Parliament obliged by passing a GAAR (sec. 86 of the Finance Act 1989 (subsequently codified as TCA 1997, sec. 811)). On legislative history, it appears that the Irish courts are prepared to go further than the U.K. courts and look at legislative material even if the statute appears clear on its face. *See* DPP v. McDonagh, 2 ILRM 468; John Ward & Brendan Mccormack, *Tax Treaty Interpretation in Ireland, in* Tax Treaty Interpretation 171, 187 (Michael Lang ed. 2001).

the statute, and for failing to construe the law so as to strike down "several blatant tax-avoidance schemes."[22] The Court's general approach is to base the income tax consequences on the "legal effect (also referred to as legal substance or legal results) of transactions ascertained under ordinary [i.e. non-tax] legal principles."[23] Adoption of a purposive approach in principle does not mean that courts will in each case make a serious effort to ascertain and implement Parliament's intent.

A litmus test for the approach of the Canadian Supreme Court is its decision in *Shell Canada Ltd.*,[24] which also illustrates well the choice that the courts in any country face between a literal application of the statute and a construction that prevents misuse of the law. The court stated the facts as follows:

> In 1988, Shell required approximately $100 million in United States currency ("US$") for general corporate purposes. To get the money it required at the lowest possible after-tax cost, Shell embarked upon a complex financing scheme that proceeded in two stages. First, Shell entered into debenture purchase agreements...with three foreign lenders, pursuant to which it borrowed approximately $150 million in New Zealand currency ("NZ$") at the market rate of 15.4 percent per annum. Shell was required to make payments of NZ$11.55 million to the foreign lenders on November 10 and May 10 of each year until 1993. The principal of NZ$150 million was to be returned to the foreign lenders on May 10, 1993.
>
> Second, Shell entered into a forward exchange contract...with Sumitomo Bank Ltd...., pursuant to which it used the NZ$150 million it had borrowed from the foreign lenders to purchase approximately US$100 million. That US$100 million was then used in Shell's business. The Forward Exchange Contract between Shell and Sumitomo also allowed Shell to, (1) exchange a specified amount of US$ for NZ$11.55 million on each day that a semi-annual payment to the foreign

---

[22] Arnold, *supra* note 7, at 1, 2. *But see* Joel Nitikman & Derek Alty, *Some Thoughts on Statutory Interpretation in Canadian Tax Law — A Reply to Brian Arnold,* 20 Tax Notes Int'l 2185 (May 15, 2000).

[23] Guy Masson & Shawn D. Porter, *Canada,* 87a Cahiers 187, 187 (2002).

[24] Shell Canada Ltd. v. Canada, [1999] 3 S.C.R. 622 (Oct 15, 1999), 2 ITLR 24⅃ (2000). *See* Tim Edgar, *Some Lessons From the Saga of Weak-Currency Borrowings,* 48 Can. Tax J. 1 (2000).

lenders was due, and (2) to exchange another specified amount of US$ [79.5million] for NZ$150 million when the time came to repay the principal to the foreign lenders.....

The Debenture Agreements and the Forward Exchange Contract all closed on May 10, 1988.[25]

As a result of these transactions, Shell was in essentially the same economic position as if it had simply borrowed US$ instead of NZ$. For tax purposes, however, Shell was able to claim substantially higher interest deductions than under a US$ loan, since the interest rate on a NZ$ loan was higher than the US$ rate. The difference was made up by a capital gain realized at the time the loan was repaid. Of course, this allowed a deferral of tax. Moreover, taxation as capital gain was preferable to treatment as ordinary income, since capital gains were taxed at a lower rate and could be eliminated by capital loss carryovers. The Federal Court of Appeal had limited the taxpayer's deduction for interest expense to the rate that would have been payable on a US$ loan, since the section allowing a deduction for interest limited the deduction to a "reasonable" rate. There were other theories also available to the Supreme Court to limit the interest deduction, including the general anti-avoidance rule (in its pre-1988 version).[26] However, the court chose not to follow any of these approaches, instead applying what it found to be the "unambiguous" provisions of the Act allowing the deduction: "a searching inquiry for either the 'economic realities' of a particular transaction or the general object and spirit of the provision at issue can never supplant a court's duty to apply an unambiguous provision of the Act to a taxpayer's transaction." The court held that the tax law was to be applied to the "legal relationship with the foreign lenders", and that this could not be recharacterized for tax purposes. "[I]t is not the courts' role to prevent taxpayers from relying on the sophisticated structure of their transactions, arranged in such a way that the particular provisions of the Act

---

[25] [1999] 3 S.C.R. at 628-29.

[26] Under the previous GAAR, Income Tax Act, sec. 245(1), "In computing income for the purposes of this Act, no deduction may be made in respect of a disbursement or expense made or incurred in respect of a transaction or operation that, if allowed, would unduly or artificially reduce the income." Alternatively, as the court below found, "the Debenture Agreements and the Forward Exchange Contract had to be considered together to determine whether the amounts Shell sought to deduct were actually 'interest'. In his view, the real 'interest' amounts could only be identified after reducing the putative interest payments by an amount equal to the foreign exchange gain...." [1999] 3 S.C.R. at 634.

are met, on the basis that it would be inequitable to those taxpayers who have not chosen to structure their transactions that way."

The U.S. courts apply the same principles of interpretation to tax laws as to other statutes.[27] The general approach is to implement congressional intent. Legislative history is frequently consulted to this end.[28] An elaborate substance-over-form jurisprudence has developed in construing the tax laws.[29]

Most civil law countries look to a classic treatise on Roman law for methods of statutory interpretation.[30] These include the grammatical (analyse the meaning of particular words), systematic (consider the provision as part of the whole law), historical (identify original intent), and teleological (contemporaneous purpose) methods. The analogical approach is also acknowledged, for situations where the statute does not give an answer and a rule must be framed by analogy to rules found elsewhere in the law. The classic maxim, *interpretatio cessat in claris*, although somewhat discredited, may still be followed.[31] For tax statutes, interpretation by analogy has generally been ruled out based on the principle of legality.[32]

---

[27] *See* 1 Bittker & Lokken (1999), chapter 4.

[28] *See id.* at ¶ 4.2.2. *See generally* James B. Lewis, *Viewpoint: The Nature and Role of Tax Legislative History,* Taxes 442 (June 1990).

[29] *See infra* 5.7.1.

[30] 1 Friedrich Karl von Savigny, System des heutigen Römischen Rechts 206-330 (1840). Savigny argued that the process of statutory construction involved a thought experiment whereby those construing the statute placed themselves in the position of the lawgiver and allowed the law to spring forth anew in their thought. *See id.* at 213. Savigny did not consider the methods as properly separate, and among which one could pick and choose, but as jointly applicable (although in a particular case one method might predominate). *See id.* at 215. *See* Winfried Brugger, *Legal Interpretation, Schools of Jurisprudence, and Anthropology: Some Remarks from a German Point of View*, 42 Am. J. Comp. L 395 (1994), *excerpted in* Mary Ann Glendon et al., Comparative Legal Traditions: Text, Materials and Cases 230-241 (2d ed. 1994). *See also* Alfred Rieg, *Judicial Interpretation of Written Rules*, 40 La. L. Rev. 49, 53-65 (1979), *reprinted in* Glendon et al., *supra*; Mark van Hoecke and Michiel Elst, *Basic Features of the Legal System, in* Introduction to Belgian Law 23, 27-28 (Hubert Bocken & Walter de Bondt eds. 2001); Bernard Peeters, *Belgium*, 78a Cahiers 221, 225 (1993); Kees van Raad, *The Netherlands, in* Ault et al. (1997) at 89; Leonard Van Hien, *Indonesia*, 78a Cahiers 353, 355 (1993) (reporting that these maxims are followed as derived from Dutch legal scholars). Modern German courts are influenced by the doctrine of K. Larenz, Methodenlehre (6ᵗʰ ed. 1991). *See* Tipke/Lang (2002) at 133. *See generally* Interpretation of Tax Law and Treaties and Transfer Pricing in Japan and Germany (Klaus Vogel ed., 1998).

[31] *See id.* at 27. The problem is that it is not possible in the abstract to determine whether words are clear without considering the context of the words and the purpos

In many civil law countries, courts have followed a fairly literal approach to interpreting tax statutes.   This may be due in part to the professional culture of judges, who are appointed early in their careers and see their role as one of applying the law as written rather than making policy.[33] In many countries, strict interpretation is seen as flowing from the principle of legality.[34]

---

of the statute. (Note, however, that *Pepper v. Hart* resuscitated this maxim by denying the use of legislative history where the words were clear.)

[32] *See* Bernard Peeters, *Belgium,* 78a Cahiers 221, 228 (1993); Faes (1995) at 5; Leonard Van Hien, *Indonesia,* 78a Cahiers 353, 355 (1993); Adrian Timmermans, *Netherlands,* 78a Cahiers 439, 446-47 (1993); *Bertellotti,* Fallos 315, 820 (Apr. 28, 1992) (Arg.).   *But see* Giovanni Galli & Anna Miraulo, *Italy,* 78a Cahiers 385, 386 (1993); Fantozzi (1991) at 180-83 (analogy allowed for tax statutes). Tipke (2000) at 177-92 finds that it is not completely clear under the decisions of the German courts whether analogy is allowed. He also points out that drawing a line between analogy and stretching the language of the statute (while staying within the possible literal meaning) is not always easy to draw. Tipke notes that analogy has been disapproved in Belgium, Luxembourg, Portugal, and Argentina allowed in Austria, France, and the Netherlands, perhaps allowed in Switzerland and Italy, and ruled out by statute in Spain, Brazil, and Mexico. *See id.* at 192-96; LGT art. 23 (analogy ruled out, but only in relation to the taxable event and to exemptions or concessions); Martín Queralt et al. (2001) at 189-92 (analogy allowed where not ruled out).

[33] *See, e.g.,* Donald P. Kommers, The Constitutional Jurisprudence of the Federal Republic of Germany 4 (1997). *See also* Mauro Cappelletti, Judicial Review in the Contemporary World 45 (1971) ("The bulk of Europe's judiciary seems psychologically incapable of the value-oriented, quasi-political functions involved in judicial review.   It should be borne in mind that continental judges usually are 'career' judges who enter the judiciary at a very early age and are promoted to the higher courts largely on the basis of seniority.   Their professional training develops skills in technical rather than policy-oriented application of statutes.")(This statement was made in connection with review of statutes for constitutionality but seems equally applicable to statutory interpretation in general.)

[34] The reasoning is that under the principle of legality a tax can be established only by law and therefore the judge should not read anything into the law that establishes the tax. Only a tax clearly called for by the law may be imposed. *See* Introduction to Belgian Law, *supra* note 30, at 349. In Belgium, this follows from articles 110 and 112 of the Constitution, calling for an interpretation *in dubio contra fiscum* generally for tax laws and *in dubio pro fisco* in the case of exemptions. *See* Bernard Peeters, Belgium, 78a Cahiers 221, 227, 231 (1993). Belgian courts have used legislative history, but have excluded analogy or teleological approaches. *See* Faes (1995) at 9-10; Dassesse & Minne 58-60 (legislative history should not be consulted where the

In some civil law countries, particularly France, it may be difficult to generalize about how courts interpret tax statutes, because judicial opinions generally do not elaborate on the reasons for adopting a particular approach to statutory construction.[35] A more pragmatic approach would be to ask whether the taxpayer or the government tends to win a disproportionate amount of the time (for example, the government tends to win often in Japan[36]).

A number of civil law countries have rejected an excessively literal approach to interpreting tax statutes. Countries such as Germany,[37] Switzerland,[38] Luxembourg,[39] the Netherlands,[40] and Austria[41] have also

---

text is clear). *See also* Minoru Nakazato & Mark Ramseyer, *Japan, in* Ault et al. (1997) at 76; Minoru Nakazato, *Japan,* 78a Cahiers 407, 410 (1993).

[35] *See* Guy Gest, *France, in* Ault et al. (1997) at 44. The general view in France seems to be that there is nothing special about interpreting tax laws, in distinction from other legislation. *See* Beltrame & Mehl (1997) at 555-56; Trotabas & Cotteret (1997) at 272. Legislative history can be consulted. *See id.* at 556. *E.g.,* Cons. const., Dec. 86-223, Rec. 184, 185 (Dec. 29, 1986). The general approach has been described as literal interpretation if the text is clear, unless this leads to an absurd result, while an ambiguous text may be interpreted under generally available methods of interpretation. *See* David et al. (2000) at 31-34. French judicial opinions tend to be cryptic; for a guide on how to read opinions in tax cases, see Gilles Bachelier & Eve Obadia, Le Contentieux Fiscal 277-90 (2d ed. 1996).

[36] *See* Minoru Nakazato & Mark Ramseyer, *Japan, in* Ault et al. (1997) at 76. This is attributed to lack of specialist knowledge, but in other systems lack of specialist knowledge can cause courts to favor the taxpayer. Perhaps it is a combination of a lack of specialist knowledge, judicial attitudes, and the types of cases that make it to the courts.

[37] *See* Albert Rädler, *Germany, in* Ault et al. (1997) at 62-63; Martin Schiessel, *Germany,* 87a Cahiers 287 (2002); Tipke/Lang (2002) at 132-41; Heinrich Weber-Grellet, Steuern im modernen Verfussungsstaat 203-07 (2001); Klaus Tipke, *Über teleologische Auslegung, Lückenfeststellung und Lückausfüllung, in* Der Bundesfinanzhof und seine Rechtsprechung: Grundfragen – Grundlagen 133 (1985). Legislative history is consulted in Germany, although there is controversy about what role it should play. *See* Peter Fischer, *Auslegungsziele und Verfassung, in* Die Steuerrechtsordnung in der Diskussion 187 (Joachim Lang ed., 1995) [hereinafter Diskussion].

[38] *See* Peter Locher, *Switzerland,* 78a Cahiers 573, 576 (1993)(discussing frequent use of legislative history); Toni Amonn, *Switzerland,* 87a Cahiers 537 (2002); Ernst Höhn, *Zweck(e) des Steuerrechts und Auslegung, in* Diskussion, *supra* note 35, at 213.

[39] *See* Sandra Biewer, *Luxembourg,* 87a Cahiers 405 (2002).

[40] *See* Adrian J.M. Timmermans, *Netherlands,* 78a Cahiers 439, 446 (1993) (Supreme Court abandoned the previous strict interpretation to tax statutes in 1921); Robert L.H. Ijzerman, *Netherlands,* 87a Cahiers 451 (2002).

accepted the idea of construing tax laws in order to fulfill the legislative purpose, even where this may require some deviation from the literal language of the text. In Germany, the concept of *wirtschaftliche Betrachtungsweise* (economic construction) was formerly codified[42] but not included in the tax code when revised in 1977. It was apparently considered unnecessary to include it in the law, and it continues to be an accepted method of interpreting tax law.[43] The extent to which the judge is allowed to deviate from the literal wording of the law in order to apply an economic approach or otherwise implement the purpose of the statute is disputed in Germany. In a 1983 decision, the German Federal Tax Court explicitly stated that such a deviation, even to the disadvantage of the taxpayer, is in principle permissible.[44]   However, since then the question has not been explicitly addressed by the courts.[45] It is noteworthy that the debate concerns only interpretations of the law that lie outside the "possible meaning of the words" of the law.[46] The legitimacy of interpreting the law within the scope of its possible (even if strained) meaning is unquestioned. The German tax court has found that going beyond the literal meaning may be justified in order to fulfill the legislative purpose (i.e. to avoid an absurd result that could not have been intended by the legislature) or to bring about equal treatment that is required by the Constitution.[47]

In the above-mentioned Germanic countries, while there is a general acceptance of applying an economic construction approach, this does not mean that this approach applies to all cases. Many situations are decided under a purely legal analysis. In each particular case, the courts must decide whether a particular concept used in the tax laws will be interpreted in a legal

---

[41] Wolfgang Gassner, *Austria*, 87a Cahiers 119 (2002).

[42] § 1 Steueranpassungsgesetz.

[43] See Tipke/Kruse, AO Kommentar, § 4, Tz. 106; Schiessel, *supra* note 37, at 288; BVerfGE 26, 327, 335 (July 15, 1969); BVerfGE 25, 28, 35 (Jan. 14, 1969); Tipke/Lang (2002) at 142-44; Moris Lehner, *Wirtschaftliche Betrachtungsweise und Besteuerung nach der wirtschaftlichen Leistungsfähigkeit, in* Diskussion, *supra* note 37, at 237. An example is leasing—the lessee under a finance lease is treated as the owner. *See* Heinrich Weber-Grellet, Steuern im modernen Verfassungsstaat 209-10 (2001).

[44] BFH, decision of Oct. 20, 1983, BStBl 1984 II, S. 221 [224]; Rainer Barth, Richterliche Rechtsfortbildung im Steuerrecht 22, 162-63 (1996).

[45] *See id.*

[46] *Mögliche Wortsinn des Gesetzes. See id.* at 34-35.

[47] *See id.* at 138.

or commercial manner.[48]   An analysis of a particular area will therefore require attention to judicial precedents on the issue in question, if available, since it is difficult in the abstract to predict whether a legal or a commercial approach will be taken in a particular situation.

In Argentina, an excessively literal interpretation of tax laws was rejected in favor of purposive interpretation as early as 1937; guidance to courts is given by the tax procedure law.[49] Elsewhere in Latin America, the general approach is strict construction of tax statutes and reliance on civil law form, except as otherwise called for by general provisions of the tax code.[50]

The tax code of Spain also contains general provisions on tax law interpretation.   These implicitly refer to the Civil Code, which calls for interpretation of laws according to "the own sense of their words, in relation to the context, the historical and legislative background, and the social reality of the time in which they are to be applied, with fundamental regard to their spirit and purpose."[51]

In the Nordic legal tradition, Denmark, Norway, and Finland— particularly the former two—have adopted an approach to interpreting tax statutes that is close to that of the U.S. and often emphasizes the underlying economic reality of transactions rather than legal form.[52] The general judicial approach in Sweden looks for the intent of the legislator, often consulting

---

[48] *See* Schiessl, *supra* note 37, at 288. This is, incidentally, reminiscent of the analysis called for by the *Westmoreland Investments* case (*see infra* 5.7.2.3).

[49] *See* Juan Carlos Vicchi, *Argentina,* 78a Cahiers 161, 164-66 (1993) (citing art. 11 of tax procedure law which calls for interpretation according to purpose and economic meaning); 1 Catalina García Vizcaíno, Derecho Tributário 169-93 (1999); Horacio D. Diaz Sieiro, *Argentina*, 87a Cahiers 71 (2002); Kellogg Co. Arg. v. F., Supreme Court, Feb. 26, 1985.

[50] *See* Ricardo Lobo Torres, *Brazil,* 87a Cahiers 175 (2002); Jorge E. Paniagua-Lozano & Hector M. Mayorga-Arango, *Colombia,* 87a Cahiers 213 (2002); Fernando Moreno Gómez de Parada, *Mexico,* 87a Cahiers 429 (2002). The Mexican Tax Code calls for strict interpretation of provisions defining the subject, object, base, and rate of the tax. Código Fiscal de la Federación, art. 5. *See* Narciso Sánchez Gómez, Derecho Fiscal Mexicano 68-71 (1999).

[51] *See* Fernando Pérez Royo & Angel Aguallo Avilés, Comentarios a la Reforma de la Ley General Tributária 31-33 (1996); Martín Queralt et al. (2001) at 186-89; LGT art. 23; cod. civ. art. 3. A similar approach prevails in Italy. *See* Fantozzi (1991) at 172-80.

[52] See Jan Pedersen, *Denmark,* 87a Cahiers 233 (2002); Jarmo Ikkala, *Finland,* 87a Cahiers 249 (2002); Bettina Banoun, *Norway,* 87a Cahiers 499 (2002); Aage Michelsen, *Polycentry in the Sources of Tax Law, in* Liber Amicorum Sven-Olof Lodin 173 (2001).

legislative history for this purpose.[53]   However, the Swedish courts tend to respect the civil law form of transactions, and are reluctant to apply form over substance except in egregious cases.[54]

Judicial precedents are not always binding in civil law jurisdictions although they are often followed in practice.[55]   Common law jurisdictions have a more firmly established concept of precedent. Lower courts are bound by the precedents set by higher court decisions. The highest court overrules its own precedents with reluctance; this reluctance is greater in the U.K. than in the U.S.[56]   The concept of precedent influences the style of judicial decisions in common law jurisdictions; courts discuss previously decided cases and   explain how the present case fits in with those decisions. This discussion generally provides insight as to the reasoning behind the decision and often makes future decisions more predictable.

In all legal families, one can therefore discern a general trend in favor of purposive interpretation of tax laws and consequently abandonment of maxims such as *in dubio contra fiscum*.[57]   The acceptance of purposive

---

[53] *See* Peter Melz, *Sweden, in* Ault et al. (1997) at 102-03.

[54] *See id.* at 105. In Finland, there have reportedly been some substance over form decisions, and there also is a general anti-avoidance rule. *See* Ahti Vapaavuori, *Finland,* 78a Cahiers 317, 318.

[55] *See* Introduction to Belgian Law, *supra* note 30, at 35; Guy Gest, *France, in* Ault et al. (1997) at 44; de la Garza (2001) at 49-51 (jurisprudence, which normally will require repeated decisions, is binding on lower courts as specified by law).

[56] *See, e.g.,* Vestey v. I.R.C., [1980] A.C. 1148, 1175-78.

[57] Explained *supra* note 9. However, maxims like this have many lives. Recently, a U.S. Court of Appeals cited approvingly the maxim that "statutes imposing a tax are construed liberally in favor of the taxpayer." The Limited v. Commissioner, 286 F.3d 324, 332 (6th Cir. 2002). This goes back to a statement by Justice Story, "[I]t is, as I conceive, a general rule in the interpretation of all statutes, levying taxes or duties upon subjects or citizens, not to extend their provisions, by implication, beyond the clear import of the language used, or to enlarge their operation so as to embrace matters, not specifically pointed out, although standing upon a close analogy. In very case, therefore, of doubt, such statutes are construed most strongly against the Government, and in favor of the subjects or citizens, because burdens are not to be imposed, nor presumed to be imposed. beyond what the statutes expressly and clearly import. Revenue statutes are in no just sense either remedial laws or laws founded upon any permanent public policy. and. therefore, are not to be liberally construed." United States v. Wigglesworth. 2 Story. 369, 373-74 (1st Cir. 1842). It seems reasonable to conjecture that Story was influenced by the British jurisprudence of the time. *See supra* note 10. Justice Story's words were later parapharased by the Supreme Court in Gould v. Gould. 245 U.S. 151, 153 (1917). *See also* Porter v.

interpretation is not, however, uniform and perhaps most importantly there is not a uniform understanding of what purposive interpretation means and of how judges should go about it.   In particular, there is an uncertain line between implementing the original intention of the legislature which passed the law (in civil law terms, the historical approach) and interpreting the law according to its contemporaneous purpose, which the judge must necessarily infer (teleological approach).   The former may rely on legislative history, while the latter may rely more on evidence of contemporary problems and on policy analysis.   Because it is somewhat free-ranging, the teleological approach grants a fair amount of discretion to the judge.   It is accepted in the jurisprudence of the European Court of Justice.[58]

The notion that it is the role of courts to interpret the law in a flexible way in order to implement a presumed legislative intent to impose tax on a broad basis, which has been a mainstay of U.S. tax jurisprudence for a long time, is certainly not universally accepted, and few courts have come close to the U.S. courts in terms of injecting numerous judge-made anti-avoidance doctrines into the law (courts in the Nordic and Germanic countries often take a similar approach to that of the U.S. courts).   The balance of this chapter focuses on anti-avoidance doctrines in a few selected countries.   While the discussion is divided between judge-made and statutory-based anti-avoidance rules, the division is to some extent arbitrary, since some of the statutory rules (in countries like France and Germany) codify previously-developed judge-made principles and are drafted in a fairly broad manner.

What patterns can be detected in how courts interpret tax law in the country?   To what extent has a purposive approach been adopted, and what does this mean in practice if it has been?

5.4 TAX AVOIDANCE: INTRODUCTION

Tax avoidance transactions provide a classic test of statutory interpretation.   The taxpayer will typically have structured a transaction that qualifies for favorable tax treatment under the literal language of the statute. The taxpayer may argue that the statutory language is clear and entitles him to the treatment sought.   On the other hand, what the taxpayer is trying to do may be inconsistent with fairness in taxation, and the court may therefore b

---

Commissioner, 288 U.S. 436, 442 (1933) ("familiar rule that tax laws are to be construed liberally in favor of taxpayers"); United Dominion Industries Commissioner, 532 U.S. 822, 839 (2001) (Justice Thomas concurring) ("tradition canon that construes revenue-raising laws against their drafter").

[58] *See supra* 4.4 note 195.

inclined to disallow the benefits if there is a sound legal basis for doing so. Sometimes this can be done by analyzing the facts and finding that the taxpayer does not meet the factual requisites for the deduction or other benefit sought. Or it may be that the characterization of the facts under private law leads to the conclusion that the private law relationship necessary to qualify for the tax benefits has not been established. Or the situation may call into play a judge-made or statutory anti-avoidance rule. Such a rule may allow the statutory language to be set aside in favor of taxation based on the economic substance of the transaction. The question is in which circumstances such anti-avoidance rules should be applied, and when will courts find that the taxpayer is entitled to the treatment sought.[59]

All countries face the problem of tax avoidance transactions, although there are significant differences in terms of the aggressiveness of both the taxpayers and the tax administration, as well as the extent to which taxpayers engage in tax evasion, as opposed to tax avoidance (see 5.5 for explanation of these concepts). The balance of this chapter discusses methods that have been adopted by the courts, legislatures, and tax administrations to deal with tax avoidance transactions.[60] The topic is closely related to the general philosophy of statutory interpretation. Sometimes, courts can deal with tax avoidance transactions by interpreting the law in such a way that the taxpayer does not qualify for the particular treatment that it has sought. For example, where a taxpayer aggressively finances a corporation with debt, seeking an interest deduction, a court might find that the instruments issued by the corporation are not properly regarded as debt (either under general law or under an interpretation of the tax laws) or that the interest sought to be deducted does not meet the statutory requirements for deduction of interest expense. Such interpretative techniques easily merge into a reading of the statute that includes broader anti-avoidance rules, and the willingness of judges to see such rules as part of the statutory framework often turns on a general willingness to adopt a purposive statutory interpretation. However,

---

[59] This is not to say that questions of tax interpretation come up only in tax avoidance situations; however, it is probably fair to say that a large portion of tax interpretation questions in the tax area arise in the context of tax avoidance transactions.

[60] *See generally* Tax Avoidance and the Rule of Law (Graeme S. Cooper ed., 1997) (discussing both judicial interpretation and statutory anti-avoidance rules on a comparative basis); 68a Cahiers (1983) (Tax avoidance/Tax evasion); 74a Cahiers (1989) (The disregard of a legal entity for tax purposes); 87a Cahiers (Form and substance in tax law). Tiley (2000) at 87-89 gives a typology of legislative responses to tax avoidance.

the linkage is not tight, in that some courts (such as Canada) have espoused a purposive interpretation without adopting judicial anti-avoidance rules.[61]

Tax law often treats differently transactions that are similar in economic terms. The economist's ideal manner of taxing income would be to tax the increment of net wealth. This could be done if we knew the value of everyone's wealth holdings – the present discounted value of expected future income streams from each asset. But since we do not know the future, neither do we know the present. Instead of taxing increments of wealth, we are forced to tax transactions. Taxable transactions are legally defined events. By manipulating the transactions that they engage in, taxpayers can legally reduce the tax that they are required to pay. This exploits the legal definition of taxable income based on transactions and legal categories.

Every day, taxpayers structure transactions so as to minimize tax liability. The question is: when does this activity cease being legitimate tax minimization and become tax avoidance which the law prohibits? One view, which used to be taken by the British courts until the early 1980s, is that as long as what the taxpayer does is within the terms of the tax law, there is nothing wrong with it, even if the taxpayer manages to find a clever and artificial way of reducing tax. If Parliament thinks that a particular transaction should not be effective in reducing tax, the remedy is for Parliament to change the law. One of the things the British people have inherited as a result of this approach is a tax law full of detailed anti-avoidance rules specifying transactions that will not be effective in reducing tax. While there is a place for such rules, they will never be completely effective in stopping abuse. Moreover, such rules contribute to the complexity of the law and form part of a cat-and-mouse game between the tax authorities and taxpayers (and their advisors). Cutting off abuses on a prospective basis only allows taxpayers to succeed for the period between the time they discover a new tax avoidance loophole, and the time that the loophole is closed by the legislature. To render loopholes ineffective, they must be closed with retroactive effect.

Experience has taught legislatures and courts in most OECD countries that they must go beyond specific anti-avoidance rules and fashion doctrines that prohibit tax avoidance with a broader sweep. These doctrines are, however, problematic because it is inherently difficult to draw a distinction between acceptable and unacceptable transactions. It is instructive to

---

[61] Cases such as *Shell* (discussed in 5.3) illustrate that despite the acceptance of a purposive interpretation in principle, Canadian courts do not consistently attempt to read the statute so as to preclude abusive transactions which circumvent the statutory purpose.

compare how effective different countries have been in dealing with avoidance transactions and in providing legal certainty for taxpayers. The dividing line between the acceptable and the unacceptable will necessarily be somewhat arbitrary, and constitutes an important feature of a country's tax culture.   As that culture develops, based on provisions in the law, administrative guidance, court decisions, taxpayer attitudes, and the practice of tax advisors and tax administrators, it will normally be possible to form a view as to whether a particular transaction will be considered consistent with the law.   But like any cultural question, there will be uncertainty at the margins, and the extent of uncertainty will vary from country to country.

A variety of techniques have been employed to deal with tax avoidance (judicial interpretation, general and specific judge-made and statutory rules, procedural requirements, penalties, and substantive changes to the tax law to make it less prone to abuse). No one approach is likely to solve the problem on its own. Therefore, disputes over tax avoidance are likely to remain a permanent feature of tax systems and those countries with less sophisticated approaches will tend to increase their anti-avoidance arsenals. However, countries have not adopted a uniform approach and so we see now and will likely continue to see substantial differences.

Tax avoidance takes on a peculiar dimension under European law. For example, the Merger Directive allows EU Member States to deny tax-free merger treatment "where it appears that the merger, division, transfer of assets or exchange of shares has, in particular, as its principal objective or as one of its principal objectives tax evasion or tax avoidance." The ECJ has held that this does not authorize a member State to enact blanket rules denying the benefit of the directive in specified cases in order to forestall the possibility of tax avoidance, but requires an "examination of the operation in each particular case" to determine whether there is actually tax evasion or tax avoidance in that case.[62]   The details of the rules for determining whether there is tax avoidance would be left to each EU Member State, provided that the results of the examination are subject to judicial review.

In a treaty context, antiavoidance rules may be found in domestic law (in which case the issue arises as to whether the domestic antiavoidance rules can be applied, *see supra* 4.5.3.2), or may be found in the treaty itself, either as general concepts such as that of beneficial owner, or as more detailed rules (particularly in more recent treaties). Since there is an extensive literature on antiavoidance rules in treaties, I will not deal specifically with this issue here.

---

[62] *See* Leur-Bloem v. Inspecteur der Belastingdienst/Ondernemingen Amsterdam 2 Case C-28/95), 1997-7 ECJ I-4190, 4206 (July 17, 1997).

A number of general and specific anti-avoidance rules are reviewed in the balance of this chapter. While it would be interesting to speculate as to the effectiveness of these rules in particular countries, this could not be done without an empirical study. To assess the overall effectiveness of anti-avoidance rules, one would have to evaluate the extent of their deterrent effect, which involves a counterfactual that cannot be observed directly, but can be inferred by becoming familiar with the attitudes of taxpayers and their advisors. One would also want to know about the extent to which taxpayers practice aggressive tax planning and the extent to which such behavior is confronted by the audit of returns. Finally, one would need to assess the role of these rules in the context of the whole system, since the opportunity for tax avoidance will depend on the entire tax system, not just on the structure of the anti-avoidance rules.

5.5 TAX AVOIDANCE AND EVASION

The terms tax avoidance and tax evasion are often used imprecisely or with varying meanings. Part of the problem is a linguistic one. In English, tax evasion is synonymous with tax fraud,[63] and means criminal[64] activity. In French, *évasion* means avoidance. Tax evasion should be translated into French as *fraude fiscale*.[65] (Confusingly, however, the French expression

---

[63] "In my view the expression tax evasion should be deleted from the vocabulary as it is a euphemism which covers its true name, which is tax fraud. Tax evasion requires falsehood of some kind." John Dilger, *Tax Avoidance from the Practitioner's Perspective, in* Tax Avoidance and the Law (Adrian Shipwright ed., 1997).

[64] One could ask whether "criminal" in this context includes behavior punishable as civil fraud. *E.g.,* Stolzfus v. United States, 398 F.2d 1002 (3d Cir. 1968); Webb v. Commissioner, 394 F.2d 366 (5th Cir. 1968) (civil tax fraud is intentional wrongdoing, with the specific purpose of evading a tax known or believed to be owing). One answer to this is that often the definition of criminal fraud is broad enough to cover virtually all "civil" fraud, even if in fact criminal penalties are only rarely applied to the full extent they could be. Another answer may be that a civil penalty may in fact be in the nature of a criminal penalty (as has been held in connection with the ECHR, for example). Thus, I would tend to stick with the concept of tax evasion as being "criminal" in nature, even if this might also include behavior that in practice is dealt with through civil rather than criminal penalties.

[65] *See generally* Charles Robbez-Masson, *Fraude et Evasion Fiscales, in* Dictionnaire Encyclopédique de Finances Publiques 854 (Loïc Philip ed. 1991). Canadian treaties use the term "fiscal evasion" in the English version and "évasion fiscale" in the French, which seem to have a different meaning. *Cf.* the French version of the OECD Model, footnote 1 (which uses the term *fraude fiscale*), *reprinted in* Philip

fraude à la loi, used in a tax context, means tax avoidance.[66]) The general meaning of tax evasion (activity that is considered criminal) should therefore be clear. There is substantial consensus that the term should be used to refer only to criminal activity, although it has not always been used with this meaning.[67]   Specifically what behavior constitutes tax evasion, however, depends on the criminal laws of each country.[68]

Tax avoidance is a more ambiguous concept than tax evasion. It can be properly used with more than one meaning, so the meaning must be derived from the context. Tax avoidance in a general sense refers to any activity aimed at reduction of tax that is not criminal in nature.[69]   Often, however, tax avoidance is used (often as part of a phrase such as "tax avoidance scheme") to connote tax minimization behavior that skirts the limits of the law or that is in fact legally ineffective in reducing the taxpayer's liability.[70]   In this latter sense, one can distinguish between tax avoidance and tax mitigation (tax planning, tax minimization):

Baker, Double Taxation Conventions (looseleaf 2001). This has caused some confusion. *See* Jean-Marc Déry & David A. Ward, *Canada, in* 78a Cahiers 259, 269 n.44.

[66] *See* Florence Deboissy, La Simulation en Droit Fiscal 65-66 (1997). *Fraude à la loi* means taking advantage of the letter of the law while seeking to violate its spirit.

[67] For example, section 482 of the U.S. Internal Revenue Code refers to "evasion" of taxes in a context that clearly would call for the use of the word "avoidance" instead. In Furniss v. Dawson, [1984] A.C. 474, 513, Lord Scarman referred to the difficulty of determining "the limit beyond which the safe channel of acceptable tax avoidance shelves into the dangerous shallows of unacceptable tax evasion."   In a later case, this usage of the term tax evasion was criticized. *See* Craven v. White, [1989] 1 A.C. 398, 507-08.

[68] *See infra* 6.11.

[69] For example, The Economist, Jan. 29, 2000, states: "Tax avoidance is doing what you can within the law." The following distinction between tax avoidance and tax evasion is drawn in a manual for revenue agents in the U.S.: "Avoidance of tax is not a criminal offense. All taxpayers have the right to reduce, avoid, or minimize their taxes by legitimate means. The distinction between avoidance and evasion is fine, yet definitive. One who avoids tax does not conceal or misrepresent, but shapes and preplans events to reduce or eliminate tax liability, then reports the transactions. Evasion on the other hand, involves deceit, subterfuge, camouflage, concealment, some attempt to color or obscure events, or making things seem other than what they are." U.S. Internal Revenue Service, Internal Revenue Manual, Audit Guidelines, sec. 913.

[70] "...the unacceptable reduction of a person's tax liability that the tax legislation was intended to cover but literally, for some reason, does not." Brian Arnold & James R.

> The hallmark of tax avoidance is that the taxpayer reduces his liability to tax without incurring the economic consequences that Parliament intended to be suffered by any taxpayer qualifying for such reduction in his tax liability. The hallmark of tax mitigation, on the other hand, is that the taxpayer takes advantage of a fiscally attractive option afforded to him by the tax legislation, and genuinely suffers the economic consequences that Parliament intended to be suffered by those taking advantage of the option.[71]

Although the precise contours of "tax avoidance" can be disputed, the following definitions of the terms tax evasion, tax avoidance, and tax minimization can be suggested:[72]

- Tax evasion[73] or tax fraud is an offense against the tax laws that is punishable by criminal sanctions.

- Tax avoidance[74] is behavior by the taxpayer that is aimed at reducing tax liability, but that is found to be legally ineffective (perhaps because of an anti-abuse doctrine or by construction of the tax law), although it does not constitute a criminal offense.

- Tax minimization (tax mitigation, tax planning) is behavior that is legally effective in reducing tax liability.

However, no definition can explain actual usage, given that the various terms have been used inconsistently and interchangeably, even within a single legal system. Moreover, the classification of particular behavior as tax evasion, tax avoidance or tax minimization, even within one legal system, may be difficult, the difficulty being compounded when one is working on a comparative basis.

Statutory anti-avoidance rules are often written or interpreted so as to apply only when "tax avoidance" is the sole, predominant, or a significant

---

Wilson, *The General Anti-Avoidance Rule – Part I*, 36 Can. Tax J. 829, 873 (1988). "Tax avoidance...involves an interpretation of the tax legislation which provides a tax benefit not foreseen or intended by the legislature, and which defeats the scheme and purpose of the legislation." 2 [New Zealand] Commission of Inquiry into Certain Matters Relating to Taxation, Report of the Wine-Box Inquiry 2:2:3 (1997).

[71] IRC v. Willoughby [1997] STC 995 at 1003.

[72] *See* Frans Vanistendael, *Legal Framework for Taxation, in* TLDD at 15, 44-46.

[73] In French, *fraude fiscale*; in German, *Steuerhinterziehung*.

[74] In French, *évasion fiscale*; in German, *Steuerumgehung*.

purpose for a transaction. Depending on the context, this may have the meaning discussed above, or may simply mean tax reduction.

What terminology is used in the country for tax avoidance? Is it used consistently? How is the distinction to tax evasion drawn?

5.6 SHAM TRANSACTIONS, SIMULATION, AND ABUSE OF LAW

In a number of civil law countries, despite the general literal approach to statutory interpretation, some anti-avoidance doctrines that were judicially developed under the civil law apply for tax law as well.[75] One of these is simulation.[76] Simulation is essentially equivalent to the common law concept of "sham transaction" (in the terminology of the U.S. courts, "sham in fact").[77] Where the taxpayer presents to the tax authorities a purported transaction, but the legal reality of the transaction is different under private law, the tax will be applied according to the actual legal reality, not the taxpayer's pretended reality. This situation is borderline between tax avoidance and tax evasion. Simulation is originally not a tax concept, but a

---

[75] David Ward et al., *The Business Purpose Test and Abuse of Rights* [1985] B.T.R. 68 surveys both tax and nontax law and find similarities among many civil law countries and the U.S. in terms of applying a doctrine of abuse of law first outside tax law and then for tax purposes, in contrast to other common law countries. Importantly as a matter of comparative law, the authors conclude: "The United States developments are similar to those of the civil law countries that have long known the abuse of rights concept. As similar doctrines have traditionally been applied in the United States in other fields of the law, it is not surprising that the concepts, under various labels, are regularly applied in tax law." *Id.* at 116-17. *See also* Stefan N. Frommel, *United Kingdom tax law and abuse of rights*, 55 Intertax 54 (1991). Abuse of law has not, however, been accepted for tax law in Italy. *See* Guglielmo Maisto, *The abuse of rights under Italian tax law: an outline*, 93 Intertax 93 (1991).

[76] *Simulation* (French), *simulación* (Spanish), *Scheingeschäft* or *Scheinhandlung* German)*, negozio simulato* (Italian). The doctrine of simulation has been codified in Germany in AO § 41(2), in France in LPF L. 64, and in Spain in LGT art. 25.

[77] Sham has been described by the House of Lords as "acts done or documents executed by the parties to the 'sham' which are intended by them to give to third parties or to the court the appearance of creating between the parties legal rights and obligations different from the actual legal rights and obligations (if any) which the parties intend to create." Ramsay v. IRC, [1981] STC 174, at 170-71, quoting Snook . London and West Riding Investments Ltd, [1967] 2 QB 786; [1967] 1 All ER 518 Diplock LJ).

civil law concept. The concept is that of legal reality, not economic reality. It means that for civil law purposes as well as for tax purposes, the intention of the parties will be followed, if this is different from the arrangement which the parties purport to make. For example, the parties sign a paper that says something is a sale, but both parties know and intend it to be a gift. While this doctrine can be used for tax purposes to look through transactions that are essentially fraudulent (for example, invoices that show one price where the true price intended and paid (under the table) is a different one), it is not much of an obstacle to careful tax planning, since tax advisors will take care that the instruments used are intended by the parties to have legal effect.

In France, as under the civil code, the tax administration has a choice as to whether to impose tax either on the basis of the real situation or on the basis of the situation as simulated by the taxpayer.[78] By contrast, in Belgium, except where specifically provided by statute, it is considered that tax must be imposed according to the actual situation.[79]

A second doctrine found in many civil law countries is known as abuse of rights, avoidance of the law, or *fraus legis*.[80] This doctrine also is based in the civil law.[81] "Abuse of rights, in general terms, is a concept which gives a remedy to a person who is injured by another person who exercises a right but in doing so acts with malice or other improper motive."[82] This general doctrine has been applied in many areas of the law, involving such diverse issues as spite fences, dismissal of employees, administration of the

---

[78] *See* Deboissy, *supra* note 66, at 267, 367-95; David et al. (2000) at 164-69.

[79] *See id.* at 367-38. (This approach is consistent with the principle of legality.)

[80] When referring to abuse of private rights the term used (in French) is *abus de droit*. When referring to avoidance of the law, it may be more accurate to refer to *fraude à la loi*, although the two terms tend to be used interchangeably. *See* Ward et al., *supra* note 75, at 68 n.1. In Spanish the corresponding terms would be *abuso de derecho* or *fraude de ley*. The latter term is used in article 24 of the Spanish tax code (LGT) which codifies the abuse of rights rule for tax purposes. *See* Pérez & Aguallo, *supra* note 51, at 45-66. Italians refer to *negozio in frode alla legge fiscale*. The *fraus legis* doctrine has its origin in Roman law, applying when someone relies on the literal language of the law in contravention of its purpose. *See* Eelco van der Stok, *General Anti-avoidance Provisions: A Dutch Treat* [1998] B.T.R. 150, 151.

[81] The famous case of the Princess of Beauffremont (Cass. civ. 18 mars 1878: 1878, 1, p. 193, note Labbé) involved a foreign divorce. The court found that the Princess had acquired nationality in the foreign jurisdiction for the purpose of committing fraud on the French law and that the foreign divorce therefore would not be recognized.

[82] *See* Ward et al., *supra* note 75, at 68 n.1.

joint estate by the husband, voting rights under company law, and adaptation of contracts to new circumstances.[83] Given the generality of the concept, it has not surprisingly been applied in different ways in civil law countries.

This doctrine has been rejected for tax purposes by the Belgian courts.[84] It has been approved by the courts in Switzerland.[85] France, Sweden, and Germany currently apply this principle largely on the basis of statutory anti-avoidance rules; in both France and Germany there is also room for judge-made rules (see below).[86] Somewhat similarly, in the Netherlands, under the *fraus legis* doctrine, the legal form of a transaction may be set aside when tax reduction was the dominant reason for the transaction, the transaction lacks economic effect, and the intended tax consequences violate the intention of the law.[87] In Japan, a doctrine of substance over form has been applied to a very limited extent by the courts.[88] Likewise, the doctrine seems to have limited if any applicability in Italy.[89]

Even though the two doctrines of simulation and abuse of law are conceptually separate, in the hands of judges, simulation often tends to expand to cover abuse of law.[90] In the *Knetsch* case, the U.S. Supreme Court called a loan agreement a "sham" even though there was no question about the genuineness of the transaction for private law purposes.[91] Similarly, the Belgian courts expanded the concept of simulation to include transactions that are not regarded as "genuine" for tax purposes, even though they are genuine under the civil law;[92] however, the Supreme Court in decisions from 1988-90

---

[83] *See* Ward et al., *supra* note 75, at 68-84; Germany, Civil Code, §§ 138, 242 (concepts of good faith, equity, and transactions in violation of good morals).

[84] *See* Ward et al., *supra* note 75, at 84-85.

[85] *See id.* at 89-91; Raoul Lenz, *Switzerland, in* International Bar Association, Tax Avoidance, Tax Evasion 75, 76 (1982) (Where a taxpayer enters into "unusual, inadequate or abnormal transactions which in any event are not adapted to economic conditions" for a tax avoidance purpose and with the result that tax is reduced, "tax authorities may apply taxation as if the transactions had taken place in the normal way").

[86] *See id.* at 85-89, 91-95.

[87] *See id.* at 95-96; Ault et al. (1997) at 90; van der Stok, *supra* note 80.

[88] *See* Ward et al., *supra* note 75, at 96-99.

[89] *See id.* at 99-100.

[90] *See* Cozian (1999) at 34-35.

[91] *See infra* 5.7.1.2.

[92] *See* Ward et al, *supra* note 75, at 85.

disapproved this doctrine.[93]   Abuse of rights cases in Belgium are now presumably governed by the general anti-avoidance rule enacted in 1993 (see 5.7.6 below). In France, the *Conseil d'État* decided in 1981 that article L. 64 of the tax procedure code, which seems on its face confined to simulation, applies to abuse of law as well. In the U.K., however, the courts seem to stick to a classical approach to the sham transaction doctrine.[94]

This tendency of simulation to slide into abuse of law can be explained by the factual context of many tax cases. The doctrine of simulation calls for rejecting the feigned transaction in favor of the true intention of the parties. However, in self-cancelling tax avoidance transactions, it seems that the true intention of the parties is to do precisely nothing of economic substance. Can it not be said, therefore, that the doctrine of simulation calls for disregarding such a transaction?

5.7 GENERAL ANTI-AVOIDANCE RULES

5.7.1 UNITED STATES

5.7.1.1   Introduction

The U.S. judiciary has long been activist in interpreting tax laws, fashioning a number of anti-avoidance doctrines to reflect the presumed intent of Congress in enacting the income tax laws. These doctrines are known under the names "substance over form, step transaction, business purpose, sham transaction, and economic substance."[95] The doctrines do not have an explicit grounding in specific language of the statute. These doctrines, which are overlapping,[96] have been developed gradually by the courts, and their contours are indistinct.   Because their application is controversial, and because they are grounded in the specific fact patterns of decided cases, it is

---

[93] *See* Jacques Malherbe et al., *Simulation in Belgian fiscal law: a modest proposal for a clear legislative solution*, 1991/92 Intertax 88, 91 (Feb. 1991); Tiberghien (1995) at 39.

[94] *E.g.,* Hitch v. Stone, 73 T.C. 600 (Court of Appeal 2001).

[95] Joseph Bankman, *The Economic Substance Doctrine*, 74 S. Cal. L. Rev. 5, 5 (2000). For a comparative review of U.S. and U.K. anti-avoidance doctrines, *see* John Tiley, *Judicial Anti-avoidance doctrines*, [1987] B.T.R. 180, 220, 433, [1988] B.T.R. 63, 108; John Tiley & Eric Jensen, *The Control of Avoidance: The United States Experience*, [1998] B.T.R. 161.

[96] *See, e.g.,* Kirchman v. Commissioner, 862 F.2d 1486, 1490-91 (11th Cir. 1989).

impossible to precisely describe them (however, I attempt a rough sketch).[97] An important reason why it is difficult to pin these doctrines down is that they are a joint product of judges who take different approaches and who do not necessarily agree with one another. Although nominally the Supreme Court has the last word on all tax cases, the Court does not agree to hear many of them, and consequently exercises only a loose control on the lower courts in this area of the law. In the U.S. system, several sets of courts deal with taxation at the federal level, each with different approaches.[98]

As John Tiley has pointed out, the U.S. anti-avoidance doctrines should be seen in the backdrop of administrative practice. Because of the detailed set of regulations, revenue rulings, other published notices, and letter rulings, it is often possible to determine whether a particular transaction will run the risk of being attacked by the IRS under anti-avoidance doctrines or will be safe from such scrutiny.[99] The uncertainty is therefore faced mainly by those who are on notice. Tiley also attributes the broad substance-over-form approach of U.S. courts to the initially broad wording of taxing statutes in the U.S.[100]

The seminal case[101] for the anti-avoidance doctrines, which—although a Supreme Court case—was essentially decided on the basis of the opinion of the appeals court judge Learned Hand.[102] The case, *Gregory v. Helvering*,[103] involved an attempted corporate reorganization in which assets were transferred to a corporation specially created for the purpose and liquidated shortly afterwards. Judge Hand found that, although the transaction met the literal requirements of the statute,

---

[97] For further analysis, *see* James Wetzler, *Notes on the Economic Substance and Business Purpose Doctrines*, 92 Tax Notes 127 (July 2, 2001); Bankman, *supra* note 95; Bittker & Eustice (2000) 12-244 to 246; David Hariton, *Sorting out the Tangle of Economic Substance*, 52 Tax Law. 235 (1999); Robert Thornton Smith, *Business Purpose: The Assault upon the Citadel*, 53 Tax Law. 1 (1999).

[98] *See infra* 6.8.

[99] *See* John Tiley, *Judicial Anti-Avoidance Doctrines*, [1988] B.T.R. 108, 143.

[100] *See id.* at 144.

[101] Although the leading case, it was not the first time that the Supreme Court used substance-over-form analysis in taxation. *See infra* note 126 [Phellis].

[102] 69 F.2d 809 (2d Cir. 1934).

[103] 293 U.S. 465 (1935). "Although *Gregory* may mean all things to all people, its essence is an instinctive judicial attitude that a transaction should not be given effect for tax purposes unless it serves a purpose other than tax avoidance." Bittker & Eustice (2000) at 12-244.

it does not follow that Congress meant to cover such a transaction, not even though the facts answer the dictionary definitions of each term used in the statutory definition...The purpose of the section is plain enough; men engaged in enterprises—industrial, commercial, financial, or any other— might wish to consolidate, or divide, to add to, or subtract from, their holdings.   Such transactions were not to be considered as "realizing" any profit, because the collective interests still remained in [corporate] solution.   But the underlying presupposition is plain that the readjustment shall be undertaken for reasons germane to the conduct of the venture in hand, not as an ephemeral incident, egregious to its prosecution.   To dodge the shareholders' taxes is not one of the transactions contemplated as corporate "reorganizations."[104]

The conclusion was therefore reached by imputing an underlying purpose to the sections of the Internal Revenue Code dealing with reorganizations.   The purpose was to provide relief for bona fide reorganizations undertaken for a business purpose. Because the particular transaction did not qualify under that test, it was not allowed by the statute.

The Supreme Court's opinion echoed this reasoning, highlighting the fact that the transaction had "no business or corporate purpose" and that it was "a mere device which put on the form of a corporate reorganization as a disguise for concealing its real character."[105] The case had within it the seeds of all the subsequently evolved anti-avoidance doctrines—the step-transaction doctrine (the transient corporation was disregarded), the business purpose doctrine, the substance over form doctrine (the Supreme Court said it was necessary to look through the "device" for its "true character"), and the economic substance doctrine (the transaction lacked the substance contemplated by the statute).

---

[104] 69 F.2d at 810-11.

[105] 293 U.S. at 469. *Gregory* was decided at a time when the Supreme Court was concerned to avoid reading too broadly the reorganization rules, realizing that to treat as reorganizations all transactions that arguably came within the literal language of the statute "would make evasion of taxation very easy."   Pinellas Ice Co. v. Commissioner, 287 U.S. 462, 469 (1933). In *Pinellas*, the Court had decided that short-term notes should not qualify as corporate securities for purposes of the reorganization rules.

5.7.1.2   *Economic substance doctrine*

Stated broadly, the economic substance doctrine holds that a transaction without economic substance is not recognized for federal taxation purposes.[106] The economic substance or "sham transaction" doctrine can be attributed to the Supreme Court case of *Knetsch v. U.S.*[107] At issue was the deductibility of interest paid in respect of nonrecourse[108] indebtedness by the taxpayer to a life insurance company, incurred to purchase a life insurance annuity policy. Under the arrangement, the taxpayer stood to receive little or nothing under the annuity, since virtually all its cash value was borrowed. Since the rate of return under the annuity was less than the rate of interest payable on the debt, the taxpayer had no prospect of making money on the transaction. The transaction simply boiled down to the taxpayer paying a fee to the insurance company in return for its arranging a transaction which (apart from the fee) had no substance other than the taxpayer's hope of being able to take an interest deduction for tax purposes.

The Court framed the issue as being whether the transaction "created an 'indebtedness' within the meaning of ...[the tax] Code, or whether, as the trial court found, it was a sham."[109] The Court concluded that the "transaction with the insurance company did 'not appreciably affect his beneficial interest except to reduce his tax.....' that there was nothing of substance to be realized by Knetsch from this transaction beyond a tax deduction" and that the transaction was "a sham."[110] It appears that in calling the transaction a sham the Court did not mean that it was a sham in the sense that the parties did not intend the documents they had signed to have legal effect. Rather, the Court found that, even if a debt technically existed under State law, it had no economic substance and so would not be respected for tax purposes. It was therefore a sham in economic terms.

It would have been better if the Court had not used the term "sham," which has traditionally been reserved for cases involving forged documents or false testimony and the like intended to give the appearance that certain legal rights or relations have been created where in fact they have not been.[111] In

---

[106] *See, e.g.,* Lerman v. Commissioner, 939 F.2d 44, 45 (3d Cir. 1991).

[107] 364 U.S. 361 (1960).

[108] Nonrecourse borrowing means borrowing that is secured by property, where the lender has no personal liability to repay the loan.

[109] 364 U.S. at 365.

[110] 364 U.S. at 366.

[111] *See supra* note 77.

any case, the terminology is now used by U.S. courts without apparent confusion. Instead of referring simply to a "sham," courts have referred to transactions as "shams, devoid of economic substance,"[112] as "shams in substance,"[113] or as "economic shams,"[114] calling shams under the traditional concept "factual shams."[115]

The D.C. Circuit has summarized the sham transaction doctrine as follows:

> first, the sham transaction doctrine is simply an aid to identifying tax-motivated transactions that Congress did not intend to include within the scope of a given benefit-granting statute; and second, a transaction will not be considered a sham if it is undertaken for profit *or* for other legitimate nontax business purposes.[116]

The doctrine stemming from *Knetsch* has also been called the "economic substance" doctrine. A leading case articulating the doctrine is *Goldstein v. Commissioner*,[117] in which the taxpayer borrowed money from a bank and invested the proceeds in U.S. Treasury obligations paying a lower interest rate than that payable on the loan. The taxpayer prepaid the interest on the loan. The transaction was not likely to be profitable, although there was a small chance of profit depending on an improvement in the bond market. The court disallowed the deduction for interest, holding that "Section 163(a) of the 1954 Internal Revenue Code does not permit a deduction for interest paid or accrued in loan arrangements, like those now before us, that can not with reason be said to have purpose, substance, or utility apart from their anticipated tax consequences."[118] In so doing, the court rejected the Tax

---

[112] Lerman v. Commissioner, 939 F.2d 44, 56 (3rd Cir. 1991).

[113] "Courts have recognized two basic types of sham transactions. Shams in fact are transactions that never occur. In such shams, taxpayers claim deductions for transactions that have been created on paper but which never took place. Shams in substance are transactions that actually occurred but which lack the substance their form represents. *Gregory*, for example, involved a substantive sham. The issue in this case is whether, assuming the transactions actually occurred as claimed, the transactions are shams in substance." Kirchman v. Commissioner, 862 F.2d 1486, 1492 (11th Cir. 1989).

[114] Horn v. Commissioner, 968 F.2d 1229, 1231 (D.C. Cir. 1992).

[115] 968 F.2d at 1236 n.8.

[116] 968 F.2d at 1238.

[117] 364 F.2d 734 (2d Cir. 1966).

[118] 364 F.2d at 740. The court did not rely on specific language in the statute in reaching this conclusion, but on the presumed intention of Congress.

Court's finding that the loan transaction was a sham: the court felt that given the recourse nature of the loan and the substantial duration of the loan arrangement, the transaction could not be ignored altogether and treated as a direct investment in Treasury securities by the lending banks, as the Tax Court had done.

More recently, in the *ACM* case,[119] the Third Circuit dealt with a transitory purchase and sale of property that it found to be reminiscent of *Gregory v. Helvering*. In *ACM*, the taxpayer purchased property (Citicorp notes) and sold it almost immediately thereafter. The reason that this property was purchased and sold was to generate artificial gains and losses (taking advantage of a technical anomaly in regulations concerning contingent sales), through a partnership which allocated the gains to foreign partners that were indifferent to this allocation since they were not subject to U.S. tax. Paradoxically, the anomaly in the regulations arose from rules devised in an effort to prevent abuse: they ended up overtaxing the taxpayer, but the drafters of the regulation had not anticipated that the overtaxation would be allocated to a foreign partner and the corresponding undertaxation allocated to a U.S. partner under the partnership rules. Noting that "ACM engaged in mutually offsetting transactions by acquiring the Citicorp notes only to relinquish them a short time later under circumstances which assured that their principal value would remain unchanged and their interest yield would be virtually identical to the interest yield on the cash deposits which ACM used to acquire the Citicorp notes,"[120] the court found that while, technically, the transaction followed the requirements of the relevant sections of the statute and regulations, it had no economic substance. The court summarized the economic substance test as follows:

> The inquiry into whether the taxpayer's transactions had sufficient economic substance to be respected for tax purposes turns on both the 'objective economic substance of the transactions' and the 'subjective business motivation' behind them.... However, these distinct aspects of the economic sham inquiry do not constitute discrete prongs of a 'rigid two-step analysis,' but rather represent related factors both of which inform the analysis of whether the transaction had sufficient substance, apart from its tax consequences, to be respected for tax purposes.... In assessing the economic substance of a taxpayer's transactions, the courts have

---

[19] ACM Partnership v. Commissioner. 157 F.3d 231 (3rd Cir. 1998).
[20] 157 F.3d at 250.

examined 'whether the transaction has any practical economic effects other than the creation of income tax losses...'[121]

The economic substance doctrine is controversial, because it is not always clear when it applies. The objective test, requiring a determination of the taxpayer's expected pre-tax profit, can give rise to particular difficulties in this respect. For example, another court has found, on facts very similar to those of the ACM case, that the taxpayer's transaction had economic substance because it anticipated that the transaction could be profitable.[122] Another recent illustration of the difficulties in applying the economic substance doctrine is found in the *Compaq* case.[123] The case involved a cross-border dividend-stripping transaction whereby the taxpayer purchased shares cum dividend and very shortly thereafter sold them ex dividend at a loss. The transaction was attractive for two reasons: a foreign tax credit was available for the withholding tax imposed on the dividend, and the market valued the dividend at its net-of-withholding-tax value, so that the taxpayer had to pay little or nothing for the right to get the foreign tax credit. While the transaction was clearly tax motivated, the taxpayer prevailed in court on the basis that the transaction was profitable on a pre-tax basis (on a pre-tax basis, the taxpayer was receiving the dividend gross of the withholding tax); therefore the transaction could not be seen as tax motivated in applying the economic substance doctrine.[124] The short holding period in the *Compaq*

---

[121] 157 F.3d at 247-48.

[122] "AHP evaluated all of the transactions in issue, including the purchase of the PPNs and the LIBOR Notes, from an investment perspective on a pre-tax basis and entered into the transactions in order to make a profit." Boca Investerings Partnership v. United States, 167 F. Supp. 2d 298 (D.D.C. 2001). This conclusion raises the difficult issue of *how profitable* a transaction has to be in order to pass muster under the economic substance doctrine. Some prospect of profitability seemed to satisfy the district court in *Boca*. The decision was reversed by the Court of Appeal. See Landon Thomas, *Court Rejects Tax Strategy Merrill Sold to Companies*, N.Y. Times, Jan. 11, 2003, at B1 (the case involved $226 million in tax).

[123] Compaq Computer Corp. v. Commissioner, 277 F.3d 778 (5th Cir. 2001). *See* Daniel Shaviro, *Economic Substance, Corporate Tax Shelters, and the* Compaq *Case*, 21 Tax Notes Int'l 1581 (Oct. 2, 2000).

[124] The taxpayer had realized a long-term capital gain in an unrelated transaction. Desiring to create a capital loss to offset part of this gain (ordinary expenses could not be used to offset a capital gain), the taxpayer purchased shares of a Netherlands corporation cum dividend and immediately sold them ex dividend. (Cum dividend means that the purchaser (in this case, the taxpayer) is entitled to receive the dividend most recently declared, and ex dividend means that the person purchasing the share from the taxpayer would not be entitled to this dividend.) Under this arrangement, the

transaction highlighted that the possibility of making a profit from holding the stock could not have been a motivation for the transaction. If the taxpayer were prepared to hold the stock for a longer period, it would have the additional argument that it was holding the stock for investment and hence had a purpose other than tax avoidance. Congress dealt with this specific type of transaction on a prospective basis by denying the foreign tax credit where the holding period does not meet a specified threshold.[125]

---

taxpayer became entitled to receive the dividend even though it owned the shares for only a brief period of time.

The difference in the purchase and sales price was approximately equal to the amount of the dividend (net of Dutch withholding tax), and so the taxpayer incurred a capital loss that was approximately equal to the amount of dividend net of withholding tax. While the dividend was taxable in the U.S., this tax could be offset in part by a foreign tax credit for the withholding tax. The overall tax consequences were a short-term capital loss of $20.6m on sale of the Royal Dutch shares, dividend income of $22.5m, and a foreign tax credit of $3.4m.

In economic terms, the transaction was largely a wash before taking commissions into account: the after-tax dividend more or less equaled the short-term capital loss. On top of this, however, the taxpayer paid a commission of $1.5 m; taking the commission into account, the transaction was uneconomic (apart from tax consequences). The Tax Court disallowed the foreign tax credit on the basis that there was no business purpose for the transaction. The court of appeals reversed, persuaded by the taxpayer's argument that, looking at the transaction on a pre-tax basis (including pre-foreign taxes), it was profitable. The gross-of-tax dividend (25.9m) exceeded the capital loss. The profitability on a pre-tax basis was due to the fact that the foreign withholding tax was fully discounted by the market, i.e. the taxpayer could purchase the stock cum dividend by paying the ex dividend price plus the amount of the dividend net of foreign tax. This made the transaction largely a wash, disregarding the foreign tax, but if a pre-foreign-tax calculation were made, then the taxpayer was making money before tax. Only a somewhat mechanical and unreflective application of the objective test could turn this transaction into one that had economic substance because it was profitable for the taxpayer. This transaction had no business purpose—it was solely motivated by the opportunity to take advantage of the allowance of the foreign tax credit. The transaction worked for two reasons: (1) the market discounted the dividend by the full amount of the foreign tax, and (2) there was an anomaly in the rules for measuring taxable income, which consider the shareholder to be taxable on a relatively large amount of dividend income just because it happens to be the nominal owner of shares for a few instants. On similar facts, another court of appeals has also held for the taxpayer on a similar basis. *See* IES Industries v. United States, 253 F.3d 350 (8th Cir. 2001).

[5] Under I.R.C. § 901(k), the taxpayer must hold stock for at least 15 days in order to obtain a foreign tax credit for tax withheld with respect to a dividend. After this

In addition to problems of how to apply the economic substance doctrine, a fundamental problem lies in deciding whether the doctrine should apply in the first place.[126] The Supreme Court declined to apply the doctrine in *Frank Lyon,*[127] a case involving a sale-leaseback of a building, in which the government argued that the sale-leaseback should be disregarded as a sham.[128] The case involved factual peculiarities: for regulatory reasons, the taxpayer was prohibited from borrowing money to finance the building. This provided a legitimate business reason for entering into the lease arrangement. The unsatisfying decision in *Frank Lyon* did not do much to clarify in a useful way how the sham transaction doctrine should be applied; the key seemed to lie in independent (nontax) reasons for the transaction: "In short, we hold that where, as here, there is a genuine multiple-party transaction with economic substance which is compelled or encouraged by business or regulatory realities, is imbued with tax-independent considerations, and is not shaped

---

change, taxpayers can still engage in a transaction like that in *Compaq*, but they will have to hold the stock for 15 days instead of selling it right away. This will require a commitment of capital and will also expose the holder to the risk of fluctuations in value of the stock. It is likely that in light of these factors there will be much less interest in this kind of dividend-stripping transaction in the future, so that probably § 901(k) dealt effectively with this particular abuse. However, if a taxpayer is willing to accept the additional market risk, it can still engage in a dividend stripping transaction by holding the stock for at least 15 days. In order to deal with the problem more comprehensively, it would be necessary to devise rules that tax shareholders on accrued dividends, just as holders of bonds are taxed on accrued interest in many jurisdictions. It is not clear, however, how the amount of accrued dividends could be determined, since dividends are determined by a vote of the board rather than automatically accruing as interest does. Alternatively, one could go further and limit the foreign tax credit by pro-rating it depending on how long the stock was held. Any such rules are not likely to be completely accurate, however, and would add complexity to the tax code.

[126] *See* Bankman, *supra* note 95, at 13.

[127] Frank Lyon Co. v. United States, 435 U.S. 561 (1978).

[128] ".... the Government takes the position that the Worthen-Lyon transaction in its entirety should be regarded as a sham. The agreement as a whole, it is said, was only an elaborate financing scheme designed to provide economic benefits to Worthen and a guaranteed return to Lyon. The latter was but a conduit used to forward the mortgage payments, made under the guise of rent paid by Worthen to Lyon, on to New York Life as mortgagee. This, the Government claims, is the true substance of the transaction as viewed under the microscope of the tax laws. Although the arrangement was cast in sale-and-leaseback form, in substance it was only a financing transaction, and the terms of the repurchase options and lease renewals so indicate." 435 U.S. at 573.

solely by tax-avoidance features that have meaningless labels attached, the Government should honor the allocation of rights and duties effectuated by the parties."[129]

5.7.1.3 *Business purpose doctrine*

Business purpose is an important element of the economic substance (or sham transaction) doctrine. In addition, in the corporate reorganization area, a business purpose requirement has been included in the regulations[130] and permeates the case law.[131] One can therefore speak of a business purpose doctrine, primarily in the corporate reorganization area, which has a life of its own separate from the economic substance doctrine. The doctrine holds that a qualifying reorganization must have a business purpose.

5.7.1.4 *Step transaction doctrine and substance over form*

In general terms, the step transaction doctrine calls for consolidating for tax purposes a transaction that involves a number of interconnected steps. Consolidating means disregarding intermediate steps as not having significance. Like the business purpose doctrine, the step transaction doctrine has evolved independently, mostly in the corporate reorganization area, also as a direct offshoot of *Gregory*.[132] The extent of its acceptance is evidenced

---

[129] 435 U.S. at 583-84. United Parcel Service of America, Inc. v. Commissioner, 254 F.3d 1014 (11th Cir. 2001) followed Frank Lyon in rejecting the sham transaction argument. The *UPS* case involved an offshore insurance affiliate. The IRS argued that the whole transaction was a sham, but the court found that the insurance company was a bona fide independent party. Here the IRS may have pushed the sham transaction doctrine too far (although there is precedent for disregarding for tax purposes a partnership that served no business purpose; *see* Kocin v. United States, 87 F.2d 707 (2d Cir. 1951)). The government's alternative argument was that much of the insurance company's profits could be reallocated from it under sec. 482: this issue was to be decided on remand.

[130] Treas. Reg. §§ 1.368-1(c), 1.368-2(g). In the U.K., section 137 of the TCGA 1992 requires that a reorganization be effected for bona fide commercial reasons and must not form part of a scheme of which the main purpose or one of the main purposes, is avoidance of tax. *See* Tiley (2000) at 707. It may be that this U.K. anti-avoidance rule was inspired by the U.S. rules.

[131] *See* Bittker & Eustice (2000) at ¶ 12.61[1].

[132] *See* Bittker & Eustice (2000) at ¶ 12.61[3].

by the *MacDonald's Restaurant*[133] case, in which the taxpayer successfully applied it against the Commissioner and contrary to the form of the taxpayer's own transaction. That case involved a merger in which the shareholders of the acquired company subsequently sold the MacDonald's shares they received in the merger. The taxpayer argued that the transaction did not qualify as a tax-free merger (even though it literally complied with the statutory requirements), because if the subsequent sale was considered as part of the reorganization under the step-transaction doctrine, then the selling shareholders did not have the continuity of interest in the surviving company which the merger rules required. The court agreed with the taxpayer, finding that the step-transaction doctrine could be applied even where there was not a legally binding commitment for the shareholders to sell their shares.[134] The step transaction doctrine has become a routine part of administrative practice, particularly in the corporate reorganization area.[135]

The substance-over-form doctrine is a more general principle of tax law of which the step-transaction doctrine is a part.[136] Courts use the doctrine to disregard the legal form of a transaction in favor of its underlying economic substance. A leading case for substance-over-form is *Court Holding*.[137] In

---

[133] McDonald's Restaurants of Illinois, Inc. v. Commissioner, 688 F.2d 520 (7th Cir. 1982).

[134] The court discussed three judicially developed standards for application of the step-transaction doctrine: "under the 'end result test,' 'purportedly separate transactions will be amalgamated with a single transaction when it appears that they were really component parts of a single transaction intended from the outset to be taken for the purpose of reaching the ultimate result.'... A second test is the "interdependence" test, which focuses on whether 'the steps are so interdependent that the legal relations created by one transaction would have been fruitless without a completion of the series.'... Finally the "binding commitment" test most restricts the application of the step-transaction doctrine... it was formulated to deal with the characterization of a transaction that in fact spanned several tax years and could have remained 'not only indeterminable but unfixed for an indefinite and unlimited period in the future, awaiting events that might or might not happen.'" 688 F.2d at 524-25.

[135] *E.g.,* Rev. Rul. 2001-46, 2001-42 I.R.B. 321.

[136] *See MacDonald's Restaurants*, 688 F.2d at 524. The U.S. Supreme Court has long recognized "the importance of regarding matters of substance and disregarding form in applying the...income tax laws." United States v. Phellis, 257 U.S. 156, 16 (1921).

[137] Commisioner v. Court Holding Co., 324 U.S. 331 (1945). *See also* Bush Brothe. & Co. v. Commissioner, 73 T.C. 424 (1979) (discussing whether the determinatic that the sale was made by the corporation is a factual question or whether instead th sale could be imputed to the corporation where a tax avoidance motive underl structuring the sale as being carried out by the shareholder).

that case a corporation owned a building and negotiated for its sale. When it became apparent that a sale by the corporation would attract a large tax, the corporation distributed the property to its shareholders in liquidation, and the shareholders then sold the property to the intended purchasers. The Court stated that:

> The incidence of taxation depends upon the substance of a transaction. The tax consequences which arise from gains from a sale of property are not finally to be determined solely by the means employed to transfer legal title.... A sale by one person cannot be transformed for tax purposes into a sale by another by using the latter as a conduit through which to pass title. To permit the true nature of a transaction to be disguised by mere formalisms, which exist solely to alter tax liabilities, would seriously impair the effective administration of the tax policies of Congress.
>
> It is urged that respondent corporation never executed a written agreement, and that an oral agreement to sell land cannot be enforced in Florida because of the Statute of Frauds.... But the fact that respondent corporation itself never executed a written contract is unimportant, since the Tax Court found from the facts of the entire transaction that the executed sale was in substance the sale of the corporation.[138]

In the particular area of corporate distributions of appreciated property to shareholders, the *Court Holding* doctrine is now irrelevant since such distributions are now taxable.[139] But the basic principle that courts apply the tax laws to the "substance of a transaction" remains a mainstay of U.S. tax law. A typical area of its application is in distinguishing debt from equity: U.S. courts do not accept a debt instrument as such but go behind it to ascertain whether it is in substance equity. The determination is highly factual. As a leading corporate tax lawyer has pointed out, however, while it is true to say that in U.S. tax law substance prevails over form, it is equally true that in some contexts form prevails over substance.[140] To tell when the form will be disregarded in favor of the substance and when the form will be respected requires a careful study of the precedents and good judgment, and the answer is not always obvious.

---

[138] 324 U.S. at 334.
[139] I.R.C. §§ 311(b), 336.
[140] Steinberg, *Form, Substance and Directionality in Subchapter C*, 52 Tax Law. 457 (1999).

5.7.2 UNITED KINGDOM

5.7.2.1   Duke of Westminster: *Tax avoidance approved*

Unlike the U.S. courts, the U.K. courts have traditionally been unwilling to fashion judge-made rules to combat tax avoidance schemes. In the classic *Duke of Westminster* case,[141] the House of Lords refused to look through the form to the substance of a transaction. This case is often cited for the proposition that taxpayers are entitled to arrange their affairs so as to pay the least tax allowed by law, but such an abstract statement fails to convey the full flavor of this entertaining case.

In order to understand the case, some background on the then-prevailing U.K. tax rules concerning annuities is needed. These rules were flawed, and have since been amended.   In considering the case, one can reflect on the extent to which it was simply a result of flawed rules for taxing annuities, or reflects a blinkered judicial approach that allowed the form of a tax avoidance transaction to be respected.   Perhaps both elements are responsible. Avoidance transactions often take advantage of structural flaws in the system. The question is whether the courts will allow taxpayers to take full advantage of those flaws.

The basic concept for the then-prevailing annuity rules was that when a taxpayer granted an annuity to another person, the transaction succeeded in assigning income of the taxpayer to that other person. This meant that the recipient of the annuity payments was taxed on them, and the grantor of the payments could deduct them from his income. Such a deduction was allowed regardless of whether the annuity payments represented a business expense by the payor.   Most other countries have, either by statute or judicial decision, recognized the avoidance potential in allowing taxpayers to so easily assign their income to another, but this had not been recognized by Parliament at the time *Westminster* was decided.   Indeed, even now the basic conceptual structure for taxing annuities remains, although it has been limited by so many exceptions that the avoidance potential of annuities has now essentially been eliminated.[142]

---

[141] [1936] A.C. 1.

[142] For example, in the case of an annuity written by one individual in favor of another outside a business context, the annuity payments are no longer taxable to the recipient and they are not deductible by the payor.

In *Westminster,* the House of Lords considered a tax planning scheme devised by advisors to the Duke which allowed him to convert wages paid to his gardeners and other household staff into tax deductible amounts. This was accomplished quite simply. The Duke executed deeds of covenant whereby he agreed to pay to each employee a weekly sum for a period of seven years. After the transaction, each member of the staff continued in employment, but his salary was reduced by the amount payable under the covenant. The House of Lords refused to agree with the government's argument that the payments were in the nature of compensation for services. Each employee but one had signed a somewhat ambiguous letter which stated that "there is nothing in the deed to prevent your being entitled to and claiming full remuneration for such future work as you may do, though it is expected that in practice you will be content with the provision which is being legally made for you for so long as the deed takes effect, with the addition of such sum (if any) as may be necessary to bring the total periodical payment while you are still in the Duke's service up to the amount of the salary or wages which you have lately been receiving."[143]

Lord Atkin (dissenting) found that this letter was contractual and established that payments under the deed were remuneration for employment. In the case of the employee who had not signed such a letter, Lord Atkin considered that "it appears necessary to treat the legal relations between him and the Duke in respect of the payment of 2000*l.* [pounds] a year as governed by the deed alone"[144]—i.e. the payment would be deductible. In other words, *even Lord Atkin was prepared to allow the legal form adopted by the taxpayer to govern*, but he found a hook in the letter signed by the employees to treat payments under the deed as contractually agreed compensation. The majority of the Court[145] was, however, unwilling to infer such a contract from the letter: "I cannot think that a letter so framed can be construed as constituting a contract that the payee would serve the Duke upon terms in contradiction of the language of the letter—namely, that he should be entitled to less than the salary or wages which he had been then lately receiving."[146] The Court also rejected the view that "in revenue cases there is a doctrine that the Court may ignore the legal position and regard what is called 'the substance of the matter'."[147] "The sooner this misunderstanding is dispelled, and the supposed

---

[143] [1936] A.C. at 11-12.

[144] [1936] A.C. at 16.

[145] Quotes are from the opinion of Lord Tomlin.

[146] [1936] A.C. 18-19.

[147] [1936] A.C. 19.

doctrine given its quietus, the better it will be for all concerned, for the doctrine seems to involve substituting "the uncertain and crooked cord of discretion" for "the golden and streight metwand of the law. Every man is entitled if he can to order his affairs so as that the tax attaching under the appropriate Acts is less than it otherwise would be....This so-called doctrine of 'the substance' seems to me to be nothing more than an attempt to make a man pay notwithstanding that he has so ordered his affairs that the amount of tax sought from him is not legally claimable."[148]

The opinion by Lord Wright left open the possibility that in other cases the *sham transaction* doctrine might be used, but rejected the application of that doctrine in this case because there was a finding by the trier of fact that "the deeds are genuine": "If the case were one in which it was found as a fact in regard to each of the deeds in question that it was never intended to operate as a legal document between the parties, but was concocted to cover up the payment of salary or wages and to make these payments masquerade as annuities in order to evade surtax, it may well be that the Court would brush aside the semblance and hold that the payments were not what they seemed. But there is no such finding by the Commissioners."[149]

5.7.2.2 Ramsay: *The tide turns*

Over time, the English courts changed their attitude. The landmark decision is *W.T. Ramsay Ltd. v. Commissioners of Internal Revenue,*[150] but there were indications of a change in approach even earlier.[151] In *Ramsay,* the

---

[148] *Id.*

[149] [1936] A.C. at 29.

[150] [1982] A.C. 300 (1981). Besides the cases discussed below, other cases of note include: IRC v. McGuckian, [1997] 3 All ER 817, [1997] STC 908, 69 TC 1 (HL) (discussing purposive interpretation of tax laws); Fitzwilliam (Countess) v IRC, [1993] 3 All ER 184, [1993] STC 502, HL (complex and to some extent self-cancelling transfer tax scheme upheld); Ingram v. IRC, [1986]Ch 585, [1985] STC 835 (*Ramsay* applied in stamp duty area); Black Nominees Ltd. v. Nicol, 50 T.C. 229, Ch. 1975 (Templeman J.) (attempt to transmute personal earnings into capital through a self-cancelling series of transactions failed); Burmah Oil [1982] STC 30; Moodie v. CIR, [1993] 1 WLR 266, HL; R v. CIR ex parte Matrix Securities Ltd, [1994] STC 272.

[151] The dissenting opinion of Eveleigh LJ in Floor v. Davis, (Court of Appeal) [1978] Ch. 295 was subsequently approved by the House of Lords in *Ramsay* and was a preview of the subsequent 1982 House of Lords decision in *Burmah Oil.* Even earlier, the House of Lords had decided a dividend-stripping case in which the loss or

House of Lords held that the prearranged steps of a tax avoidance scheme could be integrated and treated as a whole where the taxpayer had intended them to operate as such.

Ramsay involved a tax planning scheme purchased from a promoter. "The general nature of this was to create out of a neutral situation two assets one of which would decrease in value for the benefit of the other. The decreasing asset would be sold, so as to create the desired loss; the increasing asset would be sold, yielding a gain which it was hoped would be exempt from tax....At the end of the series of operations, the taxpayer's financial position is precisely as it was at the beginning, except that he has paid a fee, and certain expenses, to the promoter of the scheme. There are other significant features which are normally found in schemes of this character. First, it is the clear and stated intention that once started each scheme shall proceed through the various steps to the end....Secondly, although sums of money, sometimes considerable, are supposed to be involved in individual transactions, the taxpayer does not have to put his hand in his pocket....The money is provided by means of a loan from a finance house which is firmly secured by a charge on any asset the taxpayer may appear to have, and which is automatically repaid at the end of the operation....Finally, in each of the present cases it is candidly, if inevitably, admitted that the whole and only purpose of each scheme was the avoidance of tax."[152]

While denying that the court was applying a substance-over-form doctrine, Lord Wilberforce found: "It is the task of the court to ascertain the

---

disposal of shares sold ex-dividend was disallowed on the basis that it was not a trading loss. F.A. & A.B. Ltd. v. Lupton, [1972] A.C. 634. This decision was later explained by Lord Templeman as follows: "In *Lupton's* case the dealer was not allowed to succeed in a claim for a fiscal loss of £80 because, viewing the transaction as a whole, and taking the dividend into account he had made no loss at all." Ensign Tankers Ltd. v. Stokes, [1992] 1 A.C. 655, 670. Lord Templeman has stated that "The decisive stage in the development of this field of revenue law came with the decision...in *Chinn v. Hochstrasser* [1981] A.C. 533....The case concerned capital gains tax. Tax was payable on a distribution of a trust asset by a trustee to a beneficiary...a scheme was devised to avoid capital gains tax on the transaction. The trustees retired and were replaced by foreign trustees, an appointment was made of the shares to the taxpayer contingent on his surviving by three days and the taxpayer sold his reversionary interest to a foreign company. The taxpayer then purchased the shares from the company...This House...held that upon the true construction of the documents the trustees had disposed of the shares to a beneficiary." *Ensign Tankers*, [1992] 1 A.C. at 671-72.

[152] [1982] A.C. at 321-23.

legal nature of any transaction to which it is sought to attach a tax or a tax consequence and if that emerges from a series or combination of transactions, intended to operate as such, it is that series or combination which may be regarded."[153] Regarding the transaction as a whole, it was appropriate to find that no loss had been realized: "To say that a loss (or gain) which appears to arise at one stage in an indivisible process, and which is intended to be and is cancelled out by a later state, so that at the end of which was bought as, and planned as, a single continuous operation, there is not such a loss (or gain) as the legislation is dealing with, is in my opinion well and indeed essentially within the judicial function."[154]

As stated in a subsequent case by Lord Fraser of Tulleybelton, "The true principle of the decision in *Ramsay* was that the fiscal consequences of a preordained series of transactions, intended to operate as such, are generally to be ascertained by considering the result of the series as a whole, and not by dissecting the scheme and considering each individual transaction separately."[155] In other words, with *Ramsay* the House of Lords adopted a kind of step-transaction doctrine.[156] *Ramsay* involved a self-cancelling transaction with "no commercial justification...no prospect of a profit...[which] was designed to, and did, return the taxpayer to the position which he occupied before it began, except for the payment of the expenses of the scheme."[157] Hence it was a particularly compelling case for application of step-transaction principles.

5.7.2.3   Evolution of the Ramsay doctrine

The doctrine established in *Ramsay* was extended in *Furniss v. Dawson*.[158] Unlike *Ramsay*, the latter case did not involve a self-cancelling scheme. In *Furniss v. Dawson*, the taxpayers had negotiated for a sale of shares to a purchaser named Wood Bastow. Because a direct sale to Wood Bastow would have attracted a tax, the taxpayers decided to structure the deal

---

[153] [1982] A.C. at 323-24.

[154] [1982] A.C. at 326.

[155] Furniss v. Dawson, [1984] A.C. 474, 512.

[156] Lord Diplock's formulation was "a pre-ordained series of transactions (whether or not they include the achievement of a legitimate commercial end) into which there are inserted steps that have no commercial purpose apart from the avoidance of a liability to tax...." CIR v. Burmah Oil Co. Ltd., 54 T.C. 200, 214 (H.L. 1981).

[157] Furniss v. Dawson, [1984] A.C. 474, 522-23 (per Lord Brightman).

[158] [1984] A.C. 474. *See generally* Peter Millett, *Artificial Tax Avoidance: The English and American Approach,* [1986] B.T.R. 327.

by first transferring the shares to a newly incorporated Isle of Man company called Greenjacket, and having Greenjacket sell the shares to Wood Bastow. This would have allowed the tax on the sale to be avoided. The House of Lords held that "[t]he relevant transaction...consists of the two transactions or stages taken together. It was a disposal by the respondents [taxpayers] of the shares in the operating company for cash to Wood Bastow."[159] Or, as put by Lord Roskill, "I am convinced that there was a disposal by the Dawsons [taxpayers] to Wood Bastow in consideration of the payment to be made by Wood Bastow to Greenjacket at the behest of the Dawsons."[160] It was found that "the inserted step was the introduction of Greenjacket as a buyer from the Dawsons [taxpayers] and as a seller to Wood Bastow. That inserted step had no business purpose apart from the deferment of tax..."[161] To draw an American analogy, this case is reminiscent of *Court Holding*:[162] a sale is negotiated by one party, but instead of being carried out directly it is carried out by first transferring the property to another party because it is more advantageous for tax reasons to carry out the transaction in this manner.

In *Craven v. White* the Law Lords faced the question of whether the step transaction doctrine would be applied to combine steps which took place further apart in time, and in some cases involved a change of plans.[163] In a 3-2 decision, Lord Jauncey suggested the following formula as a "tentative guide" to applying the step transaction doctrine:

> A step in a linear transaction which has no business purpose
> apart from the avoidance or deferment of tax liability will be

---

[159] [1984] A.C. at 513 (per Lord Fraser).

[160] [1984] A.C. at 515.

[161] [1984] A.C. at 527 (per Lord Brightman).

[162] *See supra* note 137.

[163] [1989] 1 AC 398. The case involved consolidated appeals in three cases. One case had a very similar fact pattern to *Furniss v. Dawson*, with the major difference being that the parties were uncertain whether the sale to the ultimate purchaser would take place. In this case, two of the Law Lords would have held for the tax authorities. All the Law Lords held for the taxpayer in the second and third cases. In the second case, the sales negotiations were broken off, and the intermediate Isle of Man company (equivalent of Greenjacket in *Furniss v. Dawson*) was incorporated and the property transferred to it at a time when no purchaser was on the horizon. The property was sold about 2 years later. In the third case, property was intended to be sold to one purchaser, and was divided and transferred to five companies preparatory to the sale (the division was advantageous for Development Land Tax purposes), but the sale was then called off. In the following year, however, negotiations recommenced and the sale took place.

treated as forming as part of a pre-ordained series of transactions or of a composite transaction if it was taken at a time when negotiations or arrangements for the carrying through as a continuous process of a subsequent transaction which actually takes place had reached a stage when there was no real likelihood that such subsequent transaction would not take place and if thereafter such negotiations or arrangements were carried through to completion without genuine interruption.[164]

The decision in *Craven v. White* meant that taxpayers could avoid getting caught by the application of *Furniss v. Dawson* by better planning. This may not be an inappropriate result. Tax avoidance transactions generally rely on some weakness or loophole in the law. Where taxpayers exploit such loopholes by using blatant transactions with no business purpose whatsoever, courts can appropriately step in and disregard what the taxpayer is seeking to do. But a line has to be drawn somewhere as to when courts will step in to prevent the exploitation of loopholes. They cannot do so in all cases if the statute remains unamended. At some point, it is legitimate for the courts to rely on Parliament to close loopholes in the law if it considers that appropriate. If Parliament is satisfied by the judicially drawn line, it can let it stand.

Ensign Tankers (Leasing) Ltd. v. Stokes[165] involved a film production scheme in which a limited partnership in form incurred some $11m to produce a film, "Escape to Victory". Maybe the film should have been called "Escape the Taxman." Unfortunately for the investors, the film neither made money nor succeeded in reducing their taxes. The taxpayers sought to qualify for the 100 percent first-year allowance for investment in machinery or plant (which included the master negative of a commercial film). The limited partners put up $3.25m. The rest of the financing came by way of a nonrecourse loan from the production company. The production company incurred expenses, and then made transfers to the partnership under the nonrecourse loan arrangement, which promptly retransferred the money back to the production company as reimbursement for the expenses. Not only were the transfers of cash self-cancelling, and the partnership at risk only as to its cash contribution, but the profit split on film proceeds corresponded to the $3.25m cash contributed: the partnership was entitled to 25 percent of the film proceeds, with 75 percent going to the production company, until the $3.25m

---

[164] [1989] 1 A.C. at 533.
[165] [1992] 1 A.C. 655. *See* Morse & Williams (2000) at 44-47 for a history of the case.

was recovered; thereafter 100% of the proceeds went to the partnership for the purpose of repaying the loans to the production company and when the loan was paid off the partnership was entitled to a 25% share. In other words, once the smoke cleared, the partnership had contributed 3.25m in exchange for a 25% interest in the film, although in form the partnership claimed to have incurred 100% of the production costs and to be entitled to a capital allowance therefor. The lower court judge found that: "In purely financial terms, Victory Partnership was in effect a sleeping partner with a minority interest. It was putting up 25 per cent. of the cost and taking a 25 per cent. equity participation."[166]

Lord Templeman found that "the judge was quite right in his analysis of the true legal effect of the transaction. The transaction was a joint venture and contained no element of loan....a creditor who receives a participation in profits *instead* of repayment of his 'loan' is not a creditor. The language of the document in the latter case does not accurately describe the true legal effect of the transaction which is a capital investment by the 'creditor' in return for a participation in profits."[167] This was "the true effect in law of the scheme documents read as a whole."[168]

What did Lord Templeman mean by "true effect in law"? A hint can be found from his discussion of *Ramsay*. In that case, he found that "[t]he true legal effect of the two transactions treated as a whole was that the taxpayer made neither a gain or a loss."[169] In this statement the terms "gain" and "loss" are not legal terms, in the sense of terms with meanings outside the tax law: they are concepts of tax law. Thus, it appears that the term "true legal effect" means the effect in terms of tax law concepts, these being based on commercial reality.

Lord Goff's opinion supports this view. He "find[s] it impossible to characterize the money paid by [the production company] into the bank account to the credit of V.P. [the limited partnership] as, in any meaningful sense, a loan....It follows that the money paid back to L.P.I. out of the bank account cannot be regarded, on a true construction of the statute, as expenditure incurred by V.P. in the making of the film."[170] "The self-cancelling payments ...are typical examples of artificial transactions, the sole

---

[166] [1992] 1 A.C. at 666.

[167] [1992] 1 A.C. at 666-67.

[168] [1992] 1 A.C. at 668.

[169] [1992] A.C. at 672.

[170] [1992] 1 A.C. at 682.

purpose of which is the avoidance of tax. They can, in my opinion, be properly disregarded for the purposes of tax."[171]

Instead of saying that taxation should be based on the substance of the transaction rather than its form, Lord Templeman preferred to say that the "true legal effect" was that there was no loan. But this is the same thing as saying that in substance there was no loan or that the loan is an "economic sham," to use the words of the U.S. courts.

In its recent decision in *Macniven v. Westmoreland Investments Ltd.*,[172] the House of Lords reassessed the scope of the *Ramsey* principle, finding that it did not "enunciate any new legal principle"[173] that would apply in all cases but was just part of "the established purposive approach to the interpretation of statutes."[174] The Law Lords found that the "*Ramsey* approach" should apply only where concepts were used in the tax laws with a commercial meaning, as opposed to a purely legal meaning.[175] In this context, "legal" is a reference to private law.

In *Westmoreland*, the taxpayer was a company owned by a pension fund. The taxpayer borrowed money from the fund and immediately returned this money by way of payment of accrued interest on previous loans from the

---

[171] [1992] 1 A.C. at 684.

[172] [2001] UKHL 6 (Feb. 8, 2001), 73 T.C. 1.

[173] 73 T.C. at 56 (para. 1).

[174] 73 T.C. at 57 (para.6).

[175] In this decision, Lord Nicholls of Birkenhead summed up the Ramsey decision as follows: "*Ramsay* brought out three points in particular. First, when it is sought to attach a tax consequence to a transaction, the task of the courts is to ascertain the legal nature of the transaction. If that emerges from a series or combination of transactions, intended to operate as such, it is that series or combination which may be regarded. Courts are entitled to look at a pre-arranged tax avoidance scheme as a whole. It matters not whether the parties' intention to proceed with a scheme through all its stages takes the form of a contractual obligation or is expressed only as an expectation without contractual force....Second, this is not to treat a transaction, or any step in a transaction, as though it were a 'sham', meaning thereby, that it was intended to give the appearance of having a legal effect different from the actual legal effect intended by the parties... Third, having identified the legal nature of the transaction, the courts must then relate this to the language of the statute. For instance, if the scheme has the apparently magical result of creating a loss without the taxpayer suffering any financial detriment, is this artificial loss a loss *within the meaning of the relevant statutory provision*?... [A] loss which comes and goes as part of a pre-planned, single continuous operation 'is not such a loss (or gain) as the legislation is dealing with'.... [T]his is an exemplification of the established purposive approach to the interpretation of statutes." 73 T.C. at 56-57 (paras. 2-6).

fund. The statute allowed a deduction for interest only if the interest was paid. The case involved the question whether the transaction described constituted a payment that would give rise to a deduction. (It was advantageous to make a payment because the recipient of the payment (the pension fund) was exempt from tax, and because the payment would give rise to an operating loss carryover that could be used by a person who subsequently acquired the taxpayer.) The government argued that the payment should be disregarded because it had no commercial purpose—the only purpose was tax avoidance. The House of Lords rejected this argument on the basis that the requirement that interest be "paid" should be read with a legal, not a commercial meaning. It refused to accept "an overriding legal principle, superimposed upon the whole of revenue law without regard to the language or purpose of any particular provision,"[176] that tax advantages cannot be obtained on the basis of transactions without commercial purpose, finding that adoption of such a principle would not be appropriate statutory construction.

According to Lord Hoffman, the key question was whether the statute was using a commercial concept or a purely legal concept: "If the statutory language is construed as referring to a commercial concept, then it follows that steps which have no commercial purpose but which have been artificially inserted for tax purposes into a composite transaction will not affect the answer to the statutory question."[177] In this case, payment "was a legal concept and did not have some other commercial meaning."[178]

There was of course ample precedent to have decided *Westmoreland* the other way, and Lord Templeman (now retired) has criticized the decision as ignoring the precedents.[179] Only time will tell whether this decision represents a significant shift in the jurisprudence of the U.K. courts. The result of the case was not surprising. Unlike *Shell Canada,* there was apparently nothing abusive about the loan on which interest had accrued. Like the U.S. Supreme Court in *Frank Lyon,* the House of Lords may have been impressed with the business purpose underlying the initial loan transaction, and content to allow form to prevail on an aspect of an otherwise legitimate transaction. Purely artificial transactions may not benefit from such indulgence. As shown by both the U.S. and the German jurisprudence, form can trump substance occasionally even where courts generally take an

---

[176] 73 T.C. at 64 (para. 29) (Lord Hoffman).
[177] 73 T.C. 69-70 (para. 48) (Lord Hoffman).
[178] 73 T.C. at 77 (para. 69) (Lord Hoffman).
[179] *See* Templeman, *Tax and the Taxpayer*, 117 L. Quarterly Rev. 575, 581 (2001).

economic approach to construing tax statutes.[180] Ultimately, it boils down to a question of whether the courts feel that the taxpayer is abusing provisions of the law.[181] Because this judgment is somewhat subjective, the appearance of occasional pro-taxpayer decisions does not negate a jurisprudencc that generally takes a tough line against tax-motivated transactions.

What does this decision mean and where does it leave the law? Certainly it involves some change in conceptual analysis.[182] The decision might simply stand for the proposition that some concepts in tax laws are used with a purely formal meaning, and hence are not susceptible to a substance-over-form analysis. One example given of a case where a legal meaning was appropriate was that of "a legally defined concept, such as stamp duty payable on a document which constitutes a conveyance on sale."[183] It will not, however, always be predictable when courts will consider words to be used with a legal as opposed to commercial meaning. While the uncertainty may seem disquieting, it is an inevitable feature of a substance-over-form approach.

Although there was not much discussion of *Ensign Tankers* in *Westmoreland*, the latter case may clarify the former. In *Ensign Tankers* the court was applying a commercial view. In finding that there was no loan, the

---

[180] *See supra* note 127 and *infra* note 237; Bittker & Lokken (1999) at ¶ 4.3.3; Steinberg, *supra* note 140.

[181] In Miller v. Commissioner, [2001] 3 NZLR 316 (Privy Council), an appeal from New Zealand dealing with the construction of the New Zealand GAAR (sec. 99), Lord Hoffman explained the choice between using commercial and legal concepts as follows: "It may be more fruitful to concentrate on the nature of the concepts by reference to which tax has been imposed. In many (though by no means all) cases, the legislation will use terms such as income, loss and gain, which refer to concepts existing in a world of commercial reality, not constrained by precise legal analysis. A composite transaction like the Russell scheme, which may appear not to create any tax liability if it is analysed with due regard to the juristic autonomy of each of its parts, can be viewed in commercial terms as a unitary arrangement to enable the company's net profits to be shared between the shareholders and Mr Russell. (Compare MacNiven (Inspector of Taxes) v Westmoreland Investments Ltd [2001] 2 WLR 377.) Their Lordships consider this to be a paradigm of the kind of arrangemen which s 99 was intended to counteract. On the other hand, the adoption of a course o action which avoids tax should not fall within s 99 if the legislation, upon its tru construction, was intended to give the taxpayer the choice of avoiding it in that way."

[182] *See* John Tiley, *First Thoughts on* Westmoreland, [2001] B.T.R. 153.

[183] Para. 39. By comparison, in Italy, registration duties are the one area where a abuse of law principle is available. *See* Maisto, *supra* note 75; Fantozzi (1991) a 179-80. In Spain, stamp duty is imposed based on the "true legal nature of the act c contract." Soler Roch (2002) at 166.

court meant that there was no loan in a commercial sense. *Westmoreland* also clarified the decision in *Furniss v. Dawson.* "Commercially, therefore, the transaction was a transfer by the Dawsons to Wood Bastow in exchange for a payment to Greenjacket."[184] One could just as well substitute "in substance" for "commercially". While Lord Nicholls was at pains to deny that the courts were applying a substance-over-form approach ("Nor is this to go behind a transaction for some supposed underlying substance."[185]), in effect this is what they have been doing. Lord Hoffman was more forthright: "if the legal position is that tax is imposed by reference to a commercial concept, then to have regard to the business 'substance' of the matter is not to ignore the legal position but to give effect to it."[186]

It is clear from *Westmoreland,* as well as earlier cases,[187] that the Law Lords will not use the *Ramsay* doctrine as a rubber stamp on any assessment by the revenue when there is a whiff of tax avoidance in the air. *Ramsay* and subsequent cases are not "a broad spectrum antibiotic which killed off all tax avoidance schemes, whatever the tax and whatever the relevant statutory provisions."[188] But at the same time, *Westmoreland* does not appear to represent a substantial retreat by the Law Lords. They reaffirmed the earlier cases and moreover refused to accept that the rationale of these cases could be confined by any formula beyond that the courts needed to interpret the tax laws so as to give effect to the intention of Parliament.[189] If anything, this solidifies and broadens the *Ramsay* principle.

One might wonder at the implications of citation of American cases in *Westmoreland.*[190] While a broader meaning may be possible, it seems likely that the only intention was to refer to the fact that the U.S. doctrines too were based on statutory interpretation, rather than being independent of the statute.

Therefore it appears that the *Ramsay* doctrine remains alive and well after *Westmoreland*, but only subsequent decisions of the courts can confirm this and delimit the scope of application of the doctrine.[191] It is a doctrine that

---

[184] 73 T.C. at 69. (para. 46).

[185] 73 T.C. at 57 (para. 4).

[186] 73 T.C. at 67 (para. 39).

[187] *E.g.,* Craven v. White, [1989] A.C. 398, and Countess Fitzwilliam v. IRC, 67 TC 614 (H.L. 1993).

[188] 73 T.C. at 70 (para. 49).

[189] See paragraphs 7, 28, 29, 55, 56 of the opinion.

[190] Paragraphs 36, 37, 73 T.C. at 66.

[191] *See, e.g.,* Tony Foley, Case Note, *ABC v. M, a decision of the Special Commissioners*, [2002] B.T.R. 65.

is difficult to reconcile with the *Duke of Westminster* case. Lord Hoffman argued that the *Duke of Westminster* case did not apply in situations where "tax is imposed by reference to a commercial concept."[192] He did not discuss whether a commercial approach should have applied under the facts of that case. In *Ensign Tankers,* Lord Templeman said "I agree with Lord Atkin; gardeners do not work for Dukes on half-wages."[193] In *Furniss v. Dawson*, each of the Law Lords made remarks limiting the *Duke of Westminster* case. Lord Roskill was most graphic:

> 'When these ghosts of the past stand in the path of justice clanking their mediaeval chains, the proper course for the judge is to pass through them undeterred.' 1936, a bare half-century ago, cannot be described as part of the Middle Ages but the ghost of the *Duke of Westminster* [case] and of his transaction, be it noted a single and not a composite transaction, with his gardener and with other members of his staff[,] has haunted the administration of this branch of the law for too long. I confess that I had hoped that that ghost might have found quietude with the decisions in *Ramsay* and in *Burmah*. Unhappily it has not. Perhaps the decision of this House in these appeals will now suffice as exorcism.[194]

5.7.3   OTHER COMMON LAW COUNTRIES

A number of common law countries have adopted statutory general anti-avoidance rules (GAARs), including Australia, Canada, Hong Kong,[195]

---

[192] Paragraph 39, 73 T.C. at 67. *But see* Griffin v. Citibank Investments Ltd., 73 T.C. 352, 373, 377 (High Court, Chancery Division) (*Westminster* has never been overruled and remains binding).

[193] [1992] 1 A.C. at 669.

[194] Furniss v. Dawson, [1984] 1 A.C. 474, 515.

[195] *See* Shiu Wing Ltd v. Commissioner of Estate Duty, Final Appeal (Civil) No. 17 of 1999 (12 July 2000), 2 ITLR 794. This case involved the issue whether a transfer within 3 years of death was a disposition of property situated in Hong Kong. Although the property was located in Hong Kong before commencement of the transactions under scrutiny, it was first transmuted to property located outside Hong Kong by transfer to entities located offshore. The court refused to integrate all the transactions involved so as to characterize them as involving a disposition of Hong Kong property.

Ireland, Israel, Malaysia, New Zealand,[196] Singapore, and South Africa.[197] Statutory anti-avoidance rules may be considered necessary where judges have failed to interpret the law so as to cut off abuse, or where judicial anti-avoidance doctrines are not considered sufficient. The possibility of introducing a statutory GAAR has been discussed in both the U.K.[198] and the U.S.,[199] but so far no action has been taken, in part because it is not clear that a statutory rule would provide an improvement over judicial doctrines. A problem with anti-abuse rules is that they must ultimately be interpreted by courts, who can read them very narrowly: this has happened in Australia[200] and in at least one case in Canada.[201] The attitude of the courts may be

---

[196] *See generally* CCH New Zealand Ltd., New Zealand Master Tax Guide 1097-1124 (2001); CCH New Zealand, Top 100 Questions and Answers on Tax 93-98 (2001). The Inland Revenue Department announced in 1990 that it would apply the GAAR only where an "arrangement frustrates the underlying scheme and purpose of the legislation." Wine-Box report at 3:1:27.

[197] *See* John Prebble, *Trends in Anti-Avoidance Legislation, in* Asian-Pacific Tax and Investment Research Centre, Practical Problems of International Taxation 161 (1990); Income Tax Act (Act 58 of 1962), sec.103 (South Africa). The South African provision is drafted fairly broadly, but is limited to cases where tax avoidance is the principal purpose of the transaction, which could raise issues such as those discussed *infra* note 194.

[198] *See, e.g.,* Tax Law Review Committee, Tax Avoidance (1997); Tax Law Reveiew Committee, A General Anti-Avoidance Rule for Direct Taxes (1999); U.K. Inland Revenue, A General Anti-Avoidance Rule for Direct Taxes: Consultative Document (1998). In the U.K., a GAAR has been introduced for the tonnage tax. *See* Finance Act 2000, Sched. 22, para. 41; Morse & Williams (2000) at 43.

[199] *See* NY State Bar Ass'n Tax Section, Treasury's Proposal to Codify the Economic Substance Doctrine, Tax Notes 937 (Aug. 14, 2000).

[200] *See* TLDD at 47; Ault et al. (1997) at 21-22.

[201] The Tax Court of Canada has concluded that a composite transaction with an overall business purpose is not an avoidance transaction for purposes of the Canadian GAAR. *See* Brian Arnold, *Gutting GAAR*, 21 Tax Notes Int'l 2463 (Nov. 27, 2000) (discussing the Canadian Tax Court case Canadian Pacific Ltd. v. R. (Oct. 13, 2000), 3 ITLR 238 (2001), aff'd, 4 ITLR 588 (Fed. Ct. App. Dec. 21, 2001). The case involved borrowing in a weak foreign currency. The court found that there was a business purpose for the borrowing, and that the transaction could not be split up into components in order to identify component transactions that were made primarily for tax avoidance. *See also* Larry Chapman and Richard Marcovitz, *Weak-Currency Borrowing Transactions*, 49 Can. Tax J. 961, 966-67 (2001). For an overview of application of the GAAR in Canada, see Hogg et al. (2002) at 572-87.

difficult to predict. For example, in Jabs Construction Ltd. v. R.,[202] the taxpayer was involved in litigation with a business partner (Callahan) and settled it by agreeing to transfer to Callahan certain properties. Since the transfer would have led to a substantial taxable gain, the taxpayer instead transferred the properties to a private foundation controlled by the taxpayer's major shareholder, which shortly thereafter sold the properties to Callahan. Under Canadian tax law, the transfer to the foundation was allowed to take place at a value equal to the adjusted cost base of the property, so that the taxpayer did not have a taxable gain. The court held that this transaction did not involve an abuse of the Act (therefore sec. 245(4) rendered section 245 inapplicable), since the transaction did nothing more than take advantage of the rule allowing the transfer to take place at cost. The court's analysis ignored, however, the transitory nature of the foundation's ownership and the circumstance that the taxpayer had already agreed to transfer the properties to Callahan. The interposition of the foundation could easily have been seen as an abusive step taken solely for tax avoidance. However, the court refused to apply sec. 245, stating that "section 245 is an extreme sanction. It should not be used routinely every time the minister gets upset just because a taxpayer structures a transaction in a tax effective way...."

By contrast, in OSFC Holdings Ltd. v. R.,[203] the court applied sec. 245 in a case involving a taxpayer engaged in mortgage lending which was being liquidated. Because it was unable itself to use the accrued losses on its loan portfolio, the company formed a partnership with a newly created subsidiary to which it transferred a portfolio of properties. The partnership interests were then sold to a purchaser who could use the tax losses. Under the rules for partnership taxation, the arrangement shifted the losses to the purchaser. The court upheld the application of the GAAR, sec. 245. It found that the primary purpose for creation of the partnership was to obtain a tax benefit. In so doing, the court applied an objective standard, which required the taxpayer to "produce an explanation which is objectively reasonable that the primary purpose for the series of transactions was something other than to obtain the tax benefit." The court also noted that the statute "is carefully worded to make it clear that the recipient of the tax benefit need not be the same person who enters into, or orchestrates, the transaction...." Finally, the court held that the tax result sought was contrary to the scheme of the Act, so that the exception in sec. 245(4) did not apply." The decision was affirmed by the court of appeal, which found that the purchase of the partnership

---

[202] Tax Court of Canada (June 24, 1999), 2 ITLR 552 (2000).

[203] Tax Court of Canada (June 25, 1999), 2 ITLR 522 (2000).

interest was part of a series of transactions (including under the statute, related transactions) resulting in a tax benefit.[204]

An illustration of a purposive interpretation of New Zealand's general anti-avoidance rule is the *Challenge Corporation* case.[205] This case involved the purchase of the stock of a corporation with losses accrued in previous years. The purchasing corporate group sought to take a deduction for these losses on the basis of the group relief rules. Although the rules were literally complied with, the Privy Council found that the group relief rules were not intended to allow the deduction of a loss arising in a prior year, and that the purchase of the shares was therefore a tax avoidance transaction which fell afoul of the general anti-avoidance rule of the New Zealand Income Tax Act. The court stated that the group relief rules (Sec. 191 of the Act) were "intended to give effect to the reality of group profits and losses. When one member of a group makes a profit of $5.8 million and another member of a group makes a loss of $5.8 million then the reality is that the group has made neither a profit nor a loss and that the members of the group should not be liable to tax. Section 191 in these circumstances is not an instrument of tax avoidance. But in the present circumstances the reality is that the Challenge group [the purchasers] never made a loss of $5.8 mission. A loss of $5.8 million was made by Perth [the loss company] and that loss fell on Merbank [the seller] before the taxpayer contracted to buy Perth. Section 191 in these circumstances is an instrument of tax avoidance which falls foul of section 99 [the general anti-avoidance provision]."[206]

5.7.4 FRANCE

The French courts have developed, specifically for tax purposes, the doctrine of abnormal management act, an act which "makes the enterprise responsible for an expense or a loss, or deprives the enterprise of income, without being justified by a business purpose."[207] This concept can cover situations that may be covered by separate rules in other systems, for example, in the U.S. system, section 482, the concept of abnormal

---

[204] *See* Hogg et al. (2002) at 578-79.

[205] Commissioner of Inland Revenue v. Challenge Corporation Ltd., WLR, 9 Jan. 1987 (Privy Council, Appeal from the Court of Appeal of New Zealand, Oct. 20, 1986)

[206] [1987] WLR at 28.

[207] Conseil d'Etat, Jan 5, 1985. *See* Ault et al. (1997) at 47; Cozian (1999) at 92-117.

compensation, the concept of business purpose, or the concept of ordinary and necessary business expenses.

The *abus de droit* (abuse of law) rule was codified in 1941, and is currently embodied as *Livre de procédures fiscales* art. L. 64:[208]

> Acts which conceal the true purport of a contract or agreement with the assistance of clauses:
>
>> a. which lead to lower amounts of registration duty or real estate registration tax;
>>
>> b. which disguise either the earning or the transfer of profits or income; or
>>
>> c. which permit the complete or partial avoidance of the payment of turnover tax corresponding to transactions carried out pursuant to a contract or agreement,
>
> cannot be relied on as against the tax administration.
>
> The administration has the right to restore the true nature of the transaction in question....

This provision has two prongs:

- *Simulation*

- *Fraude à la loi*: where the sole purpose of a transaction is to obtain a tax benefit.

The second prong was approved by the Conseil d'Etat only in 1981.[209] The provision is not used frequently – less than two dozen cases per year are heard by the commission responsible for appeals under this article.[210] The

---

[208] *See* David et al. (2000) at 173-81; TLDD at 49.

[209] *See id.*; Cozian (1999) at 31-34. The court referred to transactions that "could have been inspired by no other motive than to avoid or reduce the fiscal burden which the interested person, if he had not entered into these transactions, would have normally borne, having regard to his situation and his actual activities." In other words, if there is any purpose for the transaction other than tax avoidance, the provision should not apply. In terms of the civil law, the doctrine has been explained as follows: "Those subject to administration may violate the spirit of the law if, solely for the purpose of obtaining the advantages linked to a situation which, by dint of a text, gives the right to such advantages, they place themselves in this situation and claim the benefit while refusing to accept the consequences which the legislator had in mind when he contemplated the corresponding advantages." R. Odent, *quoted in* David et al (2000) at 174.

[210] *See* Sébastian Moerman, *The Theory of Tax Abuse*, 27 Intertax 284, 288-89 (1999). *See generally* David et al. (2000) 173-83. In the period 1990-95 this commission (*comité consultatif de répression des abus de droit*) rendered 133 decisions. The plurality of cases (51) involved gifts disguised as sales; 45 cases involved fictitious

consultation of this commission is practically obligatory for the tax administration since absent such consultation the administration has the burden of proving abuse of law.[211] The provision is drafted poorly in the sense that it only applies in specified cases rather than generally for purposes of taxation. This can raise disputes as to the applicability of the provision.[212] On the other hand, even though the article literally applies only to contracts or agreements, it has been read to apply more broadly.[213] Judicial abuse-of-law doctrines may also apply interstitially in areas not covered by art. L 64. The procedural protections available to the taxpayer make it important for the administration to distinguish in litigation on what theory it is relying to support an assessment.[214]

The French tax administration has been frustrated by the courts in a number of cases in its attempt to apply art. L. 64. For example, the courts have refused to recharacterize under this provision the sale of the shares of a company as a sale of its assets.[215] The Court of Cassation has also refused to collapse an exchange of assets for shares which were subsequently redeemed into a sale of the assets.[216] The courts have also refused to apply the provision to transactions were there was a motivation other than tax avoidance.[217]

Perhaps the most remarkable failure of the courts to apply article L. 64 was the case of so-called "turbo funds." These involved investment funds where the taxpayer made an investment just before distributions were made and sold the shares just afterwards. Under the applicable tax rules, the taxpayer received a taxable distribution, but could offset the loss realized on the sale, resulting in a wash. However, under an administrative instruction, the taxpayer became entitled to a tax credit, so that a transaction which was approximately a wash in economic terms generated a substantial tax benefit.

---

tax credits under a tax avoidance scheme known as "turbo" funds. *See* Gilles Bachelier & Eve Obadia, Le Contentieux Fiscal 68 (1996). Nearly 90% of the decisions were in favor of the tax administration.

[211] *See* Bachelier & Obadia, *supra* note 210, at 51.

[212] *See id.* at paras. 101-103; Cozian (1999) at 61.

[213] *See* Cozian (1999) at 58.

[214] *See* Deboissy, *supra* note 66, at 78-79. For example, the administration may be in a position to apply either art. L. 64 rule or the abnormal management act doctrine, but the procedures for the two are different and the case may be thrown out on procedural grounds if the administration changes its mind. *See* Cozian (1999) at 45-46.

[215] *See* Deboissy, *supra* note 66, at 188-202; Cozian (1999) at 30.

[216] *See id.* at 74-75.

[217] *See id.* at 71.

The tax administration attempted to apply art. L. 64, but the *Conseil d'Etat* held that this provision did not apply, since art. L. 80A provided that the taxpayer could rely on administrative instructions.[218] The paradoxical result is that the taxpayer is allowed to exploit the literal language of administrative instructions even in cases where a similar attempt to exploit the literal language of the law would fail by reason of the abuse of law rule. The decision did not, however, undercut the application of art. L. 64 where administrative instructions are not involved.

5.7.5   GERMANY

In Germany, article (*Paragraph* or §) 41 of the tax code provides that transactions that are legally inoperative are taxed if they have an economic result. It also states that fictitious transactions are disregarded for tax purposes.[219] This provision should be applied fairly restrictively to transactions that are really sham transactions.[220] In the case of arrangements that are put on paper, the question is whether the parties intended these arrangements to create legal consequences. Article 41 applies only if there was an understanding for them not to. "The introduction of a so-called straw man does not lead to a fictitious transaction if a specific civil law structure must be chosen in order to attain the desired goal."[221]

A broader anti-abuse rule is found in Article 42: "The tax laws cannot be avoided by the misuse of legal construction opportunities. Where such a misuse is found, the tax consequences shall be such as would follow from a legal construction that is appropriate to the economic circumstances." A leading commentator explains that "tax avoidance is the misuse of legal constructions through the choice of a legal construction that is inappropriate

---

[218] *See* Cozian (1999) at 81-87.

[219] Abgabenordnung § 41:

(1) If a legal transaction is inoperative or if it becomes inoperative, this is irrelevant for taxation, to the extent and for so long as the parties allow the economic results of this legal transaction to take effect. This rule does not apply if the tax laws provide to the contrary.

(2) Fictitious transactions and actions are not taken into account for taxation. If a fictitious transaction conceals a different legal transaction, then the concealed legal transaction is taken into account for tax purposes.

[220] *See* Tipke/Kruse, AbgabenordnungKommentar, commentary to § 41 (looseleaf).

[221] *Id.* at para. 68.

to the economic transaction for the purpose of tax reduction."[222] Four elements are therefore involved: (1) misuse, (2) legal construction, (3) inappropriateness, and (4) tax avoidance. According to Tipke/Kruse, the concept of misuse actually includes elements (3) and (4); in other words, where these elements are not present, then a construction is simply used, not misused.[223] "Legal construction opportunities" primarily refers to opportunities under civil law, such as entering into contracts, unilateral declarations of will, and in general so-called "real acts."[224] It would also cover constructions under public law and tax law. Article 42 would not apply where the tax law depends on "a particular legal relationship as such without regard to the economic background."[225] A legal construction is "inappropriate" if it serves no economic purpose, is done only for tax avoidance purposes and does not serve other (nontax) purposes.[226] Unnecessarily complicated steps in a transaction can be considered as inappropriate constructions.[227]

Where the taxpayer has a business purpose, then the most appropriate legal construction generally will be a simple, direct, and uncomplicated manner of achieving this purpose.[228] However, article 42 does not necessarily require the taxpayer to take the most direct path; there may be more than one appropriate path to a particular goal.[229] The fact, however, that a particular legal construction is used because it has tax advantages does not render it subject to article 42, if there is a reasonable business purpose.[230] Article 42

---

[222] *Id.* § 42, para. 23. For a general discussion of § 42, as well as other aspects of interpretation of tax law, see Jörg-Dietrich Kramer, *Abuse of law by tax saving devices*, Intertax 96 (Feb. 1991). *See also* Jörg-Dietrich Kramer, *Tax Avoidance, Tax Evasion, and Tax Fraud – German National Rules*, 23 Tax Notes Int'l 1085 (Aug. 27, 2001); Franz Klein, Abgabenordnung 246-81 (2000).

[223] Tipke/Kruse, *supra* note 220, at § 42, para. 30.

[224] *Id.* at § 42, para. 28

[225] *Id.* at § 42, para. 26. An example given by Tipke/Kruse is the state of being married. There is an analogy here to the House of Lords decision in MacNiven v. Westmoreland Investments (2001), where the court held that where a term in the tax laws was used with a legal, and not a commercial meaning, anti-avoidance doctrines would not apply if the legal form was complied with.

[226] Tipke/Kruse, *supra* note 220, para. 33. BFH decision of Oct. 29, 1997, BFHE 184, 476.

[227] *Id.* para. 34.

[228] *Id.*

[229] *Id.* para. 43.

[230] *Id.* para. 39.

applies only where there is a tax avoidance purpose, but this is normally determined on an objective rather than on a subjective basis.[231]

The following specific examples of application of article 42 by the courts[232] show how broadly the provision has been read and the diversity of situations where it has been applied:

- A father makes a "gift" of a specified sum out of his capital account in a partnership to his minor child under the condition that the amount is relent to the father for use in the business under a long-term loan. This was found to be an inappropriate structure.

- "It is also abusive within the meaning of § 42 if a mother transfers an apartment to her son gratuitously and the son rents it back to her. This case is treated under § 42, second sentence, as if the mother had transferred the apartment to her son with reservation of a usufruct."

- An abusive case would be the planned acquisition of two apartments of equal value combined with their reciprocal leasing, or the lease to a family friend who leases it back to close relatives.

- If a taxpayer withdraws property from a business for no business reasons shortly before the valuation date for purposes of a tax based on the value of the business, and shortly thereafter contributes the property to the business again, this is an inappropriate transaction.

- Prepayment of expenses for services to be performed only a number of years later is inappropriate and does not count as part of business expenses for the year of payment.

- It is also inappropriate if one partnership fixes its fiscal year in such a way that it ends one year before the fiscal year of a sub-partnership, solely for the purpose of causing a one-year deferral of taxation of the income of the sub-partnership.

- Reciprocal leases to establish the fact of renting out in order to be able to deduct loans and other costs as business expenses are inappropriate constructions.

- An employer acts in an abusive manner where he splits up an employment relationship by employing his own employees through another company which he sets up.

---

[231] *Id.* para. 44.

[232] They are all taken from Tipke/Kruse, *supra* note 220, commentary to § 42. I do not include specific citations, since this can't be done properly without getting encyclopedic; those interested in the details should consult the available literature.

- There is abuse where a taxpayer transfers a partnership interest to a corporation at book value and it immediately thereafter withdraws from the partnership in exchange for a cash payment.

- "A 'chain donation' occurs where one spouse transfers a portion of his property directly to his children and another portion to his spouse, who in turn transfers it to the children....This has always been considered a classic case of tax avoidance" and will be recharacterized for gift tax purposes.

- The transfer of shares in a corporation which owns real property (instead of direct transfer of ownership of the property) has been considered tax avoidance.[233]

- The transfer of property to a corporation incorporated in a tax haven would be considered an inappropriate construction where the corporation serves no business purpose and carries out no activity independently.[234]

- The establishment of an entity in a treaty partner solely for treaty shopping purposes would also call into question § 42.[235]

As can be seen from these examples, the German courts have felt it warranted to apply § 42 to a broad range of cases, and have allowed the tax administration to use § 42 to address many different types of tax avoidance in a flexible manner. This marks a contrast with most other countries, where specific anti-abuse provisions have had to be enacted to deal with the same or similar types of tax avoidance transactions. At the same time, the open-endedness of § 42 means that it is not possible to predict with certainty in which cases the courts will be willing to apply this provision.

Recent years have witnessed a tendency on the part of the BFH to apply § 42 somewhat more narrowly.[236] For example, the court found that the provision did not apply in the case of an Irish financial services company, even though most of the activities of the company were outsourced through a

---

[233] *Id.* para. 96.

[234] *Id.* para. 98; Schaumburg (1998) at 423-30; .

[235] Tipke/Kruse, *supra* note 220, para. 101. See also the Austrian court's application of the analogous Austrian provision to the issue whether the recipient of dividends was the beneficial owner. N AG v. Regional Tax Office for Upper Austria, Decision of the Austrian Supreme Administrative Court of 26 July 2000, 2 ITLR 884.

[236] *See* Andreas Kowallik & Nicholas Hasenoehrl, *German Courts Rule on Antiabuse Law Transactions*, 22 Tax Notes Int'l 614 (Feb. 5, 2001); Weber-Grellet, *supra* note 3, at 222-25.

management contract.[237] The court also found that the sale of shares just before the end of a fiscal period was not abusive.[238]   The court also departed from its earlier jurisprudence and held that a rental on arm's-length terms to an adult child who was still required to be supported by the parents would be respected.[239] (The court suggested that the rental would not be respected where the parents and child form part of the same household.) The court justified this result on the basis that the civil code allowed the parents the choice of providing support either in cash or in kind, so that an in-kind provision of support could not be seen as abusive. Previously, the court had disregarded under § 42 the rental of housing by parents to their children whom the parents are obliged to support (the rental can be tax advantageous as it often gives rise to a tax loss).

Article 42 is not the only tool the courts use to strike down abusive transactions.   The court can apply a substance-over-form approach to interpretation of the tax laws or use other available interpretative techniques without invoking § 42, and this approach of using statutory interpretation as a first recourse before turning to § 42 has become more dominant in recent years.[240] For example, in a case where a partner withdrew money from a partnership, made a gift to a child, and conditioned the gift on the child relending the money to the partnership, the Federal Tax Court has denied a deduction for interest on the loan, on the basis that payment of interest cannot be considered a business requirement in such a case.[241] The same result followed where the loan back to the partnership was not a condition of the gift, but was part of a prearranged plan. The court has held that the existence of a prearranged plan in this context must be determined according to all the relevant circumstances, and could not be inferred from the fact alone that the loan to the partnership followed fairly closely after the gift.[242] It is interesting

---

[237] *See* BFH decision of Jan. 19, 2000, BStBl 2001 II 222. The decision involved a number of factors, including a factual view that the company was not a mere letterbox company, the interaction with specific anti-avoidance rules (the CFC rules were not applicable under the facts; *see* 5.8.1 *infra*), and the fact that the company being attacked as a tax haven entity was established in another EU State.

[238] *See* BFH decision of Oct. 11, 2000, BStBl 2001 II 22.

[239] *See* BFH, decision of Oct. 19, 1999, DStR 3/2000 107; decision of Oct. 19, 1999 DStR 3/2000 109.

[240] As Tipke/Lang put it, the purpose of §42 is to fulfill the statutory purpose. I should therefore be resorted to only after teleological interpretative tools have been shown inadequate to deal with a particular avoidance transaction. *See* Tipke/Lang (2002) at 150.

[241] *See* BFH, decision of Jan 22, 2002, DStR 17/2002 716.

[242] *See* BFH, decision of Jan. 18, 2001, DStR 12/2001.

that in a civil law country, the courts do not hesitate to develop judicially made requirements for the deduction of business interest, while in a common-law country like Canada, the Supreme Court found itself incapable of developing common-law requirements for the deduction of business interest in a case like *Shell Canada*. Blanket statements about the role of courts in civil vs. common law countries are therefore difficult to make in the tax area.

5.7.6 OTHER CIVIL LAW COUNTRIES

As discussed above (5.6), a number of civil law countries have accepted for tax purposes the concept of *fraus legis*, a theory initially developed as part of private law. In some countries (e.g., Netherlands) the doctrine is applied by the courts without specific statutory basis. This doctrine, or variants thereof, may also be codified, usually in broad terms. In particular, GAARs have been included in the tax laws of Sweden (1995), Belgium (1993),[243] Brazil (2001),[244] Portugal (1999), Finland,[245] and Spain (1995). Many other civil law countries have neither a judicial nor a statutory GAAR. (I do not attempt a complete catalogue here, however.)

Have the country's courts developed anti-avoidance rules in interpreting the tax laws? To what extent is their scope ascertainable?

5.8 SPECIFIC ANTI-AVOIDANCE PROVISIONS

5.8.1 IN GENERAL

Tax laws are full of rules aimed at cutting off avoidance opportunities. Where these take a mechanical form (for example, the denial of certain deductions), they do not present special problems of administrative or judicial discretion analogous to those involved with general anti-avoidance rules. Sometimes, however, specific anti-avoidance rules are couched in a

---

[243] *See generally* Dassesse & Minne (2001) at 70-73, 185-90. The tax administration has relied on this provision to recharacterize share repurchases as dividends, although its right to do so has been questioned. *See id.* at 187.

[244] Article 116 of the National Tax Code, allowing the tax authorities to disregard simulated transactions, was added in 2001.

[245] *See* Gustaf Lindencrona, Trends in Scandinavian Taxation 42 (1979).

form that is predicated on a tax avoidance motive on the part of the taxpayer. This kind of rule, even though its application may be limited, presents the same kind of conceptual issues as a general anti-avoidance rule. In particular it may require a determination of the presence of a tax avoidance motive or of a business purpose.[246] Examples of such rules are provided below for the U.S. and U.K.

In countries having a GAAR on the books, or where the courts apply judge-made anti-avoidance rules, the question arises as to whether specific rules are needed. Where specific rules exist, they raise questions for application of the general anti-avoidance rules, since the argument can be made that the specific rule was intended to cover the area in question, leaving no room for application of the general rule.[247] This point has been addressed recently in Germany. Earlier thinking had been that the nonapplicability of a specific anti-avoidance provision would not preclude the application of § 42.[248] However, in late 1999 and early 2000, the Federal Tax Court refused to apply § 42 in areas governed by specific anti-avoidance rules, one being the CFC rules[249] and the other being dividend stripping. In the latter case, a specific avoidance rule would have applied, but the rule provided an exception for transactions conducted on the stock exchange. In the particular case, the transactions were conducted over the stock exchange, but not anonymously. The court refused to find that the lack of anonymity should preclude the exception for stock exchange transactions, or could provide a basis for the application of § 42, given that the matter was regulated by the specific anti-avoidance rule.[250] In finding that § 42 would not apply to prevent the avoidance of a specific anti-avoidance rule, the BFH went too far, and §

---

[246] *See, e.g.,* IRC v. Willoughby [1997] 1 WLR 1072 (HL).

[247] In *Challenge, supra* note 205, the court found that New Zealand's general anti-avoidance rule applied even though there was a specific anti-avoidance rule in the relevant statutory provision. The same issue arises, albeit with additional considerations, in the tax treaty context. *See also* Hugh Appleton, *The Interaction Between Paragraph 13 and* McGuckian: *A Descent into the Maelström,* [1999] B.T.R. 86. The court in Winn-Dixie Stores, Inc. v. Commissioner, 254 F.3d 1313 (11th Cir. 2001) found that compliance with a specific anti-avoidance rule which allowed a deduction for interest in the case at hand did not preclude application of the economic substance doctrine.

[248] *See* Tipke/Kruse, *supra* note 220, at para. 20.

[249] *See* BFH decision of Jan. 19, 2000, BStBl 2001 II 222.

[250] *See* BFH decision of Dec. 15, 1999, BStBl 2000 II 527. The court stated that the specific rule takes precedence over § 42 "even then when the acquisition on the stock exchange was carried out exclusively for the purpose of taking advantage of the [exception to the anti-avoidance rule] and to avoid [the rule]."

42 was quickly amended to reverse this decision.[251] While the enactment of specific anti-avoidance rules is understandable (an abuse is observed and the government wishes to cut it off), often they present only a partial solution to the problem because tax planners can find transactions that are not covered by the rule. Such specific rules therefore tend to contribute to the complexity of the tax laws, and to a cycle of continuous refinement of such rules as the government attempts to counteract tax planners, who in turn try to always be one step ahead of the government.[252] Some specific anti-avoidance rules are, however, quite effective and have the advantage of providing greater certainty to taxpayers than necessarily open-ended general anti-avoidance rules.

Where the statute refers to a tax avoidance purpose, what does this mean?

5.8.2 UNITED STATES

Numerous provisions of the Internal Revenue Code refer to a tax avoidance purpose on the part of the taxpayer.[253] For example, Code section 269 denies a deduction for expenses of a corporate acquisition where "the principal purpose for which such acquisition is made is evasion or avoidance of Federal income tax." A number of provisions of the regulations issued to implement the Internal Revenue Code also refer to tax avoidance purpose.[254]

---

[251] A new paragraph (2) was added in 2001, stating: "Paragraph 1 is applicable [in every situation where] its applicability is not explicitly precluded by law." Even after this amendment, the courts will still be faced with the problem of how to apply § 42 in the context of specific anti-avoidance rules. This is because by its terms a transaction runs afoul of § 42 only where that transaction is abusive in nature. Where the taxpayer arranges its affairs so as to avoid the application of a specific anti-avoidance rule, the court must still face the question whether under the circumstances his arrangement is abusive or not.

[252] For example, Canada has enacted specific rules dealing with certain transactions involving weak-currency borrowing. The rules were enacted after court decisions in favor of the taxpayer. They do not provide a comprehensive scheme for taxing foreign-currency borrowing and related hedging. *See* Chapman and Marcovitz, *supra* note 201.

[253] I.R.C. §§ 170(f)(9), 269, 269A, 302(c), 306(b), 355, 357(b), 453(e)(7), 467(b)(4), 32, 542(c), 614(e), 643(f), 877, 1022(g), 1031(f)(2), 1092(c), 1256(e), 1272(a), 551, 2107(a), 2501, 2652(c)(2), 4222(c), 6015(c)(4), 6111, 6662, 7268, 7301, 7341, 872(c).

[254] *E.g.,* Treas. Reg. §1.1275-1(g)(1) (original issue discount).

For example, under Treas. Reg. sec. 1.881-3, the IRS may disregard the participation of an intermediate entity in a financing arrangement, if it participates as part of a tax avoidance plan. "A tax avoidance plan is a plan one of the principal purposes of which is the avoidance of tax imposed by section 881."[255]   A general partnership anti-abuse rule has been promulgated by regulations requiring that each partnership transaction "be entered into for a substantial business purpose,"[256]   that "the form of each partnership transaction must be respected under substance over form principles,"[257] and that "the tax consequences... to each partner of partnership operations and of transactions between the partner and the partnership must accurately reflect the partners' economic agreement and clearly reflect the partner's income."[258] The regulations go on to say that: "If a partnership is formed or availed of in connection with a transaction a principal purpose of which is to reduce...tax...in a manner that is inconsistent with the intent of subchapter K, the Commissioner can recast the transaction...."[259] Probably any one of these conditions would give the IRS sufficient authority to recast abusive partnership transactions. Collectively, they are quite formidable.

5.8.3 UNITED KINGDOM

The U.K. also has a number of specific anti-abuse provisions the application of which turns on the presence of a tax avoidance motive.[260] An example is sec. 703 of the Income and Corporation Taxes Act 1988:

> Where
>
> (a) in any such circumstances as are mentioned in section 704, and
>
> (b) in consequence of a transaction in securities or of the combined effect of two or more such transactions,

---

[255] Treas. Reg. §1.881-3(b)(1). Section 881 imposes a 30% withholding tax on income not connected with U.S. business.

[256] Treas. Reg. §1.701-2(a)(1).

[257] Treas. Reg. §1.701-2(a)(2).

[258] Treas. Reg. §1.701-2(a)(3).

[259] Treas. Reg. §1.701-2(b).

[260] *See generally* Robert W. Maas, Tolley's Anti-Avoidance Provisions (looseleaf 2002).

a person is in a position to obtain, or has obtained, a tax advantage, then unless he shows that the transaction or transactions were carried out either for bona fide commercial reasons or in the ordinary course of making or managing investments, and that none of them had as their main object, or one of their main objects, to enable tax advantages to be obtained, this section shall apply to him in respect of that transaction or those transactions.... [section 703 goes on for another 11 printed pages]

Section 703 applies to deny the benefits of transactions such as dividend-stripping or bond-washing. It can also apply to cases like the sale of shares in one controlled company to another controlled company.[261] The enumeration of the covered transactions is in some cases quite detailed, posing potential problems of interpretation, as well as being subject to the general tax avoidance purpose rule quoted above. There is a special procedure for application of the provision, involving a special tribunal (the section 706 tribunal).[262]

Sections 703 and 704 are part of Part XVII of the Act (Tax Avoidance) which occupy about 140 printed pages of the statute. Some of these contain a motive test, while the application of others is mechanical. Among these are sections 731-734, aimed at dividend-stripping. These generally deny a loss in cases where someone purchases shares or securities and subsequently sells them after receiving a dividend.[263]

At a time when capital gains were not subject to tax (i.e. before 1965), wealthy taxpayers used to buy government securities and sell them just before the next interest date, thus receiving a return in the form of untaxed capital gain. An anti-avoidance provision (sec. 33 of the Finance Act 1927) was enacted to deal with this, but it was difficult to apply in part because it contained a motive test.[264] The matter is now dealt with more

---

[51] *See id.* at para. 1.21; CIR v. Cleary, 44 TC 399 (H.L. 1967).

[52] *See id.* at paras. 1.53, 1.53A.

[53] In the case of a tax exempt body, sec. 733 imposes tax on the dividend. The provisions generally do not apply where the holding period exceeds one month. They do not apply to foreign shares bought in the ordinary course of the taxpayer's share dealing business, if no foreign tax credit is claimed. Sec. 732(4). Thus, a transaction like that in *Compaq* would be impossible in the UK.

[54] *See id.* at paras. 2.1-2.2.

comprehensively by treating the accrued interest as income of the seller (instead of as a capital gain).[265]

Under a provision enacted in 1937, when the owner of shares or securities transfers them with an option to reacquire them, he or she is taxed on the income.[266] In 1938, the provision was extended to cover a sale or transfer of the right to receive interest or dividends.[267] By contrast, in the U.S. this problem was dealt with by judicial decisions (prohibiting assignment of income).

The price differential on a agreement for the sale and repurchase of securities (repo) is treated as interest.[268]

Another provision dealing with the capital gain-ordinary income distinction is section 776, which treats gains as income in the case of real estate or an interest in real estate that is aquired with the sole or main object of realising a gain by directly or indirectly disposing of it.[269]

To stop taxpayers from selling land and leasing it back at an artificially high rent, the deduction for rent in such a case is limited to a fair market value rent.[270]

Extensive anti-avoidance rules apply to trusts,[271] leasing transactions,[272] cross-border transactions,[273] life insurance,[274] capital allowances[275] and other areas. Given the technical way in which they are drafted, they are apt to give rise to litigation.[276]

---

[265] ICTA 1988 s 713.

[266] *See* Maas, *supra* note 260, at para. 3.2; ICTA 1988 s 729.

[267] *See* Maas, *supra* note 260, at para. 3.18; ICTA 1988 s 730.

[268] ICTA 1988 s 730A.

[269] *See* Maas, *supra* note 260, at para. 4.8; ICTA 1988 s 776.

[270] *See* Maas, *supra* note 260, at para. 5.1; ICTA s 779.

[271] See Maas, *supra* note 260, chapter 7; ICTA 1988 ss 660A, 660B, 677, 678; TCGA 1992 ss 71(2), 79A, 74, 76A, Sch 4A, s 76B, Sch 4B, ss 77-79, 165(3)(b).

[272] *See* Maas, *supra* note 260, ch. 8; ICTA 1988 ss 781-785, 384(6)-(8); CAA 1990, 42; FA 1997, 12 Sch; F(No 2)A 1997 ss 44-47 (finance leasing).

[273] *See* Maas, *supra* note 260, chapters 9, 10.

[274] *See id.*, chapter 11.

[275] *See id.*, chapter 13.

[276] *See, e.g.,* Vestey v. I.R.C., [1980] A.C. 1166, which involved the question whether an anti-avoidance rule applied to the transferor of a trust only or also to beneficiaries.

5.8.4 OTHER COUNTRIES

Common law countries (at least those with complex tax statutes) typically include specific anti-avoidance rules that apply only where the tax administration can prove that the taxpayer acted with a tax avoidance purpose.[277] Typically, civil law countries do not adopt this approach. The general reluctance of civil law countries to draft specific anti-avoidance rules which depend on the taxpayer's purpose is a noteworthy difference from common law countries. The feeling may be that if there is a general anti-avoidance rule then specific rules based on a tax avoidance motive would be somewhat redundant, since transactions caught by such rules would normally be caught by the general rule. This would then be a corollary of the general tendency in civil law countries to avoid cluttering the statute with too much detail. That said, civil law countries have not been shy about enacting specific anti-avoidance rules that are mechanical in nature (for example, the rules in Germany concerning expatriation to avoid tax). Unlike the U.S. rules, which refer to a purpose to avoid tax,[278] the German rules simply apply under specified circumstances, making no reference to the taxpayer's purpose.[279] There are a few instances of civil law anti-avoidance rules that come close to being based on tax avoidance purpose. For example, article 238A of the French tax code restricts the deduction of certain forms of passive income paid to entities located in a tax haven, except if the taxpayer can prove that the payments correspond to an operation that is both "real" and "normal."

What anti-avoidance rules can be found in the statute and regulations?

5.9 PROCEDURAL ATTACKS ON TAX SHELTERS

Another approach to tax avoidance that has recently been launched in the U.S. requires certain tax shelters to register with the IRS.[280] The taxpayer

---

[77] *E.g.,* sec. 82 KH, Income Tax Assessment Act 1936 (Australia); secs. 56(4.1), 03(1), 104(7.1), 104(7.2), 129(1.2), 129(3.4), 193(7), 195(7), 256(2.1), Income Tax Act (Canada).

[78] I.R.C. § 877.

[79] *E.g.,* Aussensteuergesetz §2.

[80] I.R.C. § 6111 requires a tax shelter organizer to register the shelter with the IRS. The shelter receives an ID number, which must be included on the investor's return. The organizer must also keep a list of investors and provide this to the IRS if requested. I.R.C. § 6112.

must disclose the shelter on the tax return. This gives the IRS a list of matters to audit. Promoters of potentially abusive tax shelters must keep a list of investors, which is available to the IRS.[281] To provide a coordinated effort, the IRS created an Office of Tax Shelter Analysis.[282]

The initial attempts in the U.S. to require disclosure of tax shelters have been judged not to have been too successful, as relatively few disclosures were made on returns for 2001.[283] Legislation is being considered by Congress to clarify and increase the penalties for failing to disclose tax shelters on returns. The proposed legislation uses the concept of listed transactions. For example, in Notice 2000-51, the IRS published a list of tax shelter transactions.[284] The legislation being considered provides for serious penalties if a taxpayer engages in one of these transactions and does not disclose the transaction on its return. In this context, there is a difficult problem of definition. In order to impose a penalty on the taxpayer for failure to disclose tax shelter transactions, the transactions subject to disclosure must be defined precisely. But this is difficult to do. The U.S. Treasury has used a combination of specific examples of transactions and criteria. In an effort to reduce the burden on taxpayers, it established a number of exceptions to what needed to be disclosed, but many taxpayers interpreted the exceptions broadly and failed to disclose transactions that arguably should have been disclosed. The Treasury has now determined to eliminate some of these exceptions and produce a broader definition.[285]

Another element of the U.S. Treasury's fight against tax shelters is regulations issued under Circular 230, which governs practice of tax advisors before the IRS.[286] The regulations contain requirements for tax opinions relating to tax shelters; for example, the person issuing the opinion must take all the relevant facts and law into account.

The U.S. disclosure rules do not involve any change in the substantive rules; therefore, the matters required to be disclosed can be broadly (but precisely) defined, because an overbroad definition does not harm the taxpayer; it merely requires the taxpayer to flag certain transactions on it

---

[281] I.R.C. § 6112.

[282] *See* Announcement 2000-12, 2000-12 I.R.B. 835 (Feb. 29, 2000).

[283] *See* U.S. Treasury testimony of March 20, 2002 before the Senate Committee o Finance [hereinafter Testimony]; Sheryl Stratton, *U.S. Treasury Issues Plan Combat Tax Shelters,* 25 Tax Notes Int'l 1382 (April 1, 2002).

[284] 2001 I.R.B.-31 (August 20, 2001). *See also* Notice 2000-15, 2000-12 I.R.B. 826.

[285] *See* Testimony, *supra* note 283.

[286] Proposed regulations were issued on Jan. 11, 2001. Treasury has announced th these regulations will be revised and strengthened. *See* Testimony, *supra* note 283.

return.   The proposed legislation, however, increases penalties if the taxpayer's position is not upheld and the taxpayer has failed to make a disclosure. Severe penalties for "abusive tax positions"— with reductions for cases where the taxpayer has made disclosure — have been introduced in New Zealand as well, raising the question of how the line is to be drawn between such abusive tax avoidance and tax evasion.[287]

In 1983, the IRS announced a program whereby abusive tax shelters would be attacked even before tax returns were filed.[288]   The program involves identification of potentially abusive tax shelters by consulting newspapers and other sources. Possible steps to be taken include the issuance of warning letters to investors, the assertion of penalties against the promoters,[289] or filing an action to enjoin the promoters from marketing the shelter.[290]   The Service has been publishing with frequency notices and rulings warning taxpayers that it believes certain transactions do not work to achieve the tax benefits claimed.[291] The current thinking is that the IRS needs more help in this effort by way of disclosure requirements so that it can respond quickly to tax shelters that are being marketed.

A recent IRS approach to tax shelters involves mass settlement offers, whereby the taxpayer agrees to pay a certain portion of the tax involved, while avoiding litigation and penalties. These are targeted to specific tax shelters. An interesting feature is a taxpayer option for binding arbitration.[292]

5.10 ACCOUNTING STANDARDS

Accounting standards are not normally thought of as anti-avoidance rules, but features of some accounting standards bear an uncanny resemblance

---

[287] *See* Adrian Sawyer, *Blurring the Distinction Between Avoidance and Evasion— The Abusive Tax Position,* [1996] B.T.R. 483.

[288] *See* Rev. Proc. 83-78, 1983-2 C.B. 595.

[289] I.R.C. § 6700.

[290] I.R.C. § 7408.

[291] *E.g.,* Rev. Rul. 2002-69 (lease-in lease out transaction); Notice 2001-45, 2001-33 R.B. 129 (basis shifting tax shelter; identification as a listed transaction, *see supra* note 262); Notice 2002-65, 2002-41 I.R.B. 690 (passthrough entity straddle tax shelter).

[292] *E.g.,* Rev. Proc. 2002-67, 2002-43 I.R.B. 1; Announcement 2002-96, 2002-43 R.B. 756 (Oct. 28, 2002); Announcement 2002-97, 2002-43 I.R.B. 757 (Oct. 28, 2002). *See* I.R.C. § 7123(b).

to judicially developed anti-avoidance doctrines. The IASB Framework[293] provides that "information must represent faithfully the transactions and other events it either purports to represent or could reasonably be expected to represent....If information is to represent faithfully the transactions and other events that it purports to represent, it is necessary that they are accounted for and presented in accordance with their substance and economic reality and not merely their legal form."[294] Further, IAS 1 provides that "[f]inancial statements should present fairly the financial position...of an enterprise."[295]

These principles are applied, for example, in Interpretation SIC-27, which finds that "[a] series of transactions that involve the legal form of a lease is linked and should be accounted for as one transaction when the overall economic effect cannot be understood without reference to the series of transactions as a whole" and that "[t]he accounting should reflect the substance of the arrangement." Under IAS 17, leases are classified as finance leases or operating leases based on economic substance. A finance lease is defined as "a lease that transfers substantially all the risks and rewards incident to ownership of an asset."[296] An asset leased under a finance lease is carried on the books of the lessee and is depreciated in the same manner as property owned by the lessee.[297] Another example of the use of economic substance is the requirement to adjust the sales price of property that is sold in combination with an artificially low interest rate.[298] Financial instruments are also classified according to their economic substance, rather than legal form.[299]

Of course, these principles are not applicable to taxation in most countries. However, a few countries base their corporate income tax directly on International Accounting Standards. And many countries base their corporate income tax on national standards for financial accounting, which may have similar principles to those found in IAS.

The "substance over form" approach of IAS goes far beyond what is found in the judicial doctrines discussed in this chapter, since it calls for aggregation of transactions when called for by their economics, not only

---

[293] Framework for the Preparation and Presentation of Financial Statements (Apr. 1989), reprinted in International Accounting Standards Board, International Accounting Standards 2002, at F-1.

[294] *Id.* at F-14-F-15.

[295] *Id.* at 1-10.

[296] *Id.* at 17-8.

[297] *Id.* at 17-14.

[298] *Id.* at 17-19.

[299] IAS 32, *reprinted in id.* at 32-11.

where there was a binding commitment or prearranged plan to carry out the series. And in recharacterizing leases as financing arrangements and hybrid financial instruments as combinations of debt and equity instruments, IAS disregard legal form to an extent found in few tax laws.

At the same time, accounting standards allow considerable flexibility to accountants, providing the opportunity for either understatement or overstatement of income. To some extent, this is an inherent feature of the economic substance approach.   Because economic substance involves business judgment, there can be legitimate disagreement about how to account for a particular situation.   Thus, while the use of financial accounting standards for tax purposes would render certain tax avoidance transactions ineffective, it would open the door to "creative accounting" in other respects.

Chapter 6

TAX ADMINISTRATION AND PROCEDURE

6.1 INTRODUCTION

While there are many cross-country differences in tax procedural rules, beneath the details there is a fair amount of similarity.[1] This should not be surprising, because administrative techniques that have been found to work elsewhere have been adopted by most countries, tax administration being an eminently practical discipline.   An example of this is wage withholding. Virtually all countries require employers to withhold income tax from wages. While there are some differences in methods for the calculation of tax to be withheld and on procedures for payment of the withheld tax to the treasury,[2] the basic approach is similar.

In the context of this substantial similarity, I try to highlight here the more important differences in the law of tax procedure, recognizing that a thorough examination of the details would require a much larger study.

6.2 BASIC ATTITUDES AND PSYCHOLOGY

Substantial differences are found among countries in the operation of the tax administration, often dwarfing any differences on the books. These differences are not so dramatic among the OECD countries, although even here differences in administrative style can be significant.[3] The differences become substantial once developing and transition countries are taken into account.

---

[1] For a general overview of tax administration from an economic perspective, see John Mikesell, *Tax Administration: The Link Between Tax Law and Tax Collections in* Handbook of Public Finance 173 (Fred Thompson & Mark Green eds., 1998).

[2] *See* Van der Heeden, *The Pay-as-You-Earn Tax on Wages, in* TLDD at 564.

[3] *See generally* 65a Cahiers (1980) (The dialogue between the tax administration and the taxpayer up to the filing of the tax return). For a comparative, but now somewhat dated, study of some aspects of tax administration, see L. Hart Wright et al, Comparative Conflict Resolution Procedures in Taxation (1968).

These differences run the gamut of the operation of the tax system. While in countries like the U.S. or Germany corruption among tax officials is virtually unknown, it is rampant in a number of developing and transition countries, with other countries occupying intermediate positions. Corruption obviously plays an important role in terms of whether tax is collected according to law. Also relevant is the extent to which tax officials understand and apply tax law, and with what competence. Here paradoxically the more "advanced" countries like the U.S. might not fare so well, since their tax laws are so complex as to be beyond the ken of the average tax official. In non-OECD countries that have problems retaining civil servants because the salaries paid are hardly enough to survive on, the problem may be a low level of education and competence in the public service, rather than an excessive complexity of the law. In some countries, tax officials may routinely be subject to physical danger when they try to collect tax from taxpayers.[4] Together with these challenges, the tax administrations of many countries lack a culture of effective tax audit. Their auditors may tend to focus on formal matters such as the taxpayer's ability to produce receipts substantiating deductions, rather than probing the legal and economic issues posed by the taxpayer's return. Overall audit policy is also relevant, determining what types of returns will be selected for audit and the audit rate.[5] Post-audit, substantial differences can be found in how well the appeal function works. Finally, while in some countries the payment of a refund, if one is due, is given scarcely any attention since it is so automatic, in others the difficulty of extracting refunds from the government is one of the top tax policy issues. This has been a problem in a number of transition countries and some developing countries, and is a symptom of weak government budget systems.

Even among OECD countries, there are basic differences in the orientation of the tax administration, including changes over time in particular countries. In countries like Canada[6] and later in the U.S., political decisions were made to change the orientation of the tax administration from enforcement to taxpayer service. This has included reorganization of the tax administration according to divisions oriented to particular types of taxpayer.[7]

See, e.g., Tiley (2000) at 73 (in 1996, 26 collectors were killed and 74 injured in Russia, 6 were kidnapped and 41 had their homes burned down).

See, e.g., Albert Rädler, *Germany, in* Ault et al. (1997) at 64 (10,000 field auditors in Germany, implying a high audit rate).

See Brian Arnold, *Canada, in* Ault et al. (1997) at 33.

In the Netherlands, another country that undertook such a reorganization, the five divisions are for private taxpayers, business taxpayers (two regional divisions), large companies, and customs. *See* Matthijs Alink & Victor van Kommer, The Dutch Case: Description of the Dutch Tax and Customs Administration 88-91, 128-50 (1998).

In any country, to understand the law of tax procedure, it is important to learn about how the tax administration functions and the extent to which it complies with legal requirements.

What are the key features of how tax administration works in the country?

6.3 ORGANIZATION OF TAX ADMINISTRATION LAWS

Several typologies can be identified for the organization of tax administration laws. Some countries have separate tax administration provisions in separate substantive tax laws. This is typical for Commonwealth countries. Under such a system, each tax law is stand-alone, containing both the substantive rules and the rules of tax procedure. This is not an optimal approach, as it leads to divergence of procedural rules and duplication of legal norms. The preferred practice is to bring together the procedural rules for all taxes. Those provisions that are peculiar to specific taxes can be dealt with in separate chapters or can be grouped together with the substantive rules for the particular tax. Since 1970, the procedural rules in the U.K. have been consolidated into the Taxes Management Act, and some other Commonwealth countries have taken a similar approach.

The problem does not arise for countries which include all their tax laws in one code.[8] A number of European and Latin American countries have tax codes which contain the general rules for taxation, including procedural and administrative provisions. For these countries "tax code" has a different meaning than for those previously mentioned. It is not a compendium of all the tax laws, but rather a code of the general rules for taxation, with the specific and substantive rules contained in a separate law for each tax. Most of these codes are direct or indirect descendants of the tax code of Germany, which was initially enacted in 1919.

The internal organization of tax administration laws mostly follows the chronology of the process for determining, paying, and collecting tax. This chapter is by and large organized along the same lines.

---

[8] Countries with a comprehensive tax code include France, a number of former French colonies, the United States, most countries of the former Soviet Union, Colombia, the Dominican Republic and the Philippines. For convenience France has separated the rules of tax procedure into a separate volume called the *Livre des Procédures Fiscales* (book of tax procedures), although for practical purposes should be considered part of the tax code.

In what laws can the provisions on tax administration and procedure be found?

6.4 RETURN FILING

Corporations are generally required to file a corporate income tax return regardless of whether they have taxable income in a particular period. In part this is due to the existence of loss carryover rules, but for audit purposes too the tax administration wants to stay on top of all companies. The same is true for VAT. These requirements for corporations are pretty much universal across countries.

The filing rules for individual income tax returns are substantially different. In the U.S., there is almost universal filing, especially since with the earned income tax credit even individuals with low income have an incentive to file.[9] In most OECD countries the percentage of the population that files individual income tax returns is substantially lower. And in developing and transition countries a significant goal of individual income tax policy is to drastically limit the number of individuals filing returns so as not to distract the tax administration from more important tasks, such as collecting tax from businesses. One factor leading to a reduced number of returns in many developing and transition countries is a high tax threshold, so that few taxpayers are liable to tax. In addition, many countries calculate withholding in such a way that taxpayers' liability is satisfied and they do not need to file. Final withholding taxes may be imposed on income such as interest and dividends.

Where returns are filed, countries differ in whether the taxpayer assesses the tax himself or herself. While in the past it was common for the tax administration to assess the tax and then send a bill to the taxpayer, the general (but not universal) trend is for countries to move to self-assessment since this is much more efficient from the point of view of the tax administration.[10] It also allows the tax administration to focus on relatively sophisticated audits instead of the often tedious assessment process. The

---

I.R.C. §6012 requires every individual subject to tax to file, but any individual may file a return. It may be advantageous to do so in order to claim a refund, or simply to qualify for the statute of limitations (which expires three years after the due date, if a return is filed).

See Tiley (2000) at 66-67 (U.K.). The tax is still determined by the tax authorities in France, see Trotabas & Cotteret (1997) at 194, and Germany, see Tipke/Lang (2002) at 432.

adoption of an efficiently functioning self-assessment system is, however, still a work in progress in many countries.

What are the return filing requirements for the various taxes? To what extent is there self-assessment? What are the requirements and possibilities for amended returns?

6.5 WITHHOLDING AND INFORMATION REPORTING

Most countries have shifted the collection burden for a good deal of the taxes to the private sector in the form of withholding obligations. This is true of the individual income tax on wages, social security and other payroll taxes, and sales and excise taxes where the person collecting the tax (the seller) is not the same as the one on whom the incidence of the tax is designed to fall (the consumer). In respect of payments where the payor is not required to withhold, an obligation is often imposed to report the payment to the tax administration (information reporting).

Virtually all countries withhold tax on wages (France and Switzerland are exceptions).[11] A few countries, such as Colombia, impose extensive withholding on other types of domestic payments. Withholding on payments to nonresidents is, of course, typical, and the resulting tax normally is a final one. The main difference, therefore, lies in the extent to which withholding is used as a collection device in the case of domestic payments other than wages. Only a few countries make extensive use of withholding on domestic payments other than wages, interest, and dividends.

There are substantial differences in the extent of required information reporting. These often relate to the capacity of the tax administration to efficiently process information. The U.S. has probably the most comprehensive requirements and best system of matching individual income tax returns with information returns. It is relatively recent. As recently as the early 1980s there was heated debate over the imposition of a withholding tax on interest (which was almost implemented), but since then the IRS has dramatically improved its matching capability so that it can now fairly efficiently police compliance with the reporting of interest income, at least if the interest is earned from a domestic financial institution. With the U.S. probably at one extreme, there are substantial country differences in the extent of automatic information reporting, and this is a key factor in tax compliance concerning the types of income that lend themselves to information reporting.

---

[11] *See* OECD (1990) at 30-32.

Automatic reporting of information on interest income of course presupposes that the bank secrecy laws do not stand in the way. This is now a hotly debated issue in the OECD; the governments of most OECD countries in principle have accepted the desirability of automatic reporting of information on interest income but a few countries consider this to be an unwarranted incursion on bank secrecy. There seems to be a growing international consensus that bank account information should be accessible to the tax authorities at least in cases where a criminal investigation has been launched. However, this standard would contemplate only rare disclosure because as a rule criminal prosecutions for tax offenses are infrequent.

Virtually all OECD countries, and most other countries, have taxpayer identification numbers (TINs) (Japan does not). TINs are important in terms of being able to match information reporting with returns and verify residence for treaty purposes. Japan's lack of a TIN influenced the design of its VAT: it would have been virtually impossible to adopt the standard tax invoice method used in other countries (which allows for cross-checking invoices) without the existence of TINs.[12]

What kinds of payments are subject to withholding? To information reporting?

6.6 ADVANCE RULINGS

Because legislation is inherently ambiguous and incomplete, and must be interpreted by human beings, there is always uncertainty as to the application of the tax laws to specific transactions. The tax administration can provide published guidance on how to deal with certain issues. The extensiveness of published rulings differs from country to country. Their legal effect is generally similar; usually the taxpayer can rely on them or challenge them at his option.[13] In the case of very important transactions or investments, businesses often wish to know with certainty what the tax consequences will be. In any system, it is possible to approach the tax

---

[2] *See infra* 8.2.

[3] *See* Frédéric Douet, Contribution à l'étude de la sécurité juridique en droit fiscal interne français 190-234 (1997). French law allows taxpayer reliance on published administrative interpretations, including in situations where the administration attempts to change its interpretation of the law retroactively. In the U.S., courts accord a limited amount of deference (so-called *Skidmore* deference) to published rulings: "they are 'entitled to respect' to the extent they 'have the "power to persuade"'" Del Commercial Properties Inc. v. Commissioner, 251 F.3d 210, 214 D.C. Cir. 2001), *cert. denied*, 122 S.Ct. 903 (2002)

administration for advice. The difficulty is that almost invariably such advice, even in written form, will not be legally binding. If the tax administration disavows the advice or changes its mind, at most, the taxpayer will be able to argue that reliance on advice from the tax administration should excuse the taxpayer from application of a penalty.

Advance rulings offer a way for taxpayers to obtain legally binding advice on specific transactions. This is an area of change: in many systems there still is not legal provision for advance rulings, but more and more countries are adopting rules in this area.[14] Even where advance rulings are not recognized on a formal basis, obtaining written advice from the tax administration informally may be an important aspect of tax practice and may give rise to legal rights.[15] For those countries that have formally recognized advance rulings, the schemes are generally similar in broad terms, with the notable exception of Sweden, which has formalized the advance rulings process by making the denial of a ruling appealable.[16] A fairly recent development, started in the United States and already imitated in a number of mostly OECD countries, is the advance pricing agreement, under which the tax administration agrees to respect prices for the transfer of goods and services among members of a corporate group. This can be seen as a form of advance ruling, but it has its own procedural peculiarities, including the possible involvement of more than one tax administration so as to avoid inconsistent transfer pricing determinations.

The operation and role of rulings vary from country to country. In the U.S., rulings tend to be sought to obtain assurance of the tax treatment of large transactions. Most do not involve controversial issues and in many controversial areas the IRS refuses to even consider issuing a ruling. By contrast, in a country like Brazil rulings are more of a risk and it is apparently common for rulings adverse to the taxpayer to be issued.

---

[14] *See generally* The International Guide to Advance Rulings (IBFD: D. Sandler ed. looseleaf 2002); Adrian Sawyer, *Binding Rulings: A Comparative Perspective, in* The International Tax System 291 (Andrew Lymer & John Hasseldine eds., 2002). *E.g.* Faes (1995) at 217-21 (Belgium adopted advance rulings in 1991).

[15] *See* Tiley (2000) at 55. In Canada, rulings may not be legally binding on the administration, but in all likelihood will be treated as such. *See* Hogg et al. (2002) at 18.

[16] This means that a judicial decision on an issue can be obtained fairly quickly. See Sture Bergström, *EC Tax Law in the Case Law of the Swedish Supreme Administrative Court, in* Liber Amicorum Sven-Olof Lodin 74, 75-78 (2001) Rulings can also be appealed in Finland, *see* Re A Oyj Abp, 4 ITLR 1009 (Sup Adm. Ct., March 20, 2002), and Australia, *see* Sawyer, *supra* note 14, at 302.

In France, a ruling can be obtained against application of the abuse of law rule of art. L. 64, but taxpayers rarely apply for such rulings.[17]

Sometimes the agreement of the tax administration is required in order for the taxpayer to obtain certain tax benefits or change an accounting method.[18]

In some countries, the taxpayer may have a right to a ruling—at least on certain matters—which means that where the tax administration fails to respond to a ruling it is considered to have consented.[19]

Is it possible to obtain a binding advance ruling provided for by law? If not, are there informal procedures to get a letter from the tax administration? How do formal or informal rulings work in practice?

6.7 AUDITS

The intensity of field audits varies substantially among countries, with Germany and Japan being among the most intense, followed by the U.S., with audit intensity in the U.K. being substantially less.[20]   An important different among countries is in the nature of the audit procedure.[21]   Common law countries tend to have a fairly informal procedure for assessment of tax.[22]

---

[17] *See* Cozian (1999) at 41-42.

[18] In France, this is known as *agrément fiscal. See* Guy Gest, *Agrément Fiscal, in* Dictionnaire Encyclopedique de Finances Publiques 41 (Loic Philip ed. 1991). The French courts have been struggling with the issue of the extent of discretion that the tax administration has when exercising this discretion.   This is a matter of interpretation of the law granting the discretion; the courts tend to interpret such grants of discretion so as to provide at least some limits to the discretion of the administration. *See* David et al. (2000) at 780-95.

[19] This is the case in Belgium for specified areas. *See* Dassesse & Minne (2001) at 91-94.   One of the reasons Belgium instituted the rulings regime was to grant certainty in face of its newly enacted GAAR.

[20] *See* Walter Neddermeyer, *On-the-Spot Tax Audits—Comparative Review of Country Rules and Practices,* 1991 Intertax 388. Audits typically take a year or more in Germany, Japan, and the U.S. *See id.* It has been estimated that Germany has nearly 3 times as many tax auditors per capita as in the U.S. *See id.* at 389.

[21] *See generally* The International Guide to Tax Auditing (IBFD).

[22] For Australia, see Daihatsu Australia Pty Limited v. Commissioner of Taxation No. 2), [2001] FCA 588 (Federal Court of Australia, 24 May 2001), 3 ITLR 723 ("it the clear intention...of the 1936 Act that taxpayers not be permitted to seek judicial review of the processes leading to, and the making of, assessments by the Commissioner of Taxation. Rather taxpayers are to be confined to the objection and

The U.S. Internal Revenue Code itself contains almost no rules on the conduct of audits.[23] By contrast, civil law countries tend to take the attitude that the administration is allowed to do only what is specified in the law, and spell out the procedure for audits.[24] This is particularly the case in France and Germany.[25] In the latter countries, audits are nearly as formal as criminal procedure and tax lawyers look for procedural defects to invalidate audits and the resulting assessments. In France, if there are insubstantial errors in an

---

appeal remedy...[as long as] there was a bona fide attempt by the Commissioner to exercise the power of assessment...."). In the U.K., however, a written notice of audit must be served on the taxpayer within a year of the filing date, and a repeated audit is ruled out unless the tax authorities discover an error based on information not previously available. *See* Morse & Williams (2000) at 57-58.

[23] I.R.C. sec. 6201 provides broad authority to the IRS to make assessments of tax. Procedural is generally informal. Recent legislation has formalized the procedure to a certain extent. For example, while previously the burden of proof that an assessment is incorrect was on the taxpayer, it is now shifted under some circumstances to the government. However, the burden is not shifted if the taxpayer has not fully cooperated with the government. *See, e.g.,* I.R.C. § 6201(d). In such cases, disputes may arise about the audit process and about whether the taxpayer has been sufficiently cooperative, requiring the courts to look into the details of correspondence between the IRS and taxpayers and the sequence of events during an audit, matters which were formerly largely irrelevant to court reviews of assessments. Formal rules concerning procedure are by and large provided only after the IRS determines the amount of tax (i.e. following the audit). These start with rules concerning the notice of deficiency that must be sent to the taxpayer. I.R.C. § 6212 The Code itself does not contain rules concerning the audit process. Once the revenue agent conducts the audit and makes a determination of the tax due, he sends a notice to the taxpayer informing him of the adjustments. This is known as a "30-day" letter because the taxpayer has the right to appeal the determination within 30 days by filing a protest with the IRS appeals office. The appeals process is an informal one "Conferences with Appeals Office personnel are held in an informal manner by correspondence, by telephone or at a personal conference." IRS Publication 5. *See also* IRS Publication 556.

[24] For example, in Argentina, a formal administrative procedure known as *determinación de oficio* applies for determination of tax liability (following a informal investigatory stage). The determination of tax can be struck down for procedural irregulariries. If the taxpayer appeals to the Tax Court, no new evidence that was not already submitted in the administrative proceeding may be introduce (absent newly discovered evidence). *See* 2 Catalina García Vizcaíno, Derech Tributário 48-69, 209 (2000).

[25] Audit procedure is governed by the Betriebsprüfungsordnung, BStBl. I. S. 802 (I Dec. 1987). For discussion of cases see Franz Wasseremeyer, Finanz-Rundscha (1987) at 513.

audit proceeding, the court can strike down penalties and interest; if the errors are substantial the entire assessment may be struck down.[26]   By contrast, in Belgium, if an assessment is struck down because of procedural errors, the tax authorities may proceed to a new assessment.[27]   Even in cases where a new assessment may be brought, it may be to the taxpayer's advantage to make procedural challenges since, for example, the period of limitations may have expired.

What is the likelihood of being audited?   What is the nature of the audit procedure and its formality?   What corruption exists at this stage?

6.8 LITIGATION

In virtually all countries taxpayers have the right to appeal an adverse decision of the tax administration.   There are substantial differences in the appeal procedures in terms of the administrative and judicial bodies that hear tax cases.[28]

In France, tax cases are heard by two different court systems. Litigation on income taxes and turnover taxes is ultimately brought before the *Conseil d'État* (the supreme administrative court), while litigation on registration duties, wealth tax, and excise taxes goes to the *Cour de Cassation*, which is the supreme civil court.[29]   These two court systems have their own distinctive histories, legal cultures, and methods of recruitment, which may lead to different methods of judicial interpretation. Sometimes the two courts have different interpretations of the same statute, a case in point being France's GAAR.[30] As its name indicates, the *Conseil d'État* was created by

---

[26] *See* LPF art. L 80CA; Michel Bouvier, Introduction au droit fiscal et à la théorie de l'impôt 93 (1996); Guy Gest, *France, in* Ault et al. (1997) at 45-46; Gilles Bachelier & Eve Obadia, Le Contentieux Fiscal ¶ ¶ 78, 79, 81, 85, 105 (2d ed. 1996).

[27] *See* Thomas Delahaye, *Taxpayer Protection in Belgium: Some Remarks, in* Taxpayer Protection in the European Union 61, 65 (Dirk Albregtse & Henk van Arendonk eds., 1998) [hereinafter Taxpayer Protection].

[28] *See* Beltrame & Mehl (1997) at 594-612.   In Sweden, tax appeals are heard by administrative courts. *See* Peter Melz, *Sweden, in* Ault et al. (1997) at 107.

[29] *See* Bachelier & Obadia, *supra* note 26, paras. 191, 192 (2d ed. 1996); LPF art. L 99; ch 3, n. 32.   The ordinary courts also have jurisdiction over certain cases arising from the recovery of taxes, whether direct or indirect.

[30] LPF, article L64 (*see supra* 5.7.4). Until 1988, the *Cour de Cassation* considered that article L64 was applicable only when a transaction met the two criteria of *abus de droit* simultaneously, i.e. both simulation and abuse of law (Cass. com. 16 October

Napoleon as an advisory body to the government and it still retains that role today in addition to its judicial activities. The *Conseil d'État* is staffed by judges and lawyers many of whom have graduated from a state service school (ENA, or *École Nationale d'Administration*), as opposed to the civil courts whose legal personnel is trained first in university law schools and then only in a specialized school for magistrates (ENM, or *École Nationale de la Magistrature*). For some observers, and although this may be changing, the *Conseil d'État*'s greater proximity to government and related revenue concerns may have had an impact on its method of interpreting tax laws.[31]

Germany has a particularly strong system of appeals in tax matters, in that all appeals go to a specialized system of tax courts, consisting of 544 judges at the trial level and 66 judges at the appellate level.[32] Not only are these judges tax specialists, but the litigation procedure gives the court an active role in investigating and finding the facts of the case.[33] There is no appeal from decisions of the Federal Tax Court (*Bundesfinanzhof*), the only exception being that appeals based on constitutional grounds may be filed with the Constitutional Court.[34]

The U.K. has an idiosyncratic system of appeal to boards of review called the General Commissioners and the Special Commissioners, with subsequent appeal to the ordinary courts; the courts may also entertain applications for judicial review on the grounds that an action by the tax administration is *ultra vires,* irrational, procedurally deficient, or unfair.[35]

Italy has a three tier-system of tax commissions, with appeals to the court of appeals and ultimately to the court of cassation.[36]

Canadian tax appeals are heard by the Tax Court, with subsequent appeals to the Federal Court of Appeal and the Supreme Court; the volume of litigation seems relatively low.[37]

1984, n°734). Ultimately, however, its position became aligned with that of the *Conseil d'État* (Cass. Com. 19 April 1988, n° 86-19079).

[31] I am indebted to Delphine Nougayrède for this paragraph.

[32] *See* Dieter Birk, *Tax Protection Procedure in Germany, in* Taxpayer Protection *supra* note 27, at 55, 58 (1998).

[33] *See id.* at 60.

[34] *See id.* and *supra* 4.3.1.3.

[35] *See* Ian Saunders, Taxation: Judicial Review and Other Remedies (1996). VA? appeals are heard by a special tribunal.

[36] *See* Fantozzi (1994) at 497-542.

[37] *See* Brian Arnold, *Canada, in* Ault et al. (1997) at 31.

The U.S. has a system of possible appeals to three different sets of courts;[38] this makes it fun to be a tax litigator but otherwise has minimal benefits for society. The U.S. Tax Court is a specialized court staffed with experts in taxation. The judges understand tax well. They are not fazed by complex fact patterns, and they are not impressed by taxpayer arguments seeking to justify tax avoidance efforts. The Tax Court judges tend to try to uphold the integrity of the tax system; therefore, they are sympathetic to the government's economic substance attacks on tax shelters. (At the same time, they will reject the government's arguments that they see as inconsistent with the law, and they do so with confidence in their understanding of the law.) A second set of courts is the federal district courts. These are not tax experts. On average, they may tend to favor the taxpayer more than the Tax Court does, but litigators may consider it a risk to bring a technical tax case there. Moreover, in order to get to district court, taxpayers must first pay the tax in dispute. If the litigation takes place in the Tax Court, the taxpayer does not need to pay until the case is resolved. Alternatively, taxpayers can pay the tax and go to the Claims Court, which is also a fairly specialized court. Appeal from all of these courts lies to the courts of appeal. Court of appeal judges are not tax experts, but they do get a reasonable number of tax cases. Anyway, for technical issues, they can to some extent rely on the work of the court below, particularly if the appeal comes from the Tax Court. Because the Tax Court judges are experts, and do not like their decisions to be overturned, they tend to write opinions that can be upheld by the courts of appeal. Their opinions receive a certain amount of professional respect and most of their decisions are upheld on appeal. Because there are numerous appeals court judges, there is no guarantee of uniformity of approach. This is particularly the case with the common law anti-avoidance doctrines, since their application tends to be colored by the particular facts of the case, so that it would be difficult for the Supreme Court to keep the courts in line even if it wanted to. Because of this disparate group of judges applying the anti-avoidance doctrines, they tend to develop in a somewhat anarchic manner.

---

[38] The taxpayer may petition for redetermination of a deficiency to Tax Court without paying the tax. I.R.C. § 6213. Appeal from a decision of the Tax Court lies to the court of appeal for the circuit where the taxpayer resides. I.R.C. § 7482. Alternatively, the taxpayer may pay the tax and sue for a refund. In this case, suit may be brought for recovery of the overpaid tax in the U.S. Claims Court. 28 U.S.C. §1491(a)(1), or to the Federal district court where the taxpayer resides or has his primary place of business. 28 U.S.C. §§1340, 1346(a), 1491(a)(1) In a federal district court, the taxpayer may opt for a jury trial. Claims Court decisions are reviewed by the Court of Appeals for the Federal Circuit, while district court decisions are reviewed by the court of appeal for the relevant circuit.

On top of this, the Supreme Court has never been known to be brilliant on tax matters. So even when the Court does take a case, particularly on anti-avoidance law, which is difficult even for the best scholars to articulate and agree on, as often as not it leaves the law in as confused a state after its decision as it was before.

Best practice is to have within the tax administration a quasi-independent appeals office which has the authority to settle cases on the basis of the hazards of litigation. If such a system is in place and functioning, the vast majority of cases can be settled before they go to court.

The bottom line is the rate of success which taxpayers enjoy in court. It is difficult to evaluate statistics, since a proper evaluation would require a knowledge of the objective strength of the cases that come before the courts. However, there are some cases, as with Japan, where the low rate of success of taxpayers in court is striking.[39]   Statistics like this must of course be considered in light of the overall litigation culture, which can vary substantially from country to country.[40]

An important aspect of litigation is whether tax has to be paid pending appeal. It does not in most OECD countries.[41] Developing and transition countries with weak tax administrations often require payment of tax pending appeal so as to prevent abuse of the system via frivolous appeals.

The burden of proving that an assessment is incorrect tends to be placed fairly squarely on the taxpayer in common law countries, but in some cases is shifted to the tax authorities;[42] in civil law countries the allocation of

---

[39] *See, e.g.,* Kohji Mori, *Japan's Tax Controversy System Reviewed,* 22 Tax Notes Int'l 139 (Jan. 8, 2001); Morihiro Murata, *Resolving Tax Disputes in Japan: The Current System, Key Issues, and Future Developments,* 27 Tax Notes Int'l 211 (July 8, 2002).

[40] For example, Brazil has been described as having a "culture of intense tax litigation." Romero Tavares, *Understanding and Managing Brazil's CIDE Tax,* 2002 WTD 219-13 (Nov. 5, 2002).

[41] Collection of tax pending appeal is not suspended in Italy and Turkey. It may be suspended under certain conditions in Australia, Austria, Denmark, France, Germany, Greece, Ireland, Norway, Portugal, Spain, Sweden, and the U.K. It is automatically suspended in Belgium, Canada, Finland, Japan, Netherlands, New Zealand (one-half of tax in dispute), Switzerland, and the U.S. *See* OECD (1990) at 99. For France, see Bachelier & Obadia, *supra* note 26, at paras. 258, 325 (2d ed. 1996) (delay can be obtained if satisfactory guarantee is given by the taxpayer or if guarantee is waived) LPF art. L. 277.

[42] In the U.S. the burden is shifted to the tax authorities where the taxpayer presents credible evidence, keeps adequate records, and cooperates reasonably with the IRS. *See* I.R.C. §7491; note 23 *supra*. *See generally* John Townsend, *Burden of Proof in*

the burden tends to be more complex, and to be based on both general principles of civil procedure and specific provisions in the tax laws.[43]   In France, the tax administration has the burden of proof in certain cases when invoking the doctrine of abuse of law.[44]

One issue is whether the reviewing court can substitute its own rationale or is limited to reviewing errors below.[45]   In some countries, the concept of tax law as being of public order is seen as justifying such freedom by the reviewing court, since the concept of public order requires tax to be paid according to law and so the reviewing court must be free to apply the law without restriction.[46]

In France, the taxpayer's representation to the tax administration that a certain factual situation existed was held to bind the taxpayer; the taxpayer could not subsequently change his characterization in favor of the actual situation.[47]

In most systems, regulatory decisions cannot be challenged in court as such (the taxpayer may challenge them only in the context of an assessment), but in France decrees, regulations, instructions, and circulars may be challenged on the grounds of being ultra vires, including because they conflict with treaties or European Community law.[48]

Tax Cases: Valuation and Ranges, 32 Tax Practice 33 (Oct. 12, 2001). In the U.K. the burden of proof is on the taxpayer. *See* Morse & Williams (2000) at 58-59. So too in Canada. *See* Hogg et al. (2002) at 546-47.

[43] *See* Tipke/Lang (2002) at 783-89; Martín Queralt et al. (2001) at 369-72; Faes (1995) at 10; Dassesse & Minne (2001) at 101-03; Tiberghien (1995) at 36; David et al. (2000) at 719-33.

[44] *See* David et al. (2000) at 177. The administration would also have the burden of proving an abnormal management act. *See* Cozian (1999) at 114. The general rule for the burden of proof in France is that the party who invokes the existence of a fact in his favor has the burden of proving it, *see id.* at 230, but there are also a number of special rules. *See* LPF arts. L. 191–195A; André Heurté, *Preuve, in* Dictionnaire Encyclopédique de Finances Publiques 1219 (Loïc Philip ed. 1991).

[45] *See* Tiley (2000) at 70-71; Morse & Williams (2000) at 60 (court can reverse only for error of law, but distinguishing between law and fact is not always obvious).

[46] *See* Beltrame & Mehl (1997) at 524.

[47] *See* C. David et al. (2000) at 164-65, 166-69. In a 1974 decision, the taxpayer had registered as a VAT taxpayer but later claimed (in accordance with actual fact) that he was just serving as a nominee. The Council of State held that the taxpayer could not change his position, even if the initially reported position was erroneous. CE Sect. 20 Feb. 1974, 83 270, *Lemarchand. Lebon* 126, *DF* 1974.30.958, concl. Mandelkern.

[48] *See* Bachelier & Obadia, *supra* note 26. at paras. 214-222.

The length of time that the court process takes is also of importance to the functioning of the tax system. One extreme might be Sweden, where appeals can be taken from denial of a tax ruling, thereby allowing matters to be decided even before occurrence of the taxable transaction. Another extreme example is a 1985 decision of the Supreme Court of India, involving an individual's 1959-60 tax year.[49]

What is the procedure for administrative and judicial appeal and how good are the prospects for relief if the taxpayer has a deserving case? Must all or a portion of the tax be paid pending appeal, and is it possible to secure relief from this requirement? Is the appeals process marked by corruption?

6.9 COLLECTION

Some countries have special rules for collection of tax, especially where the tax administration is given special powers, such as powers to collect tax without court judgment. There is a remarkable lack of convergence of practice in this regard, with some countries granting extensive powers to the tax authorities and others requiring them to go to court like other creditors. For example, in the U.S., the IRS has the power to impose liens and collect tax without going to court, but this has to be seen in the context of the rules for payment of tax: the taxpayer always has the opportunity of going to Tax Court and therefore staying any collection action until the tax is finally determined.

Where the tax laws themselves contain no special rules for collection, the general procedures for collecting civil judgments will apply.[50] These procedures may also apply as an alternative to the specialized tax procedures, at the option of the tax administration. In addition, the tax collection rules must be considered in the context of the bankruptcy rules. There can be a complex interaction between the special procedural rules for tax collection and the bankruptcy procedures.[51] In addition, the bankruptcy law will typically set a priority for tax claims (where the tax administration has a power to file tax liens, it may become a secured creditor and thereby obtain a higher status for its claims). As a result, the law concerning collection procedure tends to be complex and somewhat *sui generis* for each country.

---

[49] *See* C'r of Income Tax v. J.H. Gotla, A.I.R. 1985 S.C. 1698.

[50] This is the case in France. *See* Bachelier & Obadia, *supra* note 26, at para. 443.

[51] *See generally* Barbara Morgan, *Should the Sovereign be Paid First? A Comparative International Analysis of the Priority for Tax Claims in Bankruptcy,* 74 Am. Bankruptcy L. J. 461 (2000).

What is the relationship between general rules for collection of debts and the rules for collecting tax debts?

6.10 CIVIL PENALTIES

The penalty regime is an important feature of tax practice. In planning a transaction, the tax advisor will be concerned to avoid the imposition of a penalty in the event that the tax administration and eventually the courts will disagree with the position taken by the taxpayer on the return. In the United States the penalty area has become a complex one in its own right, with a substantial array of possible penalties to sort through and often difficult issues as to whether specific transactions can be exonerated from application of a penalty.

Most countries have a simpler penalty structure. Often there is little attempt to tailor the degree of the penalty to the fault of the taxpayer. For countries with weaker tax administrations, penalties can be problematic because their imposition almost inevitably involves administrative discretion and hence the possibility for corruption or heavy handedness on the part of the tax administration. In a number of transition countries (for example, Russia and other former Soviet republics) there has been a tendency to include fairly draconian penalties in the law, without reference to the taxpayer's degree of fault.[52] The mentality seems to be that where tax has been improperly understated, the taxpayer is at fault and should be punished. But this means that even routine disagreements about the interpretation or application of the tax law can give rise to penalties. Over time, a more normal penalty structure will no doubt become accepted.

Another important aspect of penalties is procedural. Which officials have the power to impose penalties and how are they applied? Countries of the former Soviet Union have inherited a code of administrative violations, which originally was applicable to individuals who violated administrative norms (i.e. it was inapplicable to legal persons).[53] In these countries, the issue arises as to whether tax penalties should be included in the administrative

---

[52] *See* Delphine Nougayrède, Construire L'Impôt en Russie 233-37 (2001).

[53] This may have made sense in the context where all enterprises were state-owned, but no longer makes sense in a market economy. Even the reformed version of this code subjects to penalty responsible officials of taxpayers for such offenses as failure to register with the tax authorities, to submit information on opening of bank accounts, or other information relevant to tax administration, and bookkeeping violations. *See* Kodeks Rossiskoi Federatsii ob Administrativnikh Pravonarushe-niakh, Sobranie Zakonodatel'stva. No. 1. (Jan 7, 2002), articles 2.4, 15.3-15.13.

code rather than the tax code, and as to the procedure for applying penalties that are included in the administrative code. For penalties whose amount depends on the amount of underpayment of tax, it makes sense to determine the penalty in the same administrative or judicial proceeding which determines the amount of the tax, but the existence of the administrative code sometimes thwarts the implementation of the most appropriate penalty structure and procedure.

In addition to rates of penalty, it is important to pay attention to the standard of culpability (e.g., strict liability, negligence, or a higher than ordinary degree of negligence) and to what excuses are available, if any (e.g., some form of reasonable cause). This is closely related to the question whether the tax administration has the discretionary power to waive penalties, and how they exercise this power.

Countries vary in the extent to which there is administrative discretion to extend time to file, time to pay, negotiate penalties, negotiate interest, and negotiate tax.

Taxpayers contemplating entering into a tax avoidance transaction may do so even where the chances of success in court are limited. Playing the "audit lottery" may be advantageous if penalties are low. Setting penalties at a very high level on a broad basis is not a satisfactory response because the penalty may end up being excessive. Instead, penalties can be tailored, with higher levels of penalty in those cases considered abusive.[54] The U.S. has substantial experience in this area. While tailoring penalties has something to recommend it, it also results in substantial complexity for taxpayers in navigating the penalty provisions and figuring out how to comply with them. It is linked to disclosure requirements (*see supra* 5.9) in that the penalty rules can exonerate the taxpayer from a penalty if the taxpayer fully disclosed the transaction on the return in the manner specified. The U.S. is now contemplating the imposition of penalties where the taxpayer's position relating to specifically defined tax shelters is found not to be justified upon audit and (potentially) litigation.[55]

---

[54] Spain is anomalous in this respect since penalties are specifically ruled out for abuse-of-rights cases. *See* LGT art. 25(3). For discussion of abuse of rights, see *supra* 5.6.

[55] *See* Tax Analysts, Highlights & Documents, May 13, 2002, 1778-79.

6.11   TAX CRIMES

In most countries, tax evasion is a crime. Prosecution is, however, typically infrequent[56] (Germany is an exception[57]). The vast majority of countries have very broad rules on what constitutes tax evasion or tax fraud.[58] This is probably due to the recognition by legislators that attempting to enumerate carefully the offenses punishable as fraud would play into the hands of taxpayers who commit fraud in ways that are not listed.

---

[56] For example, in the U.S., there were only 45 criminal convictions in the year ended Sept. 30, 2001 (31 in the prior year and 24 in 1999. *See* Wall Street Journal, Feb. 13, 2002, at A1. In 1997-98 in the U.K. there were only about 7 income tax fraud convictions. *See* Tiley (2000) at 78.

[57] *See* Albert Rädler, *Germany, in* Ault et al. (1997) at 65.

[58] *See* Tax avoidance/Tax evasion, 68a Cahiers de droit fiscal international 230 (Australia), 246 (Austria), 267 (Belgium), 285 (Brasil), 296 (Canada), 358 (Finland), 404-05 (Greece)(where unreported income exceeds a specified amount), 422 (Hong Kong), 583 (U.K.), 603 (Sweden)(1983). Germany also has a broad definition of tax evasion. *See* AO §370. It applies when a taxpayer furnishes incorrect or incomplete information. The penalty is imprisonment up to 5 years. A higher penalty (imprisonment for 6 months to 10 years) applies in "especially serious cases". Spain also has a broad definition of tax evasion, although tax evasion is a crime only if the tax evaded exceeds a specified amount. *See* Criminal Code art. 305.

Likewise, in France, art. 1741 of the tax code broadly defines tax evasion (*fraude fiscale*) as including the failure to report amounts subject to tax, punishable with a monetary penalty and imprisonment for one to five years.

Article 198 of the Criminal Code of Russia makes it a crime for a natural person to evade tax by failure to submit a declaration, by including in a declaration data known to be distorted, or by other means, if done on a "large scale". *See* Criminal Code of the Russian Federation (William E. Butler trans. 3rd ed. 1999). "Large scale" means tax in excess of two hundred minimum amounts of payment for labor. Similar rules apply to tax evasion by legal persons. *See id.* art. 199. Russian prosecutors do not seem shy to use these provisions. Indeed, criminal investigations have apparently been launched "where a company did not pay certain taxes solely because of a difference of opinion in the interpretation" of the tax laws. E. Sergeeva, *Criminal Liability for Tax Evasion by Legal Entities, in* Law of the C.I.S.: The Bottom Line (newsletter issued by Chadbourne & Parke, Spring 2000).

In Argentina, it is a crime punishable by imprisonment from one month to three years by any means to impede the assessment or collection of taxes by misstating the taxpayer's real economic situation. *See* Law 23,771, B.O. Feb. 27, 1990. *See generally* Mirtha Elena Glatigny, Nuevo Regimen Penal Tributario y Previsional (1991). There are also other penalties, including for more severe offenses where the tax evaded exceeds a specified amount.

Nevertheless, as a practical matter, drawing the line between civil fraud and criminal fraud is not easy and almost invariably is a matter of judgment. For example, in the U.S. there is a broad definition of tax fraud.[59] While a conviction for tax fraud requires some willful commision, the filing of a false return[60] would seem to be such a commission and therefore even the failure to declare a relatively small amount could be prosecuted criminally as tax fraud. (If the amount is very small, the taxpayer could perhaps defend on the basis that he forgot.) Thus, for example, if an individual has a bank account in a foreign jurisdiction and checks the box on the return denying that he has such an account, that would be fraudulent. The difficulty is that criminal tax fraud prosecutions are rarely brought. Most cases are dealt with as civil fraud. As a practical matter, therefore, the failure to report a modest amount of interest income from a foreign bank account, while technically a felony, would be most unlikely to lead to a fraud prosecution, even if detected by the IRS.[61] It can be particularly perilous to be caught for tax fraud in China, where the death penalty has been imposed for this offense and where procedural protections may be lacking.[62]

In the U.K., some tax fraud prosecutions have recently been successfully brought against tax advisors for behavior that might be in the borderline area between tax avoidance and tax fraud.[63] These cases illustrate vividly that drawing a line between aggressive tax avoidance (with the consequence of a tax assessment for the taxpayer plus penalties for the

---

[59] "Any person who willfully attempts in any manner to evade or defeat any tax imposed by this title or the payment thereof...." I.R.C. § 7201.

[60] *See* U.S. v. Bishop, 412 U.S. 346 (1973) ("voluntary, intentional violation of a known legal duty").

[61] IRS guidelines issued in 1989 set limits in terms of amount of tax at stake below which criminal cases will normally not be brought. These are $2,500 for cases where the "specific item" method of proof is used and $10,000 where indirect proof is used. *See* Bruce Hochman et al., Tax Crimes A-2 (Tax Management Portfolio 636-2d, 2002).

[62] *See* China Sentences Seven to Death in Multi-Billion-Dollar Tax Fraud Scam, 22 Tax Notes Int'l 1228 (March 12, 2001); Karby Leggett, *Investor Finds Peril in Chinese Court,* Wall St. J., Apr. 9, 2002, at A22. Tax fraud can also take on phenomenal proportions in China. One fraud scheme was said to involve over $2 billion in tax revenues. *See* Legal Media Group, News in Brief (Dec. 17, 2001).

[63] *See* Morse & Williams (2000) at 62; R. v. Dimsey [1999] STC 846, *aff'd,* [2002] A.C. 509 (Oct. 11, 2001); R v. Charlton, [1996] STC 1418. *Dimsey* involved offshore companies that were in fact managed within the U.K. *Charlton* involved the purchase of inventory from an offshore company which charged an artificially high price.

taxpayer and perhaps also the tax advisor) and tax fraud (with the consequence that the tax advisor goes to prison) can be controversial.[64]

Switzerland has a peculiar set of rules concerning tax fraud.[65] There is a general concept of tax evasion and a subset of tax evasion known as tax fraud. While the former is a criminal offense punishable with a fine,[66] only the latter is punishable by imprisonment. Tax fraud means the use of "forged, falsified or substantively incorrect documents, such as business books, balance sheets, profit and loss statements and salary certificates or other third party certificates."[67] A false tax return is not a "false document" within the meaning of this provision.[68] This narrow definition of tax fraud is out of line with the approach of virtually all[69] other countries. It furnishes part of the explanation why the Swiss authorities have been reluctant to share information with the tax authorities of other countries, even where a tax crime may have been committed abroad.[70]

---

[64] *See, e.g.,* Amnon Rafael, *Back to Basics: Tax Evasion v. Tax Avoidance,* 27 Tax Planning Int'l Rev. 19 (2000) (Supreme Court of Israel decision striking down a conviction for behavior that it considered to be tax avoidance but not criminal tax evasion; distinction between "an artificial transaction and a fictitious transaction").

[65] *See* Direct Federal Tax Law, arts. 174-193. *See generally* Harvard Law School, International Tax Program, Taxation in Switzerland 998-1007 (1976); Höhn & Waldburger (2001) at 1005-41. There are also separate rules in each canton.

[66] The fine is normally 100% of the tax evaded, but can range from 1/3 of the tax to 300% of the tax. *See* Höhn & Waldburger (2001) at 1018.

[67] Direct Federal Tax Law, art. 186 (Tax fraud is known as *Steuerbetrug*).

[68] *See* Mario Kronauer, *Information Given for Tax Purposes from Switzerland to Foreign Countries Especially to the United States for the Prevention of Fraud or the Like in Relation to Certain American Taxes,* 30 Tax L. Rev. 47, 82 (1974).

[69] Greece also draws a distinction between tax fraud involving forged or fictitious documents and fraud merely involving an inaccurate return. While submitting a wilfully inaccurate return is a crime if the amount of tax evaded exceeds €14,673, no prosecution is brought if the taxpayer pays the tax and an administrative fine and if forged or fictitious documents are not involved. *See* Constantinos Kallideris, *Penalisation of Tax Offences in Greek Tax Law,* 29 Tax Planning Int'l Rev. 18 (2002).

[70] In the case of mere tax evasion (i.e. where a criminal offense punishable by imprisonment is not involved), it is apparently not possible for the Swiss authorities to compel a bank directly to give information, although they can require information from the taxpayer. However, a judge has a right in a tax fraud case to lift banking secrecy. *See* Maurice Aubert, *The Limits of Swiss Banking Secrecy Under Domestic and International Law,* 2 Int'l Tax and Business Law. 273, 279-81 (1984).

It is common for the criminal investigation function to reside in the tax administration. Because there is a fine line between conduct that merits: (1) a reassessment of tax, without penalty, (2) a reassessment plus a penalty, and (3) a criminal sanction, and the line can shift as the facts of a particular case become known, it makes sense for the initial investigation to be conducted within the same institution that conducts tax audits. Yet, because criminal investigations involve different procedures, as well as requirements of procedural protection for the taxpayer, the distinction between civil and criminal aspects of a case must be made.

An important practical question is the framework for identifying when a case turns from a civil case to a criminal case and what has to happen at that point.[71] For example, in the United States, the courts have found no difficulties with the concept that the tax authorities can conduct an investigation that might result in either prosecution or the imposition of a civil penalty. At the point where the IRS determines that a criminal prosecution should be brought, it turns the case over to the Justice Department, but there is no requirement that the case be turned over as soon as there is suspicion of criminal fraud.[72] Once the case is turned over, however, there are limitations on how the civil investigation can proceed. In particular, civil summonses cannot be used in aid of the criminal investigation.[73] By contrast, the Canadian Supreme Court has held that the constitutional protections for criminal investigations apply once the predominant purpose of an investigation becomes the determination of criminal liability.[74]

Germany provides even greater room for investigation of criminal tax matters by the tax administration. In principle, where no other crime besides tax evasion is involved, the tax administration carries out the investigation itself.[75] The tax authority presents the case directly to the court

---

[71] In the Netherlands and the U.K., cases of possible fraud are presented to a tripartite council with representatives of the tax administration, its invesgative division, and the procecutor's office, while in Belgium the prosecutor enters the case earlier and takes an independent decision. See A.A. Aronowitz et al., Value-Added Tax Fraud in the European Union 35-37 (1996).

[72] For further information on the conduct of tax criminal investigations in the U.S., *see* Saltzman (1991), at 12-1 to 12-13, 12-15, 12-20 to 12-44; *id.* 2001 Supp. No 2: S12-2 to S12-12, S12-19 to S12-21).

[73] *See* Developments in the Law—Corporate Crime, 92 Harv. L. Rev. 1227, 1311-1340 (1979).

[74] *See* Brian Arnold, *Canada,* 28 Tax Notes Int'l 1264 (Dec. 30, 2002).

[75] AO §386(2)(1).

where only a fine is involved.[76] Otherwise, it transfers the case to the public prosecutor's office.[77]

In Austria, the tax authorities are responsible for the imposition of most penalties, in some cases even those involving imprisonment (up to three months).[78] In the case of more severe offenses, the penalty must be imposed by the court directly.[79] In these cases, the tax administration is required to turn the case over to the public prosecutor's office.[80] The vesting in the tax authorities directly of the jurisdiction to impose criminal penalties was inherited from Germany. The German constitutional court held this procedure invalid in Germany, on the basis that the imposition of criminal penalties was a judicial function, which was reserved to the courts under the German Constitution.[81]

The relationship between civil and criminal procedure is also relevant for the privilege against self-incrimination. There is a basic contradiction between the two procedures in that civil tax procedures involve and often require cooperation by the taxpayer, while criminal procedure protects the right against self-incrimination. In this context, it should be noted that the right against self-incrimination is considerably broader under the ECHR than under U.S. law, in that it extends to legal persons and to the production of documents, not just testimony.[82] Under the ECHR, as well, major civil penalties are assimilated to criminal proceedings. The full implications of the right of self-incrimination in this context remain to be worked out for ECHR signatories.

---

[76] AO §400.

[77] *Id. See also* Aronowitz et al., *supra* note 71, at 37.

[78] *See* FinStrG § 15(3).

[79] *See id.* § 53.

[80] *See id.* § 54(1).

[81] *See* BVerfGE 22, 49 (1967).

[82] *See* Stefan Frommel, *The Right of Taxpayers to Remain Silent Under the European Convention on Human Rights, in* Taxpayer Protection, *supra* note 27, at 81, 82-83, 91-92; Funke v. France, Feb. 25, 1993, Series A, Vol. 256-A European Court of Human Rights; Fisher v. United States, 425 U.S. 391 (1976) (Fifth Amendment does not prohibit compelling the production of documents where compelled self-incriminatory testimony is not involved).

6.12 TAX AMNESTIES

The legislature may provide for the forgiveness of taxes and penalties as part of a tax amnesty program. Normally amnesties need legislative approval because they represent the forgiveness of amounts that would otherwise be due according to law. The basic idea of an amnesty is to encourage taxpayers to come forward and pay their long-past-due obligations. Amnesties should in principle be combined with a vigorous crackdown to take place immediately after the amnesty. While amnesties have sometimes been successful, on the whole they are a dangerous instrument which tends to undermine compliance with the tax laws.[83] In countries where amnesties are used frequently, unscrupulous taxpayers tend to wait for the next amnesty before satisfying their obligations. If an amnesty is used, the normal and preferable practice is to forgive penalties only, and not any portion of the principal amount of tax, although sometimes amnesties also forgive the tax.

6.13 TAX PROFESSIONALS

Tax professionals generally fall into one of three groups: accountants, lawyers, and other tax advisors.[84] The first two are almost invariably subject to independent professional regulation. The last category (which is called different things in different countries) describes professionals who may or may not be subject to regulation. In countries such as Germany and the United States, there is fairly extensive regulation of tax advisors; in other countries there may be little or no regulation.

There are three basic models for the regulation of tax professionals: (1) full regulation, as in Germany, under which, with limited exceptions, only licensed professionals may provide tax advice, (2) partial regulation, as in the United States, under which anyone is allowed to give tax advice, or to prepare a return for someone else, but return preparers are required to sign the return, and only attorneys, certified public accountants, and enrolled agents are allowed to practice before the IRS, and (3) no regulation, followed by most

---

[83] According to OECD (1990) at 90-91, only Ireland, Italy (once of 2 times used), New Zealand, and Switzerland reported good results from tax amnesties. *See also Italy: Tax Shield Program Reaps €50 Billion*, 26 Tax Notes Int'l 1174 (June 10, 2002). 14 of the 22 OECD countries had used amnesties.

[84] *See* TLDD at 161. For a discussion of the role of tax advisors in representation in tax proceedings in the Netherlands, Germany, Belgium, and the U.K., see Taxpayer Protection, *supra* note 20, at 123-45.

countries, under which the provision of tax advice is not considered a regulated activity (although there is regulation for professionals such as lawyers and accountants who provide such advice as part of the general regulation of these professionals.[85]

In the U.S., the tax profession is dominated by lawyers. Economists do play an important role in the formulation of tax policy, but it is telling that the Assistant Secretary for Tax Policy has almost invariably been a lawyer, as has the Commissioner of Internal Revenue.[86] There has been, especially in recent years, an intense competition between lawyers and accountants in the area of tax practice. While accounting firms have increased their tax practice at the expense of law firms, they have done it partly by hiring tax lawyers.

In most other countries, accountants play the dominant role in tax practice. This may account for the less significant role of tax in law schools, as compared with the U.S. U.S. tax lawyers looking for foreign advisors should therefore not be surprised to find that the best advisors in a foreign country might include more accountants than lawyers.

To what professions do the leading tax advisors belong? What model does the regulatory scheme follow?

6.14 OMBUDSMAN

The institution of ombudsman originated in Sweden, and as of 1950 existed only in Sweden and Finland.[87] In 1981, there were ombudsman offices operating in over 30 countries.[88] There is no standard system of organization for the ombudsman function, and a number of countries have several offices fulfilling this function. In countries with more than one ombudsman, there may be one that concentrates on tax matters (in Sweden one of the ombudsman handles tax among other matters), although only a few countries have established an ombudsman specifically in the office of the tax administration (these include the U.S. and the U.K.[89]). In other countries, the

---

[85] *See* Thuronyi & Vanistendael, *Regulation of Tax Professionals, in* TLDD at 151-58; The State of Taxpayers' Rights in Japan 15-31 (Koji Ishimura ed., 1995).

[86] This trend was broken with the appointment of Commissioner Rosotti in 1997. He was recruited for his management and information technology expertise.

[87] *See* 1 International Handbook of the Ombudsman 4 (Gerald Caiden ed., 1983).

[88] *See id.* at 5.

[89] *See* Leonard Beighton, *The Success of a Uniquely British Institution—The Adjudicator*, 16 Tax Notes Int'l 1439 (May 4, 1998); Marjorie Kornhouser, *When Bad Things Happen to Good Taxpayers: A Tale of Two Advocates*, 16 Tax Notes Int'l 537 (1998); Morse & Williams (2000) at 18. Portugal recently abandoned a short-lived

general ombudsman typically also has jurisdiction for taxation. The U.S. tax ombudsman has been given a rather large bureaucracy, perhaps in part for political reasons.

Other countries have gotten along without a tax ombudsman because the functions in question are by and large dealt with by existing institutions. Chief among these is the internal appellate function and the court system, which hears appeals from assessments and provide judicial review of other agency actions. External and internal audit agencies monitor whether administrative agencies are carrying out their functions properly. Finally, legal aid schemes assist low-income individuals in asserting their rights.

An alternative institution for resolution of disputes found in some countries is a commission of taxpayer representatives and tax administrators. Such commissions have fulfilled various functions in France.[90]

Is there an ombudsman to whom taxpayers who run into problems with the tax authorities can turn?

---

experiment with a specialized tax ombudsman. *See* Manuel Anselmo Torres, *Government Eliminates Office of Taxpayer Ombudsman*, 29 Tax Notes Int'l 144 (Jan. 13, 2003).

[90] They are known as *commissions départementales des impôts* or *commissions départementales de conciliation. See* Thierry Schmitt, *Commissions Départementales des impôts, in* Dictionnaire Encyclopedique de Finances Publiques 324 (Loïc Phili ed., 1991); LPF art. L. 59; CGI arts. 667, 1651; Beltrame & Mehl (1997) at 571-72.

Chapter 7

INCOME TAX

7.1 HISTORY AND ORGANIZATION

The income tax in its modern form is now over 200 years old. It originated in Great Britain at the very end of the 18[1] century,[1] and developed in the early 19[1] century principally in that country, some of the German states,[2] Sweden, and some American states. Most industrialized countries adopted it only towards the end of the 19[1] or early in the 20[1] century.[3] In many countries, war finance was a reason for adoption or expansion of the tax; but only during and after World War Two did the income tax became a "mass tax," applicable to the bulk of the population in industrialized countries.[4]

The income tax has become widespread. While there are a few small countries which have no income tax, virtually all the 183 countries that are members of the IMF have some form of income tax law.[5]

---

[1] *See* John Tiley, *United Kingdom, in* Ault et al. (1997) at 109, 110. For a brief history of the U.K. income tax law, which notes that the current law retains a surprising amount of the 1803 statute, see Morse & Williams (2000) at 21-24. *See also* B.E.V. Sabine, A History of Income Tax (1966).

[2] *See* Tipke/Lang (2002) at 212-13.

[3] *See* Ault et al. (1997) at 5-6, 25, 39-41, 71-74, 82-83, 97, 109-15 for brief history of the tax for countries covered by that study.

[4] *See* Bittker and Lokken (1999) ¶ 1.1.6; Randolph Paul, Taxation in the United States 318-19 (1954).

[5] As far as I have been able to ascertain, only two IMF member countries (The Bahamas and Vanuatu) do not have an income tax. Several countries have an income tax of only limited application. Thus, Maldives has a tax on bank profits only. St. Kitts and Nevis imposes income tax on corporations, but not on individuals. Paraguay taxes businesses only. The United Arab Emirates, Oman, and Qatar have corporate taxes, but these apply mostly to oil companies and financial institutions. *See* 29 Tax Laws of the World 96, 110 (1987). Palau has a schedular and somewhat hybrid system, which includes a tax on wages, a modified turnover tax on businesses, and a tax on the net income of financial institutions.

In the development of the tax internationally, the influence of three countries–Germany, the United Kingdom, and the United States–has been predominant. Other systems can for the most part trace their origins back to these three, in some cases in combination. For example, the original income tax law of France was influenced by that of Germany and the United Kingdom.[6]

The U.K. legislation retains to this day the schedular definition of income of the 1803 law. This law also influenced the approach of other European countries, primarily indirectly via Germany. By contrast, the U.S. adopted a global definition of income in its original 1862 law,[7] and retained this approach when the income tax was reinstated at the end of the 19th and beginning of the 20th century.

At a general level, the degree of commonality in income tax is striking, given that the theoretical possibilities for different forms of income

(margin handwritten note: Schedular vs. global)

---

[6] *See* Guy Gest, *France, in* Ault et al. (1997), at 39.

[7] Although the U.S. had a federal income tax during the Civil War and later in the 19th century, it did not play a significant role until after the adoption of the Sixteenth Amendment to the Constitution in 1913. The income tax in the U.S. had its origin in colonial faculty taxes, but these were not true income taxes, being mainly imposed on presumed incomes from various professions. *See* Seligman, The Income Tax 383-84 (1914). By contrast, "most of the state income taxes of the nineteenth century...have been true income taxes". *Id.* at 384. The federal income tax was originally imposed by the Revenue Act of 1861, ch. 45, § 49, 12 Stat. 292, 309 (repealed 1862), but this law was never enforced. The first operative federal income tax was the one enacted in July 1862. Law of July 1, 1862, ch. 99, 12 Stat. 432, 473, sec. 89. *See* Seligman, *supra,* at 435-40. The charging provision of the 1862 Act (sec. 89) read as follows: "That there shall be levied, collected, and paid annually, upon the annual gains, profits, or income of every person residing in the United States, whether derived from any kind of property, rents, interest, dividends, salaries, or from any profession, trade, employment, or vocation carried on in the United States or elsewhere, or from any other source whatever, except as hereinafter mentioned, if such annual gains, profits, or income exceed the sum of six hundred dollars, and do not exceed the sum of ten thousand dollars, a duty of three per centum on the amount of such annual gains, profits, or income over and above the said sum of six hundred dollars; if said income exceeds the sum of ten thousand dollars, a duty of five per centum upon the amount thereof exceeding six hundred dollars; and upon the annual gains, profits, or income, rents, and dividends accruing upon any property, securities, and stocks owned in the United States by any citizen of the United States residing abroad, except as hereinafter mentioned, and not in the employment of the government of the United States, there shall be levied, collected, and paid a duty of five per centum." There followed a provision about as long allowing for deductions, and somewhat lengthier provisions concerning procedure. The whole income tax law took up three pages.

taxation are virtually limitless. For example, while there has been extensive academic discussion of a personal expenditure tax, even to the extent of working out the details of such a tax, no country has one.[8] Most countries have a generally similar approach to taxing the chief forms of income (wages and business income), with a greater divergence of approach in taxing various kinds of income from capital, although the degree of variation is limited. This relatively broad similarity does not mean that there are not differences in technical detail. At the same time, there are substantial differences in policy on particular issues, more so than in the case of the VAT, which is much more uniformly applied from country to country than the income tax.

7.2 CONCEPT OF INCOME AND DEFINITIONAL STRUCTURE

7.2.1 IN GENERAL

In most countries, the legal definition of income results from superimposing a *definitional structure* (schedular or global)[9] upon an underlying *concept of income* (accretion, source, or trust concept). An archetypal global income tax employs a unitary definition of income[10] and does not distinguish among different types of income. Likewise, the method for determining net income, in particular, rules for allowable deductions, is the same no matter what the type of income. Net income is then subject to tax under a single progressive rate schedule.

On the other side of a continuum from a global tax is the archetypical schedular tax. Under a pure schedular tax, there is no single definition of income. Rather, different types of income are defined and taxed separately. The rules for determining income under each schedule are different and different rates of tax apply. Losses from one category may not be set off

---

[8] The income tax laws of many countries do, however, contain substantial expenditure tax elements (especially in respect of pension savings). Croatia adopted for awhile a business tax base that was close to expenditure tax treatment, but this was abandoned in 2000. *See* Marina Kesner Skreb, *New Corporate, Personal Income Tax Rules in Effect in Croatia,* 22 Tax Notes Int'l 2319 (May 7, 2001).

[9] In continental Europe, the terminology for schedular and global is *analytic* and *synthetic*, respectively. *See, e.g.,* Leif Mutén, On the Development of Income Taxation Since World War I, at III-8 (1967).

[10] Countries with a global definition of income include the U.S., Australia, and Canada (although there is a breakdown into five sources of income: office or employment, business, property, capital gains, and miscellaneous).

against income in other categories. Few countries have a pure schedular system any longer.[11] Global taxation makes sense as a matter of policy because it corresponds more closely to equity in taxation. But in moving away from schedular taxation, countries have not necessarily made a clean break from the schedular past. Rather, the schedular definition of income has typically been retained, but income as defined in the separate schedules is combined and taxed under a single rate schedule. (For example, losses from one category of income may normally be offset against positive amounts of income in other categories, thus achieving close to the same result as obtains under a global definition of income.)   Moreover, substantial schedular elements (most notably, final withholding taxes for certain categories of income) may be included.

In many countries,[12] therefore, a schedular definition of income underlies what is largely a global income tax.[13] Income is subject to tax under a single, usually progressive, rate schedule. While there is some commonality across countries in the categorization of income, the approaches are not uniform. Most of the differences in the legal categories arise not from fundamentally different ways of categorizing income but from the ways that the types of income are grouped together. For example, in France there is a separate category for private capital gains while in Germany these are included in the category of income from investments. This is not a fundamental difference. Virtually all countries with a schedular definition of income place wages (or, more generally, income from dependent personal services) in a separate category, as well as having a separate category for business profits.

A number of developing and transition countries, in revising their income tax legislation in recent years, have adopted an accretion concept with a global definition as an uncluttered approach. The individual income tax of such countries tends to contain strong schedular elements, however, such as special rules for employment income and final withholding on items such as interest and dividends. For some of these countries, opting for a global

---

[11] See the list in TLDD at 496 n.2. None of these are OECD countries. *See also* Var Hoorn (1972) at 7-9 (history of movement from schedular to global). Romania has since adopted a global income tax. *See* Ordinance No. 7 of July 19, 2001, *approved* by Law No. 493 of July 11, 2002.

[12] Including Belgium, France, Germany, Japan, the Netherlands, Sweden, and the U.K..

[13] For France, see CGI art. 1.   The professional income category include miscellaneous income: "sources of profits not included in another category of benefit or incomes." *Id.* art. 92. For Germany, see EStG § 2.

definition represents a break with their colonial past in favor of a more eclectic and modern approach.

Countries with a schedular definition of income often provide different rules for determining the amount of taxable income in different categories of income, including different rules for methods of accounting and allowable deductions, and exempt amounts for different categories.[14]

Within the group of countries providing a schedular definition of income, one can draw distinctions among countries according to the comprehensiveness of the definition of income. A common technique is to define income according to various categories, but then to provide that "other income" falls into a residual category. Here, one can ask how comprehensive the residual category is. This depends on the underlying concept of income. If the underlying concept is broad, and includes any accessions to wealth, then the residual category includes any accession to wealth that is not enumerated in the other categories. However, if the concept of income is more restricted, as is the case where the source concept of income is maintained, then the residual category will include only those receipts that correspond to this income concept (i.e. that are considered to flow from a source). The same words –"other income"—therefore can mean quite different things in the laws of different countries depending on the legal tradition of what the concept of income is.[15]

7.2.2 CONCEPTS OF INCOME

Three general underlying concepts of income can be identified. The *accretion* concept[16] holds that any realized accession to wealth is income. This concept applies in the United States. The concept was not spelled out in the statute, but developed through administrative and judicial practice, finally

---

[4] This approach has been criticized in Germany for "encompassing income incompletely, valuing it differently, and imposing tax differently," depending on the type of income, resulting in complexity and unfairness. Tipke/Lang (2002) at 354.

[5] For example, the statutes of both the U.S. and Canada refer to income derived from any source. But this means different things. In the U.S., it means that any accession to wealth is income, regardless of its source. In Canada, it means almost the opposite: only items having a "source" are income.

[5] The term was apparently first used by Robert Haig in 1921 (referring to the concept formulated by Schanz in 1896). *See* Paul Wueller, *Concepts of Taxable Income I*, 53 Political Science Quarterly 83, 104 n.76 (1938).

being articulated in a 1955 Supreme Court decision.[17] A second is the *source* concept, under which an item is income only if it flows from a source.[18] Finally, the *trust* concept of income is found in many Commonwealth countries. Both the trust concept and the source concept are applied together in the U.K. and many other Commonwealth countries.[19] Since the concepts are closely related, they may not always be distinguished in countries where both apply.   They both originate in a time when agriculture was the chief source of income generation. The concept of income as an annual value may indeed precede the modern income tax; for example, well before the modern income tax emerged at the beginning of the 19th century, the U.K. had taxes that were based on annual values.[20]

Under all concepts, courts have held that income must be *realized* in order to be subject to tax. Legislation in various countries has changed this result selectively, particularly with respect to financial instruments.

The source concept excludes from income such items as windfalls (e.g., lottery or gambling winnings), personal injury awards, gifts, capital gains, and certain other items that cannot be traced to a source (such as payments received after an employment has ceased).[21]   Capital gains are

---

[17] Commissioner v. Glenshaw Glass Co., 348 U.S. 426, 431 (1955) (income means "accessions to wealth, clearly realized, and over which the taxpayers have complete dominion").

[18] *See generally* Tipke/Lang (2002) at 221; Horacio A. García Belsunce, El Concepto de Rédito en la Doctrina y en el Derecho Tributario (1967). According to Beltrame and Mehl, the source concept derives from "the classical economists, according to whom income is the periodic fruit of a permanent source." Beltrame & Mehl (1997) at 136. The source concept also applies in Canada. *See* Brian Arnold, *Canada, in* Ault et al. (1997) at 27. It excludes from income such items as windfall gains, including lottery winnings, and capital gains (although the statute now includes some gains in income). The source concept also applies in France. *See* Guy Gest, *France, in* Ault et al. (1997) at 40.

[19] For the U.K., see Tiley (2000) at 131-32 (both trust concept and source concept). In Australia the trust concept applies and the source concept may have some application. *See* Richard Vann, *Australia, in* Ault et al. (1997) at 9-10.

[20] *See* Kevin Holmes, The Concept of Income 175 (2001).

[21] *See* Ault et al. (1998) at 187-88. More recent thinking in Germany follows the market income theory, under which tax reaches income earned through gainful activity carried out with a profit-making purpose. *See* Tipke/Lang (2002) at 222. This is still broadly consistent with the source theory, which is followed in Germany for incomes other than business, professional, and agricultural income. In Canada the Supreme Court concluded not too long ago that strike pay was not income since there was no source. *See* Fries v. The Queen, [1990] 2 S.C.R. 1322; Brian Arnold *Canada's Supreme Court Decides 'Reasonable Expectation of Profit' Cases*, 27 Ta

thought to result from a disposition of the source itself, and therefore are not in the nature of income. Countries vary in the strictness of application of the source concept. Perhaps the most extreme interpretation of the source concept is that the source must exist at the time that the income is received. Initially adopted by the courts in the U.K., Canada, and Australia, this view has now largely been overruled by statute in specific areas.[22]

The origins of the source concept of income have been attributed to an agricultural economy:

> The concept of income that has come down to us from the past took its character from agriculture...[I]ncome appears to be a physical fact and to consist of the annual harvest...[C]apital also appears to be a physical fact: it is the land, predominantly.... Income arises from purposeful economic activity...and recurs fairly regularly....Casual, sporadic, and unexpected gains, whether derived from the sale of land, other property not ordinarily dealt in by the recipient, gifts, or otherwise, did not fit into this concept of income....Lacking a continuing source, such as a farm or business enterprise, they arose from discrete events. Hence they could not reliably be expected to recur at regular intervals. A prudent man, the conclusion was, will therefore regard them differently from ordinary income. He will treat them as additions to his capital, not available for ordinary consumption.[23]

Notes Int'l 111 (July 1, 2002). The Canadian courts have also denied deductions for expenses incurred before a source comes into existence or after it ceases to exist. *See id.* "In *Schwartz v. The Queen*, (1996) 1 CTC 303 (SCC) [[1996] 1 S.C.R. 254], the Supreme Court held that an amount received by a taxpayer as compensation for breach of a contract of employment before the employment had begun was not income from a source." *Id.* at 112. While the continued use of the source concept has been criticized as anachronistic, *see* Dixon and Arnold, *Rubbing Salt into the Wound: The Denial of the Interest Deduction After the Loss of a Source of Income*, 39 Can. Tax J. 1473-96 (1991), it has been used by the revenue service to attack various abusive situations, for example, hobby activities. The analysis is that if the taxpayer does not have a reasonable expectation of profit then there is no business, hence no source, and hence no deductible expenses. *See* Arnold, *supra*. By contrast, in the U.S. the hobby loss problem has been dealt with by a specific statutory solution. *See* IRC § 183.

[22] *See* Brian Arnold, *Canada, in* Ault et al. (1997) at 27-28.

[23] Lawrence H. Seltzer, *Evolution of the Special Legal Status of Capital Gains Under the Income Tax*, 3 Nat'l Tax J. 18 (1950).

The trust concept of income distinguishes income (or "revenue") from capital.[24] It originated in trust law from the problem of allocating amounts between the income beneficiaries in a trust and the holders of the remainder interest.[25] When a trustee disposed of a portion of the corpus of the trust, perhaps receiving cash and reinvesting the proceeds in another asset, this transaction was not seen as generating funds that could be paid out to the income beneficiaries without depleting the trust. Payment of the proceeds of a disposition of corpus would invade the corpus, thereby eroding the value of the remainder interest.

It is not clear whether or to what extent the concept of income was borrowed from trust law to be used in tax law or whether the concepts used in trust law and tax law in the U.K. simply coincided.[26] A 1921 tax decision explicitly referred to trust law.[27] As for the earlier British understanding of income, trust law and tax law may have shared the prevailing understanding of income, which seems to have differed from that in the U.S.:

> The "trust" concept of income was the prevailing understanding of income in a society, such as England's,

---

[24] *See* Tiley (2000) at 131-32. In referring to expenditures, the U.K. terminology tends to be whether the expenditures are "on capital or revenue account." *See* Tiley (2000) at 370.

[25] A trust is an arrangement whereby one person (or a group of persons), the trustee (or trustees), holds the legal title to property in trust for one or more beneficiaries (who are said to have an equitable interest in the property). *See generally* William Fratcher and Austin Wakeman Scott, The Law of Trusts (4th ed. 1987). Trusts grew up under the courts of equity in England, and are known in common law countries. There are some analogues in civil law countries (such as *fideicommisum*) but these are not exactly the same. Some civil law countries have in recent times created trust-like institutions by legislation.

An example can illustrate how the trust concept of income arose. Suppose that a husband (H) left property under his will to be held by a trustee in trust, the income to be distributed for life to his wife (W), and upon W's death the trustees were to distribute the remaining property of the trust (known as the corpus or remainder) to W's children (known as the remaindermen). W is said to hold an income interest. Suppose that the trust comes to sell one of its assets. When the trust sells the asset at a gain and receives cash, the question is—what should the trustee do with the cash? Should it be distributed to W or should it be reinvested in the trust for eventual distribution to the remaindermen? Disputes on such questions between the remaindermen and the holders of income interests led the courts of equity to develop the idea that gains on the sale of assets should not be considered income, because they are properly to be reinvested by the trust for distribution to the remaindermen.

[26] *See generally* Holmes, *supra* note 20, at 152, 173-98.

[27] I.R.C. v. Blott, [1921] 2 A.C. 171.

where estates were typically entailed, so that the life tenant was unable to dispose of the principal....By contrast, in the early U.S. economy, entailed estates were not common, while gains on real estate were a common source of wealth.[28]

The trust concept not only deals with characterization of receipts as revenue or capital, but also provides for the characterization of expenses as on revenue or capital account. There are similarities in the way that trust law deals with expenses and how they are dealt with under generally accepted accounting principles in the business context, but the result may not be identical.

Both the source concept and the trust concept rule out taxing capital gains, but for somewhat different reasons and with different consequences. The difference lies with capital gains that arise in a business. Under the source concept, these gains flow from a source, namely the business. Thus, in continental European countries, business income is typically taxed without drawing a distinction between revenue gains and capital gains.[29] Under the trust concept, however, the exclusion of capital gains from income applies in accounting for gains from a business as much as for gains on the disposition of investment assets. Therefore, in Commonwealth jurisdictions that embrace the trust concept of income, business income is considered not to include capital gains. Legislatures have typically reversed this result by statute; the legislative structure often involves a separate capital gains tax superimposed on top of an income tax, although sometimes capital gains are included as a separate category of income subject to tax. In the U.K., taxable capital gains of companies are determined under the Taxation of Capital Gains Act, and are then included in profits subject to corporation tax.

---

[28] Seltzer, *supra* note 23, at 18-19, 22-23. Seltzer goes on to note that "Although the economy of the United States was predominantly agricultural in its early years, realized capital gains quickly took on a more conspicuous role in this country than they had abroad. Land was so plentiful and cheap that its ownership did not carry the same social prestige that it did abroad. The strong desire to keep the descent of land ownership along family lines that was so conspicuous in Europe was relatively weak in this country. The purchase and sale of lands and the accumulation of private fortunes through the profits from such transactions became common early in our history...In this environment capital gains became scarcely distinguishable from ordinary business profits for many business men and they became a familiar source of private wealth." *Id.* at 22-23.

[29] There may, however, be statutory concessions for certain gains on disposals of business assets. These concessions are motivated by policy reasons rather than the idea that these gains are capital in nature.

By contrast, in continental Europe the typical result of the source concept of income is that private (i.e. nonbusiness) capital gains are not subject to tax, unless the legislature has created a separate category of income to tax them (in derogation of the source concept). This has happened to varying degrees in most continental European countries: some countries (e.g., France) now tax all capital gains. Other countries (e.g., Germany) tax capital gains in the case of individuals who hold a substantial interest in a company,[30] as well as gains that are considered speculative because they arise from short-term trading.

7.2.3 DEFINITIONS AND CONCEPTS OF INCOME IN PRACTICE

While the source and trust concepts of income still apply at an underlying level in a number of countries, legislatures have decided in most countries that these concepts do not make sense as a matter of tax policy since they contravene principles of tax equity. Legislatures have modified the legal definitions of income to tax amounts which would not be income under the source or trust concepts. Despite this convergence of policy, however, it is necessary to understand the underlying income concept in order to comprehend the statutory scheme. The table shows the general combination of definitional structure and income concept in various countries. As can be seen, virtually all the possible combinations are represented:

	Definitional structure	*Concept*
Australia	global	source, trust
Canada	global	source, trust
U.S.	global	accretion
France	schedular	source
Germany	schedular	source
Italy	schedular	source
Japan	schedular	accretion
Spain	schedular	source
U.K.	schedular	source, trust

---

[30] The definition of what is a substantial interest has been changed recently to include more holdings. *See infra* 7.9.2.

There has been a considerable degree of *convergence* in terms of what is included in the legal definition of income, but in achieving this convergence legislatures have typically built upon old concepts, rather than discarding them completely.

A somewhat anachronistic step in the shift from schedular to global systems is so-called composite taxation. Under a composite system, separate schedular taxes are imposed (under different rates), and the amounts taxed under each schedule are then combined and subject to tax under a progressive rate schedule, with a credit being allowed for the taxes paid under the separate schedules. A number of countries (e.g., France) at one point had composite systems as part of the movement to global taxation, but composite systems can now be found in only a few developing and transition countries and no longer in any OECD countries.[31]

What is the definitional structure and underlying concept of income in the country in question?

7.3 SCHEDULAR ELEMENTS IN INCOME TAXATION

As a counter-trend to the move from schedular to global taxation, many schedular elements have for various reasons crept into global income taxes.[32] I call them schedular elements to distinguish the archetypical schedular tax, although sometimes the distinction between schedular elements superimposed on a global tax and a schedular tax that has become partially global is hard to draw. As a structural matter, these schedular elements can be built on top of a pure global income tax. Or they might take the form of a reverse evolution from a global tax. Let us look at a few examples.

Quite typical in many developing and transition countries is the taxation of interest and dividends paid to individuals on the basis of final withholding taxes (or in some cases the outright exemption of such amounts).[33] Several Nordic countries, as well as the Netherlands, are also taxing capital income at a flat rate, and Germany has proposed to do so for interest income.[34]

---

[31] For example, Chile and the Republic of Serbia (in Yugoslavia, the income tax is imposed at the level of the two republics rather than at the federal level).

[32] The same two-fold convergence was noted by Mutén in 1967. *See* Mutén, *supra* note 9, at III-8. *See also* Van Hoorn (1972) at 10.

[33] *See infra* 7.8.1.

[34] *See infra* 7.8.1.

A separate tax regime often applies to capital gains. For example, in the U.S., even though capital gains have always been considered part of income, they have been subject to one sort of favorable regime or another for most of the time (except for a brief period following the Tax Reform Act of 1986). Similarly, certain capital gains are taxed at favorable rates or are allowed to be deferred in France, Germany, and other countries.[35]

Many systems (even those with a global definition of income such as the U.S.) prohibit the deduction of losses in certain categories of income against other types of income.[36] Such limitations respond to various policy concerns. For example, in the U.S., capital losses in excess of a specified amount are generally deductible only against capital gains. This responds to the concern that taxpayers with substantial investment holdings might realize losses but not gains, thereby reducing their tax on other sources of income. Further, investment interest is deductible only against investment income in the U.S. This is motivated by the concern that taxpayers may fail to realize capital gains in the case of debt-financed holdings.   Losses from an individual's so-called "passive activities" (isn't tax jargon great?), which are business activities in which the taxpayer does not personally participate, may not be used against other income. Here, the concern is to cut off the use of tax shelters (in contrast to a business in which the taxpayer is actually working).

Finally, virtually every income tax system is studded with special rules concerning particular types of income. For example, many countries provide special treatment for expenses incurred by employees in earning employment income. In some countries a deduction is denied for such expenses; in others a threshold is provided below which such expenses are not deductible; in others, all employees are given a specified allowance for such deductions, with itemized expenses deductible only if they exceed the allowance.

The bottom line is that it is quite possible for a tax based on a global definition of income to end up seeming as schedular as, or even more schedular than, a tax that starts out with a schedular definition of income with different rules for calculating each category of income. The classification of income tax laws according to the basic definitional structure therefore tells us little about the ultimate operation of the tax. It is, however, useful in terms of understanding the tax's legal and historical structure.

In overall terms, while there clearly has been convergence as countries have moved away from a schedular system toward a global system,

---

[35] Some countries, e.g. Singapore, still do not tax capital gains. *See* Derivatives and Financial Instrument 289 (1999).

[36] *See* Ault et al. (1997) at 245-48.

we also see a general convergence in the opposite direction. No country operates a purely global system without distinguishing among different kinds of income, and over time more and more such distinctions have been adopted by different countries.

What schedular elements can be found in the country's income tax?

7.4 THE TAX UNIT

A few countries define the married couple as the tax unit (U.S., Portugal, Switzerland). Belgium taxes the couple as a unit but taxes the earned income of the lower-income spouse at progressive rates.[37] France and Luxembourg tax the entire family under a family quotient system. However, the international trend has been to move toward taxation of each individual independently (or to provide for aggregation with income splitting, but with an option for separate filing).[38] Separate taxation of spouses is the most common. In some countries, the adoption of a system other than mandatory aggregation has been motivated by constitutional considerations.[39] In other countries, administrative concerns support individual taxation; it is easier for systems that are largely based on withholding, since each wage earner's tax can be determined without regard to the situation of the person's spouse. This allows the tax withheld from wages to stand as the final tax in most cases, thereby obviating the need to file returns. By contrast, in the United States, with almost universal return filing, this is not a concern, and therefore there is a greater freedom to take decisions on the family unit, and on the applicable rate schedules, independently of administrative considerations.

In addition to administrative concerns, how to tax married as opposed to single persons involves fundamental concepts of fairness, as well as attitudes about marriage and the economics of married women's labor force participation. The topic is therefore a controversial one, lacking a unique technical solution or uniform practice.[40]

---

[37] *See* Introduction to Belgian Law 356 (Hubert Bocken & Walter de Bondt eds. 2001).

[38] *See* Beltrame and Mehl (1997) at 198-203.

[39] *See supra* 4.3.8.

[40] *See, e.g.,* Michael McIntyre, *Marital Income Splitting in the Modern World: Lessons for Australia from the American Experience, in* Tax Units and the Tax Rate Scale 1 (J. Head and R. Krever eds., 1996); Neil Brooks, *The Irrelevance of Conjugal Relationships in Assessing Tax Liability, in id.* at 35; Thuronyi, *The Concept of Income,* 46 Tax L. Rev. 45, 68-77 (1990).

What is the tax unit?   In what cases is marital status relevant for taxation?

7.5 RATE SCHEDULE

Income tax rates have been reduced substantially in most countries over the past 25 years or so.   Individual income tax rates were as high as 90 percent in the United States as recently as 1980.   These rates have steadily come down.   The rate reduction has been pursued fairly universally,[41] so that now rates in excess of 50% can rarely be found, and many countries have substantially lower rates.   In the corporate income tax area, Ireland has adopted a generally applicable low rate in lieu of targeted tax preferences. Several countries have adopted flat rates (e.g. Russia).   As long as there is a substantial personal exemption, even a flat rate system is progressive.   No country with a serious income tax has abandoned a progressive rate structure.

What is the marginal rate for most people?   What is the top marginal rate (determined by taking into account any phase-outs and the like)?

7.6 PERSONAL DEDUCTIONS

Many countries allow a deduction for personal expenses of various kinds.   The allowance of these deductions is motivated by considerations of equity, but considerations of efficient tax administration counsel against allowing them.   Virtually all systems allow dependency deductions based on family size and take them into account in the withholding calculation.   Some European countries have replaced tax relief with direct assistance.[42]   Because the amount of allowances does not change frequently for any given taxpayer, the administrative burden is not so great.   Many systems, however, particularly in developing and transition countries, allow no further deductions in order to keep the number of returns filed to a minimum.

In the U.S., virtually everyone files a return.   Allowing personal deductions therefore does not increase the number of returns that have to be

---

[41] In the U.K., the rate on employment income was reduced from 83 percent to 60 percent around 1980 and the rate on capital income from 98 percent to 75 percent. *See* Malcolm Gammie, *International Tax Avoidance: A UK Perspective, in* International Studies in Taxation: Law and Economics: Liber Amicorum Leif Mutén (Gustaf Lindencrona et al. eds. 1999) 111.

[42] *See* Beltrame & Mehl (1997) at 202.

processed. Of course, itemized deductions do complicate compliance and audit, and so a generous standard deduction is allowed in lieu of itemizing. The majority of taxpayers do not itemize. For those who do, personal deductions can be substantial.[43]

There are substantial differences among countries in the extent to which deductions other than business expenses are allowed.

Most countries allow a deduction for interest expense only if the interest is traceable to borrowing for business or investment.[44] This approach is consistent with a schedular definition of income. The U.S. allows in addition a deduction for certain home mortgage interest. With limited exceptions, the U.K. and France allow a deduction for business interest only.[45] France is stricter than most, disallowing as well a deduction for investment interest. Sweden allows a deduction for all interest, but there are special allocation rules related to the fact that capital income is taxed at lower rates.

The U.S. is virtually alone in allowing a deduction for casualty losses on personal-use property, although a substantial floor has been introduced, which limits the importance of this deduction.[46] In Germany casualty losses are sometimes deductible under the general rubric of "extraordinary expenses." A number of countries allow a deduction for medical expenses, often subject to limitation or a floor.[47] A deduction for charitable contributions, again often subject to floors and limits, is also common but not universal.[48]

A number of countries have introduced tax credits instead of deductions for some expenses of a personal nature, thereby giving relief at a rate differing from the taxpayer's marginal rate of tax.

What personal deductions are allowed? Are these available to all employees or only to those filing a return or itemizing?

---

[3] The itemized deductions include principally: state income and real property tax, interest, charitable contributions, and, to the extent they exceed specified floors, medical expenses, casualty losses, and employees' and other miscellaneous expenses. The 1986 Act also increased the standard deduction in order to reduce the number of taxpayers itemizing deductions.

[4] *See* Ault et al. (1997) at 233-36.

[5] *See* Tiley (2000) at 168; Ault et al. (1997) at 236.

[ ] *See* Ault et al. (1997) at 236-37.

[ ] *See* Ault et al. (1997) at 238-39.

See Ault et al. (1997) at 239-41.

7.7 EMPLOYMENT INCOME

7.7.1 DEFINITION OF EMPLOYEE

Virtually all countries have special rules for employment income. These respond to practical concerns about administrability of the income tax. In principle, employees could be treated the same as businesspersons, keeping the same type of books and calculating the tax liability on their own. This would not work as a practical matter because the vast majority of employees would not be in a position to keep books to the same strict standards as businesses and because their vast number would make tax control impossible. Instead, as discussed below, virtually all countries have adopted a special regime for employees under which most of the obligation for determination and payment of the tax falls on the employer. The nature of the regime for employees has little to do with the global or schedular definition of income. Although for countries with a schedular definition of income, the special regime for employment income falls neatly within the statutory scheme, even countries with a global definition of income have established special rules for employment income, often in derogation from the general rules concerning income and expenses.

The regime for taxing employees is remarkably similar across countries in its broad outlines, posing similar problems. There are, however, significant differences in the extent to which countries make a fuss about: fringe benefits (depending in part on each country's experience with their use for tax avoidance); the allowance of employee deductions (which is linked to the proportion of taxable employees filing a return); the extent of the withholding obligation; and the treatment of particular fringes and deductions.

The existence of special rules for employees requires "employee" to be defined. This is inherently problematic. Because individuals can offer their services through contractual relationships that are not employment contracts, taxpayers will try to get around the definition by structuring their service contracts appropriately, no matter how employees are defined. There will be an incentive for such legal manoeuvres if there are substantially different rules (or higher tax rates, such as for social security contributions for employees and for independent contractors (who would pay tax under the head of business or professional income).

Employees are often taxed less favorably than independent contractors. Virtually all countries require employers to withhold tax from wages, but not from payments to independent contractors. Deductions are typically limited for employees. Some countries, though, provide a flat allowance for employees. By itself, this could serve to make classification as an employee for income tax purposes advantageous in many instances although if the social security tax considerations are taken into account, independent contractors are typically better off. Social contributions must typically be withheld from wages, while independent contractors may be subject to favorable schemes or may practice "self-help" social security tax reduction.

The definition of employee in civil law countries tends to rely on the labor law (German tax law has an autonomous definition, though).[49] In common law countries, the definition tends to be based on tort law doctrines of *respondeat superior*, or on employment law,[50] and the courts are often left to resolve the issue on a case-by-case basis. The U.K. courts have struggled with short term engagements, as by actors. The matter could be resolved by looking at the nature of each engagement on its own or by seeing engagements in aggregate as a profession.[51]

Statutes typically incorporate in the definition of employee for tax purposes persons who would not be treated as employees under general nontax concepts, for example company directors or other officeholders.[52] Even if these individuals are not employees for labor law purposes, it makes good sense to subject them to withholding and other special rules that apply to employees for tax purposes.[53] Attempts to provide detail to the definition of employee include a U.S. revenue ruling, which lists 20 factors to be taken into account.[54] The political sensitivity of the issue is illustrated by the fact that in 1978, legislation was passed preventing the U.S. Treasury Department from issuing regulations that would have provided a more airtight definition.[55]

Taxpayers may find it advantageous to interpose a personal service company (PSC) between themselves and their employer. While the taxpayer would be the employee of the PSC, the PSC would not pay to the taxpayer the entire amount received from the recipient of the services. The balance might be distributed as a dividend or as capital gain, thus attracting lighter taxation

---

[49] *See* Tipke/Lang (2002) at 386.

[50] *See* Tiley (2000) at 201-02; Hogg et al. (2002) at 105-08.

[51] *See* Tiley (2000) at 203-04.

[52] For example, the U.K. taxes under schedule E emoluments from an office or employment. *See* Tiley (2000) at 200-01.

[53] *See generally* Lee Burns & Richard Krever, *Individual Income Tax, in* TLDD 495, 509-10. In the U.K., Schedule E applies to emoluments from an office or employment.

[54] Rev. Rul. 87-41, 1987-1 C.B. 296.

[55] *See* Burns & Krever, *supra* note 53, at at 510 n. 60. Another example (apparently) of politics is the exclusion of North Sea divers from Schedule E in the U.K.. *See* Tiley (2000) at 202 n.38.

than wages would. This might be particularly attractive if corporate tax rates are lower than rates for individuals. Such arrangements have been attacked in different ways in different countries. The U.S. has a number of special rules for PSCs, including accumulated earnings tax. In addition, the use of PSCs has been struck down by the courts in some cases on assignment-of-income grounds. Finally, section 482 can be used to reallocate income between the taxpayer and the PSC. The U.K. recently enacted rules under which compensation for services provided by a PSC is taxed under Schedule E (i.e. as employment income). The statutory test is whether, if the services were directly provided by the individual to the client, the relationship would be one of employment.[56] The enactment of such a specific anti-avoidance rule seems typical of the U.K. By contrast, a country like Germany may prefer to deal with the problem by applying its general anti-avoidance rule. This would hold that if the contractual relationship represents an unusual means of achieving the desired result, namely employment of the individual taxpayer by the entity to which the taxpayer is providing services, then the arrangement will be regarded as an employment for tax purposes.

What is the general approach to defining employees? Are there special statutory exceptions for officeholders and the like? Are there any special rules imposing withholding obligations with respect to payments to independent contractors?

7.7.2 DEFINITION OF EMPLOYMENT INCOME

What is employment income may seem obvious, but this is not necessarily so in systems with a source concept of income. In such systems, the question arises whether a payment made before employment begins or after it ends is income, since in these cases there is no "source" in existence at the time the payment is made.[57] In the U.K., a terminal payment in

---

[56] *See* Tiley (2000) at 205-06. See R (on the application of Professional Contractors Group Ltd and others) v. Inland Revenue Commissioners, [2001] EWHC Admin 236, Queen's Bench Division, Administrative Court (Apr. 2, 2001), 3 ITLR 556.

[57] For example, under a court decision payments remitted to the U.K. at a time when a foreign employment no longer existed and taxable on a remittance basis were not subject to tax. *See* Tiley (2000) at 209, 212. This rule was reversed by statute. The statute now provides that amounts received in respect of an office or employment that is no longer held are emoluments of the last year in which the office or employment was held. *See id.* at 225. In continental countries, the statute often provides explicitly that earnings attributable to previous employment are taxable. *See* EstG § 19(1)(2) (Germany); Tiberghien (1995) at 162 (Belgium).

connection with the ending of an office or employment is not taxed.[58] In countries where this is an issue, legislatures have not accepted this application of the source concept as a matter of policy, and have accordingly overridden judicial decisions holding that various types of payment were not income.

In addition, the U.K. courts have read narrowly the concept of emolument—remuneration for services. In *Hochstrasser v. Mayes*, the House of Lords held that compensation paid by the employer on the occasion of a relocation for the loss in value of an employee's house was not taxable as an emolument.[59] Because of the schedular definition of income, the result was that the payment was not taxable at all, since it fell into no other schedule. The U.K. courts have also wrestled with the problem of gifts made in the business context.[60] Even though there is no exclusion for gifts (as there is in the U.S.), the U.K. definition of income means that no tax would arise on a gift if it was not considered an emolument. Compensation paid by an employer for the employee's loss of a right has also been held nontaxable.[61] The U.K. courts also held a payment for a covenant not to compete to be nontaxable, but this result has been overturned by statute.[62] The disputes over the concept of "emolument" are a good example of the differences between a schedular and a global definition of income; with a schedular definition, if a particular receipt does not fit within the definition of one of the schedules, it is not income. With a global definition (as in the U.S.), receipts are considered income unless they fall within an exclusion (such as for gifts). Legislatures have dealt with this problem over time so that, by now, there are no major differences in practice between systems based on schedular and global definitions.

Does the country have a source concept of income? Does this concept allow any forms of employment income to escape tax?

7.7.3 FRINGE BENEFITS

The most vexing issue in the taxation of employment income is posed by fringe benefits.

---

[58] *See* Tiley (2000) at 207, 233-39. Likewise, a reward for past service is not taxable. *See id.* at 223.

[59] *See id.* at 220-21, who notes a similar Canadian case. The result was overruled in Canada by statute. *See* Hogg et al. (2002) at 126-30.

[60] *See* Tiley (2000) at 227-30.

[61] *See id.* at 230-32 (an example is a professional player giving up amateur status).

[62] *See id.* at 233.

Fringe benefits are significant not only for income tax but also for social security contributions. Logically, the social security wage base should be the same as the base for employment income, but as a matter of historical practice there is not consistent treatment. It cannot therefore be assumed that the income tax and social security tax rules will be the same.[63]

Conceptually, the following possibilities exist for taxing fringe benefits, all of which are applied to various benefits by different countries:

- Exclusion by statute, regulation, or judicial decision;
- Arbitrary valuation (e.g., Sweden, Germany: standard values for meals, cars);
- Deduction denial;[64]
- Fringe benefit tax;
- De facto exclusion by administrative practice;[65]
- Taxation at fair market value.

As a matter of theory, it is not clear to what extent various benefits that are a part of working conditions should be taxed as a benefit. In practice, countries do not tax benefits that are considered to arise out of working conditions.

Even where it is decided to tax a benefit, it is necessary to value it. Valuation under schedules is often employed, especially for big-ticket items. In the U.K., cars account for more than half the total tax collected on fringe

---

[63] Tiley (2000) at 241 notes that many fringes are now also subject to national insurance contributions, but this was not previously the case. Tiley notes one argument against subjecting all fringes to NIC: if NIC is applicable only up to a specified level of compensation, then it will make little or no difference to include those fringes that typically are paid to higher compensated individuals, other than causing unnecessary paperwork. This argument of course does not apply if there is no ceiling to NICs. In many countries there is not.

[64] For example, medical benefits in Sweden. *See* Ault et al. (1997) at 160.

[65] *See, e.g.,* Announcement 2002-18, 2002-10 I.R.B. 621 ("...the IRS will not assert that any taxpayer has understated his federal tax liability by reason of the receipt of personal use of frequent flyer miles or other in-kind promotional benefits attributable to the taxpayer's business or official travel. Any future guidance on the taxability of these benefits will be applied prospectively.")

benefits.[66] It is therefore not surprising that the U.K. has a fairly detailed statutory scheme for taxing and valuing car benefits.[67]

Under U.K. judicial decisions, benefits are not taxable if not reducible to cash, and if so reducible are taxed according to the amount of money the employee could have obtained. This doctrine originates in the case of *Tennant v. Smith*, which involved the question whether a bank employee who was required as a condition of employment to occupy the bank premises overnight was taxable on the value of the lodging.[68] The House of Lords decided that the employee should not be taxed because a benefit "is not income unless it can be turned to money." For most purposes, the results of this case have by now been reversed by statute in the U.K. and most other Commonwealth countries. The U.S. courts were faced with the same problem[69] and solved it by crafting an exclusion for lodging provided for the convenience of the employer (this rule was subsequently codified[70]), rather than adopting a more general principle that in-kind benefits could not be taxed unless convertible to cash.

Section 132 of the U.S. Internal Revenue Code illustrates possible approaches to fringe benefits and the pragmatic and political nature of the issue. Previous to its enactment in 1984, fringe benefits were dealt with largely through administrative practice, based in part on judicial decisions, and the status of many benefits was unclear. Section 132 attempted to provide clearer rules. This was largely successful for the fringes covered, although those not explicitly dealt with still pose problems (e.g., frequent flyer miles). To some extent the statute makes a good faith attempt to balance concerns of equity and administrability, but there are some obvious political concessions to specific industries. The general approach is to allow a fairly broad range of fringe benefits to escape tax, while limiting the value of such benefits. The following types of fringes are excluded from income:

- *Working condition fringes.* The concept is that if the employee would have received a deduction if she had incurred the expense herself, the item will not be taxable. In other words, if a particular item is

---

[66] *See* Tiley (2000) at 242.

[67] ICTA 1988, s.57 and schedule 6. These rules apply a tough valuation on the car but do not include the value of parking space, since it proved difficult to value the latter. *See* Tiley (2000) at 242.

[68] [1892] AC 150, 3 TC 158, *discussed in* Tiley (2000) at 243-46.

[69] Benaglia v. Commissioner, 36 B.T.A. 838 (1937). *Tennant v. Smith* was mentioned in the opinion, but a narrower rule was fashioned by the U.S. court.

[70] I.R.C. § 119.

necessary for work, the fact that it may incidentally provide a benefit to the employee is not taken into account.

- *De minimis fringes.*   Small items that would be unreasonably burdensome to account for are not taken into account.

- *Qualified employee discounts.*   Discounts that are limited in amount are considered a normal business practice and will not give rise to a taxable benefit. The statute provides mechanical limits on the amount of the discount that may be provided: 20% for services and the average profit margin in the case of goods.

- *Qualified facilities.*   A number of on-premises facilities have some relationship to work and are left untaxed as a policy matter: on-premises gyms, cafeterias (but only if the subsidy is limited in amount), parking and transportation benefits (subject to limits).

- *No-additional-cost services.*   This provision was written mostly for airlines in response to lobbying pressure, to cover standby flights for employees.   Few other services would qualify, since normally services would require employee time to provide.

Section 132 did not touch fringe benefits that have little to do with the employer's business operations and that were specifically excluded by statute under prior law, for example, employer-provided health and life insurance and education benefits.

Australia and New Zealand (but no other major countries) impose a fringe benefits tax at the employer level. Conceptually, this approach may make sense on a targeted basis in the case of fringes that are difficult to allocate to particular employees, but as an overall approach the fringe benefits tax is problematic. It taxes fringes at an excessive rate for most employees if the tax rate is set in line with the top marginal tax rate. It also raises problems for social security taxation and for international taxation (for example, because the tax is not imposed on the employee, the employee cannot obtain a foreign tax credit). The fringe benefits tax was adopted largely for political reasons in Australia and New Zealand. Germany has a somewhat analogous treatment for a limited category of benefits, taxing them at concessional rates at the employer level and excluding them from the income of employees. These include employer-provided meals, allowances for recovery from illness, and transportation of employees between work and home.[71] It seems that these items are either difficult to allocate to employees or are deliberately subject to favorable treatment.

taxing fringes — tax employer rather than employer [handwritten margin note]

---

[71] EStG § 40.

History, politics, and tradition have led to varying exclusions for particular items. For example, the following fringe benefits are among those fully or partially exempt by statute in Germany (in some cases up to specified caps) (besides a long list of benefits for military and other public servants and payments out of public funds): unemployment benefits and severance pay, payments on marriage or birth of a child, reimbursement for travelling and moving expenses, tool allowances, typical work clothing furnished by the employer, transportation between work and home in certain cases, kindergarden expenses, tips, certain legally required payments to employees the nontaxation of which is justified by social reasons or administrative simplicity, and the employer's share of social insurance contributions.[72]

Is there a general statutory rule on fringe benefits? What is administrative practice with respect to taxing benefits for which there is no explicit statutory or regulatory rule (is there an overall tendency of lenience)? What approaches are taken with respect to various benefits? Are there any withholding obligations with respect to fringe benefits, and under what procedures? Are the obligations the same with respect to social security tax?

7.7.4 DEDUCTION FOR EMPLOYEE EXPENSES

As a matter of equity and accuracy, it would make sense to allow employees to deduct the costs of earning employment income. However, the nature of employment is such that the costs incurred by employees are relatively small, given that the employer provides the conditions for work. It is therefore less critical (in terms of tax equity) to allow a deduction for employee expenses than it is for the self-employed. An additional and critical factor is that the vast majority of taxpayers are employees. Allowing each taxpayer to deduct expenses raises a serious issue of tax administration, particularly for countries where it is desired to tax employment income through final withholding and to avoid filing of individual returns by most taxpayers.

These factors have led the majority of countries to restrict deductions for earning income from employment. There are several possible techniques. Many countries simply deny a deduction.[73] Several countries, motivated by the unfairness of denying a deduction altogether, allow a standard deduction, with those employees who can document costs in excess of the standard

---

[72] EStG § 3 (in total there are about 70 exemptions, most of which involve payments out of public funds). Some of these are subject to exemption with progression.

[73] *E.g.,* Canada. *See* Burns & Krever, *supra* note 53, at 512 n.66.

allowance allowed to deduct the excess.[74] In the U.S., a 2% floor is imposed on miscellaneous itemized deductions (which include employment expenses). This has a similar effect to the standard allowance in terms of limiting the number of employees who itemize, but it denies a deduction to most employees, instead of allowing it to all. Finally, in the U.K., a judicial doctrine holds that expenses of getting into a position to earn income are not deductible.[75] This means that many employee expenses (commuting, clothing, child care) are not deductible.

Employee expenses can also be cut back on the theory that they are "personal" in nature, and therefore nondeductible. This involves items such as commuting costs, moving expenses, clothing, business travel, entertainment, and child care. There is substantial variation in the treatment of these items, and what may seem like a self-evident rule in some countries (for example, that no deduction is allowed for commuting expenses) is not self-evident in others (such a deduction is allowed, albeit with limitations, in Germany, Sweden, Netherlands, and France).[76]

7.7.5 WITHHOLDING

In virtually all countries (with the notable exception of France, Singapore, and Switzerland)[77], employment income is subject to withholding. Withholding typically represents 75% or more (in many developing and transition countries in excess of 90%) of individual income tax revenue. In many developing and transition countries, withholding is a final tax. This rule is designed to minimize the number of returns filed, at the cost of some unfairness. Many countries operate withholding systems designed to withhold an accurate amount of tax on a cumulative annual basis.[78] By

---

[74] These include Japan and France, *see* Ault et al. (1997) at 209-10, and Spain, *see* Burns & Krever, *supra* note 53, at 512 n. 67; Beltrame & Mehl (1997) at 197.

[75] *See* Ault et al. (1997) at 205. *See, e.g.,* Ansell v. Brown, 73 T.C. 338 (High Court, Chancery Division 2001)(professional rugby player could not deduct expenses of dietary supplements, since these placed him in a position to perform his employment duties, rather than being incurred in the performance of his duties).

[76] *See* Ault et al. (1997) at 204-21.

[77] *See* OECD (1990) at 30-32 (France, Switzerland).

[78] *See generally* Koenraad van der Heeden, *The Pay-As-You-Earn Tax on Wages, in* TLDD 564. In the U.K., personal reliefs are taken into account in calculating tax to be withheld, and in most cases employees do not have to file a return with the tax authorities, adjustments being made within the PAYE system itself. *See* Tiley (2000) at 216.

[handwritten: note how US system for withholding is different]

contrast, in the U.S., withholding is fairly flexible since it is assumed that virtually all employees will be filing returns anyway and the information reporting and matching programs of the IRS prevent evasion (at least with respect to reported wages).

Fringe benefits taxable to the employee are not necessarily subject to withholding. In the U.K., withholding originally applied to money payments only, but its application was extended to certain in-kind benefits.[79] By contrast, most fringe benefits are included in wages subject to withholding in the U.S.[80]

How are wages subject to withholding defined? Is this the same as the definition for social security contributions?

7.8 CAPITAL INCOME

[handwritten: i.e., income from capital - not sale of capital asset]

7.8.1 SCHEDULAR TAXATION OF CAPITAL INCOME

Many developing and transition countries impose final withholding taxes on interest and dividends paid to individuals. Income such as rents or royalties may also be subject to this kind of treatment. Part of the motivation is administrative simplicity: given that for the vast majority of the population their only sources of income will be wages, interest, and dividends, taxing these amounts through withholding means that most individuals will not have to file returns. Further policy reasons may concern the nature of the payments themselves. In the case of dividends, exemption in the hands of individual shareholders represents a simple way of integration,[81] and taxation at a low rate represents a simple variation on the classical system that avoids the problems resulting from the imposition of a full double tax. In the case of interest, a final withholding tax (or exemption) may be a policy response to the difficulty of taxing this type of income in an inflationary environment. In addition, taxation of this kind of income from capital may be considered difficult as a policy matter since imposition of a tax can encourage capital flight.

While most industrial countries have stuck to global taxation of capital income, there are some recent important exceptions. Some Nordic countries have pioneered the flat rate taxation of capital income.[82] Part of the

---

[79] *See id.* at 213.

[80] *See* I.R.C. §3401; Treas. Reg. § 31.3501(a)-1T.

[81] *See infra* 7.12.4.

[82] *See* Leif Mutén et al., *Towards a Dual Income Tax?* (1996).

justification was that interest deductions were eroding the capital income tax base. The Netherlands has gone even further by taxing income from capital on an imputed basis, imposing a flat 30% tax rate on an imputed income of 4%.[83]   This actually goes back to the system that the country had over a hundred years earlier.[84] It remains to be seen whether this system will survive in the face of the valuation difficulties that will be involved. Recently, the German government announced its intention to propose taxation of interest income at a flat rate, no doubt in part because of problems of capital flight to neighboring countries.

An important issue in the taxation of investment income is the allowance of deductions, the most important of which tends to be interest expense.   In the U.S. the deduction for investment interest is limited to investment income. In France, investment interest is not deductible at all.[85] In the U.K., interest is deductible by individuals only under limited circumstances, so that investment interest generally is not deductible.[86]

7.8.2 TAXATION OF FINANCIAL INSTRUMENTS

Financial instruments have always been problematic for the income tax. Tolerable rules were developed for simple instruments such as debt obligations without any original issue discount, although these rules do not precisely reflect the economics of such instruments. However, rules for taxing derivatives, OID obligations and hybrid instruments are still under development.   Probably no country has rules that are considered fully satisfactory.   The U.S., the U.K., and New Zealand are probably in the forefront in this area,[87] although arguably the Netherlands has joined these

---

[83] *See* Gerwin de Wilde, *The New Dutch Income Tax Act 2002: International Tax Implications*, 54 B.I.F.D. 227 (May 2000).

[84] *See* Kees van Raad, *The Netherlands, in* Ault et al. (1997) 81, 82 (under Wealth Tax Act of 1892 income from capital was deemed to amount to 4 percent of the value of the capital).

[85] *See* Cozian (1999) at 204.

[86] Interest is deductible on loans (1) "for a partner or employee to buy machinery or plant", (2) to acquire certain closely held company interests, (3) "to buy into a partnership", or (4) "to enable personal representatives to pay certain inheritance tax." Tiley (2000) at 168.

[87] *See* Tim Edgar, The Income Tax Treatment of Financial Instruments: Theory and Practice 152-55, 157-58 (2000). A new accruals regime for financial arrangements has been under discussion for some time in Australia, and is planned to be effective

countries in the avant-guard, even though it did so by reviving a 100-year old technique.[88] The systems in other OECD countries are not as highly developed, and a fortiori this is the case for non-OECD countries. One can expect substantial legislative development in this area over the coming years. Even though countries are building on the legal categories and rules which they have been used to for a long time, financial reality is forcing the development of new rules that break out of traditional molds, as tax policymakers and legislators realize that the failure to reform can lead to substantial erosion of the tax base. Financial innovation is also rendering out of date the international rules (embodied in treaties) for taxing income from capital, with the consequent need to revamp and renegotiate treaties (although this process has not begun to any substantial extent).

In the U.S., several forms of income are now taxed on a mark-to-market or equivalent basis. Thus, original issue discount is taxed as it accrues, according to the internal rate of return of the instrument. Market discount is taxed on an accrual basis at the taxpayer's election (the election allows full deduction of associated interest expense). Certain straddles, futures, foreign currency, and option contracts are marked to market. Partly, the reason for these rules is that with new financial instruments taxpayers can realize artificial losses. The mark-to-market rules are therefore needed to tax the gains that would otherwise go unrealized. Special rules require mark-to-market taxation for dealers in securities and derivatives. Because the U.S. rules are selective, they are highly complex.

Since 1996, the U.K. has adopted accounting rules for certain financial transactions which generally require either a mark-to-market or an accruals basis of accounting.[89] These rules apply for corporation tax, not income tax or capital gains tax. This makes sense because the rules are tied to accounting treatment: as long as the accounting rules conform to the requirements of the tax laws, the accounting results are accepted for tax purposes. One regime is established for "loan relationships." Separate regimes (but with the same general contours) apply to foreign exchange transactions and to "qualifying contracts" (interest rate contracts or options, currency contracts or options and debt contracts or options). Development of the law by judicial decision, as opposed to legislation, has proven more difficult. For example, in a recent case the court refused to aggregate two options and treat them as a single loan even though they were economically

---

July 1, 2004. See Press Release C 57/02 of Sen. Helen Coonan (Assistant Treasurer), May 14, 2002, available on website of Australian Taxation Office.

[8] *See supra* 7.8.1.

[9] *See* Tiley (2000) at 833-56.

equivalent to a loan, since any increase in the amount payable on one option would be exactly matched by a reduced payment on the other option.[90]

New Zealand has pioneered in adopting in 1987 an accruals system for taxing financial assets.[91] Under these rules—called financial arrangement rules—assets are taxed by accruing annually their yield to maturity. Publicly traded property is marked to market. Although capital gains still remain untaxed in New Zealand, the accrual regime narrowed the concept of capital gains by treating returns on financial arrangements as income. In general terms, financial arrangements include debt, debt instruments, and any other arrangements under which a person receives money in consideration for providing money to any person in the future.[92] Many transactions involving a prepayment or deferred payment for goods or services are treated as financial arrangements. Equity (including partnership interests, shares, and options) is not, however, treated as a financial arrangement.[93] Derivative instruments (for example, swaps or foreign exchange forward or futures contracts), other than some equity-related derivatives, generally will be treated as financial arrangements.

Countries (such as Germany, France, and Sweden) which base the taxation of business income on financial accounting rules have less need to legislate in detail with respect to financial instruments since they automatically incorporate for tax purposes more sophisticated accounting practices which may require mark-to-market treatment in some cases. The issue for such countries will be whether they are content with the treatment provided by financial accounting rules or will legislate special rules for tax purposes (or have the financial accounting rules changed).

7.8.3 OWNER-OCCUPIED HOUSING

In most countries, the taxation of imputed income from owner-occupied housing would seem strange, even if it might be discussed academically as a matter of theory and even if it is recognized as a matter of policy that the failure to tax such income, combined with the allowance of housing-related deductions, creates serious economic distortions. It is

---

[90] *See* Griffin v. Citibank Investments Ltd., 73 T.C. 352 (High Court, Chancery Division 2000).

[91] *See generally* Susan Glazebrook et al., The New Zealand Accrual Regime (2d ed. 1999).

[92] *See* Income Tax Act 1994 sec. EH 22(1).

[93] *See id.* sec. EH 24(1).

therefore interesting to note that several countries (including Australia, France, Germany, and the U.K.) have historically taxed such income and countries like the Netherlands and Sweden still do.[94] The approach has been abandoned by some countries because of political considerations and, on a technical level, valuation problems, combined with the fact that the allowance of deductions often led to small revenues, or even losses. The taxation of imputed income from housing is consistent with the structure of the schedular system, under which assets such as real estate are often taxed by applying an imputed return.

example
of
schedular
approach

7.8.4 POLICY ON PENSIONS AND SAVINGS

While the tax rules on pensions differ, most operate on the TEE (taxed-exempt-exempt) or EET (exempt-exempt-taxed) basis, i.e. either pension contributions are made after tax, with subsequent earnings on reinvestment and upon withdrawal of the proceeds being exempt, or the contributions are deductible and earnings exempt, but the full amount is taxed on withdrawal. Both methods are equivalent under certain assumptions, so that the treatment of pensions can be seen as an exemption of capital income on retirement savings.[95]

---

[94] *See* Ault et al. (1997) at 172-75. A dozen OECD countries have taxed imputed income. *See* Tiley (2000) at 20. All the Scandinavian countries have taxed imputed income from owner-occupied housing, although it was typical for the tax system to favor homeowners because the deduction for interest tended to exceed the imputed income. *See* Gustaf Lindencrona, Trends in Scandinavian Taxation 33 (1979).

[95] The equivalence can be seen from the following two expressions. In the first expression, an amount of wages W is invested after paying tax of t_1W. The earnings grow at the rate of return r without any tax being imposed; the expression shows the amount available upon retirement after being invested for n years. The second expression shows the result under the EET system. The amount that is invested is W (no tax is due because the pension contribution is deductible). This is then invested for n years and grows at the rate r. At the end of the n years, a tax is imposed at the rate of t_2. The two expressions are equivalent if $t_1 = t_2$, i.e. if the rate of tax during the working life is the same as the rate of tax on retirement. Where, as is common, the rate of tax on retirement is less, then the EET method proves more favorable for the taxpayer.

(1) $(1-t_1)\,W\,(1+r)^n$ (tax-free investment)

(2) $W\,(1+r)^n\,(1-t_2)$ (tax-deferred pension treatment).

Besides pensions, many countries nominally imposing an income tax provide favorable treatment for a number of forms of private saving. The result is that very little tax actually falls on capital income.

Because the issues raised are primarily matters of economics and tax policy, rather than legal culture, I will not deal with them further here, beyond noting their importance for tax policy. The extent of favorable treatment for pensions and other forms of long-term savings raises questions as to the economic nature, incidence, and distributional implications of the income tax, and certainly merits further study, including on a comparative basis.

7.9 CAPITAL GAINS

7.9.1 CONCEPT OF CAPITAL GAINS

Capital gains furnish one of the most important examples of differences in conceptualization of income tax issues across countries. I focus here on the U.S., U.K., and Germany, since these represent the main approaches taken. The distinction between capital gains and ordinary income is central to the tax systems of both the U.S. and the U.K., although the significance of the distinction has varied over time. The concept of capital gains also differs in the two countries in subtle ways. By contrast, Germany has no concept of capital gains as such,[96] although gains on the disposal of assets are subject to special treatment in different contexts.

The main difference between the basic concepts of income (accretion, trust, and source) lies in how they view capital gains. Under the accretion concept, capital gains are part of income, and if—as in the U.S.—there is special treatment for capital gains, the definition of what is a capital gain flows not from the concept of income itself but from special statutory provisions influenced by the policy considerations underlying the special treatment. Early 20th century U.S. income tax laws had no special treatment for capital gains.[97] The concepts of capital assets and capital gain were first introduced in 1921, motivated by the problem that gains accumulated over several years were being taxed at high marginal rates.[98] In general terms,

---

[96] *See* Klaus Vogel, *Germany*, 61b Cahiers 129 (1976) ("The tax law of the Federal Republic of Germany does not have a concept of 'capital gains' or a comparable legal concept.")

[97] *See* Paul, *supra* note 4, at 119.

[98] *See* Burnet v. Harmel, 287 U.S. 103, 106 (1932). As defined in 1921, a capital asset was "property acquired and held by the taxpayer for profit or investment for more than two years (whether or not connected with his trade or business), but does

under U.S. law a capital gain arises on the sale or exchange of a capital asset. The relevant concepts have undergone substantial modification and limitation in the case law and numerous statutory provisions to deal with special cases.

Under the U.K.'s trust concept, one of the principal definitional elements for the concept of income is the distinction between revenue (income) and capital. Capital gains on the disposition of assets—as well as any other receipts of a capital nature—are not taxable as income, while outlays of a capital nature are nondeductible. Judicial concepts of capital receipts therefore become central for defining the tax base (except to the extent overruled by the legislature). Previously, the distinction was critical since capital receipts were not taxed. If taxpayers could find ways to turn receipts into those considered to be of a capital nature, substantial tax savings could result. A good example of the difference between U.K. and U.S. concepts is that of a premium payment on a lease. In the U.K., a lump sum payment by the lessee to the lessor at the beginning of a lease was traditionally considered a capital sum;[99] it would not be considered a capital gain in the U.S. because it does not represent the sale or exchange of a capital asset.

The German system differs from that of the U.K. in that in Germany gains on the disposition of business assets are part of business income. There is no separate concept of capital gains in the business context, and no limitation on a deduction for capital losses. However, for policy reasons the legislature has provided for favorable treatment for gains on certain kinds of disposals of business assets (for example, the transfer of an entire business).[100]

Central to the German system is the classification of assets into business and private assets. This involves a tripartite classification. Some assets are considered as inherently business assets or private assets (where

---

not include property held for the personal use or consumption of the taxpayer or his family, or stock in trade of the taxpayer or other property of a kind which would properly be included in the inventory of the taxpayer if on hand at the close of the taxable year." Revenue Act of 1921, sec. 206, Ch. 136, 42 Stat. 227, 232-33. The current definition of capital asset is found in I.R.C. § 1221.

[99] *See* Morse & Williams (2000) at 133. *Cf. supra* ch. 4, n. 282 (premium on oil and gas lease not a capital gain in U.S.).

[100] Germany offers a reserve for reinvestment of the proceeds of certain dispositions. In France, special rates of tax apply to gains on the disposition of fixed assets (*cession d'éléments de l'actif immobilisé*). *See* CGI art. 39 *duodecies*. Gains and losses on these assets are known as *plus-values et moins values professionelles,* to distinguish them from private capital gains. *See* Guy Gest, *Plus-values et moins values professionelles, in* Dictionnaire Enclyclopédique de Finances Publiques 1149 (Loïc Philip ed. 1991).

their inherent use must be for business or private purposes), while the third category (voluntary business assets) involves assets which at the taxpayer's choice can become business assets.[101] This intermediate category includes such items as real estate that is rented out, cash, bank accounts, and equity interests in other companies. The taxpayer can take action to include such assets in the balance sheet and they thereby become business assets. Voluntary business assets are not the same as mixed-use assets. Mixed-used assets are allocated to business or private assets as follows: they are business assets if used 50 percent or more for business purposes, private assets if used for business purposes less than 10 percent, and the taxpayer has an election if the percentage of business use falls in between.[102] In this context, "business" refers to the three types of income that are taxed under the balance sheet method, namely commercial, agricultural, and professional activity. In the case of legal persons subject to corporate income tax, if they are required to keep commercial books, all their income is considered business income.[103] For these taxpayers, which represent all the commercially significant taxpayers under the corporate income tax, the question of "capital gains" does not arise—gains are taxable as business income and losses are deductible.[104] However, certain transactions are eligible for deferral of tax, taxation at a reduced rate, or even exemption (for example, gains on the disposition of shares in other companies).[105] For corporate taxpayers not keeping commercial books and for individuals, gains on the disposition of private (i.e. nonbusiness) assets are not income under the source concept.

Whenever capital gains are taxed at favorable rates or are excluded from tax altogether, taxpayers seek to characterize certain kinds of transactions as qualifying for the favorable treatment. All systems have to deal with this problem, and resolutions are often similar in practice, despite differences in the labels that tax law uses. Thus, for example, a taxpayer may

---

[101]   Goods can therefore be necessary business assets (*notwendiges Betriebsvermögen*), necessary private assets (*notwendiges Privatvermögen*), or optional business assets (*gewillkürtes Betriebsvermögen*). *See* Tipke/Lang (2002) at 320-22. France initially had similar rules, but a 1967 court case established a rule allowing flexibility to the taxpayer to determine whether to include assets in the business balance sheet. *See* David et al. (2000) at 214-28. The French terms for business assets and private assets are *patrimoine professionnel* and *patrimoine privé*.

[102] *See* Tipke/Lang (2002) at 321.

[103] *See id.* at 452.

[104] *See* David et al. (2000) at 247-50 (capital losses incurred in business are deductible).

[105] *See* Tipke/Lang (2002) at 443; Beltrame & Mehl (1997) at 158. Rollover relief is available under different circumstances in most countries.

subdivide real estate and sell the parcels, claiming that this was a capital gain and not a business transaction. In continental systems, the problem does not arise in the first place if the assets are held by a company or are otherwise business assets in the first place. But in case they are held as investment assets by an individual, the same factual problem arises as in common law countries. It is resolved by drawing somewhat arbitrary lines depending on the extent of the taxpayer's activity and frequency of sales. Another case is that of the disposition of a bond which might have accrued discount. This problem is now typically dealt with by specific statutory provisions. A third situation is the disposition of a partnership interest where the partnership holds inventory or other business property that would not be eligible for capital gain treatment on disposition. This would not be seen as a problem in continental systems which do not draw distinctions among different kinds of business assets. It has given rise to complex "collapsible partnership" rules in the U.S. A final example is that of share redemptions. A share redemption can be a substitution for paying a dividend. The U.S. has enacted specific rules characterizing certain redemptions as dividends, and the U.K. defines some redemptions as "distributions" which are taxed in the same way as dividends, but most other countries treat a redemption in the same way as the sale of the shares.[106] Liquidating distributions are treated as capital gains in some systems and as dividends in others.[107]

7.9.2 TAXATION OF CAPITAL GAINS

In most countries employing the source concept, the legislature has changed the rules so as to subject certain private gains to tax. Thus, for example, in Germany, gains on the disposition of private assets are taxable if they are speculative or represent the disposition of shares in a legal person in which the taxpayer held a substantial interest. Both concepts were recently expanded.[108] The concept of speculative gains was replaced by a more neutral term (private disposition) and the holding period extended to one year for most property and 10 years for immovable property (previously six months and two years, respectively). The previously applicable 25% threshold defining a substantial interest in a corporate taxpayer was reduced to 1% as of 2002. The German legislator has also been long aware that transactions

---

[106] John Avery Jones et al., *Credit and Exemption under Tax Treaties in Cases of Differing Income Characterization,* European Taxation 1996, 118-146.

[107] *See* Guy van Fraeyenhoven, *General Report,* 72b Cahiers 37 (1987); Van Hoorn 1972) at 84-87.

[108] *See* Tipke/Lang (2002) at 404-06.

taking the form of a gain on the disposition of property could be substitutes for interest or other capital income, and both the legislator and the courts have accordingly drawn lines around such transactions so as to subject them to tax notwithstanding the general principle that dispositions of private assets were not taxable.[109]

The U.K. (together with most other significant Commonwealth economies, New Zealand and Hong Kong being notable exceptions) has long since imposed a separate capital gains tax, which applies to both individuals and to companies. A feature of having a separate tax is that the capital gains tax may have a separate zero-bracket amount (thereby simplifying administration, since taxpayers with small amounts of capital gains need pay no tax).[110] Of interest to the tax lawyer's mentality is that this tax applies only to disposals of capital assets, and that there may therefore be receipts that are considered to be of a capital nature (and hence are not subject to income tax) and which are not reached by the capital gains tax.[111] It is therefore necessary to focus on what is meant by disposal and by capital asset (for this purpose, asset is read broadly as including all kinds of interests in property).[112] "Disposal" is also read broadly; for example, the grant of a leasehold for a premium is treated as a part disposal,[113] as is the grant of an option, or the shift of control in a company.[114] Structurally, capital gains tax is separate from income tax, and is govered by somewhat differing rules.[115] For example, accounting practice is of little relevance to capital gains tax,[116] while being important for the taxation of business profits.[117]

Among the features of the U.K. capital gains tax that differ from U.S. rules for taxing capital gains are the following. There used to be indexation for inflation, which still applies for corporations, but for individuals there is

---

[109] *See* Tipke/Lang (2002) at 390-91.

[110] This is true for example in the U.K where a not inconsiderable exempt amount of £7,200 (for 2000-01) applies. *See* Morse & Williams (2000) at 205.

[111] Under the U.K. capital gains tax, this possibility is narrowed by deeming capital sums derived from assets by their owner to arise from a disposal, even if no asset is acquired by the person paying the capital sum. *See* Morse & Williams (2000) at 212-23.

[112] *See* Morse & Williams (2000) at 208-09.

[113] *See* Morse & Williams (2000) at 212.

[114] *See id.* at 220-21.

[115] *See* Tiley (2000) at 609.

[116] *See id.*

[117] *See infra* 7.11.2.

now a partial exclusion of gain depending on the holding period.[118]   In the case of assets where rollover relief applied, a disadvantage is that the holding period of the previously held assets (or previous owner) does not apply in determining the amount of tapering relief.[119]   While somewhat draconian compared with the U.S. rules, this approach is much simpler, avoiding the substantial complexity that results from determining holding period in the U.S. The U.K. has also simplified its system by providing a generous annual CGT exemption, which means that the average taxpayer does not have to pay tax on relatively small stock market transactions. The U.K. exempts a number of gains from tax. The exemptions include gain on debt, other than "debt on a security."[120]   As a result, for example, the exchange gain on a loan in foreign currency will not be subject to tax.[121]   Capital gain of trusts is taxed to the trustee;[122] this will normally dovetail with the interests of the parties under the trust instrument, but not necessarily so. Partnerships are viewed under the aggregate approach for CGT purposes.[123]

7.9.3 REALIZATION EVENTS

Where taxed, capital gains are typically taken into account only where there is a realization event. Exceptions are found in systems such as that of New Zealand, where certain financial gains are taxed even though not realized. In the U.S. as well, certain gains (such as those on straddles) are now marked to market. In Sweden and France, short-term foreign currency claims are marked to market. We can expect to see further special rules marking certain gains to market, particularly in the case of financial assets, publicly traded property, and foreign investments.

Both in the U.K.[124] and in countries inspired by Germany's system, the withdrawal of an asset from a business is considered to be a realization event. In continental systems, this is because the status change whereby the asset becomes "private" is seen as an occasion for tax. If the gain is not taxed

---

[18] *See* Tiley (2000) at 602.

[19] *See id.* at 610, 715.

[20] *See id.* at 626. The gain on certain corporate and government bonds is also exempt from CGT. *See id.* at 709. For a discussion of the concept of debt on a security, see Morse & Williams (2000) at 219-20.

[21] *See* Tiley (2000) at 626.

[22] *See id.* at 681.

[3] *See* Tiley (2000) at 725. *See infra* 7.12.3 for discussion of the aggregate approach.

[4] This is known as the rule in Sharkey v. Wernher [1956] A.C. 58. *See* Morse & Williams (2000) at 81.

upon withdrawal, then the taxpayer could avoid tax on what should be a business gain.

We see substantially different policies on the question of whether donative transfers and transfers at death are realization events and, if no gain is realized, what basis the donee or heir receives:[125]

- Germany, Japan, Netherlands, Sweden: carryover basis.
- France. Realization (where business property transferred). Donee gets stepped up basis.
- Canada, South Africa: realization event.[126]
- U.K.: basis step up for death. Realization on gifts.[127]
- U.S.: basis step up for death transfers, carryover on gifts.
- Australia: realization on gifts. Carryover on bequests.

7.10 FORGIVENESS OF INDEBTEDNESS

Forgiveness of indebtedness presents similar issues to capital gains, albeit in a more limited context.[128] In countries (like the U.S.) with a global accretion concept of income, debt forgiveness income is taxable like any other. By contrast, in countries with a schedular definition and a source concept, the forgiveness of indebtedness must typically be analyzed according to the context in which it arises. If the debt forgiven is business debt, then the debt forgiveness gives rise to business income. If the debt is private debt, there is no source and hence no income. In the U.K. and other commonwealth countries, debt forgiveness may be considered a capital receipt and hence not subject to tax except insofar as reached under the capital gains tax.

7.11 BUSINESS INCOME

7.11.1 IN GENERAL

This section deals with the rules for determining income from a business – whether it is operated by a sole proprietorship, partnership

---

[125] *See* Ault et al. (1997) at 176.

[126] *See* Hogg et al. (2002) at 306, 315-17. There are rollovers for transfers to a spouse and transfer of a farm to a child.

[127] For certain purposes outside the capital gains tax, death does give rise to a deemed disposal. *See* Tiley (2000) at 675 n.5.

[128] *See* Ault et al. (1997) at 182-85.

corporation or other entity. Special rules for entity taxation are considered in 7.12 below.

A threshold issue is the definition of business income. In countries with a schedular definition of income it was common historically to treat professionals separately from businesses.[129] Most countries with such a distinction have now moved away from it, and the OECD has correspondingly removed the article on professional income from its model treaty, thereby including such income in the category of business income. Another dividing line in respect of business income involves the sale of property in an isolated transaction—under certain circumstances such a sale might be treated as business income and in other cases as a capital gain.[130] Finally, the issue arises whether in the case of a company all of its income is considered business income, or will its capital gains, interest income, and so on be considered as separate types of income. The general approach in continental Europe is to consider all the income of a company to be business income.[131] By contrast, in the U.K., the profits of a company are "computed according to income tax principles...under the Schedules and Cases applicable to income tax."[132] However, there are a number of special rules that apply to corporations and not individuals.[133] Moreover, the capital gains of a company are computed separately under the Taxation of Capital Gains Act. Since the U.S. has a global definition of income, the question of the nature of a corporation's income does not arise, except in the case of capital gains and other types of income for which special rules are provided. There are of course many special rules and so different types of income are taxed under different rules in the U.S., much as if they had appeared in separate Schedules and Cases.

7.11.2 ACCOUNTING METHODS – IN GENERAL

While accrual accounting is generally prescribed for larger businesses, virtually all countries allow small businesses to use the cash method of accounting or even more simplified methods. Depending on how it

---

[129] *See* Burns & Krever, *Taxation of Income From Business and Investment, in* TLDD 597, 598 n.4.

[130] *See id.* at 602-03; *supra* 7.9.1.

[131] *See* Van Hoorn (1972) at 76-78; Tiberghien (1995) at 245 (Belgium).

[132] Tiley (2000) at 814.

[133] *See id.* These include the "special rules for loan relationships, foreign exchange transactions and financial instruments... [and] the controlled foreign company legislation." *Id.*

is applied, the cash method can allow substantial deferral, particularly if outlays of a capital nature are deductible. However, since the cash method is simpler than double-entry bookeeping and since most countries want to favor small businesses, they are often allowed to use it. The threshold between those businesses allowed to use the cash method and those required to use accrual accounting differs substantially. In many civil law countries, the requirement to use accrual accounting is tied to financial accounting rules – if the business is required under the commercial code or the accounting law to use the accrual method for financial accounting purposes, the same applies for tax purposes.

For businesses required to use accrual accounting, one of the key structural features for the taxation of business income is the relationship between tax accounting and commercial accounting.[134] Country practice varies substantially, Germany being on one end of the spectrum with a very close relationship between commercial and tax accounting, and the United States on the other end, with virtually complete independence of the tax and accounting rules. There is no doubt that the German approach tends to be pro-taxpayer, by allowing accounting reserves to be deducted for tax purposes and often allowing the unrealized losses to be recognized for tax purposes by valuation at the lower of cost or market value. Countries that rely on financial accounting tend to be generous in allowing a deduction for reserves, and this can have an important effect in allowing taxpayers to reduce their taxable income. This is not, however, an inherent feature of a system linking tax to commercial accounting, since any such system will specify particular deviations between the tax and accounting rules (e.g., providing that certain expenses are not deductible for tax purposes). Moreover, it would be an oversimplification to say that the German system just bases the tax treatment on the accounting treatment. For example, court decisions have held that where the financial accounting rules allowed elections, these would be limited for tax purposes: taxable income had to be recognized for tax purposes even if its recognition for accounting purposes was optional, and deductions were allowed for tax purposes only if they were required to be taken for accounting purposes.[135] There may be interesting possibilities in a system that more

---

[134] For a brief overview, together with specific discussion of the rules in Canada, France, Germany, and the United States, see Burns & Krever, *supra* note 129, at 673-81. *See also* 62b Cahiers (1977) (Determination of the taxable profit of corporations; Otsuka & Watanabe (1994) at 10-12, 86; Lupi (2002) at 113-16 (in Italy, taxable profit determined by adjusting commercial profit according to the tax law).

[135] *See* Tipke/Lang (2002) at 310; Decision of the Bundesfinanzhof of 3 Februar 1969, BStBl. II 1969, S. 291; Hermann Clemm and Rolf Nonnenmacher, *D.

closely links tax and financial accounting, from the point of view of making corporate tax avoidance transactions more difficult,[136] and comparative study in this area may be fruitful. It may be that both the German and U.S. systems would derive some interesting insights from comparative study of the other system.

Practitioners should keep in mind that other systems can take quite a different approach on the relation between tax and financial accounting than is found in one's own system. Typically, to find out what is the precise relationship between tax and financial accounting, one needs to consult not only the law but also practice and judicial decisions. The precise nature of the relationship is often not easy to pin down, but it is fundamental to understanding the rules for the taxation of business income.

Although there are many variations in the precise relationship between tax and financial accounting in different countries, and in practice there is a continuum, as a generalization civil law countries tend to favor linking tax with financial accounting, since financial accounting rules are regulated by the government under the commercial code or the accounting law.[137] By contrast, in common law countries, financial accounting standards tend to be set by independent professional bodies. This may help to explain the loose relationship, or even virtual independence of tax and financial

---

Steuerbilanz – ein fragwürdiger Besteuerungsschlüssel?, in Der Bundesfinanzhof und seine Rechtsprechung (Klein & Vogel eds. 1985).

[136] *But see id.* In systems that are independent of financial accounting, the statute (or the regulations) often spells out in detail the tax treatment of various financial transactions. Taxpayers who parse the language carefully can often enter into transactions that take advantage of the literal wording of the rules, even though the result is unreasonable. By contrast, a system based on financial accounting without detailed rules would at least be protected by basic principles of financial accounting that call for the financial statements to reflect fairly the financial situation of the company. *See supra* 5.10. As we have seen from the Enron case, however, such protection may not be worth much in practice, since accountants can manipulate the financial accounts if they are determined to do so. Moreover, at least in the case of Germany, it seems that accounting rules, with their bias toward conservatism, may not adequately reflect the economic effect of transactions carried out with derivatives. Thus, it appears that Deutsche Bank was able to defer large taxable gains for tax purposes under German accounting rules, even though international accounting standards reflected the gains in reported profits. *See* Marcus Walker, *Deutsche Bank Gets Tax Ruling, Speeding German Restructuring,* Wall Street Journal, June 8, 2000, at A18.

[137] Court decisions may also be relevant. *See* Tipke/Lang (2002) at 306-07. In Germany, tax exercises a strong influence over financial accounting, in part because the tax court which decides what the requirements of financial accounting are.

accounting in most common law countries.   It might be considered problematic to adopt for tax purposes a standard that is set by a body not controlled by the government.

Behind the black-letter law on the relationship between tax and financial accounting is a process issue: who will decide the rules for determining the corporate tax base? The possibilities are:

- the legislature (requires detailed rules to be written into the law: a favorite option for countries like the U.S., U.K., and Australia);
- the bureaucrats (requires either detailed regulations or broad administrative discretion for tax auditors to specify in the particular case an accounting method that "clearly reflects income": the U.S. follows both approaches);
- the courts (their role in generally important in common law countries);
- accountants (their role is particularly important in most civil law countries, and in some common law countries to the extent they rely on financial accounting);
- tax lawyers (their role can be important in all systems, but less so in systems relying explicitly on the accountants).

None of the above is ideal to hold complete responsibility for determination of the corporate tax base. In every country, each of the above actors plays some role, and the system can be described in process terms according to the weight given to each. An in-depth discussion would take us too far afield,[138] so I just offer a general framework, without a thorough discussion of individual systems.

From a worldwide point of view, to the extent that countries rely on financial accounting, their tax systems will tend to become more comparable over time as financial accounting rules in different countries converge, with the adoption of international accounting standards.

In Germany and countries with similar rules,[139] apart from those cases where the cash method is allowed (largely small businesses), tax accounting is the same as financial accounting with only a few specified differences. The general rule in Germany is for tax to follow financial accounting except as specified in the tax law; but the relationship between the two is complex (for example, as discussed above, tax law may require a particular result where

---

[138] It would merit at least a good-size article on its own.

[139] Although there are some variations in detail, the relationship between financial and tax accounting in France and Sweden is similar to that of Germany.

financial accounting, left on its own, would provide options).[140]   The determination of taxable income is tied directly to the balance sheet.   Net income for the year is defined as the change in the value of net assets between the opening and closing balance sheets, corrected for capital contributions and distributions.[141]   Note that reference to the change in value of assets does not imply marking assets to market.   The valuation of assets on the balance sheet is at book value, not market value.   Of course, there may be a marking to market of certain assets if the commercial accounting rules so specify.   There are instances where the commercial accounting rules allow assets to be written down to market value or allow the formation of provisions or reserves. This allowance of unrealized losses is the principal reason why the German reliance on commercial accounting is generally favorable to taxpayers.

The two basic methods—receipts and outgoings, and balance sheet, —lead to the same result, at least in simple cases.   A question to be investigated is whether the two methods are always equivalent or can they lead to differences in result in situations where the underlying rules get more complex.

In the U.S., financial and tax accounting are almost totally separate. This means that the tax accounting rules have to be fully specified in the tax law and regulations.   Sometimes the failure to specify sensible rules for tax purposes leads to glitches.   For example, under prior law the general rule was that a deduction for an accrued expense was allowed when all events fixing the amount of the liability had taken place.   The problem with this rule was that it ignored timing: the expense might be fixed in amount but might not be payable until some time in the future.   Allowing a deduction for the

---

[140] *See supra* note 135.

[141] *See* Tipke/Lang (2002) at 300-02. For example, suppose that the opening balance has equipment with a book value of 100.   During the year, sales income of 100 is received.   Additional capital of 100 is contributed.   All available cash is used to purchase inventory.   A dividend of 10 is declared and paid.   In this case, the net worth in the opening balance is 100, and the closing net worth will be 270 (Equipment at 100, less depreciation of 20, plus inventory of 190).

Income will be determined as the difference between closing and opening net worth,   170, less the capital contribution of 100, plus the dividend paid of   10, for a total of 80.

Suppose instead that closing inventory was written down to 180 to reflect valuation at   lower of cost or market.   In this case, income would be 70 (i.e. the writedown reduces income by 10).

The receipts minus expenses method reaches the same result as income calculated according to the balance sheet calculation: receipts of 100, less depreciation (20), equals taxable income: 80.

undiscounted amount of the expense meant that in certain cases the tax savings from the deduction for a tort settlement could exceed the amount of the settlement itself. In any event, allowance of a deduction for the undiscounted amount of a settlement obligation did not reflect the actual fair market value of the obligation. This led to a requirement of "economic performance" in order for deductions to be allowed,[142] and as a result the tax accounting rules have now become stricter than commercial accounting with respect to the deduction of expenses.[143]

Another area where the U.S. has adopted tax rules differing from financial accounting is in the taxation of prepaid income. With some exceptions, prepaid income is taxed in the U.S., but for financial accounting purposes prepaid income is generally capitalized. Other countries generally follow the financial accounting treatment for prepaid income, either explicitly or by providing tax rules that achieve the same result.[144]

U.S. tax rules also differ from those of financial accounting in the case of installment sales. Financial accounting accrues income from installment sales when the sale takes place. In the U.S., deferral on installment sales used to allowed fairly broadly, but was subsequently limited.[145] Deferral is allowed in the Netherlands, and to a limited extent in Canada, but not in most countries, which follow the financial accounting treatment.[146]

The completed-contract method of accounting for long-term contracts is another area where the U.S. had special tax rules differing from financial accounting—in this case favorable to the taxpayer.[147] They were largely eliminated in the 1986 tax reform.[148]

---

[142] *See* I.R.C. § 461(h).

[143] This is not an inherent feature of financial accounting; IAS would not allow a deduction for the undiscounted amount of a future obligation.

[144] *See* Ault et al. (1997) at 257-58 (Canada taxes with a reserve. Australia follows financial accounting).

[145] *See* I.R.C. sec. § 453.

[146] *See* Ault et al. (1997) at 258-60.

[147] Under the completed contract method, both the income and expenses relating to contracts were taken into account only at the time of completion. Not only did the use of the completed-contract method result in deferral of taxation of contract profit until the time of completion (which could be lengthy in the case of large contracts, such as defense contracts), but the allowance of a current deduction for so-called "period costs" resulted in an inappropriate current deduction for expenses which, in economic terms, should have been allocable to contracts.

[148] *See* I.R.C. § 460.

Australia, Canada, the U.K., and to a lesser extent, the Netherlands, all have substantial autonomy of tax rules from accounting rules, with accounting principles being referred to by the case law to varying degrees in each of these countries.[149]

Country differences in terms of the relationship between tax and financial accounting are narrowing. In countries where the two have been far apart, they are generally coming closer together. In Germany, the two are moving somewhat further apart as the tax system adopts more and more rules that are independent of financial accounting.[150]

In order to understand how novel items might be accounted for (such as new types of financial instruments), it is necessary to ascertain the general relationship between tax accounting and financial accounting in the country concerned. This may lead one to turn to available material on financial accounting, where tax law follows financial accounting. Or, where tax law is independent of financial accounting, and there is no explicit statutory or administrative treatment of the subject, one may need to learn about any applicable case law. Of course, it is likewise necessary to examine the statute itself, as well as regulations, to see whether there is an explicit resolution of the issue.

The tax rules on inventory accounting can have an important effect on corporate tax revenues. There are substantial country differences in this respect. At one extreme is Mexico, which allows a deduction for investments in inventory.[151] Other countries, however, require closing inventory to be deducted in computing the cost of goods sold, thereby in effect requiring investments in inventory to be capitalized and recovered only as the goods are sold. While some countries require only direct costs to be capitalized, most require full absorption cost accounting, at least for larger taxpayers. The U.S.

---

[149] *See* Ault et al. (1997) at 19, 34, 255-56. The Canadian court restated the rules in 1998. They continue the autonomy of tax rules from financial accounting, while in practice ascribing greater significance to accounting rules than in the past. Rules of financial accounting are evidence of what might be acceptable for tax purposes, but this remains a matter of law to be decided by the courts. However, if the taxpayer uses a method that is consistent with well-accepted business principles (which include GAAP), the tax authorities have the burden of showing why the taxpayer's method should not be accepted. *See* Hogg et al. (2002) at 142-57. This is almost the opposite of the U.S. rule, which confers on the IRS the authority to decide what accounting method clearly reflects income. For the U.K., see Morse & Williams (2000) at 75-76. As of 1999, statute requires that trading profits "must be computed on an accounting basis which gives a true and fair view."

[150] *See* Tipke/Lang (2002) at 303.

[151] *See* Income Tax Law, art. 22.

has particularly complex and far-reaching rules in this respect, requiring many overhead costs to be capitalized.[152] While many countries permit only the use of FIFO or the average cost method, some countries allow LIFO inventory accounting. While more complex than FIFO, LIFO is quite advantageous for the taxpayer in an inflationary environment. Finally, while many countries allow closing inventory to be valued at market value, if this is lower than cost, many developing and transition countries do not allow such a rule, for fear of abuse.

A special feature of the German system is the concept of *Teilwert* (part value), which is the valuation that is generally employed when business assets are valued at fair market value (for example, in valuing in-kind distributions by a corporation to its shareholders). The *Teilwert* is the portion of the fair market value of the entire business (i.e. the amount that a willing buyer would pay) which is allocable to the specific asset in question, on the assumption that the purchaser would continue operating the business. The idea behind *Teilwert* is that the assets of a business are generally worth more as part of a going concern than the amount they would fetch in a liquidation sale.[153]

What is the relationship between tax and financial accounting in the country in question?

7.11.3 DEDUCTIONS FOR BUSINESS EXPENSES

7.11.3.1 *In general*

In principle, every expense incurred in a business context should be deductible, unless it is:

- of a personal nature, or
- of a capital nature (in which case it should be capitalized and recovered appropriately), or
- nondeductible (or partially nondeductible) for policy reasons specified by the legislator (e.g., fines, bribes,[154] taxes, entertainment, interest, pension contributions, political contributions).

---

[152] *See* Burns & Krever, *supra* note 129, at 644.

[153] *See* Tipke/Lang (2002) at 327.

[154] The OECD Council has recommended to its member countries to disallow the deductibility of bribes to foreign public officials. *See* OECD website. In France, bribes paid to foreign government officials are nondeductible under CGI, art. 392 *bis*, but bribes paid to others generally would be deductible. *See* Cozian (1999) at 126-29.

Virtually all countries follow this general structure, although there are peculiarities due to the history of the precise statutory terminology used and court decisions. Limitations on deductions such as for entertainment and automobiles have become fairly common, although the structure and percentages allowed vary substantially.[155] In the details, there are significant policy differences on some items and there are some differences due to the statutory wording[156] and judicial decisions, particularly on the dividing line between business and personal expenses and between capital and current expenses, but overall there is more harmony than divergence. One point of difference is on commuting expenses, which are considered personal in most countries, but of a business nature in Germany.[157]

It makes sense as a matter of policy to allow the carryover of business losses. Some countries allow a carryback. An unlimited carryover is frequent, while some countries allow more limited periods, usually no less than 5 years.[158] Shorter periods are found in some developing and transition countries, which may favor them for administrative or revenue reasons. It is common but not universal to find limits on loss carryovers in connection with reorganizations or changes in corporate control; such limits have often been established in response to trafficking in corporate losses.

7.11.3.2 Depreciation

The depreciation rules are second only to the tax rates in terms of their effect on the overall corporate tax burden. Depreciation policy varies from country to country and over time; it is often accelerated to encourage investment. A number of countries operate pooling systems with asset categories that make it unnecessary to keep track of the lives of individual assets, although single-asset depreciation is more common.[159] As a matter of tax administration and compliance, it is important whether depreciation lives are determined according to tables or on a facts and circumstances basis. Tables are the more modern approach, but some countries still allow a facts

[155] *See, e.g.,* Beltrame & Mehl (1997) at 163-64.

[156] In the U.S., business expenses are allowed if they are "ordinary and necessary." In the U.K., expenses must be "wholly and exclusively" incurred for the business.

[157] *See* Tipke/Lang (2002) at 290-91. The current statute allows a deduction of a specified amount per kilometer distance between work and home, up to a ceiling.

[158] *See* Burns & Krever, *supra* note 129, at 618-19.

[159] *E.g.,* Canada, *see* Hogg et al. (2002) at 271-94, and the U.K., *see* Morse & Williams (2000) at 145-46. *See generally* Richard K. Gordon, *Depreciation, Amortization, and Depletion in* TLDD 682, 714.

and circumstances approach. This can make for unproductive arguments between the taxpayer and tax authorities, unless the system is based on financial accounting and the financial accounting treatment is conclusory for tax purposes.

In the U.K., depreciation has historically been disallowed with respect to nonindustrial buildings. This has been explained as arising from the "*res* concept of capital," under which capital is viewed as a physical item yielding income. Under this concept, changes in the value of capital are irrelevant to determining income (the same concept excludes capital gains from income).[160]

7.11.3.3 *Interest*

The interest deduction has the potential to zero out the corporate tax base, particularly in the case of companies owned by nonresidents and in countries with high inflation rates but which do not have explicit inflation adjustment. Some countries deal with the problem in part by recharacterizing corporate debt as equity where appropriate under the facts. This is the approach in the U.S., and is accomplished purely under the case law. An attempt was made to deal with the matter by regulations, but this did not work. As a result, there is a gray area concerning the situations in which debt will be recharacterized as equity.

An alternative approach is to simply deny the deduction for interest expense in certain cases. Some countries deny all interest expense in excess of that corresponding to a specified debt-equity ratio.[161] In other countries, the deduction denial applies only to related-party debt. In the U.S., the deduction denial operates in the case of excessive debt to owners which are tax exempt.

The U.S. requires capitalization of certain construction-period interest (in the case of the construction of buildings, other long-lived property or property with a long construction period).[162] The same result may apply under some systems that base tax accounting on financial accounting.[163]

---

[160] *See* Seltzer, *supra* note 23, at 29.

[161] For example, interest paid to a controlling foreign shareholder is not deductible in Japan if the debt-equity ratio exceeds 3:1. *See* Otsuka & Watanabe (1994) at 22-26.

[162] *See* I.R.C. § 263A.

[163] Under IAS 23, capitalization of construction-period interest is an allowed alternative treatment. *See* International Accounting Standards Board, International Accounting Standards 2002, at 23-5 (2002).

Nevertheless, there is a substantial difference among countries as to the extent to which interest expense must be capitalized—the general approach is to treat interest as a current expense. The Canadian courts determined that interest is in the nature of a capital expense and hence not deductible in the absence of a statutory allowance.[164]

7.12 TAXATION OF BUSINESSES ENTITIES

This section considers the taxation of entities or arrangements for conducting business with multiple owners. These may be taxed as separate entities (referred to here as corporations) or may be given flow-through treatment (referred to here as partnership treatment).

7.12.1 DEFINITION OF CORPORATE TAXPAYER

Countries with an income tax almost universally impose the income tax or a separate tax on corporations (it might be called corporation tax, profit tax, tax on profit of legal persons, or just (corporate) income tax). Corporations were initially taxed under the same income tax law as individuals in the U.K. The 1913 U.S. income tax also encompassed corporations. Separate laws for individuals and corporations were adopted in Germany in 1925.[165] A separate tax on corporations—Corporation Tax—was introduced in the U.K. in 1965. Whether the tax on corporations takes the form of a separate law or is part of the same law as income tax on individuals makes little substantive difference in most current systems.

Commercial law varies substantially from one country to another in terms of what types of entities may be formed. Partly in response to differences in commercial law and partly for tax policy reasons, there are different definitions of the type of entity that is subject to a separate corporate tax (as opposed to being taxed on a flow-through basis). In civil law countries, the status of an entity as a legal person is often relevant to imposition of the corporate tax, but civil law countries do not uniformly subject entities to corporate tax if and only if they are legal persons.[166]

---

[164] *See* Hogg et al. (2002) at 246-47. Paragraph 20(1)(c) of the Act allows such a deduction; the effect of the court's rulings is that the requirements of this provision must strictly be met.

[165] *See* Harris (1996) at 90.

[166] *See* Graeme Cooper & Richard K. Gordon, *Taxation of Enterprises and Their Owners, in* TLDD 811, 888-92.

Common law countries tend to tax partnerships on a flow-through basis, but in some countries certain partnerships are taxed as corporations, and some corporations receive flow-through treatment.[167] Normally the definition of the type of entity subject to corporate tax does not give rise to problems of interpretation, although in the past the U.S. had a factually based test which has now been replaced by an elective "check the box" system for entities which are not corporations. Typically countries apply their own rules in characterizing foreign entities. This may be problematic if the foreign country's commercial law is substantially different. The differing tax rules make it quite possible for a particular entity to be treated differently in its country of incorporation and the country of residence of its shareholders, or some other relevant country where the entity does business. International tax planning often involves such "hybrid" entities.

Consolidated taxation of corporate groups is common but not universal among OECD countries, but due to complexity is not often found outside these countries. The consolidation can be comprehensive or can take the form of group relief whereby one member of a corporate group can transfer a loss to another.[168] The trend is to more widespread adoption of some form of consolidated taxation (for example, Japan and Italy have recently allowed consolidation).

7.12.2 RATES

From a policy point of view, it makes little sense to apply a progressive rate schedule to corporations. Small corporations may be (and often are) owned by wealthy individuals. While a flat-rate corporate rate structure is the norm, a number of countries apply a lower rate for smaller companies.[169] A lower rate sometimes applies to retained earnings: this is a feature of the corporate-shareholder system and is considered in 7.12.4 below. Some countries take the opposite approach—viewing corporations

---

[167] *See id.* Flow-through treatment applies to certain small business corporations as well as to investment funds.

[168] *See* Ault et al. (1997) at 343-48.

[169] These include the U.S., Belgium, Ireland, Spain, Luxembourg, and U.K.. *See* Commission of the European Communities, Company Taxation in the Internal Market, Part II, section 1.05 (2001). In the United States, the benefits of the progressive rates have been taken away for larger corporations. In effect this means that intermediate-size companies are subject to higher marginal rates over a certain band. A flat-rate schedule for corporations would make much more sense.

with small income or in a loss position with suspicion, they impose a minimum tax or a higher rate on corporations with low taxable income.[170]

Like individual income tax rates, corporate rates have come down over the years.[171] The rates for corporate income tax have historically not been as high as those for individuals, and so the rate reduction has been smaller. Statutory corporate rates in the EU vary from about 25 to 44 percent, with the exception of Ireland (10 percent).[172] Almost all countries outside the EU follow the same pattern (i.e. either within the general EU range or applying a deliberately low tax rate).

7.12.3 PARTNERSHIPS[173]

The general legal concept of partnership exists both in common law and civil law systems, but not with precisely the same meaning. In common law jurisdictions, a partnership is a relationship among persons for carrying on business in common, essentially contractual in nature rather than being a person in its own right. Civil law systems generally do not use the term "partnership" but have the concept of what could be literally translated as an association of persons or company of persons. This concept is distinct from that of a capital company. In many civil law countries, a distinction is also made between civil law partnerships (governed by the civil code) and commercial partnerships (regulated by the commercial code). In some legal systems, partnerships have legal personality, while in others they do not.

---

[170] In France, a minimum tax is imposed, with some variation depending on the company's turnover. The Netherlands imposes a higher rate on the first slice of profits. *See* Beltrame & Mehl (1997) at 174.

[171] For example, the U.K. corporate rate was 52% in 1979 and has now come down to 30%. *See* Tiley (2000) at 778. The German rate was 56% in 1977 and has gradually been reduced since then to 25%. *See* Tipke/Lang (2002) at 475.

[172] *See* Commission of the European Communities, *supra* note 169, Figure 2 (follows section 5.1). The 10% rate applies to manufacturing and other specified activities and the standard rate is 12.5% as of 2003. *See* Kevin McLoughlin, *Ireland,* 28 Tax Notes Int'l 1291 (Dec. 30, 2002).

[173] *See generally* Alexander Easson & Victor Thuronyi, *Fiscal Transparency, in* TLDD 925; Brian J. Arnold & D. Keith McNair, Income Taxation of Partnerships and Their Partners (1981)(Canada); Peter E. McQuillan & Jim Thomas, Understanding the Taxation of Partnerships (4th ed., 1999))(Canada); Ton H.M. Daniels, Issues in International Partnership Taxation: With special reference to the United States Germany and The Netherlands (1991); Sanford Goldberg, *The nature of a partnership, in* Alpert & van Raad (eds., 1993), at 155; Alex Easson, *Taxation of Partnerships in Canada,* 54 B.I.F.D. 157 (2000).

Because of this diversity of civil and commercial law, it is difficult to speak of "partnership" as a concept transcending different legal systems. Differing tax characterization of partnerships is laid on top of this. Accordingly, for our purposes, I will refer to partnerships as those entities that are given flow-through treatment for tax purposes.

A partnership can be thought of in two ways. Both imply flow through of partnership income to the partners, but the meaning of the flow through is different for each.[174] The *entity view* is that the partnership is an entity separate from the partners. The income of the partnership is therefore to be determined separately, and this income can then be allocated to the partners. The *aggregate view* is that the partnership is simply an aggregation of the partners whereby each partner is treated as an owner of a fraction of all the assets of the partnership. Under the aggregate view, the partnership does not exist independently of the partners. There is no need to determine income at the partnership level. Rather, each partner is simply allocated the partner's fractional share of partnership receipts and outgoings, and the tax consequences are determined in the hands of each individual partner.

Different systems implicitly or explicitly adopt for tax purposes either the entity or the aggregate approach or, more often, a hybrid of the two. Systems (such as the United States) adopting a hybrid approach can end up with a particularly convoluted set of rules governing partnerships. The reason for this is that either of the polar approaches—entity or aggregate—is internally coherent and allows one to solve new problems through logical application of the approach to the new situation. For example, the aggregate theory holds that when a partner leaves the partnership, the partner disposes of his or her interest in the partnership assets to the other partners. It may be complicated to perform the necessary accounting, but there is no conceptual difficulty involved. By contrast, under the entity theory, the partner is treated as disposing not of his or her fractional share of the partnership assets, but of the partner's partnership interest. This leaves the cost base of the partnership assets unaffected. While appealing from the point of view of logical coherence, strict application of either the entity or the aggregate theory may lead to undesirable consequences. A hybrid approach may be chosen to avoid these, but this loses the benefits of logical coherence and leads to a situation where instead of being able to apply a coherent theory to new situations, each new situation will require an ad hoc response, resulting in an inconsistent and complicated set of rules and the absence of a reference point when gaps must

[handwritten in margin: problem when using both entity & aggregate]

---

[174] The discussion here is a partial summary of that in Easson & Thuronyi, *supra* note 173, at 933-48. Those who wish to study the comparative tax treatment of partnerships are referred to that discussion and the references it cites.

be filled in. While some countries come close to a pure entity or aggregate approach, most countries fall in between.[175] Therefore a comprehensive cross-country comparison of partnership taxation would be somewhat complex; so far it has not been attempted—another potential doctoral thesis!

What arrangements for jointly carrying on business exist under the countries civil or commercial law? Are they subject to flow-through treatment or taxation as separate taxpayers under the corporate income tax? If they receive flow-through treatment, to what extent is the entity or aggregate approach adopted?

7.12.4 CORPORATE/SHAREHOLDER TAXATION

It has become a commonplace that traditional distinctions between debt and equity have become rather arbitrary and pose a challenge to the corporate income tax.[176] Flow-through or accrual taxation would be a difficult alternative to implement (although flow-thru is commonly prescribed for smaller and simpler enterprises). The proof is that no country has replaced its corporate income tax with a flow-through scheme.

The distortions caused by the classical system are well known:[177]

- Corporate form discouraged;
- Rental, interest, other deductible payments encouraged;
- Distributions that avoid dividend tax encouraged;
- Deductible payments to directors or employees encouraged;
- Retained profits encouraged.

While some countries have retained the classical system, a number of countries have adopted a shareholder imputation or other dividend relief system. The inconstancy of the systems is surprising. In the last few years, for example, both the U.K. and Germany fundamentally changed their

---

[175] France tends to the entity approach. For an overview of different types of fiscal transparency in France, see Cozian (1999) at 271-77. Germany started with the aggregate approach (*Bilanzbündeltheorie*), but has now moved to a hybrid approach. *See* Tipke/Lang (2002) at 364-65. This allows for a separate balance sheet for partners, for example, where they have purchased their partnership interest at an amount exceeding the "inside basis." *See id.* at 380.

[176] In this respect, some countries (like the U.S.) follow an economic substance approach and consider an instrument to be debt only if it can be considered debt under the circumstances, while other countries (like Japan) follow form. *See* Otsuka & Watanabe (1994) at 22.

[177] *See* Cooper & Gordon, *supra* note 166, at 826.

systems. I will not review the details here in light of the extensive literature,[178] but will just hit some highlights.

To recap briefly the current state of play:[179] Only a few OECD countries (including the U.S., Switzerland, and Ireland) subject dividends to full taxation in the hands of shareholders at the normal progressive rates applicable to other income (so-called classical system). Canada has a partial imputation system involving a fixed gross up and credit regardless of tax actually paid at the corporate level. A similar approach is now taken by the U.K., which has abandoned its Advance Corporation Tax (ACT) system (in part because too many excess ACT credits built up).[180] Fixed imputation in Finland and Norway has the effect of exempting dividends from tax in the

---

[178] *See id.*; Harris (1996); Ault et al. (1997) at 285-53, 505-15; European Commission, *supra* note 169. U.S. Treas. Dept., Report of the Department of the Treasury on Integration of the Individual and Corporate Tax Systems: Taxing Business Income Once (1992); A. Warren, Reporter's Study of Corporate Tax Integration (American Law Institute, 1993). See also the sources cited in these works.

[179] For a summary table, including rates (which will now, however, be somewhat dated) see IWB at 1215 (Dec. 8, 1999). *See also* Tipke/Lang (2002) at 441; Chris Edwards, *Dividend Tax Relief: Let's Go Greek!*, 29 Tax Notes Int'l 281 (Jan. 20, 2003).

[180] Prior to 1965, the U.K. had an imputation system whereby shareholders were given a credit for a fixed percentage of dividends received (at the basic rate of tax), regardless of tax actually paid at the corporate level. In 1965 a classical system was introduced. In 1973 the classical system was replaced by an imputation system. In introducing this system, a decision was made to move away from the previous system under which shareholders could receive a credit even if the corporation had paid no tax. The mechanism used to achieve this was advance corporation tax (ACT). ACT was due on payment of a dividend, and a credit for ACT was given to the shareholders. The corporation also received a credit for the ACT against mainstream corporate tax. Under this scheme, the shareholders effectively received relief for a portion of corporation tax. However, this scheme was eventually considered problematic, in part because corporations built up large amounts of excess ACT credits (excess of ACT over corporate tax). Effective April 1999, ACT was abolished. There is now a dividend imputation credit of 1/9 of the dividend. This credit is included in taxable income (i.e. the dividend is grossed up, so that a dividend of 90 will involve a credit of 10 and income of 100). This tax credit in the amount of 10% of the grossed-up dividend covers the tax liability of individuals, except those on the highest marginal rate (the "upper rate"). For those individuals the tax rate applying to dividend income is 32.5% less the 10% credit. The top rate for other types of income is 40%. The dividend is taken as the top slice of income (relevant for determining the rate on other income). Intercorporate dividends between resident companies are exempt. [I am grateful to Peter Harris for this paragraph.] *See also* Tiley (2000) at 757.

hands of individuals. Australia, New Zealand, and Mexico use full imputation systems that provide shareholders with a credit for corporate tax that is actually paid. Dividends are considered paid first out of taxable income, and so they will receive a credit to the extent of accumulated corporate tax paid, which is kept track of in a special account. France provides shareholders with a fixed imputation credit (*avoir fiscal*), while imposing a compensatory tax (*précompte mobilier*) on dividends distributed out of profits that have not borne the full corporate tax, e.g. foreign source income or preference income. The amount of compensatory tax equals the *avoir fiscal* associated with the dividend. Japan has a partial imputation system. Other EU states retaining an imputation system are Italy and Spain.[181] EU states that do not have an imputation system typically provide some form of shareholder relief. Flat or reduced rates apply in Belgium, Denmark, and Austria. As of 2001, Germany has abandoned its imputation system and split corporate tax rate in favor of a shareholder relief system taxing one-half of dividends to the shareholder, with a single low (25%) tax at the corporate level. (Luxembourg and Portugal also exempt half the dividend.) Sweden and the Netherlands retain a form of the classical system. However, in Sweden the classical system is modified in the sense that there is a flat tax of 30% at the shareholder level on all capital income, including dividends. And in the Netherlands, dividends are now no longer subject to tax as such at the shareholder level, since they are included in the flat 1.2% tax on capital. A number of developing and transition countries either exempt dividends (Greece does as well) or impose a relatively low final withholding tax (which could be regarded as a modified classical system or a shareholder relief system). Estonia has adopted a unique approach under which the corporate income tax has been completely replaced by a distributions tax.[182]

The current pattern, therefore, is that while the classical system (full taxation of dividends) is still in place in a few countries, most notably the U.S., and while a few countries operate an imputation system based on giving shareholders credit for actual tax paid at the corporate level, most countries are now operating a dividend relief system whereby dividends are either taxed with a fixed gross up and credit, or are subject to a partial exclusion or a flat tax rate. The method of shareholder relief makes some difference to progressivity: a flat rate tends to benefit upper bracket shareholders, but this may be largely a matter of appearance if in practice shares are owned almost exclusively by top-bracket shareholders (as in many developing countries).

---

[181] *See* European Commission, *supra* note 169, Box 7 (following section 4.4).

[182] *See* Erki Uustalu, *Estonia Modifies Income Tax Law*, 22 Tax Notes Int'l 1631 (April 2, 2001).

All the systems of shareholder relief provide similar incentives at the corporate level. Because shareholder relief is independent of corporate tax paid, the value of corporate tax preferences is preserved. Depending on the combination of the corporate and dividend taxes, there may be little or no disincentive to use of the corporate form (the corporate rate is typically set substantially below the top individual income tax rate). Debt finance is still encouraged if the lenders are exempt or in low tax brackets (for example pension funds, or foreigners benefiting from reduced or zero withholding under a treaty), but is not advantageous if the lenders are top-bracket residents.

As for countries using imputation systems, the key issue is the treatment of corporate tax preferences. Imputation systems currently in use tend to wash preferences out, but stack them last (i.e. distributions are considered to be made first from fully taxed income). This tends to make preferences relevant for corporations unless their distributions are high. Imputation systems tend not to give regard for foreign tax paid, thereby somewhat undermining the foreign tax credit, but again this is relevant only where distributions are treated as made out of foreign source income.

Both types of dividend relief can also be evaluated from the point of view of treatment of foreign investors. Systems allowing a shareholder credit tend to deny the credit, except as allowed under treaty. Systems imposing a flat withholding rate may treat local and foreign investors equally. Some countries impose a withholding tax on foreign investors, on top of whatever taxation applies to residents, which might be reduced under treaty. The bottom line is that both imputation and dividend relief systems tend to set up roadblocks to both inbound and outbound investment, although the details of the system need to be looked at to determine the effects. The unfavorable treatment of foreign operations under the previous regimes was part of the motivation for the recent changes in both the U.K. and Germany.

A key technical element in any corporate/shareholder tax system is the definition of "dividend." This term may be defined by reference to com-pany law or have an autonomous definition in tax law. There are substantial differences among countries in how dividend is defined.[183]

In the case of structures involving two or more tiers of corporations, there is typically relief for double taxation of dividends and often capital gains as well. The U.S. offers relief for dividends only, not for capital gains on shares in a subsidiary. The U.K. recently extended relief to capital gains, emulating

---

[183] *See generally* Cooper & Gordon, *supra* note 166, at 884-85; Marjaana Helminen, The Dividend Concept in International Tax Law (1999) (focusing on Finland, Germany, Sweden, U.S., European tax law, and double-tax treaties).

the participation exemption long provided by countries such as the Netherlands, Belgium, and Luxembourg.[184]

7.12.5 REORGANIZATIONS[185]

OECD countries typically provide nonrecognition treatment for gain that might otherwise be taxed either at the corporate or shareholder level in reorganizations. Systems for such relief may not be fully worked out in many developing or transition countries, however, so in dealing with such countries it makes sense to check whether a scheme for rollover relief exists. In the case of cross-border EU reorganizations, relief is required by EU directive.[186] However, some cross border mergers or divisions of companies are not legally possible under the company law of EU member countries, and the proposed company law directive providing for such reorganizations has not yet been approved.[187] This should be a general reminder for tax lawyers that in planning for corporate reorganizations they need first of all to ascertain what transactions are allowed under company law. Not all jurisdictions are as flexible as the State of Delaware in this respect.

7.13 TRUSTS

Trusts were created by the courts of equity under common law and have not been known in civil law countries, except where they have recently been introduced by statute.[188] Accordingly, the tax treatment of trusts is generally not well developed in civil law countries, while being fairly well elaborated in many common law countries.[189] Even in common law

---

[184] *See* Miles Dean, *New Capital Gains Tax Exemption*, 29 Tax Planning Int'l Rev. 8 (2002). A participation exemption has been adopted by Germany and is being considered by France. *See* Mathieu Pouletty, *France: Tax Authorities Considering Participation Exemption Regime,* 27 Tax Notes Int'l 31 (July 1, 2002).

[185] *See generally* Frans Vanistendael, *Taxation of Corporate Reorganizations, in* TLDD 895.

[186] *See supra* ch. 4, n. 170 (Merger Directive).

[187] *See* EU Commission, *supra* note 169, at section 3.2.1. The European Company may offer a possible vehicle to get around this problem.

[188] *See generally* Donovan Waters, *The Concept Called "The Trust,"* 53 BIFD 118 (1999); *supra* note 25.

[189] *See generally* Easson & Thuronyi, *supra* note 173; The International Guide to the Taxation of Trusts (Timothy Lyons et al. eds., looseleaf 1999-2001); Federico Maria Giuliani, *Taxation of Trusts in the Netherlands*, 26 Tax Notes Int'l 73 (April 8, 2002);

countries, the taxation of trusts is somewhat obscure. Trusts present fundamental difficulties for taxation. The general principle that one might want to apply is flow-through treatment, but it is not clear as an initial matter whether the flow-through should be to the grantor or to the beneficiaries. It is clear that in the case of a trust that is revocable at will by the grantor, it would be appropriate to tax the trust income to the grantor on a flow-through basis, or even to ignore the separate existence of the trust for tax purposes, and most countries so provide, but the difficulty is that there can be any number of trust arrangements that provide substantial control or enjoyment by the grantor, while stopping short of allowing the grantor an unrestricted right to revoke the trust.[190] In determining where to draw the line on which trusts are taxed to the grantor, countries have had to coordinate this rule with their policy on the extent to which assignment of income would be allowed.

Having dealt with the situations where the trust is treated as belonging to the grantor or the beneficiary, the problem then arises as to how to achieve flow-through treatment for trusts that are not so treated. Where the shares of each beneficiary to trust income are specified in advance, this is a feasible matter, if somewhat complex in some cases. The main difficulty arises when the trust instrument fails to specify each beneficiary's share, leaving this to a greater or lesser extent in the discretion of the trustee, or where the beneficiaries are unknown or perhaps not even yet in existence. In these cases, the only feasible approach is to tax the trustee as a proxy.

Typically, common law countries have rules which determine whether it is the trustee or the beneficiaries who pay tax on trust income. In the U.S., these rules were abused by accumulating income in the trust. The congressional response came in two stages. First, a so-called "throwback" tax was imposed in the case of certain distributions out of accumulated income. Later, the tax rate payable by trustees was increased. An alternative approach

---

Erik Werlauff, *Denmark: Trust, Anstalt and Foundation: A Comparison*, 38 Eur. Tax'n 143 (1998); Walter Ryer, *Switzerland: Trusts and Trust Taxation*, 38 Eur. Tax'n 198 (1998); Guglielmo Maisto, *Italy: Aspects of Trust Taxation*, 38 Eur. Tax'n 242 (1998); Jürgen Killius, *Common law trusts: New developments affecting the German tax-status of grantors and beneficiaries*, in Alpert & van Raad (eds., 1993), at 239.

[190] This is a case where tax law might do well to pay better attention to private law. One of the first assignments I was given in private practice involved a client who wanted to revoke an irrevocable trust. I was sent to the library to find a solution to this seemingly impossible problem, but soon was shaking my head in that there were in fact multiple ways that the trust could be revoked. The moral of the story is that tax law should not necessarily pay undue attention to private law constraints, which can often be easily circumvented as a matter of private law.

is taken by the U.K. There, the trustee is initially taxed on the trust income and the beneficiary is subsequently given a credit for the tax paid.[191] Generally, beneficiaries are taxed on amounts they are entitled to receive, regardless of whether actually distributed.[192]

7.14 INTERNATIONAL ASPECTS OF INCOME TAX

7.14.1 IN GENERAL

In the past decade or so, there has been a remarkable amount of convergence in the international area. Not too long ago, many countries (although by and large, not OECD member countries) were using a territorial approach to taxing international transactions. The territorial approach has now been almost universally[193] abandoned, as countries such as Argentina, Israel, Venezuela, and South Africa have switched to a worldwide taxation approach. In addition, there has been a substantial growth in tax treaties. The income tax treaty network among OECD countries is largely complete, but it is only very partially developed as far as most non-OECD countries are concerned. The past decade has seen an interest on the part of a number of non-OECD countries to substantially expand their treaty network (many of these are transition countries). Both among OECD and non-OECD countries,[194] there has also been much interest in international tax cooperation, although progress here has been slow. Finally, the international area has seen substantial law reform by way of borrowing law of other countries.

---

[191] *See* Easson & Thuronyi, *supra* note 173, at 951.

[192] *See id.* at 951-52.

[193] Taxing jurisdictions continuing to use the territorial system include: Bolivia, Costa Rica, El Salvador, Guatemala, Hong Kong SAR, Kenya, Malaysia, Nicaragua, Panama, Paraguay, Singapore, and Uruguay. Israel recently adopted worldwide taxation. *See* Yoram Keinan & Shlomo Katalan, *Israel's Income Tax Reform: Roads Not Taken,* 28 Tax Notes Int'l 941 (Dec. 2, 2002). By territorial approach I mean one under which residents are taxed only on domestic-source income; to be distinguished is the exemption approach under which certain foreign-source income of residents (typically business income or earned income) is exempted. *See infra* 7.14.5. Territorial taxation is basically a characteristic of schedular taxation, so the abandonment of territorial taxation goes along with the adoption of the global approach. *See* Van Hoorn (1972) at 9.

[94] *E.g.,* Juan Carlos Vicchi, *Argentina*, 86b Cahiers 325, 335 (2001).

The recent cooperation builds on the cooperation achieved in the past, primarily through the OECD, and before that the League of Nations, as well as the UN (which sponsored the UN model treaty). There is considerable general uniformity of approach to the taxation of international transactions, involving taxation by nearly all countries with an income tax both on the basis of source and residence.[195] Moreover, the foreign tax credit mechanism is almost universally used as a unilateral means to grant relief from double taxation (in combination with the exemption method in many cases). Tax treaties too are substantially uniform in broad approach, being based almost universally on the OECD Model (even the UN Model is based on the OECD model). One result of treaties is to limit source country jurisdiction. What is interesting is that a great deal of restraint is followed in source taxation, even where not limited by treaty. In other words, for policy reasons most countries have followed a fairly restrained line in broad conformity with treaties. There are, however, instances where source taxation is more aggressive than that which would be allowed by treaties, and we will focus on these cases. Likewise, there is fairly broad conformity on the definition of residence, again along the lines of definitions found in treaties.

7.14.2 Residence of individuals

As more countries tax on a worldwide basis, the concept of residence becomes increasingly important, since an individual who is considered to be a resident of a country will typically[196] be taxed by that country on all his or her

---

[195] For example, Gest & Tixier (1990) at 181 states that the French definition of residence was based to some extent on the OECD Model treaty.

[196] Some countries draw a distinction between permanent residents, who are taxed on all their worldwide income, and short-term residents not intending to remain permanently. Japan taxes short-term residents only on their domestic-source income and foreign-source income remitted to Japan. *See* Ault et al. (1997) at 370-71. Certain persons not "domiciled" or "ordinarily resident" in the U.K. may also be subject to taxation on a remittance basis. Before 1914, all U.K. residents were taxed on foreign-source income on a remittance basis. The scope of the remittance basis was gradually whittled down; it now applies only to certain types of income and to a limited class of persons. "It applies to income within Schedule D, Cases IV and V only if the taxpayer satisfies the Board that he is not domiciled in the U.K. or, that being a British subject or a citizen of the republic of Ireland, he is not ordinarily resident in the U.K." *See* Tiley (2000) at 1031. Schedule D, Case IV is income from securities. Case V covers "income from possessions" which has been held to cover any source of income. *See* Tiley (2000) at 1025. The remittance basis also applies to a limited extent for capital gains purposes (where persons are resident or ordinarily

worldwide income. An important element in most definitions of residence is presence in the jurisdiction for a specified length of time: often 183 days or more in the taxable year (sometimes 183 days in a period of 12 months ending in the taxable year). Sometimes presence in prior years is also taken into account. Although some countries rely on the physical presence test exclusively (the benefit is certainty and simplicity), many—particularly OECD countries—have additional reasons for which someone can be considered a resident, including status as a permanent resident for immigration purposes, domicile, having an habitual place of abode, and so forth.[197] In contrast with tests based on presence, some of these tests are based on a complex evaluation of the facts and not fully specified in the legislation. It has been said of U.K. law that "'residing' is not a term of invariable elements, all of which must be satisfied in each instance. It is quite impossible to give it a precise and inclusive definition. It is highly flexible, and its many shades of meaning vary not only in the contexts of different matters, but also in different aspects of the same matter."[198]

Often, one of the elements of the definition of residence will rely on concepts outside the tax law, for example, domicile, which is a concept used for conflict of law purposes.[199] It is perhaps ironic that the U.K., a common law country, uses for tax purposes the nontax concept of domicile, while in France the concept of domicile under the civil code is irrelevant for tax purposes.[200] So much for the idea that civil law countries tend to conform the civil law and tax law as much as possible!

In response to decisions of the European Court of Justice concerning discrimination, some European countries have adopted special residence rules

---

resident but not domiciled and the assets disposed of are outside the U.K). *See* Morse & Williams (2000) at 208. The remittance basis of taxation is difficult to conceptualize and apply, particularly in the modern world where transactions can be effected without an actual remittance of cash. *See* Tiley (2000) at 1030-35 for a discussion of how it has been applied in the U.K. For example, a famous case (IRC v. Gordon, [1952] 1 All ER 866, 33 T.C. 226) involved the taxpayer borrowing money in the U.K., and paying the loan back outside the U.K. with proceeds of income. It was held that this was not a remittance. (The case now has limited application, if any, for which see Tiley (2000) at 1033-35.)

[197] *See* Ault et al. (1997) at 368-70.

[198] Thomson v. Minister of National Revenue [1946] SCR 209, 224. *See generally* Tiley (2000) at 994-1003 (concept of resident for U.K. tax purposes). Canada also uses such an open-ended test, combined with a 183-day rule. *See* Hogg et al. (2002) at 60-65.

[199] *See* Tiley (2000) at 1001-03.

[200] *See* Gest & Tixier (1990) at 180-81.

that allow persons earning most of their income in the country to be treated as a resident even where they live in another country. For example, Spain allows individuals who live in another EU member country and who earn 75% of their income from employment or business in Spain to elect to be taxed as a resident.[201]

The U.S. is virtually alone in taxing all its citizens on their worldwide income, thereby, in effect, treating them as residents for tax purposes no matter where they live. The U.S. rule is softened by an exclusion for a substantial amount of earned income; moreover, if a U.S. citizen pays tax abroad on their foreign-source income this will be creditable in the U.S. In other countries, citizenship is sometimes relevant[202] for tax purposes, but will not by itself subject an individual to unlimited tax jurisdiction.

The fact that tests for residence are not harmonized means that an individual can be resident in no country—or more than one country. Tax treaties, if they exist between these countries, are usually fairly good at resolving the problem.

Does the country have one or more tests for residence? What does the statute say? Are there any cases or regulations or other explanations of the position of the tax authorities? To what extent does the test rely on concepts outside the tax law, such as domicile, which must be consulted?

7.14.3 RESIDENCE OF ENTITIES

In virtually all countries, a corporation or other legal person that is formally incorporated or legally registered as a company in the jurisdiction will be treated as resident for tax purposes. Some countries stop with this test. Others apply an additional test that looks to place of management. The scope of the place of management test differs from country to country, however. In the U.K., it is by and large equivalent to the place where the directors meet, while in Germany the day to day management of activity is the focus.[203] Canada appears to have a mixed test in practice.[204] Particularly where the place of management test refers to day to day management, it can be used to

---

[201] *See* Soler Roch (2002) at 38; Nonresidents' Income Tax Act, art. 33.

[202] Gest & Tixier (1990) at 180, note that it is relevant for purposes of art. 199 of the tax code (*quotient familial*), art. 81A (employees working abroad) and art. 150C (principal residence of French citizens resident outside of France.)

[203] Belgium includes as well the concept of principal establishment in Belgium. *See* Introduction to Belgian Law, *supra* note 37, at 357.

[204] *See* Ault et al. (1997) at 371-73. *See also* Hogg et al. (2002) at 65-67. Incorporation in Canada also gives rise to residence. *See id.*

attack the establishment of companies in tax havens. Because these companies (sometimes called letterbox companies) may carry on little or no actual activity in the country where they are incorporated, they may be vulnerable to the charge that the place of management is in fact located in the home country, thereby rendering them ineffective in shifting taxation abroad.[205]

Residence rules for various legal entities other than commercial companies, and for entities (such as partnerships or trusts) that may not be separate legal persons can present special problems.[206]

What is the formal test for residence? Is there also a test based on place of management—if so, what does this mean?

7.14.4 GENERAL APPROACH TO TAXATION OF RESIDENTS

As noted above, the vast majority of countries now subject their residents to worldwide taxation.[207] This gives rise to the potential for double taxation. It is avoided in most cases by granting a foreign tax credit for income tax paid abroad. A number of countries also exempt specific kinds of foreign source income of their residents, either unilaterally or by treaty.

Residence-based taxation requires dealing with change of residence. Most countries do not tax departing residents, and apply an historical cost approach to an individual's assets when the person becomes a resident.[208] Canada and Australia apply a general exit tax on long-term residents who become resident elsewhere, considering them to have sold their property upon emigration.[209] Several OECD countries apply more limited exit taxes.[210]

---

[205] *See* 86b Cahiers at 37, 400, 461-62, 874 (2001).

[206] *See* Easson & Thuronyi, *supra* note 173, at 946-47, 961-62.

[207] In Germany, this is called unlimited tax liability, with nonresidents being subject to limited tax liability. *See* Tipke/Lang (2002) at 216.

[208] *See* Ault et al. (1997) at 373-76. In the case of business assets located abroad, this gives rise to the somewhat messy problem of how to account for their history prior to the change in residence. Presumably, the tax rules of the new country of residence would have to be applied, thus requiring depreciation and other items to be recalculated.

[209] *See* Luc de Broe, *General Report,* 87b Cahiers 19, 32-36 (2002); Sanford Goldberg et al., *Taxation Caused by or After a Change in Residence (Part I),* 21 Tax Notes Int'l 643 (Aug. 7, 2000). South Africa follows a similar approach.

[210] *See* de Broe, *supra* note 209, at 36-44.

Only a few countries, however, allow a step-up in basis to immigrants.[211] In a number of countries, a corporation's transfer of its incorporation abroad is considered a taxable event, whether by way of exit tax or deemed liquidation.[212] However, such a transaction is not even possible under the company law of many countries, and so the issue does not arise for tax purposes. The transfer of assets to a foreign branch or foreign subsidiary may be taxable or eligible for deferral.[213]

Instead of imposing an exit tax on departing residents, some countries have special rules which continue to tax former residents under certain circumstances, particularly where the change in residence is seen as motivated by tax avoidance.[214] For example, in Spain, resident individuals who move to a tax haven continue to be treated as residents for the year of the move and the following four years.[215] In Sweden, Finland, and Norway a similar result is achieved by continuing to treat certain departing residents as residents unless they prove to have terminated substantial links with the country they have left.[216]

7.14.5 RELIEF FROM DOUBLE TAXATION[217]

The existing scheme of international tax rules can give rise to double taxation or, more frequently, double nontaxation. Double nontaxation is to some extent tolerated or encouraged by governments (to attract investment or make their companies competitive).

Virtually all countries with worldwide taxation grant unilateral double tax relief through a foreign tax credit. France and Switzerland are exceptions, allowing only a deduction for foreign taxes, except as provided by treaty. The overall limitation on the credit is most common. The U.K. has a per-item limitation.[218] Canada and Germany use a per-country limitation. The U.S.

---

[211] *See id.* at 57-58 (Australia, Canada, Denmark, and to a limited extent Austria, The Netherlands, and New Zealand).

[212] *See* Ault et al. (1997) at 376-79.

[213] *See id.* at 425-28.

[214] *See id.* at 374-76; de Broe, supra note 209, at 44-52.

[215] *See* Soler Roch (2002) at 37-38; art. 9.3 of the income tax law. A similar rule applies in Germany. *See* de Broe, *supra* note 209, at 48-49.

[216] *See* de Broe, *supra* note 209, at 44-45.

[217] *See* Ault et al. (1997) at 380-429 for a more complete discussion of credit and exemption systems on a comparative basis in the major industrialized countries.

[218] Since dividends from a single company are considered a single item, the per-item rule (in conjunction with generous indirect credit rules available in the U.K.) gave rise

has a complicated "basket" system, although it previously used a per-country limitation. Several countries allow an "indirect" credit for foreign tax paid by subsidiaries, while others deal with the issue by allowing a participation exemption.[219] While all countries limit the credit to foreign income tax, most countries do not have detailed rules for what foreign taxes qualify. The U.S. is unique in having promulgated very detailed and technical rules on creditability;[220] Australia and Germany also have moderately detailed rules,[221] while in the U.K. the tax authorities publish a list of admissible and inadmissible taxes.[222] Only a few countries specifically deny a credit for "soak-up taxes" (i.e. taxes that are imposed only on those taxpayers eligible for a credit in their residence country).[223] Countries generally (with the exception of Germany) allow carryover of excess foreign tax credits for varying periods.[224]

A number of countries exempt specific types of foreign source income, instead of granting a credit for foreign tax.[225] The U.S. exempts a certain amount of earned income of individuals. France exempts business income. Germany exempts business income, as well as extending a participation exemption, by treaty.[226] Similarly, the Netherlands offers a participation exemption and in effect exempts business income from abroad, and other countries have similar regimes.[227] Australia exempts certain foreign employment, dividend, and business income. Exemption is often conditioned

---

to so-called "mixer companies" which pooled dividends received from lower-tier subsidiaries, thereby achieving averaging. Rules limiting benefits from using this structure apply as from 2001. *See* Tiley (2000) at 1102-06; Richard Vann, *International Aspects of Income Tax, in* TLDD at 758 n.82.

[219] *See* Ault et al. (1997) at 397-402.

[220] *See* Treas. Reg. § § 1.901-1, 1.901-2, 1.901-2A.

[221] *See* Ault et al. (1997) at 387-88.

[222] *See* Tiley (2000) at 1096.

[223] *E.g.,* sec. 6AB(6), Income Tax Assessment Act 1936 (Australia) (credit absorption tax) ; U.S. Treas. Reg. § 1.901-2(c)(2) (soak-up tax); Income Tax Act sec. 126(4) (Canada).

[224] *See* Ault et al. (1997) at 396-97. The U.K. now allows carryover of unused credits. *See* Tiley (2000) at 1107.

[225] *See* Ault et al. (1997) at 402-06.

[226] As do Belgium, Denmark, Luxembourg, The Netherlands, and Spain. *See* Jean-Marc Tirard, Corporate Taxation in EU Countries 8 (1994). Belgium taxes at 25% of the normal corporate rate business profits subject to tax abroad, except where they are exempt by treaty. *See* Dassesse & Minne (2001) 885-88.

[227] *See* Paul Vlaanderen, *Why Exempt Foreign Business Profits?,* 25 Tax Notes Int'l 095, 1101 (March 11, 2002).

on the income being subject to tax (sometimes specifying comparability or a minimum threshold of tax) in the foreign country.[228]

Tax sparing (credit for a notional tax paid) is offered by a number of countries by treaty as a benefit to developing countries, although this practice has come under criticism in recent years.[229] The U.S. has a longstanding policy of refusing to grant tax sparing.

Application of both the foreign tax credit limitations and exemptions for foreign-source income require an allocation of expenses as between foreign-source and domestic income. This is particularly problematic with respect to overhead expenses such as general administrative expenses, research and development, and interest. The U.S. has detailed rules which apportion such expenses between foreign and domestic income, which are applied on a consolidated basis to corporate groups. Other countries generally have much more liberal and less detailed rules in this regard.[230] Particularly in respect of interest expense, the use of a tracing approach (which is typical) allows substantial planning opportunity to the taxpayer.

Another issue in calculating the foreign tax credit limitation is foreign losses. The U.S. has complex rules attributing foreign losses to other baskets of foreign income (and recharacterizing income subsequently earned in the basket which generated the loss). Australia has even tougher rules disallowing the use of foreign losses against domestic income. Germany limits the deduction for foreign losses.[231] Most other countries have not developed specific anti-avoidance rules on this issue.

7.14.6 TAXATION OF NONRESIDENTS

Given the extensive literature on comparative income taxation of nonresidents,[232] it seems otiose to attempt even a summary treatment here. For purposes of this book, it should suffice to note that, even though there are differences in country practice, the taxation of nonresidents is characterized

---

[228] *See* 86b Cahiers de droit fiscal international 70, 363, 409, 436, 485 (Australia, Austria, Belgium, Canada, Denmark, Finland, Luxembourg, Netherlands, Spain, Sweden).

[229] *See* Ault et al. (1997) at 478-80; Toaze, *Tax Sparing: Good Intentions, Unintended Results*, 49 Can. Tax J. 879 (2001); *supra* ch. 2, n. 18.

[230] *See* Ault et al. (1997) at 391-94, 406-08.

[231] § 2a EStG.

[232] *E.g.,* Arnold & McIntyre (1995); Ault et al. (1997) at 431-58; Richard Vann *International Aspects of Income Tax, in* TLDD at 718; Easson (1999); Rohatg (2002); Vogel (1997).

by overall similarity, largely due to a network of tax treaties on which there is substantial international consensus. This general consensus antedates the more recent trend in favor of global (vs. territorial) taxation of residents, since all countries were applying a territorial approach to taxation of nonresidents.

The overall approach followed by developing and transition countries is not fundamentally different from that of OECD countries. Source taxation of nonresidents is of course of great importance for this group of countries. A major issue here is the extent to which countries give up taxing rights in order to attract foreign investment.[233] To the extent that developing and transition countries want to tax nonresidents, the main difficulties lie in untangling the accounting of multinationals, a task that tax administration officials are often not up to.

7.14.7 ANTI-AVOIDANCE RULES

The international area is full of anti-avoidance rules.[234] These have often been pioneered in the U.S. and copied in other countries, although many have also sprung up independently in various countries as a response to particular problems of abuse. Despite substantial imitation, most of these rules apply in only a limited number of countries. Given the increasing consensus in international taxation, it can be expected that the adoption of such rules will spread further. Some countries are adopting even more aggressive rules than those found in the U.S. Given the rapidly changing rules, I can give only examples of some rules to look out for. One problem that such rules pose arises in connection with treaties. Where such rules are in place at the time a treaty is negotiated, provision can be made for them in the treaty. However, given the slow pace of treaty negotiation, legislative developments often overtake treaties. The question then arises whether the anti-avoidance rules are consistent with treaty obligations.[235]

---

[233] *See supra* 2.4.

[234] *See, e.g.,* Sébastien Moerman, *The French Anti-Avoidance Legislation,* 27 Intertax 50 (1999). *See generally* Roy Saunders, International Tax Systems and Planning Techniques (1997).

[235] *See* Brian Arnold & Patrick Dibout, *General Report,* 86b Cahiers 21, 81-88 (2001). For example, the French supreme administrative court has held that France's CFC rules (CGI art. 209B) were incompatible with treaties providing for the taxation of the profits of an enterprise of a State solely in that State. *See* Re Schneider SA, Appeal no. 96-1408, Administrative Court of Appeal, Paris (Jan. 30, 2001), 3 ITLR 529, *aff'd,* Judgment of June 28, 2002 (Conseil d'Etat), 4 ITLR 1077; Marcellin Mbwa-Mboma, *France-Switzerland Treaty Overrides CFC Regime, French Tax*

Transfer pricing rules are a special form of anti-avoidance rule allowing the tax authorities to adjust the price of transactions taking place between related persons.[236] The U.S. transfer pricing provision (section 482) applies to both domestic and foreign transactions, although in many countries transfer pricing rules apply to international transactions only. Given the extensive literature on transfer pricing, it does not seem appropriate to hazard generalizations here, other than to note the increased importance of transfer pricing adjustments and the increasingly widespread adoption of transfer pricing rules. The complexity of the issues makes it difficult for tax officials of developing and transition countries to deal with transfer pricing, although increasingly the authority to do so is being placed on the books. Within the framework of the OECD, a fair amount of consensus has been reached on how transfer pricing adjustments are to be made, although there are substantial national differences in both legislation and the administrative style in which the legislation is applied. As with many other issues, the U.S. stands out from other countries, with a relatively aggressive administrative style and substantially more transfer pricing litigation than other countries.[237]

The current scheme of international taxation makes it tempting to establish subsidiaries in tax havens or low-tax countries and arrange matters so that income is taxed to them. If repatriation of this income is deferred, so is tax payable in the parent company's residence country. To some extent, transfer pricing rules can address this problem, by redetermining the amount of profit properly allocable to the low-tax subsidiary. But applying transfer pricing rules can be difficult, even for sophisticated tax administrations.

(margin note: tax haven)

Court Rules, 27 Tax Notes Int'l 143 (July 8, 2002). The reasoning is that taxation of a shareholder on the profits of a CFC is taxation by the shareholder's state of the profits of the CFC and hence is precluded by the treaty. A counterargument (which may have greater or less force depending on how the CFC rules are structured) is that taxation of a shareholder on profits of an enterprise located in another state does not violate the treaty, since it is in the nature of flow-through taxation of shareholders, and does not constitute taxation of the enterprise itself. A contrary holding would prevent any flow-through taxation of shareholders, partners, or beneficiaries in situations where the source state regards the flow-though entity as a separate taxable person. The opposite conclusion was reached in Finland in Re Oyj Abp, 4 ITLR 1009 (Sup. Adm. Ct., March 20, 2002), which also held the CFC legislation compatible with European law (freedom of establishment).

[236] *See generally* Jill C. Pagan & J. Scott Wilkie, Transfer Pricing Strategy in a Global Economy (1993).

[237] *See id.* at 30-31, 172. For history of the lead role of the U.S. in this area, see Joseph H. Guttentag, *Passing the Torch on Transfer Pricing, in* Liber Amicorum Sven-Olof Lodin 119 (2001).

Therefore, controlled foreign corporation (CFC) rules have been established as a backup to transfer pricing and as a way of preventing siphoning off of profits into low-tax jurisdictions which might even withstand transfer pricing scrutiny.[238]

CFC rules tax domestic shareholders of CFCs on income earned by the CFC; they are a form of look-through taxation. Where the CFC is just a shell company with no business purpose, the same thing can be done under the anti-avoidance rules of countries like Germany by disregarding the CFC and taxing the shareholder directly on its income.[239] Over 25 countries have adopted CFC rules since the U.S. first adopted such rules in 1962.[240] Even though countries adopting CFC legislation based their laws on those of other countries, the resulting laws exhibit a fair amount of diversity, in part because countries balanced the policy interests involved in different ways. In many of the countries with CFC legislation (particularly the U.S.), the rules are technical and highly complex, and they offer opportunities for tax planning.

The definition of CFC varies: most countries restrict CFCs to those controlled, directly or indirectly, by residents, while some treat as CFCs foreign corporations in which a resident has a substantial (10 percent or 25 percent) interest.[241] With the exception of a handful of countries, constructive ownership rules apply.[242] Most countries' rules involve the designation of low-tax countries or regimes.[243] In most countries as well, the nature of the income earned by the CFC is important in applying the rules. Passive income, income from transactions with related parties, and income from selling property or rendering services outside the CFC's country of establishment are particularly targeted, but the scope and precise definitions of "tainted" income differ. Assistance from related parties in earning the income is sometimes a factor. In addition to these rules focusing on definition of a CFC, identifying

---

[238] For a recent analysis of the CFC rules of 19 countries, on which the summary description here is based, see Arnold & Dibout, *supra* note 235, and sources cited herein.

[239] *See supra* 5.7.5.

[240] *See* Arnold & Dibout, *supra* note 235, at 38 n.5. In addition to those listed by Arnold & Dibout, basic CFC-type rules may be found in Kazakhstan, Tax Code, art. 30 (2001); Tajikistan, Tax Code, art. 152 (1998); Georgia, Tax Code, art. 66 (1997); and Azerbaijan, Tax Code, art. 128 (2000). Because such countries do not have much legitimate outbound investment activity, CFC rules can be drawn broadly so as to deter use of tax havens for tax avoidance. In part, such rules serve as a backup for transfer pricing rules.

[241] *See* Arnold & Dibout, *supra* note 235, at 41-43.

[242] *See id.* at 43.

[243] *See id.* at 44-48.

tainted income, and so forth, the CFC rules must contain all the necessary mechanics for look-through treatment, such as relief for foreign taxes, for losses, for subsequent dividend distributions, and for subsequent capital gains on disposition of the CFC's shares.[244]   CFC rules are therefore doubly complicated.

Because they are limited to cases of substantial ownership, CFC rules do not deal with the deferral of tax by investment in foreign investment funds. Australia, Canada, France, Germany, New Zealand, and the United States have enacted special legislation to eliminate the benefit of deferral for such investments.[245]

An obstacle to the application of transfer pricing rules is that they are applicable only to related parties. However, taxpayers may fail to disclose relatedness or may take advantage of technical definitions of related parties (particularly if these have loopholes) to escape these rules. Some countries have dealt with this problem by providing special transfer pricing rules in the case of any transactions with a party located in a tax haven, or by denying outright a deduction for such payments or imposing a withholding tax on them.[246]   Typically, in the case of a deduction denial, these rules allow the taxpayer to come forward with evidence substantiating the bona fides of the transaction. France has enacted a rule against the assignment of personal services income to tax haven companies.[247]   Several countries have enacted rules aimed at the transfer of property abroad to trusts or similar arrangements.[248]

Companies can be established so as to be treated as residents under the tax laws of two countries. This is typically done in order to be able to deduct losses in both jurisdictions. Several countries have enacted rules to

---

[244] *See id.* at 64-67.

[245] *See id.* at 44; Lee Burns & Richard Krever, Interests in Nonresident Trusts 79-12? (1997); Code Général des Impôts, art. 123 bis (France); Brian Arnold, *The taxation o investments in passive foreign investment funds in Australia, Canada, New Zealan and the United States, in* Alpert & van Raad (eds., 1993), at 5.

[246] *See* 86b Cahiers 36, 67-69, 325, 407, 421 (Argentina, Belgium, Brazil, France Peru, Portugal, Spain). Poland has established special documentation rules fc transactions with persons in a tax haven. *See* Janusz Fiszer, *Poland Decrees Tighte Rules for Transactions with Tax Havens,* Tax Notes Int'l 2337 (May 7, 2001).

[247] *See* Ault et al. (1997) at 460.

[248] *See* Robert W. Maas, Tolley's Anti-Avoidance Provisions, ch. 9 (looseleaf 2001 Ault et al. (1997) at 460-61 (France); Burns & Krever, *supra* note 245; I.R.C. §§ 67 679.

prevent this kind of transaction, often by refusing to treat such companies as residents.[249] The matter is also dealt with through tax treaties.

Double benefits can also be sought by arbitrage which takes advantage of divergent characterization rules in two countries.[250] Where such double benefits involve application of a treaty, the treaty can include special provisions precluding a double exemption or providing for a tax credit mechanism in lieu of the otherwise normally applicable exemption.[251] Special anti-avoidance provisions of this kind have, however, been included only in a few recently negotiated treaties.

Treaties can also be abused through treaty shopping. The mere interposition of a nominee holder in a treaty country is now dealt with in many treaties though a beneficial ownership requirement. More elaborate anti-treaty-shopping clauses have been included in a number of recent treaties, particularly those involving the U.S., although the vast majority of existing treaties do not have such clauses. Treaty abuse has also been attacked through unilateral rules.[252] The U.S. has promulgated regulations under which treaty benefits are denied to intermediate entities receiving U.S.-source income where "[t]he participation of the intermediate entity in the financing arrangement is pursuant to a tax avoidance plan."[253]

7.15 INFLATION ADJUSTMENT

Inflation rates have gone down throughout the world but even low inflation rates can have significant effects on tax systems that are not adjusted

---

[249] *See* Ault et al. (1997) at 379-80. The countries with special rules include Australia, Canada, the U.K., and the U.S. *See also* Friedrich E.F. Hey, *Germany's New Consolidated Loss Rules Target Dual-Resident Companies*, 25 Tax Notes Int'l 151 (March 18, 2002).

[250] *See, e.g.,* 22 Tax Management Int'l Forum (June 2000). U.S. regulations deny treaty benefits to foreign hybrid entities in order to prevent double non-taxation. *See* Robert Goulder, *U.S. Tax Officials Clarify Regulations for Payments to Foreign Hybrids*, 21 Tax Notes Int'l 2017 (Oct. 30, 2000); T.D. 8889, 2000-30 I.R.B. 124 July 24, 2000).

[251] *See* Arnold & Dibout, *supra* note 235, at 78-79.

[252] *E.g.,* § 50d(1a) EStG (Germany) which denies treaty benefits in cases of companies with no substantial activities where the owners would not have been entitled to the benefits themselves. Rädler, *Limitation of Treaty Benefits in Germany*, International Studies in Taxation: Law and Economics: Liber Amicorum Leif Mutén 297 (Gustaf Lindencrona et al. eds., 1999) argues that this provision violates European law.

[253] Treas. Reg. § 1.881-3(a)(4). *See* supra 5.8.2, note 255.

for inflation.[254] The effects of inflation can be divided into three categories: (1) inflation erodes amounts expressed in the law in national currency, (2) inflation erodes the value of tax obligations, and (3) inflation affects the measurement of the tax base.[255] The first of these is straightforward. It is more a political than a technical tax issue, since as a technical matter inflation adjustment need not be written into the law: the legislature can simply periodically adjust upwards amounts fixed in national currency in the law. In many countries, this is the approach followed: amounts are fixed in the law and periodically the legislature changes them. The result of this approach, however, is that, if the legislature does not make changes relatively frequently, any amounts fixed in the law are eroded over time. The legislature may also choose not to adjust amounts exactly for inflation, but to redistribute the tax burden when it makes adjustments to, say, the tax rate brackets. This effect of inflation (and the legal means available to deal with it) are not peculiar to taxation, but affect all laws which specify nominal amounts (for example, levels of fines in criminal laws or levels of registration fees in a company law). In principle, a generally applicable law could be enacted providing for automatic adjustment of all amounts stated in domestic currency in specified laws and regulations. However, countries which have adopted automatic indexation for tax typically do not apply this approach to every amount stated in the law in national currency.[256]

The second effect described above—erosion of tax liabilities—is typically dealt with by charging adequate interest. Explicit adjustment of the tax obligation between the time it arises in an economic sense and the time the tax falls due legally may also be provided for, but this is less usual and typically done only in hyperinflationary countries.

The real problems arise with the third effect—distortion of the tax base. They are most complex in the case of the income tax.[257] It is easiest to think of inflation adjustment in terms of the balance sheet and the profit and loss statement derived therefrom. Since profits equal the difference between

---

[254] Suppose that the real interest rate is 4% and the inflation rate is 2%. The nominal interest rate will then be around 6%. At a tax rate of 33⅓%, the tax on interest income will be 2, which is effectively a rate of 50% of the real interest income.

[255] For a detailed discussion (on which this section draws), *see* Victor Thuronyi *Adjusting Taxes for Inflation, in* TLDD 434.

[256] The U.S. applies automatic adjustment primarily to the rate brackets, personal exemptions, and the zero-bracket amount. Belgium applies automatic adjustment to most—but not all—amounts in the income tax law that are stated in national currency. *See* Tiberghien (1995) at 234-35.

[257] This is discussed comprehensively in Thuronyi, *supra* note 255.

the net worth in the closing and opening balance sheets (plus dividends declared, less contributions to capital),[258] an inflation-adjusted determination of profit simply requires adjusting all these elements and expressing them in terms of end-of-period currency values. Adjusting opening net worth is easy: just take the beginning value and adjust for the inflation that took place during the year. As for closing net worth, inflation adjustment requires restating the value of all the assets and liabilities included on the closing balance sheet. Finally, dividends declared and capital contributions made must be adjusted for the inflation occurring between the date of the dividend declaration (or capital contribution) and the end of the year.

The above approach works for businesses only—individuals do not keep balance sheets. But conceptually, the same approach could apply as if the individual kept a balance sheet. (Of course, tax administration considerations would preclude actually applying such a system in practice.)

How does actual country practice stack up against this conceptual benchmark? In terms of business income, comprehensive inflation adjustment has been practiced by a number of Latin American countries (as well as Israel), although several have dropped inflation adjustment as inflation rates have come down. Other countries generally have adopted ad hoc or partial inflation adjustment. For example, LIFO may be authorized or accelerated depreciation provided, both of which tend to compensate for the effects of inflation. Explicit adjustment for capital gains[259] or inventories[260] is also allowed by several countries. One problem with these ad hoc and partial approaches is that they tend to adjust the asset side but not liabilities. This can lead to serious distortions, because if the full nominal amount of interest expense is deductible while gains are adjusted for inflation, negative tax rates can easily result. Of course, the distortions are not so large as long as inflation is kept quite low, as it now is in most OECD countries.

7.16 INCOME AVERAGING

Not too long ago, individual income tax rates could reach very high levels (see 7.5) but they have come down substantially nearly everywhere. A steeply progressive rate schedule makes some sort of income averaging

---

[258] *See supra* note 141.

[259] U.K., France (for real estate), Australia. *See* Ault et al. (1997) at 41-42, 113; Beltrame & Mehl (1997) at 156. In the U.K., as of 1998, for individuals inflation adjustment has been replaced by a partial exclusion depending on the holding period. *See* Tiley (2000) at 610. Indexation still applies for corporations. *See id.* at 602.

See Beltrame & Mehl (1997) at 151-52 (Denmark, France, Ireland, U.K.).

provisions important. But income averaging has problems of both complexity and abuse.[261] Some countries do not have general averaging provisions, while others that previously had averaging rules have eliminated them or reduced their scope consequent on the reduction in tax rates.[262]

7.17 PRESUMPTIVE METHODS[263]

The extent to which presumptive or notional[264] methods are considered a normal part of income taxation constitutes an important conceptual difference between countries.

Some tax systems (the U.S. is an example) make no use of presumptive taxation. All taxpayers with business income are required to keep adequate records and report tax on their actual income and expenses. Cash accounting for smaller businesses may be allowed, but that is the extent of simplification. Only in a few cases are taxpayers allowed to take presumed amounts into account for tax purposes, one of these being travel expenses, where a per-day allowance may be deducted instead of keeping track of actual costs. Presumptive determination of taxable income can, however, be made as a result of an audit, if the taxpayer has failed to furnish adequate information.

By contrast, many developing and transition countries make extensive use of presumptive methods, particularly in taxing small businesses and agriculture. Israel has been particularly advanced in the use of these methods.[265] A few OECD countries (e.g., France,[266] Spain, Turkey) also make use of presumptive methods (such methods were important historically; in the early 19th century and even earlier, they were the predecessor of the income tax[267]). These methods often involve flat rates of tax on small businesses, traders, and even professionals which may be based on physical

---

[261] *See* Burns & Krever, *supra* note 53, at 548-50.

[262] The U.S. substantially cut back its income averaging rules in the Tax Reform Act of 1986, which also reduced the top tax rates. The U.K. never had a general averaging rule, but maintains specific rules for items such as royalties, life insurance policies, and farmers. *See* Tiley (2000) at 192-94. Canada eliminated averaging in 1988. *See* Hogg et al. (2002) at 47.

[263] *See generally* Victor Thuronyi, *Presumptive Taxation, in* TLDD at 401.

[264] Income from land used to be assessed on a notional basis in the U.K. *See* Morse & Williams (2000) at 129. *See also* Holmes, *supra* note 20, at 540-55.

[265] *See* Thuronyi, *supra* note 263, at 424-25.

[266] *See* Beltrame & Mehl (1997) at 188-94.

[267] *See* Ault et al (1997) at 82; Edwin Seligman, The Income Tax (1914).

characteristics such as square meters occupied and often involve no reliance on accounts kept by the taxpayer. The rationale for such approaches is that any accounts kept are likely to be unreliable. Presumptive taxation of this kind simplifies tax administration but the danger is that it oversimplifies. Because small businesses can always opt to keep proper accounts, they will tend to use the presumptive methods only if they are advantageous. Unless detailed preparation is undertaken, the presumptive methods are likely to be arbitrary and not to correspond very well to the taxpayer's actual income.

Another approach to presumptive taxation—for big business as well as small—is to institute a minimum tax based either on a percentage of turnover or assets. Both have been used in Latin America, and a minimum tax based on assets has become a fixture of the Latin American tax landscape, for better or worse. Unlike presumptive taxation for small business, an asset tax does not require any detailed work by the administration in designing the rules, since these are fairly simple and generally applicable to all taxpayers.

In most OECD countries, a minimum tax based on assets or turnover would be considered a violation of tax fairness and hence has not been applied with any frequency. A minimum tax based on assets was a feature of the Italian corporate tax historically. The alternative minimum tax (AMT) applicable in the U.S. is somewhat different, because it takes the form of an alternative tax base (taxed at a lower rate), involving different accounting rules (in particular, tighter limitations on deductions) than the regular tax base. The AMT does not make much policy sense: normally, if a decision is made that a particular deduction rule is too generous, the remedy would be to tighten up the rule. The reason that this was not done in a straightforward manner in the U.S. has to do with the tax policy process. While consensus could not be obtained to repeal various deductions outright, lawmakers were able to agree on a compromise, under which the deductions would be scaled back in the context of an AMT. Enactment of theAMT served the political goal of assuring that all taxpayers with substantial income would pay at least some tax, albeit at rates lower than those applicable for purposes of the regular tax.

In many developing countries, agriculture (sometimes with the exception of larger farms, which are subject to normal income tax rules) is subject to taxation on the basis of land area, rather than being taxed on actual income. Although taxes on agricultural land were important historically, they have become quite a minor revenue source.[268] In part, this is due to poor administration. Agricultural land taxes require a large up-front investment if

---

[268] *See* Richard Bird, The Taxation of Agricultural Land in Developing Countries (1974).

they are to be properly administered. Moreoever, taxes designed with too much sophistication in mind (progressive tax based on size of land holding, or use of many factors to estimate productivity of land), have tended to founder in maladministration, despite the impeccable theoretical considerations unpinning the design.[269]   Such taxes therefore present the prospect of a modest revenue source if simply designed and well administered, and are certainly a better way of taxing small-scale agriculture than accounts-based taxes.   They will not, however, be suitable for all situations (e.g. nomadic herding or jungle-fallow cultivation).

---

[269] *See id.*

Chapter 8

VALUE ADDED TAX

8.1 IN GENERAL

VAT[1] is noteworthy as a modern tax phenomenon. Although theoretical discussions developed the idea of the tax before World War II,[2] it was first adopted only after the war, and in most countries only since the 1970s or even more recently.[3] The tax is therefore much younger than the income tax, which is over 200 years old. The VAT has spread rapidly and is now imposed by all OECD countries with the exception of the U.S., as well as by a majority of developing and transition countries. It can be expected that virtually all countries will adopt the VAT before too long; for technical reasons, however, the tax may not be suitable for some of the very small island countries[4] and, for political reasons, the United States will likely continue to refrain from adopting this tax.[5]

---

[1] For discussion of the name, see David Williams, *Value-Added Tax, in* TLDD 164, 167-68. The tax is called by other names in various countries, for example consumption tax in Japan, and goods and services tax (GST) in Canada, New Zealand, and Australia. Whatever the name in the local language, it is almost invariably referred to by its acronym (e.g., VAT, GST, TVA (in French), IVA (in Spanish), NDS (in Russian), DRG (in Georgian)).

[2] *See* Schenk & Oldman (2001) at 5-6.

[3] *See id.* at 26-27; Ebrill et al. (2001) at 4-5; Van Hoorn (1972) at 22-24.

[4] *See* Ebrill et al. (2001) at 166-75.

[5] Proposals for a VAT have been considered in the U.S. at least since the early 70s. In an interview of Jan. 4, 1971, President Nixon stated: "I had considered the possibility of a value-added tax as a substitution for some of our other taxes, and looking to the future, we may very well move into that direction." *See Report of the Special Subcommittee of the Committee on General Income Tax Problems on the Value-Added Tax*, 24 Tax Law. 419, 419 (1971). See also the reports of the special committee in The Tax Lawyer of Fall 1972 (26 Tax Law. 45), Winter 1975 (28 Tax Law. 193) and Spring 1976 (29 Tax Law. 457) and citations therein. Despite these proposals, VAT has never gained much political support in the U.S. It was rejected in the Treasury Department's 1984 tax reform report. Political opposition to the VAT

Economically, the VAT has virtually the same incidence as a retail sales tax. The difference is administrative. While a retail sales tax is collected at the final stage only (sales to the final consumer), the VAT is collected at all stages of production and distribution. This means that it is not critical to tax all sellers, particularly small traders who sell to final consumers. Because these traders pay tax on the goods they buy from manufacturers or wholesalers, most of the tax has already been paid; thus, ignoring their value added does not make too much difference. Excluding small traders allows tax administration efforts to focus on a smaller number of taxpayers while still achieving a fairly comprehensive coverage for the tax.

In some countries, the VAT replaced turnover taxes, which suffered from the problem of cascading: tax included in the price of inputs to businesses was again subject to tax (often more than once) when the outputs produced with those inputs were sold. While it is possible to deal with cascading under a sales tax by exempting sales to other taxpayers, the VAT avoids this problem elegantly by giving a credit for taxes paid at earlier stages. Largely because of this technical advantage, VAT has supplanted turnover and sales taxes, although in some countries[6] sales taxes coexist with VAT (for example, there may be a national VAT, together with local retail sales taxes). Although as a matter of theory VAT can take different forms, everywhere except Japan VAT is of the consumption-type, invoice credit method.

The rise of the VAT has eclipsed the sales tax. Retail sales taxes continue to exist, for example in Canada and in the United States, but almost invariably at rates below 10 percent.[7] The manufacturer's-level and wholesaler's-level forms of sales tax are nearly gone.

---

could come from all sides. Many liberals do not like this tax because they are afraid it will make the tax system less progressive (if substituted for more progressive taxes). Many conservatives do not like it because it is a potentially large revenue source and could lead to bigger government. Many ordinary people simply do not like the idea of having to pay a new tax. States may view it as an encroachment on their sales taxes. Moreover, its introduction would create transition problems, by placing a burden on those about to retire who have tax-paid savings under the income tax and would now be hit by the VAT on their retirement expenditures. Retired people in the U.S. have substantial political clout and would undoubtedly make introduction of a VAT difficult. Since there is no pressing need in the U.S. to introduce a VAT, it is difficult to see politicians embracing it in the face of these potential obstacles.

[6] *E.g.*, Canada.

[7] *See* Ebrill et al. (2001) at 23-24.

8.2 VAT BASICS

Those familiar with the VAT can skip this section, which summarizes the basic rules of VAT. The operation of the VAT will not be described here in detail, since comparative literature on this topic is readily available.[8]

The VAT is a tax on transactions. It is structured in such a way that the total tax base is more or less equal to domestic consumption (usually less, given exemptions). Taxable transactions are the supply of goods or services made within the jurisdiction by a taxable person acting as such, except for those that are exempted. Goods are typically defined as tangible property, with the exception of money and land. The supply of goods is the transfer of ownership of the good for consideration. The taxable value of the supply is usually the amount of the consideration. However, certain transactions are taxable even where there is no consideration, for example where a taxpayer withdraws items for personal use or transfers them to employees for free or at a reduced price. In these cases, the taxable value is typically the fair market value of the good. In cases of transfers to employees, VAT raises questions similar to those posed by fringe benefits under the income tax. For example, if the employer operates a cafeteria, where employees are allowed to eat for free, will the employer be entitled to an input credit for the food and other items (input credits are explained below) or will the employer be required to calculate the fair market value of the meals provided and be deemed to have received this amount and be liable to pay VAT on it?

VAT laws typically define supplies of services more abstractly and comprehensively than supplies of goods. A supply of services is anything done (or not done) by a taxable person acting as such for consideration. This definition is to some extent saved from being overbroad by the exemption for financial services. Financial services are exempt in most VAT systems because of the practical difficulty of identifying the amount of consideration for a particular service. But this exemption does double duty by in effect narrowing the definition of services subject to tax. For example, if a corporation engages in a recapitalization whereby outstanding shares are exchanged for shares of a different kind, literally the exchange of shares would be a service subject to VAT. However, it is exempt because this kind of transaction is considered a financial service. Common sense suggests that this kind of transaction should not be included in the VAT base, since the

---

[8] *See* Williams, *supra* note 1; Schenk & Oldman (2001).

reshuffling of company shares does not enter in to total domestic consumption.

Where the service provider receives a payment from the service recipient, the services might nevertheless be considered as not provided for consideration if there is no direct link between the services and the payment.[9]

In addition to supplies of goods and services, VAT laws tax the import of goods. VAT on imports is taxed according to customs procedure, so customs legislation is relevant to understanding how the tax on imports operates in practice.

The mechanism used to bring the total VAT base more or less in line with domestic consumption is the invoice-credit mechanism. Taxpayers who have an invoice showing VAT paid with respect to domestically supplied goods and services (or imported goods), are allowed a credit for VAT paid to their supplier (or upon import). The invoice-credit mechanism relieves intermediate goods or services of tax burden. Typically, a credit is allowed only for goods or services that are acquired for use in a business of making taxable supplies. Inputs to exempt activities are not eligible for input credit. One exception to this rule is for exports. While exports are exempt from tax, an input credit is allowed.[10] Exports therefore bear no VAT burden.

In some systems, the exemption for exports takes the form of a zero rate of tax ("zero rating"). While a zero tax rate may seem peculiar, the reason for this is to be consistent with the rule that no input credit is allowed for inputs to exempt supplies. To allow the credit, exports must be made taxable, but since it is desired to relieve exports of tax burden, the rate of tax must be zero. Other systems accomplish the same thing by distinguishing between exemptions with credit, and exemptions without credit. Exemption with credit is equivalent to zero rating. There is no difference between the two systems beyond a terminological one. Another terminological difference

---

[9] For example, in Apple and Pear Development Council v. Commissioners of Customs and Excise, Case 102/86, March 8, 1988, [1988] ECR 1443, [1988] 2 CMLR 394, the taxpayer, whose activities promoted the apple and pear trade, was financed by mandatory fees levied on members of the trade. The court held that there was no direct link between these fees and the benefits to any particular producer arising from the taxpayer's activities. In Tolsma v. Inspecteur der Omzetbelasting Leeuwarden, Case C-16/93, [1994] ECR I 743, [1994] 2 CMLR 908 (March 3, 1994), the ECJ found that a street musician was not taxable on contributions made from passers-by.

[10] Example: Jack produces widgets for export. When Jack receives a monthly bill for electricity to be used in widget production, this shows an amount due of 120, 20 of which is shown as VAT. When Jack files his monthly VAT return, he is entitled to a tax credit of 20, and so receives a check from the government for this amount (plus all other input credits which Jack claims on the return).

is that some systems use the term credit to describe the reduction of tax liability for the tax on inputs while others speak of an input tax deduction. Again, there is no substantive difference. Unlike the income tax, where there is a significant difference between a deduction (which reduces the tax base) and a credit (which reduces the tax itself), the VAT does not really have a unitary tax base. Rather, outputs are subject to tax, possibly at various rates, but always including at least one positive rate and the zero rate, and the tax liability is computed by subtracting from output tax the allowed tax on inputs. There may also be additions and subtractions to reflect items such as changes in previously accounted for transactions. Thus, deductions, in those systems which use that term, operate in the same manner as credits, i.e. directly on the amount of tax. In Europe, the U.K. uses the term zero-rating and credit, while France speaks of exemption (for exports) and deduction of tax. The European directives typically follow the French terminology.

Most businesses, except for very small ones, are VAT taxpayers. The usual approach is to provide a turnover threshold. Once the turnover of a business exceeds the specified threshold, it is required to register and pay VAT thereafter on all its turnover. In addition, businesses with receipts below the threshold are typically allowed to register if they want. They may want to do so where their customers are mostly other businesses. Being a taxpayer allows them to claim a credit for their inputs. While they are required to charge output VAT to their customers, their customers can claim a credit for this VAT. Only a registered taxpayer is allowed to issue an invoice allowing the customer to obtain a VAT credit. An invoice must be issued with respect to every taxable transaction, although a simplified invoice can be issued for sales at retail.

The VAT applies only with respect to supplies made by a taxpayer acting as such. So if an individual is registered as a taxpayer and sells personal belongings (i.e. the sale takes place outside the scope of the business), the sale is not subject to VAT. In the case of property used partly for business and partly for private purposes, VAT does not apply to the private portion of the sale.[11] Similarly, employment services are excluded from the scope of the tax. In principle, it would be possible to treat employees as taxpayers, but this would be administratively cumbersome; no country does it. The fact that employees are not taxpayers gives rise to tax planning opportunities, however. Suppose that person X is engaged in an activity that is exempt from VAT. If X engages Y to provide a service to X, Y must charge VAT (assuming that Y's supplies exceed the threshold for

---

[11] *See* Finanzamt Uelzen v. Armbrecht, Case C-291/92, [1995] ECR I 2775 (Oct. 4, 995).

registration). X, being exempt, is not allowed to claim an input credit for this tax. If instead X gets the job done by hiring employees itself, then no VAT arises because the employment services are excluded from the scope of the tax. Of course, hiring employees may not be advantageous from an income tax or an employment tax point of view, but this is a matter to be weighed in the total balance in making a decision. From the point of view of the VAT alone, it is clearly advantageous for an exempt person to engage in self-supply in this manner.

The jurisdictional basis for VAT is typically expressed as covering supplies that take place within the jurisdiction. Like the income tax source rules, the concept of place of supply is an artificial and technical one. For goods, their physical location at the time they are transferred or shipped to the customer is usually relevant. For services, the rules differ depending on the type of service. Some services are sourced at the place where the services are actually carried out. Others are sourced at the place where the customer is located. Services relating to immovable property are sourced where the property is located.

Usually, a taxpayer providing services that are considered to be provided within the jurisdiction and hence subject to tax will be operating in the country through a fixed place of business and hence subject to VAT registration requirements. However, it is possible that the services are provided cross-border by a supplier based abroad. In this case, the typical rule is that where the recipient of the services is an individual customer, the transaction escapes tax. However, where the customer is a business, the business is typically required to impose a "reverse charge". It is called a reverse charge because the taxpayer is the reverse of the normal situation: it is the customer rather than the supplier that must pay the tax. Because a credit can be immediately claimed for the tax, though, no cash usually need be paid to the government. One exception is where the customer is engaged in providing exempt supplies and hence is not entitled to a credit (or a full credit) for the tax paid on the supply. In this case, the reverse charge leads to a tax liability.

VAT is a remarkable tax in that the taxpayer might be permanently in a position of receiving refunds from the government, and never making any payments. This will happen if the taxpayer is an exporter, because while its export outputs will not be taxable, it will be entitled to a credit for its input VAT. Taxpayers who do not regularly export most of their production might also find themselves in a refund position in months where their input credits exceed their output tax, for example where they have bought some expensive equipment.

The taxable period is normally the calendar month. VAT is a fairly simple tax to keep track of, since it is calculated just on the basis of output

VAT (determined on the basis of sales during the month) minus input VAT (determined on the basis of purchases and imports during the month). The method of accounting is usually a form of accrual method: the time of the taxable transaction is the earlier of the time that the invoice is issued or payment is received (if goods are shipped but an invoice is not issued in a timely manner, then VAT will arise at the point that that the invoice is required to be issued). The calendar month can be used because the calculation of VAT does not require the taking of inventories, the calculation of depreciation, and the like. Each month can be dealt with on its own.

VAT must be audited to detect fraud. If the taxpayer does not engage in fraud, there is not much else to audit, i.e. in the case of honest taxpayers VAT audits will normally result in no change, unlike income tax audits where there is always some room for dispute about this or that accounting treatment.[12]

The following examples illustrate the VAT basics:

Alan (A) is a consultant and provides taxable services to Bakery (B) for 100. If the VAT is 20%, then Alan charges 120, and remits 20 of tax to the government. (Assume that Alan has no inputs.)

Bakery produces bread which it sells to City Restaurant (C) for 1,000 plus 200 VAT. In addition to A's consulting services, B has other inputs (flour, utilities, etc.) on which it has paid VAT, for a total VAT paid of 110. The amount that B must remit to the government is $200 - 110 = 90$.

C produces sandwiches using the bread and sells them to final consumers for a total of 2,000 plus VAT, charging VAT of 400. It deducts the 200 in VAT paid to B, plus VAT paid on other inputs of 150, and pays 50 to the government.

The government's VAT take on the sandwiches is therefore 400. Only 50 of this is received from C. The rest is received from A, B, and other suppliers of intermediate goods and services. Therefore, while the VAT collects the same amount as a retail sales tax imposed on C,[13] the tax is collected throughout the production process.

---

[12] There are a few exceptions, one being the allocation of input credits between exempt and taxable supplies.

[13] Under a retail sales tax, the sale from A to B might be exempt on the basis that it is not a sale to a final consumer. The sale from B to C might similarly be exempt, or perhaps B would not be a taxpayer under the retail sales tax at all if it makes no retail sales. C would therefore suffer no input tax. It would collect sales tax of 400 on its sales.

Variations:

1. Suppose that bread is exempt from tax (sandwiches are not). In this case, B will not charge VAT to C, but C can claim no input credit. Therefore the tax that C must pay increases. The exemption actually increases government revenue on sales of sandwiches,[14] because it results in a break in the "chain of credits". The input VAT that B pays cannot be claimed by anyone as a credit. Of course, because retail sales of bread outweigh sales to other VAT taxpayers, the net effect of exempting bread is to reduce revenues overall.

2. Suppose instead that A is a nonresident. In this case, A will be beyond the jurisdictional reach of the country and will not be a VAT taxpayer. But when B pays 100 to A, the VAT law will typically impose a "reverse charge" on B, i.e. will make B liable for the tax as if it had supplied the service to itself. Where B can claim an input credit for the tax imposed, there is a wash, but if bread is exempt then the reverse charge makes a difference.

3. Suppose that C is a tax evader and does not report its taxable sales (or is a small business and its turnover is below the VAT registration threshold). While the government does not receive any revenue from C (assuming that C gets away with it), notice that a tax of 350 is still collected in respect of C's sandwiches, in the form of tax paid by suppliers to C.

8.3 SIMILARITY OF VAT LAWS

While there are differences in VAT from one country to another, compared with the income tax VAT laws are remarkably similar. This similarity is largely due to the newness of VAT and to its introduction on a harmonized basis in the EU. Unlike with direct taxes, the EC managed to standardize the main features of VAT as part of European harmonization. It issued several VAT directives, the most comprehensive being the 6th Directive.[15] All VATs in Europe are required to be consistent with these

---

[14] Because B is exempt, B will not charge VAT to C, but will include the 110 in nonrecoverable VAT on B's inputs in the selling price to C, thus charging C 1,110 for the bread. C's costs accordingly increase by 110. Assuming that C passes this cost increase through, C's price goes up to 2,110 plus 422 in VAT. C pays 272 in VAT (422 less 150 input tax). The total VAT paid is 110 (inputs to B) + 150 (inputs to C) + 272 (C's payment) = 532. Note that even if C were to absorb the added cost, the government's revenue would still go up if bread were exempted. In this case the VAT paid would be (400 less 150) = 250 paid by C, plus 150 in inputs to C plus 110 in inputs to B for a total of 510.

[15] Council Directive of May 17, 1977, on the harmonization of the laws of the Member States relating to turnover taxes – common system of value added tax:

Directives, and most other countries with VATs have broadly followed suit, with a few minor departures.[16] The 6th Directive allows some variation from country to country, but these differences are small. The result is a VAT that is largely uniform throughout Europe. Outside the EU, many countries have followed the EU model more or less closely.

Among OECD countries, there really are only two substantial divergences from the EU model, New Zealand and Japan. New Zealand, while keeping the basic structure of the invoice-credit method, has adopted a substantially broader base than in the EU and a single rate.[17]

Japan's tax has several important differences from Europe, not the least of which is its single low 5-percent rate, compared with typical rates of 16 percent or more in Europe.[18] While both Japan and the EU have VATs of the credit-subtraction form, the EU uses the invoice-credit method while Japan uses a different method, which is more closely related to financial accounting. The difference is not that great, in that in Europe tax administrations do not rely heavily on tax invoices to police VAT compliance.[19] Moreover, the fact that Japan does not use the tax invoice

---

uniform basis of assessment, (EC) 388/77 [1977] OJ L145/1, as amended, *consolidated text reprinted in* European Union Law Guide (Philip Raworth ed., looseleaf, updated to March 2000) *and in* Schenk & Oldman (2001) at 557-672. See Ralph Kilches, Sammlung des Europäischen Mehrwertsteuerrechts (1998) for a collection of the directives and the ECJ decisions on VAT, together with an introduction.

[16] For example, in Switzerland, leases of goods and work on goods are treated as supplies of goods rather than as services. *See* Waldburger et al., *Taxation in Switzerland*, 3 Tax Planning Int'l EU Focus 10, 11 (Jan. 2001).

[17] New Zealand adopted the tax in 1985. *See* Schenk & Oldman (2001) at 27. Most EU countries have more than one rate of VAT, as permitted by the VAT directive. Single rates are maintained by Denmark (25%) and Norway (23%). Although the UK has only one positive rate of tax, it should probably be classified as a two-rate jurisdiction, because it applies a zero rate to a number of internal supplies. *See* Ebrill et al. (2001) at 9-12.

[18] *See* Alan Schenk, *Japanese Consumption Tax After Six Years: A Unique VAT Matures*, 69 Tax Notes 899 (Nov. 13, 1995); Ebrill et al. (2001) at 9-13.

[19] *See* Schenk, *supra* note 18, at 905. This is not to say that invoices are not important. They are required as a matter of law, unless specified exceptions for simplified retail invoices apply or unless the tax authorities use their discretion to waive the invoice requirement. *See, e.g.,* Pelleted Casehardening Salts Ltd v. Commissioners of Customs and Excise, VATTR (MAN/84/287), 2 BVC 205, 192, *reprinted in* Schenk & Oldman (2001) at 190-93, holding that the Commissioner had not improperly exercised his discretion to refuse to accept evidence of petrol

method does not mean that Japanese taxpayers do not need to keep records of purchases. Rather, the difference lies in the fact that Japanese taxpayers are allowed to credit VAT on inputs by deriving this amount from total purchases, instead of adding up amounts shown on each invoice.[20] This means that an input credit is allowed even for purchases from exempt small businesses. No credit is allowed, however, for purchases of exempt goods or services. The allowance of a credit for notional VAT on purchases from small business means that the small business exemption has real value. Moreover, the threshold for exemption of small businesses is generous.[21] Other ways that Japan is generous to taxpayers include the fact that accounting methods used for income tax can generally also be used for VAT (including the use of the fiscal year, or in some cases calendar quarter, in contrast to the monthly taxable period commonly found in other countries). Moreover, small businesses (those over the exemption threshold but whose turnover is below a specified threshold) are allowed to compute VAT input credits under a simplified method which allows a credit for a specified percentage of sales.[22] All of these generous and flexible rules make sense in light of Japan's low rate; in the context of rates seen in Europe, such generosity would give rise to substantial pressures. Japan's rules, therefore, probably make sense for Japan, given its low rate and assuming a policy of wanting to give a modest preference to small business. They keep the administrative costs of the VAT down and allow its administration to be closely linked to that of the corporate income tax. But they are probably not exportable to countries imposing much higher rates of VAT.

VAT is a significant area of European law. Unlike customs duty, which is imposed in Europe under a uniform statute, VAT is imposed under separate laws in each European country, but these laws are harmonized by the 6th Directive. This structure means that questions of VAT law often involve two statutes: the national law and the 6th Directive. If the taxpayer feels that the national law is inconsistent with the 6th Directive, the matter can be litigated.[23] National courts can also construe VAT statutes so as to be

---

purchases for purposes of the input credit other than the required invoices. The input credit was denied because the taxpayer did not have the proper invoices.

[20] *See* Schenk, *supra* note 18, at 906. Use of tax invoices would have been virtually impossible without taxpayer identification numbers. *See supra* 6.5.

[21] *See* Schenk, *supra* note 18, at 904.

[22] *See id.* at 908.

[23] *See supra* 4.4.1.

consistent with the 6th Directive.[24] The VAT raises the question as to whether hamonization is best accomplished through directives (implemented by separate laws in each country) or through a uniform regulation (for example, the Community Customs Code). Another issue is whether the enactment of the 6th Directive, coupled with the unanimity requirement to make decisions on taxes, has ossified tax policy somewhat in respect of this tax. It may well be that an ossified policy is a good thing, if it has prevented negative changes from being made and reduced the frequency of legislative change. But it has also possibly made Europe less dynamic in terms of VAT policy than it could be. Innovations have tended to be made in other countries, for example, New Zealand, Israel, Japan, or South Africa.

Significant departures from the standard approach can be found in countries outside the OECD. Some countries deny an input credit for capital goods[25] or delay payment of refunds.[26] Bangladesh extends VAT only to the manufacturing stage, while Pakistan does not tax services.[27] Non-standard exemptions can be found in many countries—in Georgia, even the Georgian alphabet (which has several more letters than the Latin alphabet) was insufficient to accomodate the list of VAT exemptions.

8.4 SCOPE OF TAX

8.4.1 TAXABLE ACTIVITY

The type of activity subject to VAT is broadly defined in a similar way, using terms such as economic activity, taxable activity, or business.[28] There may be subtle differences in these concepts from country to country. In Europe, the relevant concept is "economic activity."[29] In cases involving activities such as that of a holding company or trade association, where the taxpayer was seeking to obtain an input credit, the European Court of Justice

---

[24] *E.g.*, Stirling v. Commissioners of Customs and Excise, [1985] VATTR 232, [1986] 2 CMLR 117 (Edinburgh VAT Tribunal), *reprinted in* Schenk & Oldman (2001) at 114.

[25] At least eight countries, including China and Brazil, fail to give a full and immediate credit for capital goods. *See* Ebrill et al. (2001) at 1, 18, 64.

[26] This is often the case in Latin America, where credits must often be carried forward, *see id.* at 18, as well as in the former Soviet Union.

[27] *See id.* at 2.

[28] *See* Schenk & Oldman (2001) at 105-13.

[29] 6th VAT Directive, *supra* note 15, art. 4(1), (2).

has interpreted this concept narrowly, so as to deny the input credit.[30] The Council of State of France has held that the sale of gold bars held for investment by a company was not an economic activity subject to VAT.[31] Peculiarly, and departing from standard jurisprudence under the income tax, the ECJ has also held that certain illegal activities were not subject to tax, being outside the "circuit of economic commerce."[32] Generally, only supplies that are for consideration are subject to tax, although there are exceptions to this rule for self-supplies and certain other transactions.[33] The restrictive rules on input credits in the EU probably make little sense in the context of a tax designed to reach total domestic consumption.

---

[30] In Polysar Investments Netherlands BV v. Inspecteur der Invoerrechten en Accijnzen, Case C-60/90, [1991] ECR I 3111 (June 20, 1991), the ECJ held that the mere acquisition and holding of shares was not an economic activity where the taxpayer was not involved in the management of the companies whose shares it held. The court therefore denied an input credit to the taxpayer for the VAT paid on accounting and other professional services. Similarly, in Wellcome Trust Ltd. v. Commissioners of Customs and Excise, Case C-155/94, [1996] ECR I 3013 (June 20, 1996), the ECJ denied an input credit for legal, tax, and investment advice relating to the sale of shares held by the trust. The court found that the trust was not a VAT taxpayer since the holding of a portfolio of shares was not an economic activity. *See also* Floridienne SA v. Belgian State (Nov. 14, 2000).

[31] *See* Sudfer, Conseil d'Etat, 29 dec. 1996, Dr. fisc. 1996, No. 6, comm. 221, *discussed in* Cozian (1999) at 498-99; Gunnar Rabe, *The EU VAT System—Time for a Change?, in* Liber Amicorum Sven-Olof Lodin 222, 232-33 (2001).

[32] *See* Mol v. Inspecteur der Invoerrechten en Accijnzen, Case 269/86, [1988] ECR 3627 (ECJ July 8, 1988) (amphetamines); Witzemann v. Hauptzollamt München-Mitte, Case C-343/89, [1990] ECR I 4477 (ECJ Dec. 6, 1990) (import of counterfeit currency—customs duty also not chargeable on this illegal act), Criminal Proceedings Against Goodwin, Case C-3/97, [1998] ECR I 3257 (ECJ May 28, 1998) (counterfeit perfumes are taxable—the ECJ distinguished earlier cases on the basis that counterfeit perfumes "are not goods which cannot be placed on the market because of their intrinsic nature" and "the possibility of competition between counterfeit products and goods which are lawfully traded cannot be ruled out." [1998] ECR at I 3271); Fischer v. Finanzamt Donaueschingen, Case C-283/95, [1998] ECR I 3369 (ECJ June 11, 1998) (the unlawful operation of games of chance falls within the scope of VAT since it is in competition with games of chance lawfully played).

[33] *See* Schenk & Oldman (2001) at 123-38; Williams, *supra* note 1, at 168-69, 199-202.

8.4.2 GOODS AND SERVICES

The VAT typically applies to supplies of goods and services.[34] In VATs of countries of the former Soviet Union, reference is typically made to "goods, work, and services" instead of "goods and services". The distinction does not lead to significant substantive differences, since the operatives rules for works and services tend to be the same.

8.4.3 DEFINITION OF TAXABLE SERVICES

Some countries have defined taxable services by listing. In some cases, this was a transitional matter, since originally only limited types of services were included in the tax base, consistent with capacity to administer the tax (or the political will to impose it). The standard approach currently is a broad negative definition (provision of services is any activity done for consideration which does not consist of the supply of goods). One can expect the "listing" approach to disappear over time. Listing will be needed, however, to specify services that are exempt or that are taxed at a lower rate.

The requirement of consideration is sometimes difficult to apply, for example, in the case of foreign exchange transactions where there is not a specific consideration charged, the provider of foreign exchange services making a profit on the spread between buying and selling rates. In such cases, it has been determined that there was consideration and hence the transaction was within the scope of VAT.[35]

8.4.4 SUPPLIES BY GOVERNMENT AGENCIES AND NONPROFITS

As an example of innovation outside the EU, New Zealand is unusually broad in taxing services provided by government agencies and nonprofits, although nonprofits enjoy zero rating to the extent financed by donations.[36] The EU generally exempts government services provided by public authorities acting as such.

---

[34] In Australia the law refers to "supplies" and this in turn is defined to include supplies of goods and services and a range of other supplies that may not fall within the ordinary meaning of goods or services. In European VAT laws, services are typically defined to mean any transaction that is not a supply of goods. *See* 6th VAT Directive, *supra* note 15, art. 6.

[35] *See* Schenk & Oldman (2001) at 126-38.

[36] *See id.* at 76, 309-12.

8.4.5 IMMOVABLE PROPERTY

Immovable property (land and buildings) gives rise to an important element of private consumption. In principle, one could tax this consumption by imputing income to the ownership of durable items and treating the consumer as self-supplying these services to himself. However, the VAT does not work this way as an administrative matter (the general approach is to keep the number of taxpayers to a minimum). Therefore, more practical approaches have been taken to taxing immovable property. A general approach for housing would be to tax it when first sold, and to ignore subsequent sales. The 6th Directive allows some flexibility on taxing immovable property and so countries have adopted different approaches. In practice, this may be the area of greatest difference in VAT law among the European countries. A few countries tax certain construction materials and construction services at lower rates.[37] Several exempt, zero rate, or tax at a lower rate the sales of new residential construction.[38] While sales of existing residential real estate are uniformly exempted, sales of commercial real estate are taxed in several countries (mostly outside the EU).[39] In addition to the VAT treatment, however, to get the whole picture it is important to keep in mind differing rates of real estate transfer tax that may apply.[40]

8.4.6 INTERNATIONAL TRANSACTIONS

VAT could theoretically be imposed either on an origin or on a destination basis. An origin tax is imposed according to the place of production, while a destination tax is imposed by the jurisdiction where the product is consumed. In fact, countries almost uniformly use the destination

---

[37] *See* Sijbren Cnossen, *VAT Treatment of Immovable Property, in* TLDD 231, 238-39.
[38] *See id.* at 239-41.
[39] *See id.* at 240-41.
[40] *See id.*

basis.[41] This means that for imported goods, VAT is collected by the customs authorities[42] according to customs procedures.

Challenges are posed for goods sold in electronic commerce, as well as for services sold internationally. Services are hard to tax on a destination basis because the country where the services are consumed may have trouble finding out about them. There can be no physical controls as with goods. Moreover, it may be difficult to define under what circumstances services are provided for nonresidents. For example, the New Zealand statute zero-rated services provided "for and to" nonresidents. A New Zealand court held that advertising placed in a local paper for a nonresident customer would be considered provided "for" residents if it related to goods and services provided by residents. For example, image advertising by nonresidents for promotion of a brand name would not qualify for zero-rating "where the goods or services referred to in the advertisement are sold in New Zealand."[43] The taxation of international services is an area of flux and development, but as with the rest of VAT it can be expected that the rules that eventually will be adopted by countries will end up being largely consistent, at least in general outline. There is room here for international agreements, which currently are lacking. The EU recently took an important step with respect to e-commerce, requiring nonresident sellers of downloadable products to consumers to register in an EU country and to pay tax at the rate of the country where the customer lives.[44]

There also tend to be important gaps in the taxation of international transport services. For competitive reasons, the country in which such services originate tends to tax them in the same way as exports, but countries do not typically tax the import. The result is that these services are zero-rated, which tends to favor them. There is no reason why these services should not be taxed in the same way as others, and perhaps eventually they will be.[45] For

---

[41] The origin method was used for about 10 years after the collapse of the Soviet Union for trade within that area, but has now been largely replaced by the destination method.

[42] In the case of supplies delivered by mail, the postal authorities may also exercise tax administration functions, as with customs duties. *See, e.g.,* The Postal Packets (Customs and Excise) Regulations 1986, SI 1986/260, Feb. 14, 1986, as amended (U.K.), *reprinted in* 5 De Voil Indirect Tax Service 5326 (looseleaf, as updated 2002).

[43] Wilson & Horton Ltd v. Commissioner of Inland Revenue, [1994] 3 NZLR 232 (Ct. App. Auckland), *reprinted in* Schenk & Oldman (2001) at 279-85. The New Zealand statute was subsequently amended.

[44] *See* Joann M. Weiner, *European Union,* 28 Tax Notes Int'l 1277 (Dec. 30, 2002).

[45] *See also* Kaneko, *Proposal for International Humanitarian Tax – A Consumption Tax on International Air Travel,* 17 Tax Notes Int'l 1911 (Dec. 14, 1998).

the moment, countries are quite uniform in failing to tax international transport, although the details of the definition of exempt international transport vary.

An important issue for businesses with sales in many countries is whether activities conducted in or in relation to a particular country will consist of "doing business in" that country and hence give rise to liability to register for VAT.[46] The applicable test for this purpose may be similar to the permanent establishment rule under the income tax, but treaties generally will not apply, since such treaties usually do not cover VAT, and there may be differences between the VAT and the income tax rules.[47] A more transparent practice, which is followed in some countries, is to use the same permanent establishment concept for both the VAT and the income tax.

8.5 EXEMPTIONS

Exemption under the VAT can be given in two forms. The first is zero-rating. This means that sales are subject to no tax, but input credits are fully allowed. The effective tax burden on final consumption is zero. The second is called exemption, which means that the sale is not subject to tax, but a credit for inputs is denied. Determining the amount of input credits to deny as allocable to exempt outputs can be perplexing, particularly in the case of taxpayers engaged in financial and investment transactions.[48] This means that

---

[46] See, for Canada, Schenk & Oldman (2001) at 93 n.12. For purposes of the sales tax in the U.S., a state has been held to have jurisdiction to tax only over taxpayers with a physical presence in the State. (Congress could, however, override this result by legislation.)

[47] Chile has withholding for income tax purposes rather than a reverse charge under the VAT, but this may change as Chile enters into more tax treaties that would prohibit such a charge.

[48] For example, in Sofitam SA v. Ministre chargé du Budget, Case C-333/91, [1993] ECR I 3513 (June 22, 1993), the ECJ determined that dividends received should be excluded from the pro-ration formula used to determine input credits in the case of a mixed holding company (i.e. a company which holds shares in other companies and at the same time carries out other activities), thereby allowing a full deduction for input VAT. In BLP Group v. Commissioners of Customs & Excise, Case C-4/94, [1995] ECR I 983 (April 6, 1995), the ECJ denied an input credit for banking, legal, and accounting advice rendered in connection with an exempt transaction (sale of shares). In Régie Dauphinoise-Cabinet A. Forest SARL v. Ministre du Budget, Case C-306/94, [1996] ECR I 3695 (July 11, 1996), the ECJ found that interest on investment of funds received from clients was part of remuneration for services and hence subject to VAT, even though exempt. The court distinguished dividends, which were not

some tax is effectively imposed (how much depends on the extent of inputs).[49] Exemption can even in some cases be worse treatment than taxation. This is the case where the exempt goods are an input into someone else's production. Exemption means that the purchasers can take no input credit for the tax embedded in the product. Despite their drawbacks, exemptions are varied and widespread.[50]

Exemption also means that the exempt entity or activity has an incentive to engage in self-supply. Some countries (particularly developing and transition countries) would not consider it a problem – for them, just getting taxpayers to pay the amount of VAT due under the law is difficult enough, without worrying about possible incentives to avoid tax by vertical integration. Other countries have enacted detailed and specific anti-abuse rules that reach at least the more important cases of self-supply, such as where the taxpayer constructs its own building.[51]

In OECD countries, zero-rating of internal supplies is practised to a significant extent in only a few countries (U.K., Canada, Ireland, Mexico).[52] There are significant differences among countries with a VAT as to what items are exempt.

Because of the structure of the VAT, exemption is inherently problematic. Exemption may in some cases be a backdoor way of achieving similar results to a lower rate (even a zero rate). The optimal structure of exemptions is by no means settled and much policy discussion and change can be expected in this area over the coming years, since many exemptions are difficult to justify as a policy matter.

---

remuneration for economic activity. These amounts were therefore to be included in the denominator of the fraction used to allocate input credits between taxable and exempt services.

[49] Accordingly, in Australia, the term "input taxed supplies" is used instead of exempt supplies.

[50] *See* Ebrill at al. (2001) at 83-100.

[51] *See* Schenk & Oldman (2001) at 77 n.38, 351; Sixth VAT Directive, article 5(7)(a), which allows member states to treat self-supplies as supplies made for consideration, and, for the UK, The Value Added Tax (Self-supply of Construction Services) Order 1989, *reprinted in* Butterworths Orange Tax Handbook.

[52] *See* Schenk & Oldman (2001) at 78 n.41.

8.6 RATE STRUCTURE

A single rate for VAT is typically recommended for reasons of administrative and legal simplicity, and many countries have taken this approach. However, nearly half of countries with a VAT have more than one rate.[53] Most countries adopting the VAT more recently have opted for a single rate.[54] Unlike exemptions, lower (or zero) rates of tax are consistent with the basic structure of the tax and are intellectually coherent. Therefore it can be expected that there will be considerable debate in the future on single vs. multiple rates, the extent of zero rating, and the levels of concessional (or higher) rates of tax. Indeed, there is no reason to expect a fixed and stable answer to this question, given that rates can be varied relatively easily.

8.7 ADMINISTRATION

The customs authorities are almost invariably involved in collecting VAT on imported goods. With respect to VAT on domestic transactions, in the vast majority of countries it is administered by the same department involved in administering income tax, in a few countries it is administered by the customs department, and in several countries by a separate VAT department.[55] This will make a procedural difference for taxpayers and may influence the extent to which VAT audits, for example, are coordinated with income tax audits.

8.8 SPECIAL ISSUES

8.8.1 FINANCIAL SERVICES AND INSURANCE

In principle, there is no reason why financial services should not be subject to VAT. To the extent provided to final consumers, these services should be part of the tax base (being part of consumption), and to the extent provided to businesses, they should be part of the chain of VAT credits, thereby ensuring no loss of credit for the inputs to those financial services. The reason that financial services have typically not been taxed is that there is often not an explicit charge for those services and therefore the tax would be

---

[53] *See* Ebrill et al. (2001) at 68.

[54] *See id.* at 68-69.

[55] *See id.* at 65-66.

difficult to determine. Instead of charging explicitly for financial intermediation services, financial institutions do so indirectly through such means as charging higher interest rates on loans to borrowers and paying lower rates to depositors. The EU took a decision in the 6th Directive to exempt financial services, thereby precluding experimentation on the part of member countries.[56] Innovative approaches to taxing financial services and insurance have therefore been found only outside the EU (countries like South Africa, Israel, New Zealand, and Australia).

Some financial transactions should be excluded from the VAT base. When customers pay interest, the interest is not part of consumption expenditure.[57] Therefore, to the extent that the VAT is intended to encompass personal consumption only, interest payments should be taken out of account for VAT in any event, even if financial services in general are taxed. Moreover, consider a transaction such as the issuance of shares for cash to an individual. The cash payment does not represent consumption, and therefore should not be included in the VAT tax base. Such a transaction typically falls under the exemption for financial services, but it might be better to exclude it from the scope of VAT altogether. It is included by broad definitions of goods and, particularly, services, since the latter are defined as anything done for consideration which is not the transfer of goods. What about the associated brokerage services? Again, I would argue that they are not consumption. In incurring the brokerage services, the individual is acting as an investor, not a consumer. The brokerage services provide value only insofar as they enable an individual to increase the value of his or her portfolio, which can eventually be sold and used to finance consumption. When consumption occurs, it will of course be subject to VAT.

The actual treatment of brokerage services responds to this theory only in part. For example, in the U.K., services for the negotiation of a trade in securities, together with incidental investment advice, are an exempt

---

[56] The Sixth Directive does, however, provide an option for member countries to give financial institutions the option to be taxed under the VAT. This is allowed by Germany, France, and Belgium. *See* Sijbren Cnossen, *VAT Treatment of Financial Services, in* International Studies in Taxation: Law and Economics: Liber Amicorum Leif Mutén 91, 98-99 (Gustaf Lindencrona et al. eds. 1999).

[57] The point is subject to some academic debate (I may be in the minority). I have argued that interest expense is not part of consumption and should therefore in principle be deductible for income tax purposes. *See* Victor Thuronyi, *The Concept of Income*, 46 Tax L. Rev. 45, 88-90 (1990). (That does not mean that I would necessarily support allowing a deduction for personal interest under the income tax that we have today.)

financial service, but the provision of investment advice on its own would be taxable.[58]

While EU countries uniformly exempt financial services, some other countries have made a stab at taxing financial services in various ways. The approach taken in South Africa has been to charge VAT on services where there is an explicit fee charged.[59] This is of course not totally satisfactory since it creates an incentive not to charge explicit fees where possible. The approach of Israel is to charge a VAT based on the modified addition method (that is, instead of trying to figure out how much was charged for a service, one infers a fee by calculating the total of wages and profits).[60] One problem with this approach is that it does not cater for an input credit for financial services provided to businesses. New Zealand exempts financial services but has recently proposed to zero-rate such services which are provided to businesses.[61]

Insurance services (other than life insurance) are taxed in New Zealand, Australia, and South Africa; Israel taxes insurance under the same scheme as for financial services generally.[62]

Thus, we see that on this cutting-edge issue, it is countries outside the EU that are taking the lead, perhaps because they are not constrained by the unanimity requirement that applies under European law for making tax policy changes. The problematic nature of an exemption for financial services suggests, however, that changed rules can eventually be expected on this point in the EU.

8.8.2 SMALL BUSINESSES

It is typical to provide a registration threshold so that small businesses are not required to register and become VAT taxpayers.[63] An exempt small business is disadvantaged in selling to a taxable business, since its customer

---

[58] *See* 2 De Voil Indirect Tax Service 5188 (looseleaf, updated to 2002). The 6th Directive, art. 13, refers to "transactions...in shares."

[59] *See* Schenk & Oldman (2001) at 363-64.

[60] *See id.* at 337, 362-63. Argentina also taxes financial institutions under the addition method. *See* Ebrill et al. (2001) at 20.

[61] *See* Discussion Document, GST and Financial Services (Oct. 8, 2002) (available at www.taxpolicy.ird.govt.nz).

[62] *See id.* at 389, 396-403.

[63] *See* Schenk & Oldman (2001) at 119-120; Ebrill et al (2001) at 113-24; Williams, *supra* note 1, at 177-79.

cannot take an input credit for the VAT that is embedded in the price. Japan deals with this problem by allowing a deduction for the implicit tax in purchases from exempt small business.[64] An alternative (which is widely allowed) is to provide for voluntary registration of small businesses. A liberal registration policy can, however, lead to administrative problems, because individuals can abuse it by becoming registered, claiming input credits for what are essentially personal-use items, and never recording taxable sales (or substantial taxable sales). Some countries try to avoid this problem by requiring a certain turnover threshold before a taxpayer can register.[65]

While the concept of providing an exemption for small business makes sense from the point of view of tax administration, countries vary substantially in the level of the threshold. Differences in the level of the threshold can be expected on the basis of differences in income levels, but the current differences can not all be explained in this way. It can be expected that countries with thresholds that are too low or too high will review them and that eventually the country differences will diminish as experience with tax administration is gained and shared.

For those small businesses that are VAT taxpayers, simplified regimes often apply, for example allowing the use of cash accounting or the use of a tax period that is longer than for larger taxpayers.

8.8.3 AGRICULTURE

As a matter of theory, there is no need for special provisions concerning agriculture, and a number of countries have none, but political and practical considerations have led many countries to adopt favorable treatment of agriculture in one way or another. The EU provides special simplified schemes for agriculture.[66] Outside the EU, exemption for agriculture, or for smaller producers, is widespread.[67] Exemption for agricultural producers has also often led to exemptions for agricultural inputs (since exemption means that the producer bears the burden of tax on inputs).

---

[64] *See* Schenk & Oldman (2001) at 75-76.

[65] *E.g.,* Bulgaria, Value Added Tax Act, State Gazette No. 153, Dec. 23, 1998, art. 110.

[66] *See* Sixth VAT Directive, *supra* note 15, art. 25.

[67] *See* Ebrill et al. (2001) at 65.

8.8.4 CASH VS. ACCRUAL METHOD

Unlike the income tax, where accrual accounting has become the norm, at least for large companies, it is not obvious whether it is better for VAT to be accounted for on a cash or accrual basis. This is more a question of administrative practicality. While most countries use the accrual method, the cash method is also used. Japan has some liberal rules for dealing with installment sales.[68]

8.8.5 DENIAL OF INPUT CREDIT FOR NONBUSINESS USES

The VAT raises the same issues as income tax in terms of allowance of an input credit for items that can be considered personal consumption (e.g., food, entertainment, vehicles).[69] Denial of a credit effectively taxes these as consumption items. This can be expected to be a constant source of tax policy debate and contention between taxpayers and tax authorities.

8.8.6 REFUNDS

In principle, VAT refunds are simple. It is very easy for a particular taxpayer's VAT to be a negative amount, for example where a large capital equipment is purchased and subsequent sales have not as yet materialized. Indeed, in the case of exporters, VAT can be a negative amount on a permanent basis. The logic of VAT calls for refunds to be paid promptly, subject only to proper verification of the legitimacy of the claim for refund. In practice, in many countries with weak tax administrations and poor budgetary practices, refunds are very difficult to effect in a timely manner, if at all. Some governments are so strapped for cash that they simply do not have the money to pay refunds. It is tempting for governments to see VAT refunds as a drain on resources and to find ways to avoid paying them. For governments in such a weak position, the lack of timely refunds is the Achilles heel of the VAT. Where refunds are not paid, the VAT becomes a kind of turnover tax, and loses its economic structure.

A closely related question is input credits for capital goods. Some countries have limited these input credits, or have required them to be amortized. Whether from an inability to pay refunds or otherwise, denial of such credits makes no sense as part of the logic of the VAT.

---

[68] *See* Schenk & Oldman (2001) at 158.

[69] *See id.* at 196-203.

Neither of the above is a problem in Europe, or in countries with sound fiscal systems. Unfortunately, in a number of developing and transition countries, VAT refunds are a problem. The remedy lies not so much in the VAT itself as in an overall improvement of budgeting systems.

8.8.7 INTERJURISDICTIONAL ISSUES

In federal states (and in the EU) one of the key policy issues will be how to coordinate the VAT with respect to transactions that cross jurisdictional boundaries. Some innovative ideas have been developed in this respect that go beyond the traditional origin-destination dichotomy and one can expect this to be a fertile area for development in the coming few years.[70]

---

[70] *See* Ebrill et al. (2001) at 176-96; Richard Bird & Pierre-Pascal Gendron, *VATs in Federal Countries: International Experience and Emerging Possibilities*, 55 B.I.F.D. 293 (July 2001).

Chapter 9

OTHER TAXES

9.1 EXCISES

Excises are imposed on targeted commodities, the standard ones being alcoholic beverages, tobacco products, petroleum products, and automobiles.[1] These all are characterized by fairly inelastic demand and the element of "sin" or externality in consumption. The main policy issue concerns rates: how high should they be, and should they be structured as specific rates (a given amount per unit) or *ad valorem* rates (percentage of the price). Both economic logic and administrability favor specific rates, except perhaps for cars. High inflation means that specific rates are eroded, but this can be corrected for by adjusting them periodically. In practice, both types of rates are used, sometimes in combination.

Many countries impose excises on products going beyond the standard list. In the U.S. Internal Revenue Code, virtually any miscellaneous tax —including, for example, taxes on certain prohibited transactions by private foundations—is called an excise. The trend in most countries seems to be to reduce the number of miscellaneous excises.[2]

The standard products are subject to high excises in virtually all countries. In the case of hard liquor, the tax typically exceeds the cost of the product itself. This makes tax administrative controls important. The tax is typically administered according to procedures analogous to those for customs. For example, the production premises for alcoholic beverages are like a customs warehouse. When product leaves the warehouse, that is a taxable event, unless the product is transferred into another bonded warehouse. Similarly, import of goods is a taxable event, unless one of the special customs regimes (transit goods, transfer to a bonded warehouse, etc.) applies.

---

[1] *See generally* Ben Terra, *Excises, in* TLDD at 246; Cnossen (1977).

[2] *See* Ken Messere, *Tax Policy in Europe: A Comparative Survey,* 40 Eur. Tax'n 526, 535 (2000).

While using customs-type procedures assures the strictest control, not all countries administer all excises in this way. In the U.S., some excises are imposed at the manufacturer's level, while others are imposed on the retailer (gasoline is typically taxed at the pump—this accommodates a state or local tax that can be added to the federal tax).

Smuggling is always a problem with excises, particularly where the tax is high as a percentage of the price and where the level of tax differs substantially in neighboring jurisdictions. One remedy would be to impose excise on an origin basis, with a clearing house mechanism to redistribute the tax burden on a destination basis. This has not been tried (yet). It might be particularly suitable for tobacco.

9.2 WEALTH TAXES

9.2.1 NET WEALTH TAXES

Net wealth tax can be distinguished from property taxes in that property taxes are imposed on the gross amount of property, without reduction for debts, and usually are imposed only on certain kinds of property, while net wealth tax is a more or less comprehensive tax on net worth, i.e. the value of property reduced by debt. Net wealth taxation may seem like a good mechanism to address inequality of wealth holding, but in practice few countries have imposed this tax, most of these being in Europe. Not too long ago, the tax was repealed in Germany, in response to a decision of the Constitutional Court holding the tax unconstitutional because of its uneven application to different types of property.[3] This leaves the net wealth tax in place in only a handful of countries, mostly in Europe.[4] Only Switzerland receives substantial revenue from this tax.

As shown by the German example, the main problem with net wealth tax is evenness of application. Evenhandedness is difficult to achieve because of the difficulty of valuing property such as real estate and small businesses.[5]

---

[3] *See supra* 4.3.7.2.

[4] In Europe: Finland, France, Liechtenstein, Luxembourg, Norway, Spain, Sweden, Switzerland, and outside Europe: Bangladesh, Ghana, India, Nepal, Pakistan, and Suriname. Netherlands abolished its net wealth tax upon introduction of the new income tax scheme taxing imputed income. *See supra* p. 256.

[5] Experience with the net wealth tax in Europe is reviewed in Moris Lehner, *The European Experience With a Wealth Tax: A Comparative Discussion*, 53 Tax L. Rev. 615 (2000).

9.2.2 DEATH DUTIES AND GIFT TAX

Like net wealth tax, estate and gift taxes are imposed on a net value, namely the net amount transferred (in the case of gifts) or the net value of the estate. Death duties can take the form of an estate tax or an inheritance tax.[6] The former taxes the estate as a whole, while the latter taxes the share received by each beneficiary, at rates which typically differ depending on the relation between the beneficiary and the decedent. In practice, the distinction between the two is blurred. Estate tax typically has an exemption for transfers to a spouse and often has reduced rates for transfers to children or orphans. It is a difficult tax to administer, for valuation and other reasons.

Although this tax arguably plays an important role in assuring the equity of the tax system, a number of countries have repealed the tax, including, recently, the United States.[7] Estate and gift taxes still apply in a number of countries, however.

9.3 PROPERTY TAXES

Many countries impose taxes on land and buildings.[8] The tax is particularly suited to imposition by local governments, given that the revenue base cannot move out of the local jurisdiction. A tax on rural land sometimes serves the function of taxing imputed income from agriculture, which may be lightly taxed or exempted from income tax and VAT.[9] Particularly where the

---

[6] Inheritance tax applies, for example, in Belgium. *See* Introduction to Belgian Law 361-63 (Hubert Bocken & Walter de Bondt eds., 2001). Inheritance tax is apparently more common than estate tax. *See* Messere, *supra* note 2, at 533. The U.S. has an estate tax (although it seems to be in the process of being repealed), as does the U.K. (although it is called inheritance tax).

[7] Because of budgetary gimmicks, the tax is slated to disappear but then again reappear. Its fate presumably will be decided by the political composition of the Congress and by who holds the presidency.

[8] For a survey emphasizing historical, economic and political factors, see Land-Value Taxation Around the World (Robert Andelson ed. 3d ed. 2000) [hereinafter cited as Andelson].

[9] For example, Argentina has a tax on rural land, albeit at a low level. *See* Andelson *supra* note 8, at 62. *See generally* Jonathan Skinner, *Prospects for Agricultural Land Taxation in Developing Countries, in* Tax Policy in Developing Countries 139 (Javad Khalilzadeh-Shirazi and Anwar Shah eds., 1991).

tax rates are relatively low, the tax base for rural land may not be its assessed value, but rather derived from the area of the parcel, its location, and the quality of the land as set forth in a table. Often the classification of land according to its quality does not make fine distinctions; many developing and transition countries do not have the administrative resources needed for a more sophisticated tax scheme. In most countries, it is typical to tax both buildings and the land, particularly in the case of urban land.[10] In OECD countries, the tax may be imposed at much more substantial rates than in developing and transition countries, and valuation may in principle be based on fair market value of each parcel. However, valuation is the Achilles heel of this tax, often getting out of date with consequent problems of inequity.[11]

An attempt has been made in a number of Latin American countries to tax increases in land value benefiting from public works, but with little success except in Colombia.[12]

The total revenues from property tax are typically quite low in developing and transition countries, compared with the potential.[13] There is, however, presumably a limit on how high rates can be set in the absence of market-based valuation, without running into problems of unfairness. In Africa, the bulk of property taxation falls on urban rather than agricultural land, in part because of the framework of rural land tenure, which may not involve registration of title in individual names.[14] Some countries have imposed progressive rates depending on the size or value of the parcel.[15] Because of the avoidance opportunities that this leads to, the results of progressive taxation have often been problematic, especially for rural land where sham subdivision of parcels to avoid the tax is difficult to police.[16]

---

[10] *E.g.,* Canada, Chile. *See id. passim.* In Chile, improvements on agricultural land are exempt for up to 10 years. *See id.* at 90. In Jamaica, tax is imposed only on land, not improvements. *See id.* at 118-19. *See* Joan Youngman & Jane Malme, An International Survey of Taxes on Land and Buildings 48-49 (1994).

[11] *E.g.,* Andelson, *supra* note 8, at 67-68 (Canada); at 88 (Chile).

[12] *See id.* at 97-108.

[13] *E.g.,* about 1 percent of revenues for Jamaica. *See id.* at 118.

[14] *See id.* at 274.

[15] *E.g.,* Jamaica, where rates vary from 1 per mil to 30 per mil depending on the assessed value of the parcel. *See id.* at 117-18.

[16] *See* Richard Bird, Taxing Agricultural Land in Developing Countries 211, 218-22 1974).

9.4 SOCIAL SECURITY TAXES

Social security taxation is widespread.[17] The revenues are often enormous; for many individuals, social security tax liability exceeds income tax liability. Generally, social security contributions are not called taxes. They are a tax in the U.S. In France, the "generalized social contribution", which is a tax, is also designated to social security funds, in addition to social security contributions themselves.[18] Social security rates are very high in a number of transition countries, causing serious compliance problems in light of weak administrative capacity. Apart from the rates and overall pension and social insurance policy, the most important issues from a tax structural point of view are the integration of social security tax with the income tax withheld on wages. There is a fair amount of country difference on this point.[19] The U.S. is probably on one extreme, with virtually complete integration. The social security tax is a tax and is collected as part of the income tax system. It is either withheld at source or, for income from self-employment, is self-assessed on the individual's income tax return. The base for withholding is virtually the same as for withholding of income tax. By contrast, in a number of countries social security contributions are not considered a tax, are collected by a different agency (i.e. not the tax authorities), and the base differs from the individual income tax base in substantial ways. I would like to be able to report that there is a strong trend toward greater integration; I think there is such a trend but it is slow.

9.5 STAMP AND FINANCIAL TRANSACTIONS TAXES

The stamp tax is so-called because it was originally imposed by affixing stamps to documents. It is typically imposed on transactions requiring notarization. It is called stamp duty in the U.K. and typically in those Commonwealth countries that still have it, but it goes by many other

---

[17] *See generally* The International Guide to Social Security (Henk Bedee et al. eds. 1995) (survey of 29 countries); David Williams, *Social Security Taxation, in* TLDD at 340.

[18] *See* Loïc Philip, *Contribution Sociale Generalisée (CSG), in* Dictionnaire Encyclopédique de Finances Publiques 473 (Loïc Philip ed. 1991); Cons. const., Dec. 28, 1990, Dec. No. 285 DC.

[19] In the U.K., a substantial amount of integration was achieved in 1999. *See* Morse & Williams (2000) at 124-25.

names in different countries.[20] Stamp duty applies in many countries to the issuance of securities; transfers of securities and other financial instruments may also be reached by a separate tax. More broadly, taxes on financial transactions might also reach foreign currency conversions or banking transactions. All of these taxes have in common the (usually flat rate) imposition of a tax on a contract or transaction.[21]

One of the most common targets is the transfer of immovable property; the rate in some countries is quite high.[22] In the U.S., this tax is imposed by local governments (typically at the county level) and is called the real property transfer tax. It applies to the transfer of any long-term interest in immovable property, including a long-term leasehold. It may also apply to a mortgage.

Because a flat-rate, low level tax on immovable property transfers is easier to collect than a tax on capital gains, the stamp duty may be a complete or partial substitute for other taxes that may apply to immovable property transfers, such as income tax or VAT.

Stamp duty in the U.K. is an old tax, having first been imposed in 1694, and being currently imposed under fairly old statutes, the Stamp Duties Management Act 1891 and the Stamp Act 1891.[23] The application of stamp duty has been narrowed, and it currently applies mostly to conveyances of real estate and transfers of securities, although it can also apply to transfers of

---

[20] *See* Beltrame & Mehl (1997) at 294-96; Trotabas & Cotteret (1997) at 223-29. In France, there is a distinction between stamp duty and duties on real estate transactions and other notarial acts. *See* Pierre Beltrame, *Timbre (Droit de), in* Dictionnaire Encyclopédique de finances publiques 1506 (Loïc Philip ed. 1991); Pierre Beltrame, *Enregistrement (Droits d'-), in id.* at 734. For Italy, see Roberto Pignatone, *L'Imposta di Registro, in* 4 Amatucci (1994) at 159. For Belgium, see Tiberghien (1995) at 483-543, 601-24 (droits d'enregistrement, d'hypothèque, de greffe, et de timbre).

[21] *See* Parthasarathi Shome & Janet Stotsky, *Financial Transactions Taxes,* 12 Tax Notes Int'l 47 (1996).

[22] The Belgian rate of 12.5% was lower to 10% in 2002 for the Flemish region. *See* Brent Springael, *Belgium,* 28 Tax Notes Int'l 1261 (Dec. 30, 2002); Introduction to Belgian Law 363 (Hubert Bocken & Walter de Bondt eds., 2001). In France, the rate was lowered from 8% to 4%, which is still quite high. *See* Messere, *supra* note 2, at 535. In Germany, the rate is 3.5 percent *(Grunderwerbsteuer). See* Tipke/Lang (2000) at 672. The rate in Spain falls mainly on the plain (mainly 6 or 7% depending on the region). *See* Soler Roch (2002) at 171.

[23] *See* Michael Quinlan, Sergeant and Sims on Stamp Duties and Stamp Duty Reserve Tax 5 (11th ed. 1995).

other property, including intangible property (generally, the tax will not apply if the value is less than £60,000).[24] Stamp Duty Reserve Tax is a back-up to stamp duty and applies only to securities. "Stamp duty is chargeable on instruments and not on transactions."[25] As a result it is a highly technical tax. Nevertheless, form is not everything. The label placed on an instrument does not determine the liability to tax; generally, the true legal effect of the instrument as a matter of private law will be determinative.[26] As its name implies, stamp duty was once paid by affixing stamps to an instrument at the time of its execution. This method is largely obsolete, and nowadays the Stamp Office uses impressed stamps.[27] Strangely, there is no legal obligation to stamp an instrument, but there are penalties for late stamping, and an instrument that is not stamped may not be relied upon.[28] The jurisdiction of the tax extends to instruments executed in the United Kingdom or to property situated, or matters to be done, therein.[29]

In many jurisdictions, the equivalent of stamp duty seems less mysterious than its U.K. incarnation because the only object of the tax is transfers of real estate. This is true for many States of the United States, for example. Typically the tax is paid on recording of the deed, so it is part of the real property transfer system. It is therefore fairly easy to collect and does not involve many disputes.

In the former Soviet Union, the stamp tax is called "state duty". It applies to a miscellany of transactions, most requiring notarialization, such as contracts and property transfers, but also applies to court filing fees and passport services.

Stamp taxes are also typically applied to the issuance and transfer of securities, as well as to corporate formation and other reorganizations.[30]

---

[24] *See id.* at 39-40.

[25] *Id.* at 21.

[26] *Id.* at 23. It is in this sense that the statement "regard should be had to the substance of the transaction rather than to its form," *id., citing Great Western Rly Co. v. IRC,* [1894] 1 QB 507, at 513, should be understood.

[27] *See* Quinlan, *supra* note 22,. at 31-32, 34.

[28] *See id.* at 8-9.

[29] *Id.* at 11.

[30] *See* Van Hoorn (1972) at 5-6. For a description of the tax in Spain, which falls on the transfer of both real and personal property, corporate reorganizations, and notarial documents, and is coordinated with the VAT (so that transactions subject to VAT are excluded from stamp duty), see Solar Roch (2002) at 166-75.

Security transfer taxes apply in a number of jurisdictions, typically at low rates (they have, for example, been imposed in Sweden, Switzerland, and the U.K.).

Some countries have imposed tax on foreign currency conversions.

The application of stamp taxes to contracts was fairly common as a historical matter, but few countries impose such a tax today. In Austria, stamp duty applies to transactions such as loan agreements, lease contracts, and guarantees.[31]

Taxes on banking transactions have over the past few years proved a popular revenue source in several Latin American countries, probably because they are easy to collect and quickly generate revenue for governments in fiscal crisis.[32] Some states of Australia also impose the tax, given that they have few revenue options.

9.6 CUSTOMS DUTIES

Customs duties used to be an important revenue source in nearly all countries[33] but their significance in OECD countries has vastly diminished. They are still a key revenue source in a number of developing countries. Customs duties remain important for trade regulation, however. And customs procedure is still of great tax importance in virtually all countries, since both VAT and excise are collected at the border by the customs authorities, for the most part under customs valuation rules and procedures.[34] In the U.S., which does not have a VAT and which has lowered its customs barriers, this tax significance does not exist. However, more broadly, customs duties themselves satisfy even narrow definitions of "tax", since they are a compulsory payment to the government that does not constitute consideration for a service. It is therefore curious that tax scholars tend not to consider customs as part of their field and leave it to trade lawyers. Customs codes and tariffs also are typically contained in separate legislation from taxes. Customs duties (as well as VAT and excises on import) tend to be collected by an

---

[31] *See* Friedrich Rödler, *Austria Considers Limiting Scope of Stamp Duty*, Tax Notes Int'l 2489 (June 5, 2000).

[32] *See* Isais Coelho, Liam Ebrill, & Victoria Summers, *Bank Debit Taxes in Latin America: An Analysis of Recent Trends*, IMF Working Paper 01/67 (May 2001).

[33] *See, e.g.,* 1 Bittker & Lokken (1999) at ¶ 1.1.2; Hogg et al. (2002) at 18-19.

[34] For a discussion of the relevance of customs valuation and procedure to VAT in the EU see Lyons (2001) at 35-37.

agency different from that responsible for inland revenue (although this is not uniformly the case and a number of countries have found that it makes sense to consolidate tax and customs under one roof, particularly given the importance of VAT).

While much of customs law is similar to tax law, parts of it do verge off into areas such as trade law and criminal law (relating to such matters as drugs and other controlled material that is prohibited from being imported). Customs officials do have a number of tasks unrelated to collecting tax or duty (such as agricultural inspection, health inspection, and import control).

The part of customs law that is concerned with tax is remarkable from the point of view of comparative law because it is the most highly harmonized part of tax law. In the EU, customs law is even more highly harmonized than VAT, because it is governed by a regulation, the Community Customs Code (CCC),[35] rather than, as in the case of VAT, directives. While directives must be implemented through national laws, regulations are effective on their own, requiring no implementing legislation by member countries. The CCC does have quite an extensive implementing regulation, but it is issued by the European Commission.[36]   The community customs duty is collected by national authorities, and there are national laws that supplement the CCC on matters such as procedure, appeals, and criminal penalties.[37]

There are a number of other customs unions throughout the world besides the EU (in Latin America, southern Africa, west Africa, former Soviet Union, and Carribean).[38]

Outside the EU, there has been substantial harmonization of customs law through a number of international agreements over the years, and two international organizations, the WTO and the World Customs Organization, are in place to help manage the system.   The classification of goods worldwide is based on the Harmonized Description and Coding System, which is used by over 176 countries.[39] The Harmonized System assigns a six-

---

[35] Council Regulation (EEC) 2913/92 [1992] OJ L302/1, as amended.   For a discussion of its content see Lyons (2001) at 84-95.

[36] *See id.* at 97-100.

[37] *See id.* at 102-06, 448, 453. In implementing the appeal requirements under the CCC, the UK renamed its Value Added Tax Tribunal as the Value Added Tax and Duties Tribunal. The harmonization of appeal procedures has proved difficult, since harmonized requirements under the CCC would have threatened the unity of some countries' harmonized appeal systems for taxes and customs duties.

[38] *See id.* at 2-4.

[39] *See id.* at 113-15.

digit numerical code to all tangible goods. It is a remarkable feat of taxonomy. Countries using the system can reflect further distinctions made by their law by using additional digits (for example the EU uses 10 digits to implement the TARIC (*tariff intégré de la Communauté*)). Customs valuation rules (which are also relevant for the VAT) have been harmonized within the framework of the GATT. These are based on the transaction value or, in certain cases, the market value of identical or similar goods.[40] Without getting into the details, much of the rules on customs procedure, as well as those on determining the origin of goods, have also been harmonized by international agreement.[41]

The success of international agreements harmonizing customs law furnishes a marked contrast to tax law. Even though customs is arguably tax, it seems to have been considered to be part of trade, and hence seems to have been successfully included in trade agreements. Perhaps countries have not seen customs harmonization as threatening to fiscal sovereignty, given the relatively small fiscal importance of customs duties. And of course customs harmonization has had behind it a general pressure to reduce barriers to trade, including barriers of a procedural nature, which have enjoyed a wide acceptance internationally. The harmonization of customs law began before the wide acceptance of VAT. It has had the perhaps unintended consequence of harmonizing *de facto* most of the VAT rules dealing with imports and exports. This has been beneficial for development of the VAT.

9.7 TAXES ON MINERAL EXTRACTION

Countries with oil and gas and other mineral deposits often derive substantial revenues from this sector. The taxes can take various forms.[42] Some revenues are of course earned by the normal income tax, but often there are special surtaxes for the oil and gas sector. There may also be royalties (which may or may not take the form of taxes), excess profits taxes, and others. Where the mineral resources are publicly owned, the line between nontax royalties (including signing bonuses and other fees) and taxes is rather

---

[40] *See id.* at 242-70. Where parties are related, the customs rules are similar but not identical to transfer pricing rules used for income tax purposes.

[41] *See id.* at 6-11, 194-202, 275.

[42] See for a discussion of policy alternatives David Nellor & Emil Sunley, Fiscal Regimes for Natural Resource Producing Developing Countries (IMF PPAA/94/24) 1994). *See generally* Van Meurs & Assocs., Ltd., World Fiscal Systems for Oil (2d ed. 1997).

indistinct. It is the combination of the two that determines the division of revenues between the state and the mining company.

9.8 MISCELLANEOUS TAXES

While a small group of taxes typically represents the lion's share of revenue, most countries have numerous other miscellaneous taxes, of greater or lesser revenue significance. These are so varied that a complete catalogue would be an exercise in and of itself. Even though such an exercise would have significant amusement value, it is not attempted here. Just to mention a few:

Turnover taxes are common in a number of countries, and can raise substantial revenue even at a low rate. Although these taxes do not make a lot of sense where there is a VAT, turnover is a tempting revenue target.

Motor vehicles are typically required to be registered, and a fee is typically charged. Whether this is a tax could be debated. In developing and transition countries, the licensing and other taxes on motor vehicles (there could also be an excise on importation or sale) can furnish significant revenue as well as an important element of progressivity for the tax system, given that the distribution of motor vehicle ownership can be highly unequal. The tax is also fairly easy to administer and makes sense from that point of view.

Some countries have a (usually local) tax on dogs, which is said to be justified by externalities.

Export taxes are still imposed by some (usually developing) countries, typically on a narrow range of primary products.[43]

Taxes of narrow scope are imposed on a number of products or services, including sugar, matches, electricity, tea, coffee, ice-cream, gambling of various kinds, CDs, television advertisements, plastic bags and bottles, and televisions, sometimes for environmental or other regulatory reasons.[44] Taxes on a very narrow base are sometimes used in place of penalties, where it is desired to discourage certain activities.

---

[43] *See* Bird, *supra* note 16, at 299-301. While still significant in some developing countries, their role has diminished. *See* Tax Policy Handbook 212 (P. Shome ed. 1995).

[44] *See* European Commission, Inventory of Taxes Levied in the Member States of the European Union (17th ed. 2000).

Appendix 1

RESEARCH TOOLS FOR COMPARATIVE TAX LAW

In contrast to the large volume of literature which can easily be found on domestic taxation in many countries, sources for researching comparative tax law are scarcer and harder to find (particularly those available in English). Having said that, there is still a considerable amount of material available, although an in-depth study involving non-English-speaking countries will almost invariably require a reading knowledge of the local language. For a discussion of materials in German, see Tipke (1993) at 66-76.

Hugh Ault et al., *Comparative Income Taxation: A Structural Analysis* (Kluwer Law International 1997) is an excellent introduction and overview on comparative income tax law, covering the U.S., U.K., Canada, Australia, Germany, Sweden, Japan, Netherlands, and France. Of particular interest, as the subtitle suggests, is the analysis of basic structural differences for the countries covered. Because it is authoritative and conveniently written in English, I cite this book frequently for a more in-depth discussion of some topics that I deal with only summarily (and its existence allowed me to deal fairly lightly in this book with the income tax). *Comparative Income Taxation* differs, however, from this book in several respects. First, it is confined to the income tax, while I cover other taxes as well as more general issues such as constitutionality, interpretation of tax laws, anti-avoidance, and different aspects of the legal context for tax law. These topics are touched on in the Ault book only lightly, mostly in the introductory section containing country descriptions. Second, this book is shorter than the Ault book as I try to focus on key differences between countries. Finally, the coverage here is in principle global. *Comparative Income Taxation* is a good complement to this book, since it offers (1) an overview for nine key countries, and (2) much more detailed discussion of the income tax than is found here. My expectation is therefore that many readers will want to use the books together, and I have written this one accordingly.

Tax Law Design and Drafting (V. Thuronyi ed., Kluwer 2000) (also published in paperback in two volumes by the IMF and available for purchase at the IMF website: www.imf.org), like this book, covers most of the broad aspects of tax law, not just income tax. It includes analysis of different systems, although the focus is on principles in designing and drafting tax laws of particular relevance to developing and transition countries. At the end of volume 2, there are two bibliographies. One is a basic (i.e. limited) bibliography of books useful in studying comparative tax law (it does not, however, generally include Kluwer and IBFD publications, for which see below). In putting the list together, I emphasized books in English to the extent possible. The second bibliography is a list of national tax laws of IMF member countries. While this list will get out of date, it includes publishers and so should give you an idea of where to look to find the current laws. The introduction to this bibliography discusses additional sources and provides help in how to find tax laws of a given country (pp. 1026-1031). *TLDD* has a different orientation than this book. Its basic purpose is to serve as a reference source for those thinking about tax policy in developing and transition countries, with specific emphasis on the detailed design and drafting of the law. In doing so, it necessarily looks at taxation from a comparative perspective, but it does not set out—as this book does—to treat comparative tax law systematically. Despite its orientation to developing and transition countries TLDD has also been used as part of teaching materials in courses on comparative tax law.

I consider both *Comparative Income Taxation* and *TLDD* to be complementary to this book. I hope that, for students, this book will enable them to read these books, as well as other materials, with greater understanding. As for practitioners who are pressed for time, my hope is that this book serves as a relatively brief introduction which presents the essentials.

Tax Laws of the World is the most comprehensive collection of tax laws in English. The translation is not the best and it is generally somewhat out of date, but it is nevertheless useful for the student who does not necessarily need the most current amendments. Use it with caution, however.

The International Fiscal Association publishes annually 2 volumes of the *Cahiers de droit fiscal international* (don't worry, even through the title is in French, most of the text is in English). Each volume covers in a reasonable degree of depth a particular topic on comparative tax law, usually connected with international taxation. There are country reports for a broad range of countries and a general report ties the country reports together. I have argued that, like most things, the methodology could be improved.[1] If you are researching a topic that happens to have been covered in one of the Cahiers, you are in luck (a cumulative list of topics covered appears in each volume).

Tax Notes International is a weekly publication with news on international tax law and on developments in particular countries. There is

---

[1] See Thuronyi, *Studying Comparative Tax Law in International Studies, in* Taxation: Law and Economics: Liber Amicorum Leif Muten 333 (Kluwer 1999).

now a CD containing back issues which can be searched. There is also an index and the publication is available electronically through Lexis, Westlaw, and Taxbase (Tax Notes' own website). Because the focus is on current developments, not everything is covered in a systematic way; however, there is a lot of useful information and the topic you are researching may well have something written about it. The coverage includes also non-OECD countries.

Several other periodicals regularly include articles on comparative tax:

> *Bulletin for International Fiscal Documentation*
> *Tax Planning International Review*
> *Tax Management International Journal*
> *EC Tax Review*
> *Tax Management International Forum.*

Other periodical articles can be found by consulting one of the available indices, several of which are available electronically: Index to Legal Periodicals, Legal Resource Index, Legal Journals Index, and Index to Foreign Legal Periodicals.

The *Tax Management* foreign income portfolio series (published by the Bureau of National Affairs) has portfolios covering a couple of dozen countries (entitled "Business Operations in [country]"). They cover both tax and business law.

The *International Bureau for Fiscal Documentation* is perhaps the most prolific publisher on comparative taxation. A good deal of this is descriptive rather than analytical, but it does provide an extensive source of information in English about most countries, usually reasonably up to date. They also publish the main Latin American tax laws on a CD, although only in the original language. See their website to search for their publications: www.ibfd.nl. This website also provides access to an online catalogue of books in the IBFD library.

Kluwer Law International publishes numerous quality studies in international and comparative tax law. You can find their publications from their website: www.kluwerlaw.com. Updates to this book will be posted there.

The *Harvard World Tax Series* covers a number of countries and is notable for its depth of analysis and the fact that it is accessible, being written in English. Even though it is seriously out of date, it can still be consulted today, although it is necessary to update the information from more current sources.

An increasing amount of material is becoming available on the web, including the full text of some tax laws. However, we seem to be far from the point where most countries' tax laws are available in this manner. Some links will be included in the updates to this book (see Preface).

General guides for international research include:[2]

ACCIDENTAL TOURIST ON THE NEW FRONTIER: AN INTRODUCTORY GUIDE TO GLOBAL LEGAL RESEARCH (Littleton, Colo.: F.B. Rothman, 1998) (includes some specific information on tax research)

GERMAIN'S TRANSNATIONAL LAW RESEARCH: A GUIDE FOR ATTORNEYS (Ardsley-on-Hudson, N.Y.: Transnational Juris Publications, Inc., 1991-). See the chapter on taxation, pg. IV-318. Contains references to sources for international taxation as well as some information on foreign tax systems. The last update was 6/99, but it is still useful for basic sources.

FOREIGN LAW: CURRENT SOURCES OF CODES AND BASIC LEGISLATION IN JURISDICTIONS OF THE WORLD (Littleton, CO: F.B. Rothman, 1989-). The electronic version of this resource is called FOREIGN LAW GUIDE, available by subscription on the web.

General foreign and comparative research guides available on the web include:

Researching Foreign and Comparative Law, Georgetown University Law Library
http://www.ll.georgetown.edu/intl/guides/foreign/

Foreign Legal Research, University of Michigan Law Library
http://cgi.www.law.umich.edu/library/refres/foreign/foreign.htm

Transnational Legal Research, University of Michigan Law Library
http://cgi.www.law.umich.edu/library/refres/transnatl/transnatl.htm

Foreign and Comparative Law Research Guide, Duke Law Library
http://www.law.duke.edu/lib/ResearchGuides/foreign/foreignframe.html

A Selective List of Guides to Foreign Legal Research, Columbia Law Library
http://library.law.columbia.edu/foreignguide.html

TAX TREATIES DATABASE (CD-ROM) (IBFD). Contains the full text of more than 2,200 treaties for the avoidance of double taxation

---

[2] I am indebted to Marci Hoffman of Georgetown University Law Library for this information.

together with over 2,000 protocols, supplementary agreements and exchanges of notes. www.ibfd.org

TAX TREATIES ONLINE (Oceana Online) (subscription web database). Contains more than 1,800 international tax treaties for 185 countries. http://www.oceanalaw.com/default.asp

WORLDWIDE TAX TREATIES (CD-ROM) (Arlington, VA : Tax Analysts). Also available on the web. Contains more than 4,400 tax treaties, amending protocols, and similar documents. www.tax.org

Appendix 2

GENERAL ANTI-AVOIDANCE RULES

Australia. Income Tax Assessment Act 1936. [excerpts]

Section 177A

"...'scheme' means:
(a) any agreement, arrangement, understanding, promise or undertaking, whether express or implied and whether or not enforceable, or intended to be enforceable, by legal proceedings; and
(b) any scheme, plan, proposal, action, course of action or course of conduct;..."

Section 177A(5) "A reference in this Part to a scheme or a part of a scheme being entered into or carried out by a person for a particular purpose shall be read as including a reference to the scheme or the part of the scheme being entered into or carried out by the person for 2 or more purposes of which that particular purpose is the dominant purpose."

Section 177D.

"This Part applies to any scheme...where...
(a) a taxpayer (in this section referred to as the "relevant taxpayer") has obtained...a tax benefit in connection with the scheme; and
(b) having regard to—

(i)   the manner in which the scheme was entered into or carried out;

(ii)   the form and substance of the scheme;

(iii)   the time at which the scheme was entered into and the length of the period during which the scheme was carried out;

(iv)   the result in relation to the operation of this Act that, but for this Part, would be achieved by the scheme;

(v)   any change in the financial position of the relevant taxpayer that has resulted, will result, or may reasonably be expected to result, from the scheme;

(vi) any change in financial position of any person who has, or has had, any connection (whether of a business, family or other nature) with the relevant taxpayer, being a change that has resulted, will result or may reasonably be expected to result, from the scheme;

(vii) any other consequence for the relevant taxpayer, or for any person referred to in subparagraph (vi), of the scheme having been entered into or carried out; and

(viii) the nature of any connection (whether of a business, family or other nature) between the relevant taxpayer and any person referred to in subparagraph (vi),

it would be concluded that the person, or one of the persons, who entered into or carried out the scheme or any part of the scheme did so for the purpose of enabling the relevant taxpayer to obtain a tax benefit in connection with the scheme or of enabling the relevant taxpayer and another taxpayer or other taxpayers each to obtain a tax benefit in connection with the scheme (whether or not that person who entered into or carried out the scheme or any part of the scheme is the relevant taxpayer or is the other taxpayer or one of the other taxpayers)."

Section 177F

"(1) Where a tax benefit has been obtained, or would but for this section be obtained, by a taxpayer in connection with a scheme to which this Part applies, the Commissioner may –

(a) in the case of a tax benefit that is referable to an amount not being included in the assessable income of the taxpayer of a year of income—determine that the whole or a part of that amount shall be included in the assessable income of the taxpayer of that year of income; or

(b) in the case of a tax benefit that is referable to a deduction or a part of a deduction being allowable to the taxpayer in relation to a year of income—determine that the whole or a part of the deduction or of the part of the deduction, as the case may be, shall not be allowable to the taxpayer in relation to that year of income;

and, where the Commissioner makes such a determination, he shall take such action as he considers necessary to give effect to that determination.

...

(3) Where the Commissioner has made a determination...in respect of a taxpayer in relation to a scheme to which this Part applies, the Commissioner may, in relation to any taxpayer (in this subsection referred to as the 'relevant taxpayer')—

(a) if, in the opinion of the Commissioner—

(i) there has been included, or would but for this subsection be included, in the assessable income of the relevant taxpayer of a year of income an amount that would not have been included or would not be included, as the case may be, in the assessable income of the relevant taxpayer of that year of income if the scheme had not been entered into or carried out; and

(ii) it is fair and reasonable that that amount or a part of that amount should not be included in the assessable income of the relevant taxpayer of that year of income,

determine that that amount or that part of that amount, as the case may be, should not have been included or shall not be included, as the case may be, in the assessable income of the relevant taxpayer of that year of income; or

(b) if, in the opinion of the Commissioner—

(i) an amount would have been allowed or would be allowable to the relevant taxpayer as a deduction in relation to a year of income if the scheme had not been entered into or carried out, being an amount that was not allowed or would not, but for this subsection, be allowable, as the case may be, as a deduction to the relevant taxpayer in relation to that year of income; and

(ii) it is fair and reasonable that that amount or a part of that amount should be allowable as a deduction to the relevant taxpayer in relation to that year of income,

determine that that amount or that part, as the case may be, should have been allowed or shall be allowable, as the case may be, as a deduction to the relevant taxpayer in relation to that year of income;

and the Commissioner shall take such action as he considers necessary to give effect to any such determination.

..."

...

Belgium. Income Tax Code, art. 344, §1. [translation]

"The legal characterization given by the parties to an act (or to separate acts carrying out a single transaction) may not be relied on as against the administration of direct taxes where the administration proves, by means of presumptions or other methods of proof described in article 340, that this characterization has a tax avoidance purpose, unless the taxpayer proves that this characterization is due to legitimate financial or economic reasons."

Canada, Income Tax Act 1990, s 245 [excerpts]

"(1) **Definitions.** In this section,

'**tax benefit**'.— 'tax benefit' means a reduction, avoidance or deferral of tax or other amount payable under this Act or an increase in a refund of tax or other amount under this Act;

'**tax consequences**'.— 'tax consequences' to a person means the amount of income, taxable income, or taxable income earned in Canada of, tax or other amount payable by or refundable to the person under this Act, or any other amount that is relevant for the purposes of computing that amount;

'**transaction**'. — 'transaction' includes an arrangement or event.

(2) **General anti-avoidance provision.** —Where a transaction is an avoidance transaction, the tax consequences to a person shall be determined as is reasonable in the circumstances in order to deny a tax benefit that, but for this section, would result, directly or indirectly, from the transaction or from a series of transactions that includes that transaction.

(3) **Avoidance transaction.** — An avoidance transaction means any transaction

(a) that, but for this section, would result, directly or indirectly, in a tax benefit, unless the transaction may reasonably be considered to have been undertaken or arranged primarily for *bona fide* purposes other than to obtain the tax benefit; or

(b) that is part of a series of transactions, which series, but for this section, would result, directly or indirectly, in a tax benefit, unless the transaction may reasonably be considered to have been undertaken or arranged primarily for *bona fide* purposes other than to obtain the tax benefit.

(4) **Where subsec. (2) does not apply.**—For greater certainty, subsection (2) does not apply to a transaction where it may reasonably be considered that the transaction would not result directly or indirectly in a misuse of the provisions of this Act or an abuse having regard to the provisions of this Act, other than this section, read as a whole.

(5) **Determination of tax consequences.**—Without restricting the generality of subsection (2),

(a) any deduction in computing income, taxable income, taxable income earned in Canada or tax payable or any part thereof may be allowed or disallowed in whole or in part,

(b) any such deduction, any income, loss or other amount or part thereof may be allocated to any person,

(c) the nature of any payment or other amount may be recharacterized, and

(d) the tax effects that would otherwise result from the application of other provisions of this Act may be ignored,

in determining the tax consequences to a person as is reasonable in the circumstances in order to deny a tax benefit that would, but for this section, result, directly or indirectly, from an avoidance transaction.

....

(7) **Exception.—** Notwithstanding any other provision of this Act, the tax consequences to any person, following the application of this section, shall only be determined through a notice of assessment, reassessment, additional assessment or determination pursuant to subsection 152(1.11) involving the application of this section.

............"

Hong Kong, Income Tax Ordinance. [summary]

Sec. 61 allows the tax authorities to disregard "artificial or fictitious" transactions. Sec. 61A deals with transactions carried out for "the sole or dominant purpose" of obtaining a tax benefit, and allows assessment in such cases to be made by disregarding the transaction or "in such other manner as the assistant commissioner considers appropriate to counteract the tax benefit which would otherwise be obtained."

Ireland, Taxes Consolidation Act, 1997, sec. 811. [summary]

The drafting of this provision is verbose (8 pages), but it boils down to providing broad authority to the Revenue Commissioners to make appropriate adjustments if a taxpayer enters into a tax avoidance transaction, being a transaction entered into primarily to gain a tax advantage. There is an exception for a transaction "undertaken or arranged for the purpose of obtaining the benefit of any relief, allowance or other abatement", where the transaction would not result in an abuse of the relevant provision of the tax laws, "having regard to the purposes for which it was provided."

Malaysia, Income Tax Act, 1967 sec. 140. [summary]

This provision is similar to Singapore's (*see infra*) and is based on the pre-1981 Australian GAAR (ITAA sec. 260).[1]

New Zealand, Income Tax Act 1994 (as of Jan. 1, 2002) [excerpts]

Sec. BG 1 Avoidance

BG 1(1) ARRANGEMENT VOID A tax avoidance arrangement is void as against the Commissioner for income tax purposes.

BG 1(2) ENFORCEMENT The Commissioner, in accordance with Part G (Avoidance and Non-Market Transactions), may counteract a tax advantage obtained by a person from or under a tax avoidance arrangement.

Defined: Commissioner, income tax, person, tax avoidance arrangement

Sec. GB 1 Agreements Purporting to Alter Incidence of Tax to be Void

GB 1(1) Where an arrangement is void in accordance with section BG 1, the amounts of gross income, allowable deductions and available net losses included in calculating the taxable income of any person affected by that arrangement may be adjusted by the Commissioner in the manner the Commissioner thinks appropriate, so as to counteract any tax advantage obtained by that person from or under that arrangement, and, without limiting the generality of this subsection, the Commissioner may have regard to—

(a) Such amounts of gross income, allowable deductions and available net losses as, in the Commissioner's opinion, that person would have, or might be expected to have, or would in all likelihood have, had if that arrangement had not been made or entered into; or

(b) Such amounts of gross income and allowable deductions as, in the Commissioner's opinion, that person would have had if that person had been allowed the benefit of all amounts of gross income, or of such part of the gross income as the Commissioner considers proper, derived by any other person or persons as a result of that arrangement.

---

[1] *See* Arjunan Subramian, Malaysian Income Tax Manual 721 (1990).

GB 1(2)   Where any amount of gross income or allowable deduction is included in the calculation of taxable income of any person under subsection (1), then, for the purposes of this Act, that amount will not be included in the calculation of the taxable income of any other person.

GB 1(2A) .Without limiting the generality of the preceding subsections, if an arrangement is void in accordance with section BG 1 because, whether wholly or partially, the arrangement directly or indirectly relieves a person from liability to pay income tax by claiming a credit of tax, the Commissioner may, in addition to any other action taken under this section—

(a) Disallow the credit in whole or in part; and

(b) Allow in whole or in part the benefit of the credit of tax for any other taxpayer.

GB 1(2B) For the purpose of subsection (2A), the Commissioner may have regard to the credits of tax which the taxpayer or another taxpayer would have had, or might have been expected to have had, if the arrangement had not been made or entered into.

GB 1(2C) In this section, **credit of tax** means the reduction or offsetting of the amoujnt of tax a person must pay because—

(a) Credit has been allowed for a payment of any kind, whether of tax or otherwise, made by a person; or

(b) Of a credit, benefit, entitlement or state of affairs.

[section GB 1(3), dealing with certain sales of shares as part of a tax avoidance arrangement, omitted]

Sec. OB 1 Definitions

In this Act, unless the context otherwise requires,-- ...

"arrangement" means any contract, agreement, plan, or understanding (whether enforceable or unenforceable), including all steps and transactions by which it is carried into effect: ...

"liability", in the definition of "tax avoidance", includes a potential or prospective liability to future income tax:...

"Tax avoidance", in sections BG 1, EH 1, EH 42, GB 1, and GC 12, includes—

(a) Directly or indirectly altering the incidence of any income tax;

(b) Directly or indirectly relieving any person from liability to pay income tax;

(c) Directly or indirectly avoiding, reducing, or postponing any liability to income tax.

"Tax avoidance arrangement" means an arrangement, whether entered into by the person affected by the arrangement or by another person, that directly or indirectly—

(a) Has tax avoidance as its purpose or effect; or

(b) Has tax avoidance as one of its purposes or effects, whether or not any other purpose or effect is referable to ordinary business or family dealings, if the purpose or effect is not merely incidental:

Singapore, Income Tax Act, sec. 33. [excerpts]

"(1) Where the Comptroller is satisfied that the purpose or effect of any arrangement is directly or indirectly –

    (a) to alter the incidence of any tax which is payable by or which would otherwise have been payable by any person;

    (b) to relieve any person from any liability to pay tax or to make a return under this Act; or

    (c) to reduce or avoid any liability imposed or which would otherwise have been imposed on any person by this Act,

the Comptroller may...disregard or vary the arrangement and make such adjustments as he considers appropriate, including the computation or recomputation of gains or profits, or the imposition of liability to tax, so as to counteract any tax advantage obtained or obtainable by that person from or under that arrangement.

(2) In this section, 'arrangement' means any scheme, trust, grant, covenant, agreement, disposition, transaction and includes all steps by which it is carried into effect.

(3) This section shall not apply to –

    (a) any arrangement made or entered into before 29th January 1988; or
    (b) any arrangement carried out for bona fide commercial reasons
and had not as one of its main purposes the avoidance or reduction of tax."

South Africa, Income Tax Act, sec. 103. [summary]

Where a transaction having the effect of avoiding or postponing tax is carried out in a manner which would not normally be employed for bona fide business purposes and solely or mainly for the purposes of obtaining a tax benefit, then tax is determined as if the transaction had not been entered into or "in such manner as in the circumstances of the case [the tax authoritiy] deems appropriate for the prevention or diminution of such avoidance."

Spain [translation]

General Tax Law, art. 24(2).

The facts, deeds, or legal transactions executed in fraud on the tax law shall not impede the application of the tax rule that is avoided, nor shall they give rise to the fiscal advantages which they were used to try to obtain.

Civil code, art. 6.4

Acts carried out with the help of the text of a rule which pursue a result that is prohibited by the legal order or which is contrary to it shall be considered carried out in fraud on the law and shall not impede the proper application of the rule which was sought to be avoided.

Appendix 3

BIBLIOGRAPHY

This is a basic bibliography of recommended books for the study of comparative tax law. The footnotes in each chapter list additional sources to be consulted on specific issues. The emphasis is on books available in English, but books in other languages are included where comparable material is not available in English.

Argentina

Jarach, Dino, Finanzas Públicas y Derecho Tributario (2d ed. 1996)

Reig, Enrique J., Impuesto a las Ganancias (10th ed. 2001)

Australia

Cooper, Graeme S., Richard Krever & Richard Vann, Income Taxation: Commentary and Materials (4th ed. 2002)

Lehmann, Geoffrey & Cynthia Coleman, Taxation Law in Australia (5th ed. 1998)

Kobetsky, Michael et al., Income Tax: Text, Materials & Essential Cases (3d ed. 2001).

Woellner, Robin et al., Australian Taxation Law (11th ed. 2000)

Austria

Doralt, Werner & Hans Georg Ruppe, Grundriss des österreichischen Steuerrechts (2000)

Belgium

Coppens, Pierre & André Bailleux, Droit Fiscal (2d ed. 1992)(2 vols.)

Dassesse, Marc & Pascal Minne, Droit Fiscal (5th ed. 2001)

Faes, Pascal, Belgian Income Tax Law (1995)

Malherbe, Jacques, Droit fiscal international (1994)

Tiberghien, Albert, Belgian Taxation: An Outline (5th ed. 1987)

Tiberghien, Albert, Manuel de droit fiscal (16th ed. 1995)

Brazil

Xavier, Alberto, Direito Tributário Internacional do Brasil (5th rev. ed. 2000)

Canada

David, Irene J. et al., The Complete Guide to the Goods and Services Tax (7th ed. 1997)

Edgar, Tim et al., Materials on Canadian Income Tax (12th ed. 2000)

Hogg, Peter W. et al., Principles of Canadian Income Tax Law (4th ed. 2002)

Krishna, Vern, The Fundamentals of Canadian Income Tax (6th ed. 2000)

Chile

Massone, Pedro, El Impuesto a la Renta (1996)

France

Castagnède, Bernard, Précis de fiscalité internationale (2002)

Cozian, Maurice, Précis de fiscalité des entreprises (25th ed. 2001)

Cozian, Maurice, Les grands principes de la fiscalité des entreprises (4th ed. 1999)

David, Cyrille et al., Les grands arrêts de la jurisprudence fiscale (3d ed. 2000)

Direction Générale des Impôts, Précis de fiscalité (appears annually)

Douvier, Pierre-Jean, Droit Fiscal Dans les Relations Internationales (1996)

Gambier, Claude & Jean Ives Mercier, Les Impôts en France: traité pratique de la fiscalité des affaires (25th ed. 1993)

Gest, Guy & Gilbert Tixier, Droit fiscal international (2d ed. 1990)

Harvard Law School, International Program in Taxation: Taxation in France (1966)

Lambert, Thierry, Contrôl fiscal: Droit et pratique (2d ed. 1998)

Trotabas, Louis & Jean-Marie Cotteret, Droit fiscal (8th ed. 1997)

Germany

Harvard Law School, International Program in Taxation: Taxation in the Federal Republic of Germany (1963)

Knobbe-Keuk, Brigitte, Bilanz- und Unternehmenssteuerrecht (9th ed. 1993)

Lange, Joachim & Klaus Tipke, Steuerrecht (17th ed. 2002)

Schaumburg, Harald, Internationales Steuerrecht (2d ed. 1998)

Tipke, Klaus, Die Steuerrechtsordnung (1993) (3 vols.) and (vol. 1: 2d ed. 2000)

Vogel, Klaus, Klaus Vogel on Double Taxation Conventions (3d ed. 1997)

Hong Kong

Flux, David & David Smith, Hong Kong Taxation Law and Practice (2000)

Ireland

Corrigan, Kieran, Revenue Law (2000)

Italy

Fantozzi, Augusto, Diritto Tributario (1994)

Lupi, Rafaello, Diritto Tributario, Parte generale (6th ed. 2000)

Lupi, Rafaello, Diritto Tributario, Parte speciale: I sistemi dei singoli tributi (7th ed. 2002)

Japan

Gomi, Yuji, Guide to Japanese Taxes 1996-97 (1996)(appears annually)

Ishi, Hiromitsu, The Japanese Tax System (1993)

Ministry of Finance, Tax Bureau, An Outline of Japanese Taxes (2000) (appears annually)

Otsuka, Masatami & Kenju Watanabe, Butterworths International Taxation of Financial Instruments and Transactions: Japan (2d ed. 1994)

Mexico

Margain Manautou, Emilio, Introducción al Estudio del Derecho Tributario Mexicano (14th rev. ed. 1999)

de la Garza, Sergio Francisco, Derecho Financiero Mexicano (19th ed. 2001)

Netherlands

te Spenke, Gerrit, Taxation in The Netherlands (3d ed. 1995)

Russia
Karasseva, Marina, Tax Law in Russia (2001)

South Africa
Clegg, David & Rob Stretch, Income Tax in South Africa (looseleaf)
de Koker, Alwyn, Silke on South African Income Tax (looseleaf)
Meyerowitz, David, Meyerowitz on Income Tax (looseleaf)

Spain
Albiñana, César, Sistema Tributario Español y Comparado (2d ed. 1992)
Martín Queralt, Juan et al., Curso de Derecho Financiero y Tributario (12th ed. 2001)
Pérez Royo, Fernando, Derecho Financiero y Tributário (9th ed. 1999)
Soler Roch, Maria Teresa, Tax Law in Spain (2002)

Sweden
Harvard Law School, International Program in Taxation: Taxation in Sweden (1959)

Switzerland
Harvard Law School, International Program in Taxation: Taxation in Switzerland (1976)
Höhn, Ernst & Robert Waldburger, Steuerrecht (9th ed. 2001)
Oberson, Xavier & Howard Hull, Switzerland in International Tax Law (2d ed., 2001)
Rivier, Jean-Marc, Droit fiscal suisse: L'imposition du revenue et de la fortune (1980)

United Kingdom
Maas, Robert W., Tolley's Anti-Avoidance Provisions (looseleaf 2001)
Morse, Geoffrey & David Williams, Davies: Principles of Tax Law (4th ed. 2000)

Salter, David & Julia Kerr, Easson: Cases and Materials on Revenue Law (2d ed. 1990)

Tiley, John, Revenue Law (4th ed. 2000)

Whitehouse, Chris et al., Revenue Law – Principles and Practice (19th ed. 2001)

United States

Andrews, William D., Basic Federal Income Taxation (5th ed. 1999)

Bittker, Boris, James S. Eustice & Gersham Goldstein, Federal Income Taxation of Corporations and Shareholders (7th ed. 2000)

Bittker, Boris & Lawrence Lokken, Federal Taxation of Income, Estates and Gifts (3d ed. 1999 with supplements)

Garlock, David C. et al., Federal Income Taxation of Debt Instruments (4th ed. looseleaf 2000)

Graetz, Michael & Deborah Schenk, Federal Income Taxation: Principles and Policies (4th ed. 2001)

Hopkins, Bruce, The Law of Tax-Exempt Organizations (7th ed. 1998 with supplements)

Isenbergh, Joseph, International Taxation: U.S. Taxation of Foreign Persons and Foreign Income (3d ed. looseleaf 2002)(4 vols.)

Klein, William, Joseph Bankman & Daniel Shaviro, Federal Income Taxation (12th ed. 2000)

McDaniel, Paul R. et al., Federal Income Taxation (4th ed. 1998)

McKee, William S., William F. Nelson & Robert L. Whitmire, Federal Taxation of Partnerships and Partners (3d ed. looseleaf 1997, with supplements) (2 vols.)

Mertens, J., The Law of Federal Income Taxation (looseleaf)

Saltzman, Michael, IRS Practice and Procedure (2d ed. 1991 with supplements)

Willis, Arthur et al., Partnership Taxation (6th ed. 2002 looseleaf)

General and multi-country

Alpert, Herbert H. & Kees van Raad eds., Essays on International Taxation (1993)

Amatucci, Andrea, Trattato di Diritto Tributario (1994)

Arnold, Brian J. & Michael J. McIntyre, International Tax Primer (2002)

Ault, Hugh et al., Comparative Income Taxation: A Structural Analysis (1997)

Baker, Philip, Double Taxation Conventions and International Tax Law (2d ed. 1994)

Beltrame, Pierre & Lucien Mehl, Techniques, politiques et institutions fiscales comparées (2d ed. 1997)

Cnossen, Sijbren, Excise Systems: A Global Study of the Selective Taxation of Goods and Services (1977)

David, Cyrille, Geerten Michielse (ed.), Manuel René Theisen, Martin Wenz & John Tiley, Tax Treatment of Financial Instruments (1996)

di Malta, Pierre, Droit fiscal européen comparé (1995)

Easson, Alex, Taxation of Foreign Direct Investment: An Introduction (1999)

Ebrill, Liam et al., The Modern VAT (2001)

Edgar, Tim, The Income Tax Treatment of Financial Instruments (2000)

Farmer, Paul & Richard Lyal, EC Tax Law (1994)

Harris, Peter, Corporate/Shareholder Income Taxation and Allocating Taxing Rights Between Countries (1996)

Lindencrona, Gustaf et al. eds., International Studies in Taxation: Law and Economics: Liber Amicorum Leif Mutén (1999)

Lyons, Timothy, EC Customs Law (2001)

OECD, Taxpayers' Rights and Obligations: A Survey of the Legal Situation in OECD Countries (1990)

Pagan, Jill & J. Scott Willie, Transfer Pricing Strategy in a Global Economy (1993)

Rohatgi, Roy, Basic International Taxation (2002)

Sandford, Cedric, Why Tax Systems Differ: A Comparative Study of the Political Economy of Taxation (2000)

Schenk, Alan & Oliver Oldman, Value Added Tax: A Comparative Approach in Theory and Practice (2001)

Sommerhalder, Ruud, Comparing Individual Income Tax Reforms (1996)

Tait, Alan A., Value-Added Tax: International Practice and Problems (1988)

Terra, Ben & Peter Wattel, European Tax Law (3rd ed. 2002)

Thuronyi, Victor, ed., Tax Law Design and Drafting (softcover (2 vols.): IMF, 1996 and 1998; hardcover (1 vol.): Kluwer 2000) [cited herein as TLDD]

Tirard, Jean-Marc, Corporate Taxation in EU Countries (2d ed. 1994)

Van Hoorn, J., Jr., *Taxation of Business Organisations, in* 13 Int'l Encyclopedia of Comparative Law (Alfred Conrad ed. 1972)

Vogel, Klaus, Double Taxation Conventions (3rd ed. 1997)

Zweigert, Konrad & Hein Kötz, Introduction to Comparative Law (Tony Weir trans., 3d ed. 1998)

INDEX

218 n.41; tax share in GDP, 11; taxation of gains (gifts and bequests), 266; treaty interpretation, 117 n.233; VAT, 305, 317, 321, 323, 324

Austria

anti-avoidance rules and treaties, 118 n.242; bibliography, 353; constitutional construction, 66 n.23; constitutional decisions, 94; dividend taxation, 283; effect of treaties, 112, 113 n.219; fraud procedure, 227; retroactivity, 94; stamp duty, 335 n.31; statutory interpretation, 145 n.32, 146; tax fraud, 223 n.58; tax payment pending appeal, 218 n.41

Azerbaijan

supremacy of treaties, 113 n.219

Bank secrecy, 211

Bankruptcy, 220

Belgium

abuse of rights, 159-60; agreements with taxpayer, 71 n.46; bibliography, 353; constitutional construction, 66 n.23; constitutional decisions (equality), 96; corporate income as business income, 267 n.131; delegation to executive, 70 n.42; dividend taxation, 283; exemption of foreign business income, 293 n.226; GAAR, 195; judicial precedents, 149 n.55; legal effect of circulars, 124 n.268; principle of annuality, 72 n.49; rank of treaties, 112, 114 n.223, 115 n.226; real property transfer tax, 333 n.22; residence of entities, 290 n.203; stamp duty, 333 n.20; statutory interpretation, 144 n.30, 145 nn.32, 34; tax haven transactions, 298 n.246; tax law and private law, 126 n.278; tax unit, 243; taxation according to actual situation, 158; treaty interpretation, 115 n.228

Brazil

advance rulings, 212; bibliography, 354; contribution relating to royalties, 52-53; definition of tax, 48 n.9, 52-53; emergency decrees, 71; GAAR, 195; influence of German scholarship, 4.n.11; litigation, 218 n.40; rank of treaties, 115 n.227; retroactivity, 81 n.80; statutory interpretation, 145 n.32, 148 n.50; tax fraud, 223 n.58; tax haven transactions, 298 n.246

Bribes, deduction for, 16

Burden of proof, 218-19

Business income, 266-77

Canada

anti-avoidance rules and treaties, 118 n.242; bibliography, 354; complexity, 17; concept of tax and fee, 50; constitutional decisions, 98; constitutional distinction between direct and indirect taxes, 56-57;

constitutional remedies, 66 n.22; definition of income, 233 n.10, 235 n.15, 236 n.18, n.21, 240; dual resident companies, 299 n.249; foreign investment funds, 298; fraud procedure, 226; GAAR, 184-87, 347-48; gain realization on gifts and bequests, 266; imputation, 282; income averaging, 302 n.262; incorporation of treaties, 112; interest deduction, 277; interpretation of treaties, 115 n.228, 117 n.233; legal effect of interpretation bulletins, 124; legal effect of rulings, 212 n.15; orientation of tax administration, 207; per-country limitation, 292; provincial taxation, 74-75; residence of entities, 290; statutory interpretation, 135 n.7, 140, 141-44; suspension of tax pending appeal, 218 n.41; tax and financial accounting, 268 n.134, 272; tax appeals, 216; tax fraud, 223 n.58; tax on land and buildings, 331 n.10; tax share in GDP, 10

Capital gains, 15, 236-37, 239-40, 242, 260-66

Casualty losses, 245

Chile

bibliography, 354; composite income tax, 241 n.31

China, 37-38

death penalty for tax fraud, 224

Churches, 132

Civil law, relation to tax law, 28, 125-28

Civil law countries

differences to common law, 24-25; drafting style, 18; role of precedent, 149; sources of law, 62; structure of specific antiavoidance rules, 201; tax and financial accounting, 269; tax study, 13

Code of conduct (EU), 21

Codes, civil, transplantation, 4 n.12

see also Tax codes

Collection of tax, 220-21

Colombia

statutory interpretation, 148 n.50; withholding, 210

Common law countries

attitude to tax study, 12-14; complexity, 18; definition of employee, 247; definition of tax, 49-50; differences to civil law, 24-25; role of precedent, 149; structure of specific anti-avoidance rules, 201; tax and financial accounting, 269

Comparative method, 3-7

historical, 4-5

Comparative tax law

literature, 6; reasons for studying, 1-2

Complexity, 17-20

New Zealand

> appeal to Privy Council, 27 n.32; capital gains, 264; constitutional review by courts, 65; financial instruments, 258; foreign investment funds, 298; fringe benefits tax, 252; GAAR, 185 n.196, 187, 349-51; imputation, 283; simplification, 19; statutory interpretation, 138 n.11, 141; suspension of tax pending appeal, 218 n.41; treaties, incorporation of, 112; VAT, 305 n.1, 313, 315, 317, 319, 323, 324

Nigeria

> constitutional limits on taxation, 73 n.52

Norway

> constitutional review, 97; departing residents, taxation of, 292; imputation, 282-83; net wealth tax, 329 n.4; statutory interpretation, 148; tax payment pending appeal, 218 n.41; treaties, incorporation of, 112; treaties, override of, 114 n.220

OECD Commentary, 119-20

Ombudsman, 229-30

Pakistan

> constitutional limits on taxation, 73 n.52; income tax and zakat, 132; net wealth tax, 329 n.4; VAT on services, 315

Paraguay

> income tax, limited scope of, 231 n.5; retroactivity, 81 n.80; territorial system, 287 n.193

Partnerships, 279-81

Penalties, 221-22

Pensions, 259-60

Personal deductions, 244-45

Personal service companies, 247-48

Peru

> retroactivity, 81 n.80

Poland

> constitutional decisions, 96; tax havens, anti-avoidance rules for, 298 n.246; treaties, supremacy of, 113 n.219

Portugal

> dividend taxation, 283; GAAR, 195; married couple as tax unit, 243; ombudsman, 230 n.89; statutory interpretation, 145 n.32; tax havens, transactions with, 298 n.246; tax payment pending appeal, 218 n.41; treaties, rank of, 113 n.219, 115 n.226

Presumptive taxation, 302-04

Private law

see Civil law

Property tax, 58, 330-31

Public law, 60

Reenactment doctrine, 123, 137

Religion and religious law, 129-32

Remittance basis taxation, 248 n.57, 288 n.196

Reorganizations, 285

Retroactivity, 76-81

Austria, 94; of judicial decisions (U.S.), 66 n.22

Romania

income tax, 234 n.11; retroactivity, 81 n.80; treaties, supremacy of, 113 n.219

Rulings, 211-13

Russia, 33-36

bibliography, 356; constitutional decisions, 100; penalties, 221-22; retroactivity, 81 n.80; regulations, 122; tax fraud, 223 n.58; tax law and private law, 125 n.275; treaties, rank of, 113 n.219

Saudi Arabia

income tax and zakat, 132

Schedular taxation, 15, 233-34, 241-43

capital income, 255-56

Sham transaction, 157, 159, 163-64

Simulation, 157

Singapore

capital gains, 242 n.35; GAAR, 351-52; territorial system, 287 n.193; wage withholding, absence of, 254

Slovenia

constitutional decision (equality), 96; retroactivity, 81 n.80; treaties, supremacy of, 113 n.219

Soak-up taxes, 293

Social security taxation, 16, 53, 58, 332

fringe benefits, 250 n.63

Sociology, 6

Source concept of income, 27, 31, 236-37

Sources of tax law, 62-63

229; schedular definition of income, 234 n.12, 236 n.19, 240; simplification, 19; social security tax, 332 n.19; *stare decisis,* 149; statutory interpretation, 137-40; tax academics, 12 n.38; tax and financial accounting, 273; tax appeals, 216; tax advisors, prosecution of, 224-25; tax fraud, 223 n.58; tax fraud procedure, 226 n.71; tax payment pending appeal, 218 n.41; tax rates, 244 n.41; Taxes Management Act, 208; treaties, incorporation of, 112; treaties, interpretation of, 117 n.233; trusts, taxation of, 286-87; VAT appeals, 336 n.37

UN Model, 121 n.254

Unity of legal system, 61-62

United States, 28-29

advance rulings, 212; anti-avoidance doctrines (judicial), 160-71; anti-avoidance rules (specific), 197-98; audit procedure, 214 n.23; bibliography, 357; burden of proof, 218 n.42; capital gains, 260-61, 263, 264-65; classical system (corporate/shareholder), 282; collection powers of IRS, 220; complexity, 17-18; constitutional jurisprudence, 68-70, 74-75, 78-79, 82, 91-92; constitutional limitation on direct taxes, 55; corporate income, character of, 267; deductions, itemized, 245 n.43; dual resident companies, 299 n.249; employee, definition of, 247 n.54; equal protection, 82, 91-92; estate tax, 330 n.6; financial instruments, 257; foreign earned income exclusion, 293; foreign hybrids, 299 n.250; foreign investment funds, 298; foreign losses, 294; foreign tax credit limitation, 292-93; foreign trusts, 298 n.248; fringe benefits, 251-52; gains (gifts and bequests), 266; income, definition of, 235 n.15, 240; income averaging, 302 n.262; income tax history, 232 n.7; interest deduction 276; key country to study, 9; legislative process, 20-21; married couple as tax unit, 243; ombudsman, 229; penalties, 221-22; reenactment doctrine for regulations, 123; religion, state aid to, 129; retroactive effect of judicial decisions, 66 n.22; return filing requirements, 209 n.9, 244-45; rulings, legal effect of published, 124, 211 n.13; standing, doctrine of, 65 n.20; *stare decisis,* 149; state taxation, 74-75; statutory interpretation, 144, 150; study of taxation, 12-13; suspension of tax pending appeal, 218 n.41; tax, concept of, 50; tax academics, 12; tax and financial accounting, 268 n.134, 271-73; tax advisors, regulation of, 229; tax appeals, 217-18; tax fraud, 224; tax fraud procedure, 226; tax law and private law, 127; tax share in GDP, 10; tax shelters, procedural attacks on, 201-03; treaties, effect of, 112; treaties, interpretation of, 116-17; treaties and anti-avoidance rules, 118; treaty override, 113 n.220; treaty policy, 120-21